STARLINGS LAUGHING

STARLINGS LAUGHING
A Memoir of Africa

June Vendall Clark

WILLIAM MORROW AND COMPANY, INC.
New York

The author and publishers wish to thank the following for permission to quote extracts from: "Old Man River," *Show Boat,* by Jerome Kern and Oscar Hammerstein, copyright © by Polygram Music Publishing Ltd. "Lord of the Dance" by Sydney Carter, copyright © 1963 by Galliard Ltd. Permission granted (United States only) by Galaxy Music Corp., Boston. L. P. Hartley's *The Go-Between,* published by Scarborough House, Chelsea, Michigan 48118.

First published in Great Britain by Doubleday, a division of Transworld Publishers Ltd.

It is the policy of William Morrow and Company, Inc., and its imprints and affiliates, recognizing the importance of preserving what has been written, to print the books we publish on acid-free paper, and we exert our best efforts to that end.

Library of Congress Cataloging-in-Publication Data

Clark, June Vendall.
    Starlings laughing : a memoir of Africa / June Vendall Clark.
        p.   cm.
    Includes index.
    ISBN 0-688-10540-8
    1. Botswana—Description and travel. 2. Natural history—Botswana. 3. Clark, June Vendall—Homes and haunts—Botswana. 4. Moremi Wildlife Reserve (Botswana) I. Title.
    DT2448.C53 1991
    968.83—dc20   90-25117
                                                                                      CIP

Printed in the United States of America

First U.S. Edition

1 2 3 4 5 6 7 8 9 10

Richard, my love,
this book is for you

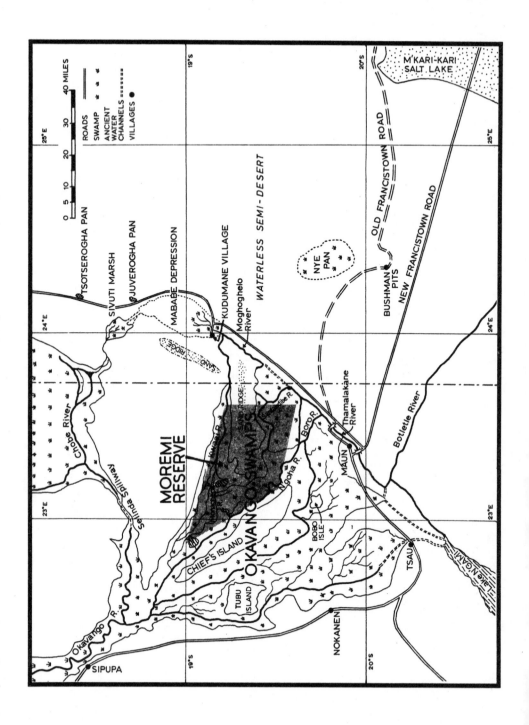

Contents

Acknowledgements

The author and publishers wish to thank the following for permission to quote extracts from: 'Ol' Man River', *Show Boat*, copyright Polygram Music Publishing Ltd; '*Lord of the Dance*' by Sydney Carter, reproduced by permission of Stainer & Bell Ltd, London, England; L. P. Hartley's *The Go-Between*, published by Hamish Hamilton.

Foreword

When I was still June Kay I lived for eight years in a tent, on an island, in the Okavango Swamp delta of north-western Bechuanaland.[1] Bechuanaland itself is land-locked, only a little larger than Texas, sharing boundaries with the Republic of South Africa on the south, Namibia on the west, and Zambia, Angola and the territory now known as Zimbabwe to the north and east. And ninety per cent of it is covered in the glaring, white salt sand of the Kalahari Desert, a land of fantastic mirages and shifting dunes, carrion-seeking vultures and scavenging jackals, where the greatest enemies of man are thirst and heat stroke. Yet, far up in its north-western corner, crowded against the Angolan border, lies the huge, sweet-water swamp of the Okavango River, and the Okavango is the last great wilderness area left on earth.

When my former husband Robert and I first went there in 1958, the wildlife was still so prolific that the unchecked slaughter of game was only just beginning to have a serious impact. We began by simply absorbing the wonder of living in one of the few regions of Africa which hadn't yet been plundered and corrupted – but gradually we were forced to recognize the hideous cruelties that were being inflicted on the entire animal population by unrestricted hunting parties.

The random, gleeful slaughter we witnessed by one particularly brutal safari party finally galvanized us into action: we began a long, gruelling struggle to persuade the local tribes – who owned the land and depended on game animals for their food and livelihood – to create the Moremi Wildlife Reserve, the first of its kind in Africa and the forerunner of eight similar reserves in Bechuanaland.

[1] Bechuanaland (Protectorate) – now Botswana.

It was the high point of my love affair with the wild, and with Africa, and the end of it. This was no sunlight-and-chiffon romance, but a frightening blend of exaltation and bloody torment, and it left me emotionally drained, financially bankrupt, with a shattered marriage, and no future in a country that had moved out of my grasp.

But while it lasted I was alive to a degree that few people ever know, and in a way which the new Africa has made it impossible to repeat.

This book is not only about animals. When I lived there, the southern half of Africa was at one of the starkest, most radical points of transition from colonial status and white rule, and it was the people I knew who left the most profound memories. This book is mainly about them: about Tembo of the elephant totem and Leonard of the Lozi tribe; Kisi and drunken Rodger; the nomadic hunter Kweri and Tamai, who was the understudy witchdoctor; Ix from the Zankuio village and her man who burnt the 'lion leaves'. It is also about the man I should have married when I first met him in 1951 – a better idea from my point of view than it might have been from his.

In the days when old Tembo's starlings were laughing at the moon, Botswana was still the Bechuanaland Protectorate and Rhodesia was a long way from becoming Zimbabwe. Blacks, by definition, were Africans. People of mixed race were Coloureds. With a fine disregard for continents, all white people were Europeans, whether they hailed from Slough or Scandinavia, Cincinnati or Cape Town. To avoid stumbling into a tangle of anachronism, I have used the old names in all cases. I hope the purists will forgive me.

June Vendall Clark

The Rock

There was a rock in the Matopo Hills where I used to go when I needed courage, or guidance, or simply the strength to carry on with a marriage that had gone disastrously wrong.

The Rock was a glassy slope running up to the knee of a granite kopje that crowded against the left-hand side of the house. Its steep side had been used to form one side of a stone fishpond. Robert had built the pond and smoothed the inner surface with cement; the Rock itself had been smoothed by a million years of erosion.

To the unbeliever, there was nothing remarkable about the place. It sheltered no secret cave like the one underneath the right-hand kopje, where an old, thick female puffadder slid through the dark and a family of mocking chats fluted from the high, sunlit boulders near the rainwater tank. Below the tank, on the far side, stood a lone paper tree with a hole in its trunk. A pair of glossy starlings nested in the hollow every spring. Their plumage was sleek and silky, the colour of smoked amethyst.

No such gorgeous creatures visited my Rock, although in the hot weather a few male agama lizards, in garish breeding finery of orange and violet and blue, scuttled across the blistering surface and bobbed their heads in a frenzy of reptilian lust. Nor was my Rock a sacred place, like the colossus of 'Njelele, where Chaminooka, the Matabele Rain God, lived with his imprisoned thunder. Mine seemed to be just another rock in a landscape of rocks, and its mysteries were known only to me. It was my secret place, and the tabernacle of my secret God.

I did not go there during the daylight hours, or when anyone was watching. I went alone, by night, to sit on the warm slope when the curious, hot, ferny smell that granite has was still seeping from the stone. I listened to the African night, a myriad tiny sounds.

★ ★ ★

A nightjar flutters down and lands a few feet away. I am as still as the stone itself, not daring to move in case I frighten her. Her eyes glow red, in a fugitive beam of light from the house. She flirts her wings and is gone. One stippled feather remains on the Rock as evidence of her visit. In the valley below a fish rises in the dam, plops over. The eddies circle in moonlight. My mind slowly empties itself of the cares of the day.

There have been ten years of days like this one – with another ten to run, although I do not know that tonight as I sit on my Rock, groping for peace and wishing it would envelop me as if I were shawled in moonlight. And, at last, my hidden God speaks softly, answering some questions but failing bleakly to settle the most agonizing of them all. Because I know, now, that my marriage should never have taken place – and it is ten years and three children too late to reverse a headstrong decision that had hurled me straight from a convent school into the reluctant arms of the first man who ever kissed me. Nor can I turn my back on it and simply walk away, because I have been brought up to believe that marriage is forever.

★ ★ ★

Sometimes, during our early years, it had seemed to be all right. Once, when we were rich, he brought me an oriental rug and an Alsatian dog puppy. Then, when we became poor, I gave him a five-cell torch and the skin of a civet cat, which cost me two shillings and sixpence. But we hadn't ever listened to the same music, or laughed at the same things.

There were many nights on the Rock when peace evaded me, when the doors of the tabernacle remained stubbornly shut. On such nights as that all I acquired were half a million mosquito bites and a lot of resurrected memories.

★ ★ ★

Memories. How far back does memory reach? For me, real memory, picture-memory, begins with my fourth birthday party, when I wore a dress trimmed with lace and carried a posy; it was my first birthday in Africa, and that was the only birthday party I ever had. But I still catch misty echoes of an earlier time, of

14

hand-fed pigeons and the sound of peafowl lumbering up into the trees at sunset, and the hard brilliance of the night sky over a flat rooftop in the pink granite city of Jaipur where my father, Lancelot Brassington-Burn, was a consulting engineer to His Royal Highness, the Maharajah.

India

On the night I was born, in the Lady Willingdon Hospital in Madras, someone had carelessly left a window open in an adjoining ward, and a fruit bat had managed to entangle itself in the netting stretched across the frame to deter the creatures of the night. Some of the hospital staff were trying to disentangle it, with shouts and curses and broomsticks.

My newly acquitted mother, Frances, lying on the narrow bed, was still drowsy from the morphine that was used, in those innocent days, to ease the pains of childbirth. Lance was looking tense. Surgeon-General Hinkstone, who had been called in when things started to go wrong, took me from the crisply starched nurse and handed me to my father.

'She's fine,' he said. 'Just fine. Those forceps marks won't last. But I'm sorry, old chap, you can't possibly call her Nigel Douglas Murdoch Brassington-Burn. Try June. Call her after Lady Inverclyde, the dancer. Very suitable, considering the month.'

'She's got red hair,' said Lance, wonderingly. 'I don't want to let her go, ever. She's all mine.'

Frances opened her eyes. 'Mine too,' she said feebly.

'No,' Lance said emphatically. 'If we have any more children they can be yours. This one is all mine!'

I wish he hadn't said that.

There *were* no more children, and in Lance's mind I became the son he had so passionately longed for. His *mores* had been formed in the Benedictine monastery of Ampleforth in Yorkshire, in the few golden years between the turn of the century and the outbreak of the First World War. He struggled hard to imbue me with the simple moral values that had been so clearly laid down by authors like John Buchan, Rudyard Kipling and Dean Farrar, and he became desperate when he felt that I was slipping away from him.

Poor, confused, forty-year-old Frances still dreamed of a daughter who was wholly feminine. She tried frantically to undo Lance's rigid teaching, and to smother all my own increasingly wayward inclinations under a froth of frilled petticoats, lace dresses and brown velvet bonnets.

It was predictable that they should both fail.

They were an ill-matched couple, cruelly brought together by pure chance. Lance had fought with distinction in the war, and afterwards he tried to wipe out the memories of the Somme and the bloody beaches of Gallipoli by chartering a pearling schooner in Broome, Northern Australia. Later he joined his brother Douglas, who was trading in gold-dust and ivory in West Africa, and then went prospecting on his own account. But he had two sisters in England, and when they wrote begging for money he went back to the engineering firm of Metropolitan Vickers, who had employed him before the war.

They, in turn, posted him to India. There he met Frances, who had been sent out on what used to be called the 'Fishing Fleet', the regular detachments of young girls of modest fortune, whose chances of finding a husband in Britain had been sharply curtailed by the war. Frances, in her late thirties and no great beauty, went to stay with distant relatives in one of the hill stations, where Lance happened to be recuperating from an attack of malaria. Since neither of them fitted well into the usual social round they tended to be thrown together, and eventually, because he somehow felt that it was expected of him, Lance proposed. Not quite believing her luck, Frances accepted instantly.

If it were possible to wind the clock back and start my life again, I would love to relive those first few precious years in India. The memories I still hold are not as sharp as the images of that birthday party; they are half-lost and smudged by time. Yet somehow I managed to absorb an awareness of India that has never left me. India and I still belong to each other. I feel at home there.

I seem to have spent most of my first two years in the sidecar of Lance's vast Harley-Davidson motorcycle combination, hurtling noisily through tiger-haunted jungle and across the desert plains of Rajputana, where the kirtled women walk like queens to draw water in cool clay pots from the stone-lined village wells. There were camel trains lurching and gurgling through the heat, with brass bells clanging and loaded with merchandise for distant bazaars. Lean yellow *pi* dogs scattered snarling away from the wheels as we roared past. Frances used the opportunity to add to the store of mostly inaccurate information with which she tried to fill my small head.

'You must never talk to *pi* dogs,' she yelled after one encounter. 'They all have rabies and they're dangerous even when they're dead.' That was one of the more reliable fragments of folk wisdom she passed on. She also warned me that the exquisite, iridescent tailfeathers of the peacock were marked with the Evil Eye and if you looked at them they would shrivel you up. Certainly, whenever we passed peafowl in the jungle she would close her eyes and turn her head away. In fact, this interesting and exotic belief was one she shared with Mina, my ayah.

Mina was a flitterwit, with a vast repertoire of folk mysteries hidden in her small but active brain. 'The peacock belongs to Kali,' she said fearfully. 'If you have the feathers, it means that you have killed her bird and she will send you terrible punishings.' The Great Goddess Kali Mata is one of the most implacable deities in the Hindu pantheon.

But worst of all the demons was the evil Leg Man, who lived under the bed, in the fluffy dark. He was invisible in the daylight, but at night he came out to gnaw at the flesh of disobedient children – beginning at the toes and progressing upwards – if ever they climbed out of their cots and ran about barefoot after sunset.

'Why doesn't Leg Man eat Sahibs and Memsahibs too?'

'The long skirts of the Memsahibs get in the way of his teeth and the legs of the Sahibs are too hairy to eat.'

For once, there was an element of reason behind the story. India was, and is, infested with poisonous snakes and it was better that a child should wet its bed for fear of a *djin* than that it should step on a cobra in the dark, or put its hand on the deadly little krait that likes to knot itself around door handles.

But the worst, most wantonly irresponsible advice anyone ever gave me came from Frances, years later, in Africa, when I was a sentient twelve years old and curious about the Facts of Life.

'You will never be able to have children, my dear,' said Frances, scarlet with embarrassment. 'You're too small, you see. When your father and I – when you were conceived – I never . . . felt anything. I could never understand why you were born at all.'

I stared at her, blankly uncomprehending. What she was trying to tell me was that a woman who failed to reach orgasm was sterile.

Oh, God.

What had taken us to Africa was the great slump. When the Metrovic company began to feel the first effects it took the sensible precaution of firing all its most capable – and better-paid – employees. Lance was one of these. There was nothing for it but to head back to England to – to what? There were no jobs there either, and in the meantime he had a wife, a child and two selfish and venomously expensive sisters to support. But in one of his rare strokes of good fortune it turned out that Frances had two step-uncles who jointly owned one of India's greatest newspapers, the *Calcutta Statesman*. They gave Lance £2,000 – worth £50,000 in today's terms – to start a new life elsewhere. He invested it in an engineering business in Southern Rhodesia's second city, Bulawayo.

Charles Cumings, who had sold Lance the business, died aboard ship on his way back to England, having strained his heart in a tug o'war. It is just possible that somewhere along the route the steamship carrying Lance from England to South Africa passed the liner conveying the body of Mr Cumings home for burial.

At all events, soon after the train from Cape Town brought Lance to Bulawayo he discovered that he had sunk his windfall in some obsolete stock, a little fast-fading goodwill, and a great many bad debts. And my mother and I were on our way out to join him.

guBulawayo

> '*I have been killed by my people. I shall call this place guBulawayo, the place of slaughter.*'
> LOBENGULA, LAST KING OF THE MATABELE NATION

The warring Matabele were an offshoot of the powerful Zulu nation, and the last Matabele king was Lobengula, a bloody-minded tyrant who believed in avenging the smallest wrongs with death by torture. When he ascended the throne, three of the existing *impis* (regiments) rashly refused to acknowledge his suzerainty, and the Matabele War followed. Lobengula set up his kraal[1] in the arid south-west of the territory that was later to be known as Southern Rhodesia. The site he chose straddled the Matsheumhlope[2] (White Stones) river, a sullen little gulch that usually refused to flow at all unless it had been flushed out by heavy rain. Here was fought a devastating battle between the rebel legions and the battalions which remained loyal to the king.

---

[1] A settlement, usually built of wattle-and-daub; in this case, Lobengula's military headquarters.
[2] Pronounced Majum-slopey.

Lobengula emerged victorious, and he celebrated the defeat of the rebels by calling in a score of witchdoctors to 'smell out' their leaders, though the wisest of these had already taken their own lives. The triumph was not long. In 1893 Lobengula was driven into exile by the advance guard of Cecil Rhodes's Colonial forces, and the first frail little European settlement was created on the site of his kraal, on the banks of the Matsheumhlope. A year later this pioneer village was upgraded to the status of a 'town'. As things turned out, the honour was a little premature. The river was indulging in one of its frequent arid periods, and there was only one general store to supply the community. Worse, the bloodshed was by no means over: two years later the Matabele rebelled against the invaders, and the slaughter that followed eclipsed even the horrors of the civil war.

There are rich mineral deposits in Rhodesia, and by the time my father arrived there in the hot summer of 1928 Bulawayo had evolved into the focal point of the country's mining community. It was still a small town, but a busy one, neatly laid out in precise squares on the Roman grid system. The streets were lined with mauve-flowering jacaranda trees, and they were exceptionally wide because the Colony's founder, Cecil John Rhodes, had decreed that they should be broad enough to allow a full span of sixteen oxen to turn in its own length. Even in the twenties the huge, long-horned beasts, bred for endurance and fed on the dry-country mopani bush, were still being used to haul produce in from the surrounding farms. The creaking wooden wagons, moving at around three miles an hour on level ground, were laden with yams, cabbages, bright crates of oranges and sweet-smelling sacks of crushed maize. Sometimes the loads were topped with big, pink-fleshed watermelons, and the African children would throw sticks and pebbles at the stoic oxen, hoping to startle them into a brief jog, enough to dislodge a melon. Usually, the oxen simply plodded steadily on, the bells round the necks of the two lead animals clinking tinnily.

Only a few of the European settlers owned cars in those days; most of them, my father included, rode bicycles or travelled in rickshaws pulled by muscular Africans who decked themselves out in huge ostrich-feather head-dresses, with long-furred armlets made from waterbuck skins and leather anklets studded with little brass bells. Even old Father Kendall from the Roman Catholic church used to make his rounds on a bicycle, his faded black cassock flapping around his ankles and, often, an escort of half a dozen yapping curs trying to make him fall off. The Africans walked, barefoot and hatless in the scorching streets; a handful, the most fortunate ones, owned and rode donkeys.

For the first few months, Lance lived in an annexe to the Bulawayo Club. This was a sprawling colonial bungalow, the sort of building featured in every film epic of Empire from *Gunga Din* to *Zulu*. It had a deep wooden verandah right across the front, and the wide sash windows were fitted with mosquito-gauze screens in the summer to keep out the multitudes of flying insects that swarmed in the wake of the rains, to drain blood from humans and animals alike. A tangle of purple bougainvillea clung to the south side, straining away from the prevailing wind, and somebody had donated seven tubs of scarlet geraniums to serve as a garden.

Lance was glad enough to cycle back to the cool, paraffin-lit refuge in the evenings, to sprawl in one of the deep armchairs in this profoundly masculine institution, leafing through back numbers of *Punch* and the *Tatler*, drinking the one brandy-and-soda of the day that his light purse would stretch to. The Club's doors were, of course, firmly closed against women, and most especially – the ultimate abomination – women with babies, so Lance eventually had to find a proper home. He explained his predicament to the Town Clerk, with whom he sometimes played poker after dinner, and one of the other men in the poker school chimed in to say that his widowed aunt was going on indefinite leave to Dear Old Blighty. The house was therefore up for sale, but the aunt was getting desperate and would probably agree to let the place on a long lease.

111 Jameson Street was quite close by. My father signed the long lease, engaged a black cook named Jacob, who wore a chef's tall toque and made marvellous pastry, and then wrote to Frances, telling her to join him.

So we set sail, my mother and I. In those days, Cape Town was still a lovely, gracious city, in one of the most spectacularly beautiful settings anywhere in the world. But because we could not afford to linger, we boarded the first available train for the four-day journey to Rhodesia. Our baggage included several rolls of butter muslin, to be tacked over the windows to keep out the swirling red desert dust of the Karroo, whose flanks we would have to pass.

It was December, high summer and also the rainy season. By ten o'clock every morning the shade temperature had hit the 90°F mark and the metal fittings of the carriage were too hot to touch. The muslin, well dampened in an effort to tame the furnace heat inside our two-berth compartment, collected every particle of the flying dust and the smoke from the huge steam locomotive, and it soon became encrusted with grey and ochre mud. At every station the train was besieged by hawkers who tried to sell us all sorts of wonderful things: bulky necklaces made from black and red mahogany beams, big cold watermelons, round hand-woven baskets containing tiny pullets' eggs lovingly nested on a little dry grass, statuettes of guinea fowl carved from soft wood and stained with charcoal to simulate feathers, cowhorns fashioned into slim bone birds, karosses made from the silvery pelts of hyrax. When the train stopped at Kimberley Frances bought sweet thin-skinned peaches and some honeypot grapes.

In those days, passengers used to put their footwear outside the doors of their compartments for the train staff to clean. Later that night, I crept out of my bunk and filled everybody's shoes with grapes while they slept.

I was destined to live in Africa for forty years and, inevitably, I adopted the full canon of Colonial beliefs and customs. *Never shut your door on a stranger, because the next water-hole is twenty-five miles away and has probably dried out; it might be your turn, next time. When a servant rubs the side of his nose and says 'As a matter of fact, Madam . . .' get ready for it. He's lying. Always shake your shoes out before putting them on in the morning, to get rid of spiders or scorpions.* Even in England, I always shake my shoes out before putting them on, but it has nothing to do with spiders. It's in case some child has put grapes in them.

When we finally arrived in Bulawayo we were met at the station by Lance and conveyed, in a procession of rickshaws, to Jameson Street. The house was a bungalow with a red-painted, corrugated iron roof and pale yellow pebble-dash walls. It had a wide verandah running round two sides, a bucket lavatory in a shed at the back next to the Sanitary Lane, a beautiful black-leaded, wood-burning Dover stove in the kitchen, and five towering fir trees in the front garden. The trees exuded a clear white gum that Jacob's plump wife, acting as a temporary nanny, told me snakes ate. In the garden next to ours there was a red-flowering bauhinia which was said to be poisonous to every living thing except elephants – of which there were lamentably few in the quiet little mining town.

A near neighbour was Charley Blanckenberg, who bought engineering supplies for the Goldfields. He lived five doors away and was the father of four rather toothy children. He was a kind man, and happy to order equipment from Lance. In return, Lance rewarded him with a £5 note taken from the cash drawer every Christmas.

Once we had carefully examined every corner of our new home, from the high-ceilinged front room to the beaded fly curtain that hung against the back door, and the bright yellow curtains in the dining room, Lance took me out into the garden and planted a young tangerine tree that he had been saving in my honour. He called it Belle Étoile and gave me a fourpenny packet of zinnia seed so that I could make my own flower garden in the little square of ground that he had reserved for me, at the foot of the tree.

I loved Number 111. My mother did not, although she reacted against it less violently than a woman reared wholly in England would have done. Nevertheless, she wasted no time in hurrying off to the Roman Catholic church two convenient blocks away. Perhaps she needed reassurance from the white congregation, who had somehow managed to survive the shock of having to use bucket privies. She certainly said an entire rosary for something or other, because she was still fumbling with her beads when she got back to the house. She had also eagerly snatched up every available shred of gossip.

Mrs Fortune was a Pillar of the Church, but she suffered cruelly from the vile attentions of her unrepentantly lickerish husband, so that she had to spend a good deal of her time recounting all her ordeals into the unamused ear of Father Kendall in the confessional. Do you know, said Frances, *that poor woman, he forces her to take her corset off and leave the lights on every time they . . . Mr S., who actually lived in our street, played the church organ, but his wife was said to drink methylated spirits and their little girl had adenoids. Florrie Blanckenberg was so poor that she only had one pair of bloomers, which meant that she had to stay indoors when they were drying on the washing line. There was poor, blind Mr Colin – what a dreadful woman she must have been, to fling sulphuric acid in his face and burn out his eyes, just because he had refused to cast aside his wife for her sake. And Mrs Robinson's husband – whisper, whisper – careful, not in front of the child. What a terrible thing, I wonder where he caught it.*

On my second day in Bulawayo I met the dreaded Mr Mortley, the local Sanitary Inspector, in charge of the 'Shit Sammies', the gang of labourers whose job it was to collect buckets of night soil from the outside privies. All children were forbidden ever to set foot in the Sanitary Lane, but by standing on tip-toe, I managed to lift the latch on our back gate and had just succeeded in retrieving a stray kitten when Mr Mortley descended on me, cursing fearfully.

I stared up into a mottled red face, then let my gaze travel slowly down towards his feet. Before I was halfway there, he suddenly struck his right leg with a resounding thump. It sounded like somebody hitting a table top.

'Wood!' he roared. 'That's what it is. Wood!'

It was true! At last I had incontestable proof that there really was a Leg Man. Poor Mr Mortley must have climbed out of his cot and gone running about barefoot in the dark, *and Leg Man had eaten one of his legs before his ayah could get there and switch the light on!*

Childish Things

'When I was a child I spake as a child . . .'
ST PAUL TO THE CORINTHIANS

During that first year in Africa I was too young to understand why the firm in which Lance had sunk all his capital was faring so badly, or why he so often pushed his breakfast away, untouched, as though he felt the food would choke him. The grown-ups used to talk in strained voices about the Recession and then, later on, about the World Slump and the Great Depression. All that I knew was that my Saturday pocket-money had been cut from a generous threepence to a single penny, and that one morning my mother had even raided my money-box in order to pay the milkman. My weekly comic books, *Chick's Own* and *Tiger Tim*, no longer dropped through the letterbox, and when Frances admired some sugar-topped buns in the baker's window my father hustled us away because we couldn't afford them. They cost a halfpenny each. I shared her disappointment and wept, loudly and ostentatiously, for days.

But I did notice, with the curious, selective intuition of childhood, that Lance's auburn hair was turning very grey, quite suddenly.

In desperation, Lance arranged a small loan with his bank and bought a half-share in a gold mine, the Solo. It was just outside the little town of QueQue, named by the Africans after the ringing, metallic 'queque' call of the plover which used to scoop saucer-shaped nests in the sand around the local waterhole. Lance's partner in the enterprise was a Major Johns and, because my father was still very much of a loner and did not make friends easily, nobody bothered to tell him that the Major was a member of the Dishonourable Regiment of Remittance Men, that corps of ne'er-do-well sons who were paid by their shamed families to stay away from England on pain of having their monthly dole severed. Of course the Major ran true to type, and the Solo proved to be riddled with arsenic ore that needed to be expensively roasted off before any of the gold could be extracted. And in any case there was no roasting plant in Rhodesia then, nor was there for many, many years. The entrance to the mine was boarded up and bats roosted in the darkness of the main shaft.

When Major Johns was found shot dead in a tin shack some time later the police didn't pursue their enquiries very far and the district coroner recorded a verdict of suicide. A good many people would have been happy to see the major dead – and perhaps none more so than the husband of a pretty girl who lived in the nearby African township.

As a small family we might, just *might*, have weathered the financial storms better if Lance had not been forced to recognize the fact that he could no longer afford to support two households: wife and child in Africa, two sisters and a young nephew back in England. He wrote to his sisters and explained that they would have to come out and join us. They resisted the idea as long as they possibly could and then, with bad grace, they exchanged the ordered safety of England for the nameless horrors of a land which they believed to be infested with snakes, blood-sucking insects, cannibals and German missionaries.

My aunts, Elsa and Mabel, were flamboyant and overbearing, and they bitterly resented Lance's marriage. They had always regarded him as their own, exclusive berry patch, and within a week the decibels at Number 111 had risen above the pain level. They never attempted to hide their dislike of my mother, and poor, frightened Frances cowered away from them. Lance, who needed to concentrate on the task of keeping us all fed, took to spending more and more time at the office as the temperature of the family rows steadily increased.

It was at this stage that Lance's brother Douglas arrived – also rather reluctantly – from West Africa. Douglas was six foot and two inches tall and weighed twenty stone, most of which he carried before him in a huge, solid stomach. He'd had blackwater fever twice and, even more enthralling, he used to beat his chest and make chimpanzee noises to entertain us, at which point my mother usually scuttled from the room. He turned up in Bulawayo wearing a silk top-hat, with forty pairs of hand-made shoes and three dozen silk shirts in his luggage, and he smoked gold-tipped State Express cigarettes. He also nursed an unquenchable desire for soups made from ground peanuts. My mother's meagre and uninspired menus did not please him, and after six identical dinners of beef rissoles, exhausted cabbage and rice pudding he added to the unending family turmoil by striking up an alliance with his sisters against Frances.

Douglas was an odd mixture of the greedy and the generous. He stole my sweets when I wasn't looking and ate the solitary chocolate éclair that I'd been given as a special treat for my birthday. But then he bought me a pink enamel brush-and-comb set, and ordered the local bookstore to let me have all the books I needed and send the reckoning to him. One day, as we sat on the verandah counting the corpses of the flies we had killed with a long-handled wire swatter, he told me the story of a baby gorilla that had died in his arms, of pneumonia. Then, when I cried, he fished in his pocket for a handful of loose change and sent me to spend it in the sweetshop. I came home with a bagful of jelly babies and fruit bonbons, and he snatched the packet from me and ate half of them.

The discord at Number 111 finally reached an intolerable pitch. After one particularly violent slanging match the aunts swept indignantly out of the house to set up their own establishment in a bungalow near the town park. Since they had no money, and since there were few paid vacancies for harpies in Bulawayo, they graciously permitted Lance to go on paying their bills for them. Once more, he was paying to support two households.

Douglas stayed on at Number 111. One morning I heard him talking to my father in the front bedroom. He was standing, shirtless, in the light from the window. Unnoticed, I peeped in and saw purple blotches on his back. His voice was thick with apprehension. 'Lance,' he said, 'look at this.'

'I'm not sure,' Lance said, but his face was ashen. 'See Standish. See him today.'

Mr Reginald Standish-White, surgeon, and a family friend, wasn't sure either, at first, and then he shook Douglas's hand as he turned to leave. He noticed that the big man's fingers were curiously limp. Douglas had leprosy.

My uncle vanished abruptly from my life, doomed to spend three horrifying years in the Leper Settlement outside Fort Victoria in the east of Rhodesia. No one would ever explain why I was never allowed to touch his letters, or to handle the books he sent me, or why my parents examined my skin so often. The leprosy bacillus can take up to seven years to show itself, and in that era people still believed that it was highly contagious. Worse, it carried the taint of Biblical superstition and dread: a 'social' disease as loathsome, as shameful as syphilis.

But Dr Moiser cured Douglas eventually, with the only treatment then available: injections of chalmugra oil. He also saved his patient's sanity by setting him to keep the settlement's account books, and persuading him to start a stamp collection. When Douglas died of a heart attack several years later, his stamps were auctioned for £4,000. Today, they would fetch perhaps twenty times that sum.

By the end of the 1920s, it began to look as though trouble had become a permanent guest in our uneasy house. Standing up in my cot, I listened night after night to the sound of Lance pacing up and down the verandah, up and down, until at last I grew heavy-eyed and lay down on the blue blanket with a yellow duck appliquéd on it, to sleep without bothering to tuck myself up.

The bitterest blow of all was still to fall. Lance had somehow contrived to scrape together £2,500 of reserve capital, a safety net to be saved for only the direst of emergencies. There was a dire emergency now. He went to see the bank manager, to arrange for the money to be transferred to his working account.

'*What* reserve?' Mr Howes asked bleakly. Then he saw my father's face and added more gently, 'I'm sorry – but you did give your sisters full signing powers, didn't you? There *is* no money left.'

My aunts had been living extremely comfortably. On Lance's money. We were on the rocks.

Frontier Children

In the days of Rhodesia's innocence, formal schooling began much later than it does now. Children seldom went to school until they were at least six, more usually seven, and very few parents ever gave them any preparatory grounding in the academic basics. It seemed a lot more important to teach them where to dig for water in a dry river bed, how to treat snakebite, and what to do if you were caught between the arms of a veld fire.

I learned these lessons early. Lance showed me how to follow the tracks of cattle along the arid bed of the Matsheumhlope, until the prints came together at a place where there was a faint blush of green grass on the nearby banks, and a hollow had been clumsily hoofed out in the sand. There, he took the shovel he had been carrying and began to dig. Ten or twelve inches down, and the sand began to change colour, from pale gold to the shade of demerara sugar, and a little murky fluid welled up in the bottom of the hole.

'Cattle can smell water,' he said. 'Wild animals, too.' He showed me a tiny, sharp slot, pointed and delicate as an arrowhead. 'After the cows had gone, a duiker came to drink.'

For the second lesson he waited until the grass was high and August-dry. He dressed me up in rompers so that there would be no billowing skirts to catch alight, and took me out to a place well away from the town where there were no houses, huts or sheds that might be damaged by the dangerous game he was going to teach

26

me, which he knew I had to learn. He set me down in a patch where the grass was shortest.

'Wait here,' he said, 'and no matter how frightened you feel don't move until I tell you.'

He walked some distance away from me and took out a box of matches to light a tuft of grass, then ran the flaming torch around me in a wide semicircle. Once he was sure that the veld was well alight he raced back to me and set fire to the grass at my feet.

'Let it burn until there's plenty of room for you to stand on,' he shouted, above the roar of the fires and the noise of my crying. 'Then stamp out the edges and run into the middle of the patch that's already been burnt and you'll be on a safe island. One of the arms of the fire will run with the wind, and the other will work up against it. By the time the arms are nearing each other they won't go any further, because you have already burnt the grass on your island. Always remember that. Always make yourself a safe island.'

He picked me up and started stamping out the small flames that were still flickering at the edge of my safe island. When we got home, my mother was furious because my new tussore silk rompers were speckled with ash. Lance never told her what we had been doing, though, and neither did I, because the way to live through a bush fire had become my proud secret and I wanted to keep it to myself.

Rhodesia was – is – ideal territory for snakes. They range from the slow, malign puffadders and the swift, deadly night adders and cobras that inject haemotoxins to poison the bloodstream, to the swifter and even more deadly black mambas. Provided that you have the right serum to hand, you stand a chance against the first category, but against the mamba you have almost no hope at all, even if you possess the special mamba serum, because its venom is a neurotoxin, which courses through the nervous system and stops the heart in an agonizing spasm.

The FitzSimons Snake-Bite Outfit came in a shiny red oblong tin box and contained a tourniquet, a safety razor blade, a tube of permanganate of potash crystals, a hypodermic syringe and two ampoules of serum to counter the haemotoxins. If you wanted mamba serum you had to buy that separately. In fact, few towns-people bothered to keep any serum at all in their medicine chests because most of the garden snakes had been killed off by feral cats and the savage little yellow mongooses, known as meerkats, which were sometimes courageous enough to invade the suburbs. But no one who lived out in the countryside, miners, farmers and traders, would ever have been foolish enough to do without a FitzSimons kit, plus two spare ampoules in case there was a second snake waiting to strike.

27

Lance's dream of teaching me the techniques needed to outwit Africa by practical example was hampered in one respect by the fact that, during my period of bushcraft tuition, nobody in Bulawayo had the decency to get themselves snake-bit. If they had, I am sure that Lance would have hurried me to their side, little red snakebite box in hand. As it was, he had to content himself with showing me how to tighten the tourniquet around my arm. He also pricked two fang punctures on the side of a green apple, lanced neatly through them with the razor blade, sucked out the imaginary venom, spat, and then rubbed permanganate crystals into the incisions. Finally he filled the syringe with water in lieu of serum, and showed me where, and how, to inject.

'Round the side of the bite, *on both sides*, then higher up on the limb until the two ampoules have been used up. Double the dose for a child, or a dog. You *must* stop the venom from reaching the heart or the brain.'

'What happens if you're bitten just over the heart, or on the head?'
He sighed. 'You die.'

★ ★ ★

When Jacob's plump wife decided it was time to return to her home kraal to sharpen the plough for the next season's planting – and also, while she was about it, to bear yet another dark-eyed, chubby-cheeked infant – a full-time nanny was engaged. Bessie Lindeboom, of mixed race, shy, sixteen, was hired for the modest wage of £4 a month, but before she was allowed to set foot in the house Frances took her on one side and warned her, on pain of instant dismissal, never, *ever*, to let me play with white children, in case they tainted my pure English accent with a Colonial twang.

Bessie took the warning to heart and kept me, religiously, from the companionship of all children of my own race. I struck up friendships instead with the black children of Jacob the cook, and the houseboy, and the gardener, and Bessie's half-breed sisters, and the bright-eyed brown children of the Indian Fruit Sammy. They did not spoil my accent, which remained true to the cold tones of the English upper classes, but they did teach me Sindebele, the language spoken by the local Africans. For a while, I spoke it rather more fluently than I did English.

Sometimes the four Blanckenberg children would pass our gate, laughing and hitting each other with their school satchels. I used to stare at them hungrily, wishing myself into their company, and once I was brave enough to wave at them. Bessie saw me, and snatched me away, fearful of losing her job if I was seen talking to them.

28

Lonely, I found some solace in animals. There was a wired-in run, full of white rabbits and guinea pigs, in a yard right next to the Post Office. On Saturdays, I took to calling at Mrs-Hart-the-Fruiterers to beg discarded lettuce leaves for them. I was not supposed to feed them, but the melancholy man who tended them never seemed to mind. There was a new set of animals in the run almost every week and once, when I asked where a particular guinea pig had gone, the one with a black patch over its right eye, he told me, evasively, that the people from the hospital had called for it. I said I hoped it wasn't too sick.

Margot Blanckenberg, who was riding her scooter down the pavement, overheard me. 'Silly!' she said scornfully. 'Don't you *really* know what happens to them? They're taken to the hospital and then they're cut up into little pieces, so that the doctors can see what their insides are like. *Everybody* knows that!' She scooted on, and I burst into a storm of crying, which lasted all that day and most of the next.

In the morning I had a temperature of 105° and red patches on my skin, but it had nothing to do with what Margot had told me. I had scarlet fever.

In those days scarlet fever was often a killer, but somehow I survived it with nothing worse to show but a badly peeled thumb. As soon as I was well enough to get out of bed, Lance, who was still furious at the guinea pig story, decided it was time I had a dog. My mother protested. To her way of thinking, dogs meant fleas, hydrophobia, and unspeakably promiscuous behaviour in the middle of the high street during the rush hour.

'Junie's *afraid* of dogs!' she wailed.

Lance said nothing, but that afternoon he bundled me on to the front seat of a hired car, and drove me out to a wonderful place called Crowhurst, which was a sort of *al fresco* tea garden, set in the heart of an orchard full of flowering tangerine trees. The honey flow was in full spate and myriads of golden bees, glowing like embers sparked off by the late sun, were raiding the creamy-white flowers for nectar. I had my face buried in a mug of milk when a little fox terrier bitch trotted up and dabbed a cold nose against my knee.

'She likes you,' the proprietress said. 'Our Jess doesn't usually take to children. It's her puppies you'll be seeing when you've finished your tea.' I didn't answer her, because Jess had reached up and was helping me to finish a buttered scone.

There were seven puppies in a box in the corner of the tool shed and I spent a long time quarrelling with my father about which of them I wanted. In the end, we came away with two smooth-coated dog pups, full brothers, Bones and Rags, and God knows what treasured possession Lance must have sold to pay for them because pedigreed stock was not cheap, even in those days. Bones grew up to be a hooligan, pure and simple, and by the time he was six months old he was cutting his teeth on the upper lip of Larry, the big airedale owned by the District Nurse who lived next door. He was also as compulsively randy as the late Lloyd George; no bitch was safe. For his part, Raggie did not fight, except when he was dragged into the foray by his brother. He was also sexually reticent to the point of total celibacy. In fact, Raggie was an *avant-garde* dog, born forty years before his time. He was gay.

The fox terriers dropped out of my life when the two aunts, who had by then been living in Bulawayo for four tempestuous years, returned to England with them, but by the time I was nineteen years old I was running my own cocker spaniel kennels. They brought me unimaginable joy and, at times, almost unendurable heartache. But perhaps that is what all serious love affairs are made of.

The enchanted childish freedom of digging for water during the dry season, and singeing my pants in self-ignited grass fires, ended abruptly on the morning after my fourth birthday. Bessie Lindeboom carried a small folding wooden table out into the front garden, and set it up in the shade of one of the five great fir trees. One of Jacob's children had been scratching the tree bark with a nail, so that the air smelled of resin and impending rain. While I was poking my finger into the pine-scented gum, Bessie went back into the house and returned with a high stool.

'Up,' she said, lifting me on to it. 'Today your lessons start, and here is your first exercise book. Write *on* the lines, like *this*, not between them, and after your eleven o'clock milk I will teach you the twice-times table. If you learn it properly by lunchtime you can have an extra helping of jelly for pudding. It's *green* jelly today, and Jacob made it specially for you, because you are not a baby any more!'

I looked at the muddy whites of Bessie's brown eyes, at her lank brown hair and her floppy brown hat, and decided that I hated her. What I wanted, more than anything else in the whole world, was to go and play with Vivian Blanckenberg, who was riding her new tricycle up and down in the road outside, making tooting noises at stray cats. In the end, though, the thought of green jelly won, and I began to trace out the copperplate letters from the copy-book.

What Bessie couldn't teach me, Lance did. He schooled me in Greek mythology, in all its horror and wonder, and made me memorize Macaulay's *Lays of Ancient Rome*. Together we devoured Rudyard Kipling and at night I lay awake reliving the stories of the day, wishing that I too, like Mowgli, had such friends as the black panther Bagheera; Baloo, the old brown bear who ate only nuts, roots and honey; Akela, the lone wolf, and Kaa, the gigantic rock python. Sometimes I woke during the night, half-hoping to hear the long, desolate howling of the wolf pack in the Seeonee Hills.

Frances, too, generously spent all her small dress allowance on buying membership tickets for the Bulawayo Library, and every night she read to me from one of the classics that she'd retrieved from the endless, dusty shelves that few other people in Bulawayo ever visited. By the time I was seven I had outgrown Bessie's store of knowledge and, in any case, she wanted to leave us to get married. She did leave us, and she did get married, and the next time I saw her, a few years later, she was crying outside the Catholic church and she looked ninety years old.

It was still unthinkable, of course, that I should be allowed to go to one of the local schools and be exposed to the common speech of the other white children. It put even more strain on the family finances, but after a search my parents found a proper governess for me. She was a magnificent woman, an Afrikaner, and her name was Mrs Algernon de Blois Spurr. Mrs Spurr was built like a Percheron mare and had a mouth as wide as a toad's, but whatever she might lack in beauty and grace she made up for in her robust skill at hammering learning into the heads of the thickest pupils. She had a rare, God-given gift for making lessons interesting.

Custard-apples, Crimson Velvet

Suddenly, our luck changed.

Lance imported the first steam-driven road roller ever seen in the town and sold it to the Bulawayo Municipality. It was a great, black, chugging monster with a brass-bound funnel, and it smelled deliciously of hot tar. It also contrived, somehow, to deposit iridescent puddles of tarry water on the road. I indicated, with imperious waves of the hand to the envious Blanckenberg children, that the roller really belonged to *me* and that *I* was allowed to ride on it at will. Which was a lie, but an acceptable one when my pride was at stake.

The profit from the sale enabled Lance to sell his bicycle and invest in a motor car, a glossy maroon Chevrolet with detachable mica windows that could be clipped back on whenever the weather was cold or wet. At the same time, the lease on 111 Jameson Street ran out and, without telling either my mother or myself, Lance took a new house in the suburb of Kumalo, where all Bulawayo's most eminent citizens lived.

The Chev hurtled us importantly up Selborne Avenue, past the Park with its lush cascades of bougainvillea and golden shower; past the pathetic little tree-hidden zoo, a dismal fenced-in acre of scrub that housed a sad old lion, a peacock, and one small antelope; past the open commonage where white ants built towering mud skyscrapers, and on into the elite area with its population of doctors, lawyers and the small but choleric Mr Sydney Veets, the feared and fearsome editor of the *Bulawayo Chronicle*.

The new house stood well back from the road, in a garden that was burning with colour and shaded by huge, spear-leaved rubber trees. Curiously, there was no street name and the house had no number; nor did we ever give it one. It was always just the-house-on-the-corner-of-Edward-Road-and-George-Avenue, and we adored it.

For the first time, I had a bedroom of my own, furnished with pale, apple-green chests, chairs and a dressing table that I found I could use as a desk if I cleared the hair-brushes and dreadful lustre-ware vases off it. Prodded by Mrs Spurr, I began to write stories: stories about animals. One was about a caged eagle that had at last regained his freedom; there was an epic about two male leopards that had fought for possession of a leopardess in the distant Matopo Hills, and a tale about a white tick bird that roosted on a dead hippo. June Lawson, who edited the children's page in the *Chronicle*, ran them all under bold titles and paid me an enormous five shillings for each, which I spent on birdseed for the flocks of blue-breasted waxbills and sparrows and – if I was lucky – the scarlet masked-weavers that congregated daily under my window.

But there was something wrong between my parents – if, indeed, their relationship had ever been wholly right. It wasn't helped by the fact that Frances was the most ardent of Roman Catholics and that Lance, who had once dreamed of becoming a Benedictine monk, had apostatised from the Faith and withdrawn into a lonely shell, with only his growing horde of cats for company. The cats had, in fact, become an obsession. In his youth Lance had been brought up with gundogs and his later preoccupation with cats had begun when Bessie Lindeboom brought him a half-Persian kitten called Brom, which is Dutch for purr. Brom died of feline influenza, but he was succeeded almost immediately by an over-fecund black female stray, which simply wandered in from nowhere one morning and climbed confidently on to my father's knee. Still mourning for Brom, he hadn't the heart to turn her out, and that was the start of a feline folly that lasted until his death.

Lance refused to castrate any of the toms because, he said, it destroyed their birthright, and neither would he ever drown kittens. Eventually there were over a hundred cats of all kinds, squalling, urinating, brawling and producing litters of yet more kittens all over the house. Francie's occasional attempts to beautify our home withered under their perpetual onslaught. The beautiful hand-woven curtains she had bought were shredded, the leather furniture was stained with reeking cat pee, all the fragile, elegant ornaments shattered. Finally she retreated in despair to her own bedroom and kept the door firmly shut. From then on, her meals were brought to her on a tray and when she entertained her friends in what she lightly christened her *sanctum sanctorum* she set out the few pretty, unbroken things that were still left to her.

It was a miserable existence for both of them, but I suspect now that even the Almighty Himself might have found it difficult to apportion the blame fairly. As Lance retreated further and further into his own cloudy world, the cats provided an emotionally undemanding substitute for human relationships. He was disillusioned with what life had offered him, with love, and with marriage, but he could not and would not break his vows to my mother. He had sworn to cherish her until death did them part, and he did not cherish her. He hated her, but he felt himself held fast in the most rigid of Roman Catholic doctrines, which denied them both the kindly release of divorce. Poor, sad, frightened, scatter-brained Frances, who had so much wanted to create a nice, artistic home, and have a host of interesting friends, faded fast under the implacable force of his resentment.

And I? I loved Lance, but I could not bring myself even to like my mother. With the cold uncharity of a child I found her conceited, self-pitying, ineffectual, stupid. Once, when I chided her for using disparaging words about something or someone, she said proudly 'I've always *been* a grouser, I've always *been* a grumbler.' We had no meeting of the minds, ever.

It's a lot too late, now, to repine, but I wish I'd been kinder.

I spent four happy, rewarding years with Mrs Spurr, and when I was twelve she was proud enough of her handiwork to enter me for the Junior Beit Scholarship. This was a formidably competitive award founded by Sir Alfred Beit, eldest son of a prosperous Hamburg merchant. In 1875 an Amsterdam diamond house sent the young Alfred out to South Africa as a buyer, and by the time he was twenty-two he had built himself a staggering fortune. Later he joined forces with Cecil Rhodes and together they founded De Beers Consolidated, a company which gave them what amounted to effective control of the entire South African diamond industry. After the death of Rhodes in 1902, Beit turned to philanthropic works, and one of these was the Beit Trust for University Education in Britain, Hamburg, South Africa and Rhodesia. When he himself died four years later the bulk of his estate was left 'to the peoples of Rhodesia, whether native or immigrant, to be used for the building of railways and bridges.'

After I'd completed the examination papers there were several weeks to wait before the results were announced, so to ease the strain a little I was allowed to spend a long weekend with some grown-up friends who had rented a farmhouse fifteen miles outside Bulawayo, in the belt of scrub bush that still fringed the town. I loved this place. It was a big, sprawling bungalow, with the inevitable mosquito-mesh screens over windows and doors and a roof made of corrugated iron, so that when it hailed the cold little stones bouncing over our heads sounded like a million tiny drummers. There were two custard-apple trees in the garden and the creamy-textured fruit was sweet and stealable. I sucked on the centres and spat out the pips while I fed the chickens. The big bronze rooster ran after them hopefully, then turned and stalked back disgustedly to the sunflower seeds. Sometimes, the family's half-tame duiker ram wandered over and nudged at my fingers, hoping for alfalfa.

The house had no power-supply, and at night I went to bed by candle-light, holding the big brass candlestick tightly, in case I spilled hot wax on the deeply polished floors.

My mother had made me a new crimson velvet dress for my stay and as we sat down to dinner one momentous evening Ronnie Napier, who had recently gone into partnership with Lance, smiled enigmatically and handed me a sealed white envelope. Puzzled, I slit it open with my bread knife and pulled out a new and uncreased £1 note and a thin sheet of paper on which was scrawled, in my father's spidery writing, 'To a very good girl, from a very proud Daddy.' For a moment I was almost sick with pride and happiness. I had won the scholarship.

But there was a bleaker side to my triumph. The Junior Beit paid for three years of my formal schooling, but it also meant that I would be away from home, on my own in a totally unfamiliar environment, for the first time in my life. For a good many Colonial children in those days this was a familiar stage in their development, but at least most of them had already learned to co-exist amicably: the years of isolation had left me totally unprepared for normal, communal living.

Because Lance's beloved Jesuits had been replaced in Rhodesia by German Dominican missionary fathers there was no possibility of my being sent to the local church school: after years of trench warfare in France and the grinding destruction of his comrades in Gallipoli, the Germans were still the Enemy for him. Nevertheless, he wearily bowed to Francie's tearful insistence that I should be given a good Catholic grounding, and I was sent up to the capital, Salisbury, to a convent school run by Dominican nuns.

Without exaggeration, I have to say that I hated every waking second of the time that I spent there, although many of my woes were of my own making. To begin with, I was cordially detested by most of the other girls, because I was a prig and a swot, my hair was red and naturally curly and – worst of all – I spoke a clear, hard English that was offensive to Colonial ears. I might have saved the situation by being good at games, but I could never get a tennis ball over the net, I couldn't swim (I still can't), and the thought of playing hockey reduced me to floods of resentful tears and lies about having a headache. Frances rapidly became bored with the endless litany of misery in my letters, but her early cosseting had been bound to produce bitter fruit: I was miserably uncomfortable in the company of white children.

As it was, whenever the school set out in a crocodile for the ritual walk on Sunday afternoons I was always left at the end of the procession with a morose, shuffling nun as my sole companion. I nursed my hurt in silence, and invented brothers for myself. Sometimes they were sheep farmers, tall and rangy, sometimes English aristocrats exiled to a life of crime as bushrangers in Australia, and shooting it out with the Chief of Police beside a billabong.

These were, after all, the only men with whom I had ever been allowed to associate, because Frances had always rigidly prohibited anything in the shape of a boyfriend. 'Don't make yourself cheap, dear.' Fatal words, too frequently repeated, that in the end signposted a short cut to disaster.

Prohibition must have accounted for a lot of drunks. On my fourteenth birthday I saw, at a distance, and discovered a passion for, Bobby Myers, whose father was 'Bullet' Myers, formerly the Middle-Weight Wrestling Champion of the World. However, not only did Bobby both fail to notice me or to return my love, but I doubt if he even realized that it was on offer. This phantom affair lasted until the day I found out that he had already pledged his heart to a tubby blonde named Dessie, whose small brain was amply counterbalanced by vast breasts. I broke down at the news and, ignoring one of my most inflexible rules, for once I confided in Frances, who only repeated – for perhaps the ninetieth time – 'Don't make yourself cheap, dear.' I only wished I'd had the chance to.

There seemed to be nothing for it but to become a nun, so I spent that week's pocket money on a rosary with yellow glass beads and a gilt crucifix. To the Mother Superior's intense relief, however, my plans were pushed to one side by more momentous events. The Second World War broke out.

A Distant War

The war washed over us with barely a ripple. Rhodesia's farms, mines and factories could produce almost everything the country needed. The farms raised beef and dairy cattle, poultry, pigs, sheep and goats and the feedstuffs to fatten them on, as well as maize, wheat, potatoes and yams, oranges, grapefruit, lemons, pawpaws, peaches, plums, apples and most other orchard fruits. There were tin, gold, coal and asbestos mines, mills to roll out mild steel, and big breweries to keep the beer flowing. Factories made furniture, cookware and hand-thrown pottery. There was plenty of good tobacco. With no coastline the fish naturally had to be imported, but regular supplies were sent up by rail from the rich Cape waters, or from the Moçambiquan ports of Lourenço Marques and Beira.

True, there was petrol rationing, but by pooling their transport most people got by without having to walk much further than from the garden gate to the front door. True, the only available lipstick to be had was a criminally bad Argentinian brand, which melted, and the razor blades, manufactured in Brazil, were generally blunt. There were no silk stockings in the stores, but in possibly the most glorious climate in the world south of the equator, it was no great hardship to go without them. But that was about the limit of our deprivation and, looking back, it is hard to believe that one of the bloodiest, most horrible conflicts in history should have touched us so lightly.

It was only when the war grew older that it began to bite, and boys who had been Father Kendall's acolytes in the Roman Catholic church were trained into eager young recruits and sent away to the distant battlefields. The settler population was small, and the number of names appearing on the casualty lists was disproportionately large.

I tried to join one of the women's auxiliary units and was turned down when the recruiting officer checked with Lance on my age, which was fourteen. The whole interview might have gone better if I hadn't been wearing a gym slip.

At the end of 1940 the scholarship money had run out, but by then Lance was reasonably prosperous and selling all the mining equipment he could lay hands on, so I was sent to the Loretto Convent in Cape Town for the last year of my schooling. The Order was an exceptionally strict one, and all the senior girls were primly isolated in separate bedrooms. This, as a delighted Frances saw it, saved me from having to associate too closely with children of a commoner clay, whose South African accents were even worse than the Rhodesian variety. But it didn't prevent me from smuggling a guinea pig into my room and taking it into chapel one evening, stuffed down the front of my school tunic. Scarlet with rage, the Reverend Mother Superior expelled me.

I was sent back to Bulawayo on the four-day train. Light rain had fallen on the Karroo and the ground was covered in pink vlei lilies. Between them, picking their way from clear puddle to clear puddle over the bright sand, were herds of springbok. I wished, bitterly, that I could get out and walk among them and never see people again.

That night I went out to the open observation platform at the end of my carriage to commune with the high, frost-white stars and to watch the leap and flicker of a scrub fire far out on the horizon. Hundreds of miles away, beyond the perimeter of that fire, a small boy who I had never known was growing up in a prim little sheep town on the banks of the Great Fish River. He had watched thousands of his uncle's sheep die in a drought that lasted for years, and he learned to read everything he could lay his hands on in the Cradock library, where his redoubtable mother was librarian. On occasions, when he was doing neither of these things, he went out to hunt the yellow cobras hiding under the rocks of the three high granite krantzes that ringed the farm, with a small Hottentot girl acting as adviser and guide. One day, he found eight cobras. He pinned them to the ground with a forked stick and beat their brains out with a stone. Then he hurried back to his uncle's farmhouse and triumphantly hung the corpses over the front gate. When his uncle returned from the weekly eighty-mile trip to collect mail and supplies, he thrashed the boy soundly for risking his life. Apparently it did no good. The boy was already his own man.

His name was Richard Vendall Clark, and it was a long time before I met him. Perhaps if I *had* known him at the critical time life would have turned out differently. Probably not, in all honesty. The reaction against the long isolation had made me headstrong and rebellious.

The New Recruit

The high seas were thickly sown with U-boats and all civilian travel between Southern Africa and England had been prohibited, except in the direst emergencies. There could be no question now of my being sent to a finishing school in Britain, and I went back to study with a delighted Mrs Spurr for the last half of 1941. She crammed me very efficiently, and I passed the university entrance exams with honours. I have to admit that I heard the news of my success with equanimity, because I had always assumed that I *must* go on to university. This was not vanity, either, because I had always enjoyed studying and although I was pleased when I took top grades – which I usually did – I also knew that I had worked hard to achieve them. I had no very clear idea of what university life would be like, except for a vague image of cloisters, capped and gowned students and loftily remote professors, and I knew I wanted to read English literature.

Lance had planned to send me to one of the South African colleges as soon as the new term started, but Frances had other ideas, with the usual terrible consequences. She had managed somehow to concoct a weird rumour that all new girl students had to have their hair shaved off, then stand naked in the middle of the campus before suffering a variety of sexual indignities. Incredibly, although I am certain that Lance dismissed these fevered fantasies out of hand, he allowed her to persuade him that I needed a six-month break from my studies in order to prepare myself for these ordeals. The truth of the matter was, of course, a lot more mundane. She wanted to show me off to her friends in the Royal Air Force canteen where she was doing volunteer work as her contribution to the war effort.

With an astounding lack of sensitivity, the combined Air Ministries of Great Britain and Rhodesia had chosen the old agricultural showgrounds in Bulawayo as a base for the Initial Training Wing of the Royal Air Force; before the war, prize farm animals were paraded there before being sent off to the slaughter-yard. To begin with, most of the trainees were young white Rhodesians, some South Africans, and young men sent out from Britain, but later they were joined by extravagantly bold Polish pilots, some Australians and a handful of Greeks. Most of the town's more prosperous families did their best to entertain the trainees, even if only to invite them home for hot baths and well-cooked meals. Frances, of course, would not allow herself to be outdone, and for weeks our bathroom was cluttered with wet socks, cigarette butts stubbed out in the soapdish, and half-finished cups of tea.

She was wise enough not to ask her visitors to full-scale meals because her kitchen skills remained uncertain, but they enjoyed the tea, delicate sandwiches and cake, and the chance just to sit peacefully, in a line along the verandah wall, and soak up the sun without having anybody shouting orders at them. Although he was not, by nature, a sociable man, Lance did feel obliged to make an effort to entertain them, but unfortunately he overcompensated for his shyness by launching into long tales of life in the trenches during the First World War, with details that they probably didn't want to hear. In a roundabout way, I suspect, Lance was actually trying to reassure them, but after a while the young men stopped coming, and my father was hurt.

Then, one day, a batch of new recruits arrived from the Middle East, and while Frances was dispensing bitter, long-stewed tea from a brass urn in the canteen, one of them wandered over to talk to her. He had an unusual, high-pitched voice, but he sounded cultivated – and that immediately disarmed her.

His name was Robert Kay, he was twenty-four years old, and he was handsome. 'He looks just like the young Laurence Olivier!' she enthused, when I arrived home from a last, celebratory tea with my beloved Mrs Spurr. Still preoccupied with thoughts of honours degrees and prizes for English literature I was only half-listening, so I didn't take in Frances's final remark: 'My dear, you must meet him! I've invited him home for tea! This afternoon!'

Robert set out to charm Frances and treated me with the condescension of a sophisticated young airman being polite to a shy sixteen-year-old still gauche enough to wear a wide-brimmed Scarlett O'Hara hat indoors. For my own part, I think I recorded him as darkly good-looking and – fatally – intriguingly mysterious. He disclosed very little of his background, though he did admit to being the son of a retired colonel of the Royal Norfolk Regiment, and that his mother was a Welshwoman who was always known as Toby. He didn't say anything about a wife.

He stayed about an hour and for most of the time he talked to my father, courteously enough it seemed. I heard almost nothing of their conversation, so I didn't know then and can never know now what they said to each other that afternoon. Perhaps Lance detected a disturbing note in the curiously alto pitch of Robert's voice which might have indicated a degree of sexual ambivalence – or perhaps Robert boasted about his girlfriends, which would have been one of the deadliest social sins in Lance's eyes. To men of his background it was still an inviolable rule that no Gentleman ever discussed women or religion.

It's hard now to believe just how seriously such social conventions were taken then, but the colonies were even starchier in their attitudes than the most purse-mouthed prig in the Mother Country. Divorcees were totally excluded from polite circles, unwed mothers were considered little better than whores and treated accordingly, and a man who swore – however mildly – in female company would excite enraged comment for weeks.

No matter how hard I pressed Lance later to explain his reaction, he simply refused to discuss the matter. What I do remember, and with stark clarity, is the fact that when Robert finally left, Lance watched him walk away down the front path, then turned on my bewildered mother and said in a voice that was stiff with rage: '*That boy would be better dead!*'

'This one is all mine!'

'If we have any more children they can be yours,' Lance had said to my mother on the night of my birth. 'This one is all mine!'

Lance was a curious man, impossible to understand fully. He had built a steel cage around himself, and from inside it he looked out at a world he despised and distrusted. It was as if the most ascetic of anchorites had been forced to leave his desert cell and set up home in Babylon. He had no friends at all, absolutely none, and he discouraged even the politest overtures from neighbours or business acquaintances. What he wanted was solitude and a refuge from emotion, but he never saw, or permitted himself to see, that he was compelling me to share his prison. I knew that he expected me to marry one day, but at the same time he shied violently away from the thought of anyone who might remove me from his sphere of influence, or his love.

And Robert? In his own way he was as contradictory as Lance. He was certainly just as self-absorbed, but he also longed to be gregarious, the centre of attention. He was a womanizer, too, but one who in fact despised women and didn't know what to do with those who fluttered into his butterfly net – except, perhaps, just to pin them in his specimen case. But in a community where dullness was the most prized virtue, he did have a certain dash and glamour. The majority of Bulawayo's males had migrated there from Britain because they knew that their modest abilities as bank clerks, minor lawyers, insurance adjusters or quantity surveyors would earn them a far higher style of living than they could ever have expected at home, and this didn't make for sparkle. Whatever else he was, Robert wasn't boring. But he was also dangerous.

Friday

'I danced on a Friday when the sky turned black,
It's hard to dance with the Devil on your back.'
SHAKER HYMN, LYRICS BY SYDNEY CARTER

Within twenty-four hours Lance had retained a private detective in London to make enquiries into Robert's background. The report, when it arrived, was not encouraging. Although his parents had finally married three years after his birth, Robert had been born out of wedlock. When he was fourteen years old the Kay family's fortunes had vanished in the crash that followed the exposure of the notorious British fraudster Clarence Hattray, and the shock had combined with a kidney ailment to kill the Colonel. Robert had to be taken away from the Italia Conti School of Drama, where he appeared to have been a promising pupil, and a job was found for him as a Blue Button messenger on the London Stock Exchange. From there, he progressed to the Royal Norfolk Regiment, but was requested to resign his commission after an acrimonious disagreement with his commanding officer concerning unpaid bills in the Officers' Mess. Round about this time he met, and ill-advisedly married, Violet, who worked in a West End night-club. The marriage lasted for three months, which was as long as it took her to discover that her new husband was unable to keep her in diamonds and hand-made chocolates. She left him, and returned to a former lover.

Robert resolved his dilemma for the moment by joining the British Palestine Police, an organization which then had a reputation for exceptional ruthlessness. When the Second World War was two years old, he applied for a transfer to the Royal Air Force and was posted to Bulawayo.

'A most unsuitable friend for your daughter,' the detective concluded. Lance folded the report carefully, slid it back into the airmail envelope and stood up, touching the edge of the breakfast table with two fingers, as if he needed to steady himself. 'June is not to see that young man again,' he said quietly.

But, of course, I did see him again. In a stubborn act of defiance, Frances arranged for me to work with her in the RAF canteen, and whenever she saw him she encouraged Robert to join us. It might have been done in a spirit of mild spite, but she should have been warned by Lance's scorching disapproval. And what began in the open, ended clandestinely.

For sixteen years my routine had been unvarying. I studied diligently for hours on end each day and, as a treat, I was occasionally taken to the museum and allowed to sketch the exhibits. Because I was never permitted to have friends of my own age, I never learned the rules of the game, how to handle personal relationships. I was totally trusting, but out of a howling ignorance, rather than any exceptional nobility of soul.

At the time, I understood none of this. All I knew for sure was that I had somehow to escape from Lance's loving despotism, and so I flung myself into a love affair with Robert, which began with a bewildering and unsought pregnancy and progressed from there, mainly downhill, to a stormy, tear-soaked marriage that lasted twenty-five years.

The ceremony took place in a grim little register office, and my parents did not attend. There were no celebrations, and not even the pretence of a honeymoon. Two days later I went down with a virulent attack of malaria, and lost the child. And that was the beginning of the end of my own childhood.

I still hadn't learned to link cause and effect, though, because within six weeks I was pregnant again, and this time for the full nine months.

★ ★ ★

'Your baby's going to be a girl,' the midwife said. 'I can always tell. Her heartbeat's the same as yours.' I had been in labour for four days and even the usually impassive matron was beginning to look glum.

'I don't want a girl,' I whispered. 'I want a son. Christopher Rupert. It has to be a son.'

'Bear down,' the nurse said. 'The head's coming. At last.'

Leslie Elizabeth was born, as I remember for some odd reason, on the day that the volcanic island of Pantelleria fell to the Allies. I was seventeen.

There is nothing to be gained, now, by raking over the cold ashes of that unhappy period, and there are still people alive who could be needlessly hurt by too close a chronicle of events. There were faults on all sides, and Robert and I probably had the dice loaded against us from the start. But the one incontestable fact is that my husband

and my father never for an instant stopped loathing each other, and I was bound by loyalty to both of them.

Far Lamorna

'Keep this with you for the night.' Our journalist host, Jack Hughes, handed me a shotgun. Like Jack, the gun had seen better days. 'You've chosen a bad spot for leopards. This is where they always come down from the hills, especially during the first quarter of the moon.'

I looked out into the ink-blocked shadows of tree and boulder. Hanging above the granite ranges was a silver sickle and as I stared at it, mesmerized with fright, a long, eerie wailing arose from the rocks and screamed a warning message to the night sky. 'Leopard! 'Ware Leopard!'

This was wonderful, I thought bitterly. Here I was, but a tender maid, not yet nineteen, who had lived in a town for most of my life. I was wearing high-heeled shoes, a corn-yellow linen dress and pearl and aquamarine earrings – heirloom jewellery. What in hell was I doing here, in the heart of the wild country of the Matopos, at dead of night, camping out in a borrowed tent, trying to prevent the pole I was holding from shaking while Robert hammered the pegs into the hard earth. He finished his task, no thanks to me, and I ducked inside the tiny shelter, laced all the ventilation flaps down and, still with trembling hands, piled up all our suitcases to form what I hoped would be a defensive barrier. I prayed that Jack Hughes had been joking, or at least exaggerating, that the screaming hyrax had made a mistake, or that at worst the leopard was a very small one. This was an especially misguided idea, as I found out later; young leopards are usually accompanied by their mothers.

All that night we suffocated stoically in the closed tent, and in the morning we did not speak to each other very much for quite a long time.

Jack Hughes had woken us at first light, shouting that the sun was up and up must we, and what about a mugful of coffee? Jack was unshaven, a ragged man, slightly built and not very tall, with curiously light blue eyes and wispy, dust-coloured hair.

His clothes were truly astonishing, in the sense that a street sweeper would have spurned them. His crumpled felt hat was stained with grease, cigarette burns and God knows what other traces of the cowshed, and half the brim had been torn away. His khaki shorts, frayed at the edges, were held up by a single strand of string. A grubby, sleeveless undershirt, part-covered by a knitted grey pullover that had long since begun to unravel at the elbows. Bare feet in open sandals, broken toenails.

In its squalor, the wattle-and-daub hut in which he lived rivalled his grimy clothing. The interior was piled high with bundles of old press cuttings and newspapers that had been stacked there so long that the lower layers had been reduced to mouse confetti. No electricity, no running water, no lavatory; there was not even what we used to call a 'long-drop loo'. One treasure: a giant cowrie shell, carved all over with bas-relief pictures of Japanese country scenes, used to weigh down the latest stack of unanswered letters, brown-envelope bills, and demands stamped 'Final'.

And yet . . . he owned his land, all three thousand acres of it, and he raised bloodstock Jersey cattle, and pure-bred Pekin ducks which were housed in a temple of beautifully quarried granite through which he had diverted one of the rare small streams that ran through the Matopos. He wrote in a fine, carefully scrivened hand, and his prose should have placed him at the top of his profession. It never did, and I never asked him why.

When he had finished his coffee, he kicked a log of wood into the smouldering fire, and spat. 'Come on, greenhorns,' he said. He walked us across his land until we came to a barbed-wire fence, strung erratically between hardwood posts cut from the mopani tree and tough enough to resist the termites.

'Top end of a farm belonging to a retired army officer,' he said, jerking a stubbled chin towards the property. 'It's cut off from the rest of his land by a range of small kopjes. He's never used it and he might just let you have it cheap if he's short of cash – and he usually is. It's only about three hundred acres.'

I avoided meeting Robert's eye. I was not going to live *here*, not in a place where leopards came down from the hills during the first or any other quarter of the moon. And yet I followed him when he climbed through the wire strands, and went on following until we came to a place where the land fell away sharply to a long valley. The country had an enervated beauty that was wholly African, full of lapis lazuli shadows. It was autumn and the grass had ripened to saffron yellow, and was raked and tumbled and sheeted by mountain winds. Behind, around, above, towered the granite chain of the Matopos, an antique land of kopje and crevice, whale-backed dwala and plunging rocks, vivid with the close-growing lichen that ran through every shade from aquamarine to scarlet, peopled by baboons and porcupine and ant-bears and jackals and rock pythons and poison snakes and dung-beetles and wild bees and tiny red-velvet spiders that came out after the first rains.

44

As I stood poised on the slope above the valley a small, russet squirrel ran down the face of a nearby rock, stopped, and looked up sharply into my face, half startled, half curious. I can still see him, his bright brown eyes fixed on me, his bushy tail erect, my first friend in the Matopos. He lived among the boulders next to which we built our first small cottage. I had contrived an uneasy peace between Robert and my father after Leslie's birth, and a sceptical Lance had given us the £100 we needed to buy the land from the retired soldier. We called it Far Lamorna.

The war still had a year to run, so Robert had little time to spare from his flying instruction. For all that, though, he still managed to build us a one-roomed hut. He used what we called the 'pole-and-dagga' method, a framework of saplings plastered with clay, whitewashed and thatched with good grass from the veld. He put down a red concrete floor and somehow wheedled Frances into sewing us chintz curtains and bed covers, because he had acquired a wife who invariably ended her attempts with the needle by spearing her own finger ends and spotting the cloth with blood.

I loved this cottage. It smelled of raw linseed oil and woodsmoke, and the scent of the sweet sultan which I planted under the windows drifted up and filled the room with fragrance. The morning glories grew twelve feet high, and covered the roof with electric blue and crimson trumpets. I bought six budgerigars, twelve Rhode Island Red pullets and one pregnant white rabbit: an interesting if unconventional nucleus of livestock for a farm.

Robert's instruction period ended, and he was transferred to an operational training unit in Kenya. I went to work for Lance in Bulawayo, because he no longer trusted me on my own. He had asked me, caustically, what exactly I intended to farm – a crop of boulders, perhaps, or was I going to rear the rock hyrax for their fur?

'Pigs,' I said. 'I've seen such a beautiful black pig. Could you let me have part of my salary in advance, so I can buy him?'

Lance stared at me, in wordless disbelief. I tried to reassure him.

'Not just one pig,' I said. 'I want to buy one every month so I can breed from them and sell the piglets.'

'Jesus!' said Lance. It was the only time that I ever heard him take the name of the Lord in vain.

All my weekends were spent at Lamorna. Before lunch every Saturday little Leslie and her nanny and I roared out in the tiny Austin 10, a two-seater car with a rumble seat that I had bought for £7. We loaded it with chicken feed, fertilizers, cement, canned milk and pumpkin for the infant. There was never quite room enough for the pumpkins in the car, so we used to tie them onto the roof. They always fell off and burst apart on the rocky road.

Because our land was not properly fenced, duiker and porcupine raided my small garden. I replanted everything with laborious care, to the delight of the thieving baboons that infested the surrounding hills.

Baboons live in a hostile environment and in the drought-stricken Matopos their main enemies were the farmers, who shot them out of hand in order to protect their crops, which these ground-apes raided savagely, pulling up everything that they could not eat. Man apart, they have only two other natural enemies – leopards and the great rock python, *Ginyambila*, who will steal the young monkeys from the trees or lie in wait for them when they come down to drink. The anarchic troops run anything up to two hundred strong and they are wanton killers, destroying anything young and vulnerable that comes within their reach – including my cocker spaniel puppy Wendy, who was foolish enough to romp after the troop in play. We found her after three days of searching the veld – and buried the shreds that were left.

I was less than enchanted when Jack Hughes, wishing to be kind, foisted a half-grown and only semi-tame baboon on me. At the end of its first sullen week the dog-faced brute bit Tembo, my elderly cook, when he went to feed it. I unchained the morose beast with absolutely no regrets, letting it go back to its native kopjes and hoping, uncharitably, that it would provide some leopard with an easy meal.

In those days, when the world was sometimes still a little carefree, it was not necessary for white women – even if they lived alone on isolated farms – to hire armed guards. I kept a loaded .22 rifle beside my bed so that I could scare off night-prowling animals, and Tembo assured me that he, and Tiye the chicken boy, and Seepho who looked after the two pigs, and Sixpence who tilled the soil and planted the crops, could easily deal with anything less formidable than an enraged bull elephant. The stonemason, old Kundachavey, who had actually fought in Lobengula's impi Mpondo Nkomo (Horns of the Cow), and was still afraid to use his spear in case it should wake memories of blood, armed himself with a sledgehammer and slept in a grass hut within shouting distance of the cottage. I was a lot safer at Lamorna than I would have been in any town.

Starlings Laughing

Tembo was teaching me to cook. Domestic skills had formed no part of my school syllabus, and I had left Mrs Spurr with a number of geometric theorems etched into my consciousness, but a comprehensive ignorance of cooking, laundering and how to wire an electric plug.

'You should buy an oven,' Tembo advised. 'A small one, the kind that is named Dover, and small so I do not have to spend too much time making it clean. We can cook outside *now*, while the days are still dry, but when the rain comes it will drown any fire that is in the open.'

He went away, and returned with two forked sticks cut from a mopani tree, and a green pole from a 'paper' tree to lay between them.

'Now,' he said, deftly skewering a chicken on the improvised spit, 'because this pole is still green it will not burn through. We will sit here and turn the chicken slowly-slowly over this small fire until the legs come away from the body. Then it can be eaten.'

Duiker liver, first fried in the fresh farm butter I used to make myself and then simmered in canned Nestlé milk mixed with orange juice, wild guinea fowl braised in canned Heinz celery soup, venison cutlets, pot-roast francolin, even a clear jelly boiled up from ripe marula fruit; Tembo made them all.

'This fruit,' he informed me, judiciously skimming the froth from a panful of bubbling, lemon-coloured marulas, 'has everything for everybody. Inside there is a big stone, with three little plugs. The baboons bite out these plugs to get the sweet nut behind them. I, too, eat marula nuts. When the stones are empty the children pick them up and string them to make necklaces. When the jelly is cooked, you will eat it with meat, and I will also make jelly for myself as soon as I have enough money for the sugar. The elephants like the fruit *very* much when it is rotten and lying on the ground. It makes them drunk later, and very dangerous. I have seen them stagger and fall, after they have eaten marulas.' At this point he grunted and changed the subject. His own name, Tembo, meant 'Elephant', and because they were his family totem he did not choose to speak disrespectfully about them.

'How did you learn to cook, Tembo?' I asked, absent-mindedly wiping my greasy fingers on the seat of my khaki trousers.

47

'By eating,' he said.

We sat on logs beside the fire and finished cooking the chicken. The moon was white in the morning sky. Tembo looked up at it.

'*iKwesi yena shaka lapana nyanga*,' he said. 'The starlings are laughing at the moon.'

'Tell me?' I asked.

He chuckled derisively. 'I thought *you* would understand. The Moon, poor fool. She tries to hide from the Sun in the daytime. People do that, too.'

The magic of the Matopos was taking hold of me.

The glaciers of the Ice Age had never touched this land, but the rocks still looked as though they had been worn smooth by ice, because that is the way in which African granite weathers. It was as if some giant force had hurled the great egg-shaped boulders haphazardly together and then suddenly abated, leaving them unchanged and unchangeable, slippery as mountains of glass that would wear only a little more in the next million years. This was the oldest granite in the world. The boulders had been prodigally piled one on top of the other, and in wet weather the slopes were seamed with blue water lichen where the little streams ran away and wasted themselves in the sandy soil at the bottom. The colours were ink-green, indigo and burnt ochre, spiked here and there by the brilliant red blossom of wild aloes, and in summer the heat rose from the earth in shimmering waves.

The Matopos also acted as a magnet for troops of earnest young archaeologists who came out to scrape up stone arrowheads and to photograph the figures that had been painted on the living rock by the little Bushmen who now survived only in legend. They tended to be especially excited by one particular rock face on which some forgotten artist had shown a number of pin-men who were brandishing spears while energetically copulating horse-fashion with their even more graphically detailed women.

This was not lion country, so the leopard, bright, richly rosetted, was Lord of the Matopos. He lived in the hills, and he was a more vivid animal than the light-coated leopard of the plains. At sunset he came down to drink from the pools that caught his reflection as still as a painting. At night I heard him coughing in the veld, and sometimes he was answered by the alarmed barking of baboons which had seen or scented him. The silky grey hyrax chattered in fright as he passed them and francolin, fat and dumpy in brown feathers, heckled from the underbrush.

There were other animals, too. Jackal – shy, red, foxy – lived under falls of dead timber, and the black-faced vervet monkeys vied with the baboons for possession of the trees, forming long monkey-garlands, holding hands in silhouette against the moon.

48

The aardvark, which Africans had christened 'the witches' horse', dug down deep into the warm brown earth to where the white ants tunnelled endlessly, and flicked his long sticky tongue back and forth, destroying the Socialist State of Ant. Sometimes, just at dawn, wild bush pigs came to raid the maize field, with a porcupine looting behind them, rattling his black and white quills like dice in a shaker. There were red hares in the hills and grey hares in the open spaces, and the great rock python *Ginyambila* preyed on them all.

★ ★ ★

There came an afternoon when I sensed that something was wrong. Tembo and Leslie and I had been walking the firebreak that ran along the northern boundary of our land, for no particular reason except that it was a time of day that appealed to us. We could listen to the early-evening fussing of francolin, scolding from thicket to thicket, and watch the first of the day-birds flighting in to roost. I hoped, as always, to see cattle egrets, flying chalk-white against a storm sky, but it was too early in the year for that.

There were times when Tembo and I felt no need to talk. He had been born in the bush, and I had grown into it, and we both possessed that vital instinct for danger. There was danger now. The old man had stopped beside me, scuffing his bare feet in the pale fawn dust. His eyes, following mine, were boring into the thicket twenty-five yards ahead of us. It had been an innocent enough copse this morning when I had visited it, alone, hoping to discover some treasure for my garden: the bulbs of the red hermanthus lilies, perhaps, or some tiny, unscented wild violets. The inner depths were concealed under a dense umbrella of lantana bushes, and in the late afternoon heat nothing stirred. There were no sounds, for even the birds had left the place.

I was carrying an old Bonehill shotgun that Robert had bought for a fiver from Jack Hughes, who was broke. Without a word, Tembo snatched it from me.

'You should stop trying to shoot,' he hissed. 'One day you will hit something and then we will *all* be in trouble. Take the baby and go back to the house.'

My stomach lurched over. I grabbed Leslie's small, sticky hand and we started to walk back down the firebreak, careful not to run. After twenty yards I felt her hanging back, dragging at my hand.

'What's there?' she demanded.

'Leopard,' I said. 'The same one that killed two of Ted Sankey's calves last month. You know about him. We heard him twice last week and again last night. He's big and old, and Tembo says that his coat has faded to the colour of straw.'

She dug her nails into the palm of my hand. 'Do leopards eat people?'

'Some people,' I said, 'particularly if they don't clean their teeth twice a day.'

'I *did*,' she said defensively. 'I even used your toothbrush this morning because I lost mine in the fishpond. Will the leopard eat you first, because you're bigger than me?'

'Probably,' I said, aching to run.

She brightened. 'I *like* leopards,' she said.

★　★　★

The early morning coffee and Tembo arrived together. He looked grumpy.

"maGerimani is here,' he announced. amaGerimani (Many Germans) was Ted Sankey's head cattle man. 'He says that our leopard went on to their land last night and killed two more calves in the pen. One it took away and ate, one it did not eat. He wishes compensation. Five shillings.'

I could not somehow imagine Ted Sankey, my delightful Cornish-born neighbour, demanding five shillings for two bloodstock calves which had been slain by my own particular leopard. Leopards were a common problem right across the Matopos, and there were all too many of them. Even so, most farmers generally preferred to leave them alone. For one thing, they were the only natural enemies of the baboons, and it was a lot cheaper to lose the odd calf than to face the onslaught of troops of baboons in the maize fields.

Still, I knew when I was beaten. Tembo had stood his ground last night, while Leslie and I had scuttled for home.

'All right,' I sighed. 'What do you want five shillings for?'

He smiled, immensely relieved. 'For sugar money,' he replied. 'The marulas are ripe. Two-and-sixpence sugar, six pounds marulas.'

'Where does 'maGerimani come into this?'

'I owe him the other two-and-sixpence. For beer.'

My Son, My Son!

Late in 1946 I had to confess to Lance that I was pregnant again. He was not pleased, but he only sighed, paid me six months' salary, and told me to go back to my absurd farm and knit bootees. I was content to go, but quite unprepared for what turned out to be a summer of calamities. As the heat increased, the crevices between the rocks became a spawning ground for venomous snakes, but it was not until Christmas that the hazards of living in the Matopos revealed themselves in full, and by then I was seven months into my pregnancy.

Supervised by Tembo, who had appointed himself foreman, a couple of African idlers were hired to build us a kitchen. The pole-and-dagga hut had been stoutly built and neatly thatched, and it housed the tiny cast-iron Dover stove that Tembo had been hankering after for so long. The mistake we made was that we failed to place the usual protective sheath of asbestos lagging around the metal chimney, which led straight through the thatch. A second mistake was to locate the kitchen only a few paces away from the cottage, *and* on the windward side.

I had spent most of Lance's gift on baby clothes and, because I was no longer working, we had very little money to spare. As often as not, our evening menu depended on what Robert had managed to shoot earlier in the day. On the morning after the final sheaf of thatch had been laid in place he took the Bonehill and went to look for francolin. I kept myself busy feeding the chickens their usual mixture of sunflower seed, crushed corn and a hard grain called rapoko, and Tembo was diligently mixing the next day's floor-polish in a battered can. He had raised the task of polishing to an art, and he could produce a brilliant shine on the cottage floor with a mixture of red stoop polish plus paraffin and candle wax. To complete the blending process, however, it was necessary to mix the ingredients over a high flame. Unfortunately, instead of putting the can on the outside fire which we normally used to heat our bathwater, he set it on the new Dover stove.

As I scattered the last handful of grain among the busy hens I heard the sudden roar of blazing thatch. The kitchen roof was burning furiously, and sheaves of flaming grass, caught in the updraught, were whirling into the sky. Within seconds the heavy thatch covering the cottage was also well alight.

51

There was very little we could do, but we began by freeing the budgerigars so that they would not be roasted alive in their cages. I opened the wire doors and the bewildered little birds whirred past me in a skein of emerald and blue. Then Tembo and I began dragging out anything we could lay our hands on before the bone-dry roof collapsed in on us; half-choked by smoke, I noticed the old man carefully putting the paper Christmas decorations in a place where the flames couldn't reach them. Then he picked up a pale green pottery salad bowl, a favourite of mine, filled it from the canvas water bag we used to hang on a thorn tree, and tried to hurl the lot on to the roof. The bowl crashed back to the ground in fragments, and what was left of the roof followed it. When Robert got back from his hunting an hour later, I was poking about disconsolately among the smouldering ruins and Tembo was sitting on a rock, crying.

Robert was furious, but mainly because the green salad bowl had been broken.

For a while we lived in a borrowed tent. Then my mother came out to join us for a weekend's carefree camping. After she had unpacked she set about cleaning her hand mirror in methylated spirits and then threw the used polishing cloth into a pit full of dry leaves that I was hoping to turn into compost. Because she thought the pit looked untidy she dropped a lighted match on to the cloth. That was the end of the tent, and everything in it.

Lance heard the story from a sobbing Frances. The next day a truck arrived at Lamorna, towing a second-hand caravan. The driver unhitched it, handed me a receipt made out in my favour, and a brief note from Lance: 'At least you'll have some sort of a roof over your head'. When Lance was really angry he never bothered to sign his letters. He had not signed this one.

★   ★   ★

The rains were late in breaking and, because their normal prey had scattered in search of water, the leopards became especially troublesome. A week before my baby was due, they killed my donkey foal, little Humar, who used to trot up to the caravan door every morning and wait for his bottle of milk. He had no mother to suckle him. A cobra had seen to her.

Robert, who believed firmly that any experience at all was useful, insisted that I come with him on a reprisal raid. For himself he borrowed a very old and inaccurate .303 rifle from Ted Sankey, and he armed me with his nine-inch hunting knife.

'If a leopard does come for you, try to get the knife in behind its left shoulder,' he counselled me earnestly. 'The *left* shoulder, remember. The heart side. Now get a move on.'

We knew the gully where one big male leopard laired. He would leave it, sometimes, to scour the land for calves or the occasional unwary duiker, but today he was at home. I sat on a rock facing the hump-backed granite kopje and watched him lazing on a ledge in the late sunlight, while Robert stalked him from behind. I felt some sorrow, because, old or not, this leopard was still a beautiful creature.

It was a still afternoon, and sounds carried a long way. I heard a dry branch crack under Robert's weight, followed by the sharp metallic click of a safety catch. The leopard heard it, too. People had been hunting him for years, and there were buckshot pellets embedded under the skin of his right foreleg, so he had a score to settle. He stood up, and his tail twitched. Then he turned his head and looked full at me.

The temperature was over 90°F, yet I felt frozen. *Please God, not now. Not just now. I don't know how to use this knife. If You will save me just this one time, I promise that I will never . . .*

I had made that promise so often before, about one thing or another, and I had always broken it, so I have no way of knowing whether God believed me this time. In the event, however, the leopard slid off the rock on to a lower crag, sprang away in a beautiful, arcing bound, landed in the valley, and then casually strolled past me, barely twenty-five yards from where I was sitting, while the baby inside me kicked in protest against my constricted stomach muscles. As the big, powerful animal passed gracefully into the long grass, I pressed my hands hard against my diaphragm, fighting an intense desire to throw up.

'You were lucky,' Robert said heartily as he scrambled down to join me. 'You don't often get a chance to see leopards in broad daylight.'

'Yes,' I said, fighting the nausea. 'I was lucky.'

★   ★   ★

The next day was a Sunday and, very cautiously, because there was no longer much room between my stomach and the steering wheel, I drove the thirty-three miles to my parents' home in Bulawayo. I was still upset, and I wanted to talk out my fear with someone who had not been there, had not seen the leopard sitting on the rock or the useless knife in my hand.

Lance was sitting on the verandah with a sleek tortoiseshell cat on his lap. The cat opened jade green eyes as I came up the steps and slid silently away without a backward glance.

'Don't worry,' said Lance. 'She'll come back. She just doesn't like strangers.' He stood up, and pulled out a chair for me. 'What is it?'

I sat down and took his hand and fiddled with his fingers and told him about everything, from the fat blue flies that had been buzzing around the carcass of my donkey foal to the twig that had snapped under Robert's foot, and the snick of the safety catch on the rifle, and the way the sun had made golden pools of light on the leopard's rosetted coat, and the whirring detonation of harlequin quail rocketing out from the long grass as the leopard stalked away down the long valley, leaving me in a churning agony of fear.

'When exactly is the child due?' he asked, and his face was unreadable.

'Next week,' I told him. 'One more week.'

'A week.' His voice was harsh. '*One week*! And he takes you on a leopard hunt.'

He said nothing more for the moment, but rose and went into his bedroom. I heard him open the door of his wardrobe, which was where he kept his .45 Webley revolver. He broke it open and I heard the rattle of the cartridges in the cardboard carton where they had been kept since the end of the First World War. There were more clicks, and I guessed he was loading the gun. He did not bring it with him when he rejoined me, so he had probably put it away somewhere it would be easy to find if he needed it. I then began at last to get some measure of the hatred between my father and my husband.

'If that bastard ever puts you in danger again I'll kill him,' said Lance.

★   ★   ★

My son was born a week later. His eyes were blue and his hair was blond and his name was Robert Tristram and Lance brought me pink carnations because it was not the season for roses. He sat beside the bed and lifted my hands and held them against his face and I could feel that he was crying. I cried too, for I had a son – a son! – so nothing could ever go wrong again. I have wondered, since, if Absolom's mother felt the same.

★   ★   ★

For a time Robert had a job with a government department that specialized in creating satellite townships for African workers in the new factories, with rudimentary houses built mainly from asbestos sheeting. Robert was an intensely practical man and this work suited him well, but inevitably he quarrelled with the foreman in charge of the project and he was dismissed. Once again, I was the sole breadwinner.

Lance's rage was absolute and, inevitably, I was caught in the crossfire between his anger and Robert's arrogant refusal to accept any form of criticism. Because my husband was now out of work, there was no prospect of paying back the money that Lance had lent us to buy the Chevrolet Imp coupé that was our only means of transport between Lamorna and town. Wearily, Lance wrote off yet another debt. A new row blazed.

Both of them constantly demanded my undivided loyalty and, between them, they were doing a fair job of tearing me apart.

The Cuckoo Chick

'If you could be alarmed into the semblance of modesty, you would charm everybody. I exhort you to restrain the violent tendency of your nature. The whole effort of your mind is to destroy. Because others build slightly and eagerly, you employ yourself in kicking down their houses, and contract a sort of aversion for the more honourable, useful and difficult task of building well yourself . . . Do not such repeated attacks wear in some little degree the shape of persecution?'

THE REV. SYDNEY SMITH TO FRANCIS JEFFREY,
EDITOR OF THE *EDINBURGH REVIEW*, C. 1802

When the cuckoo chick expels the offspring of its reluctant hosts from the nest, it is acting through a programmed instinct for survival, and not through spite. Perhaps some people are like that.

Shortly after Tristram's birth I began to detect for the first time what seemed to be a strange contradiction in my husband's character. He was a superb, totally instinctive and innovative creator of structures: houses, barns, chicken runs, cattle pens, power-generating plants, barbed-wire fences, cement-collared wells, earth dams, tiled roofs and stone-faced fireplaces. None of those things fazed him. He could, and did, work brutally long hours without ever complaining, laying brick or tiles in the glare of a Tilley paraffin pressure lamp long after the last of the daylight had gone. Often, his hands would be raw from cement burns.

But there was another side to him. With people he became a destroyer, a despoiler, who took a harsh delight in demolishing those small conceits that most of us need to create in order to live comfortably with ourselves. It did not make him popular, but whenever anyone showed that their feelings had been hurt or their vanity outraged, he would shrug and laughingly dismiss it all as 'just my Puckish sense of fun'.

In over a quarter of a century, however, I never once heard him laugh at himself.

★　★　★

My three hundred acres of granite were bisected by the old Antelope Mine road which ran between Bulawayo and the Limpopo River, far down on the border of Portuguese Moçambique. Only about a tenth of the land was arable, and until we sank a well in the long valley below the house our sole water supply bubbled up from a tiny spring that dwindled to a reluctant trickle in the dry weather. There was another valley, lying along the base of the farm on the far side of the road and walled off from the rest of the world by the stumps of what had once been a great mountain range.

The folk who farmed in the Matopos generally based their herds on ratios of eight acres to a sheep, ten to a cow, and they were very nearly right. The coarse grass in the vleis[1] was only sweet just after it had been burned off, just before the rains, and the cattle used to survive by browsing on the leaves of the mopani trees during the summer, and on whatever grazing they could find among the scrub bushes on the kopjes during winter. Sometimes, when the rains were late, the cows would snatch at anything that was green in colour and then die from veld poisoning having eaten the fleshy succulents that sprang from the earth in defiance of drought. The long-horned ranch cattle were hardy enough, but serious farmers who raised pedigree dairy herds had to supplement the meagre natural diet with feed concentrates all the year round. Most of the dairymen used, in fact, to run what were known as 'cream-and-pig' operations; the rich cream from the Jerseys was sent to Bulawayo in the big cargo trucks, and the skim that remained was fed to pigs which were destined to end up as bacon in the refrigerated warehouses of the Cold Storage Commission.

I was proud of my four plough oxen and my seven cows, but the milk yield was too small to justify either cream production or pigs, so I started up a small herd of black-headed Persian sheep and two hundred chickens – a mixture of Light Sussex, which were good to eat and dutiful brood hens, and Black Australops, which laid well. The birds were penned at night, but during the day they were allowed to forage in the orchard, where they ate the windfalls from

[1] Water meadows

the peach trees and aerated and manured the soil. They also helped to save the local genet cats and jackals from starving to death in bad years, which wasn't exactly how I'd planned the enterprise.

We did have one five-acre field on the level ground between the house and the road, and after the oxen had dragged out the tree stumps and the brush had been cleared Robert fenced it in with heavy-gauge steel diamond-mesh netting. In this field we grew our vegetables, corn, potatoes, alfalfa for the livestock, and strawberries for our table. It was a light, sandy soil, so that the crops needed constant irrigation to keep them from drying up – except in the one freak year when the heavens opened and drowned out three acres of precious potatoes just before they were due to be harvested.

There was a tree in the Matopos called the M'hlandlovu, 'Elephant Leaf', which bore great bosses of crepe yellow flowers every spring, and these yielded the nectar from which the wild bees made their main honey crop. In a moment of inspiration, Robert bought in swarms of domesticated Italian five-barred golden bees from an apiarist in Bulawayo and installed them in six hives, in the shade of a wild mahogany tree overlooking the earth dam he had built. His bees soon found the M'hlandlovu, the pungent, paper-white blossoms of the dombeya and the purple flowers of the alfalfa, and for a while the honey they produced was the only profitable crop on the farm.

We poured far more money into the ground than ever came out of it. Still, at least we had plenty of fresh vegetables, tender table birds, big brown eggs, all the butter and cream we could eat and delicately flavoured mutton. And we could have had them all for a fraction of what they cost us if we'd bought them direct from the Farmers' Cooperative in Bulawayo.

Rodger, alias Mzenge

One Sunday a tall, craggily handsome African strode up the sand track that led from the road to the burnt-out shell of the cottage and asked for work. He was dressed in tattered khaki shorts and an undershirt that had seen a good many better days. He also looked as if he could do with a square meal.

I went to Tembo. 'Do you know this man?'

'Oh yes,' he assured me. 'Everybody knows Rodger Mzenge Jackson Sibanda. *Everybody.*' He paused for dramatic emphasis. 'Even the police.'

'Come back next Sunday,' I told the stranger. 'I have to think.'

I drove over to check with the District Commissioner at Kezi, which was Rodger's home kraal. He laughed for what seemed an unnecessarily long time.

'Yes, I know him,' he said at last. 'Everybody knows Rodger-alias-Mzenge-alias-Jackson Sibanda. He's a murderer, and a thief. Served six months for ivory poaching. Got a slightly longer stretch for castrating his wife's lover. Man bled to death. Judge let him off lightly because according to tribal law he'd been seriously provoked and was too much of a gentleman to harm the woman – apart from giving her a couple of white eyes. He'd steal your last button, but apart from that he'd never let you down. I'd trust him with my life, never my cash. You employing him?'

'Yes,' I said.

Rodger sang as he ploughed the greasy furrows, occasionally pausing to curse his beasts, lovingly. The great oxen turned their mild eyes on him and steamed and sweated in the strong ploughlands, nibbling delicately at the new shoots of grass whenever he rested them. They dropped great clots of dung, fertilizing the field as they went.

'Hup, skellum![1] Hup, skellumami! Get on, my skellum! Get on, my devil! You, with the big feet, move to the whip! You, the lazy one, pull or I'll kill you!'

Jamroot, the vindictive ox, had been incompetently castrated, and he still had one of his testicles, plus half a bull's temper. He tossed his head up and down next to White and their long horns clicked together, but the beasts pulled. Rodger loved his oxen, and they worked for him as for none other. The share cut through the earth, slicing it cleanly and leaving long arteries open to take the pearly seed of the corn.

Under Rodger's big, knotted hands, the level ground on my farm was transformed from stubbled bush into orderly fields that rustled with silver-green stalks. He hoarded the manure from the chickens and when it had rotted down sufficiently he dug it into the garden and planted pumpkins, bright yellow custard-squashes, scarlet runner beans and good, conical cabbage. When the crop looked unpromising, or if foraging cattle broke through his fence, he never had any hesitation in calling on his tribal gods for aid. He tied the leaves of the wild ground orchid, *Tigridia*, to the fence posts in order to ward off rain until his day's work was finished, and he sent away to a distant witchdoctor for a handful of hyena bones, which he burnt to windward of the crops to discourage malign spirits. Nor would he ever allow me to keep tame guineafowl, in case the cook stirred up evil by accidentally burning their feathers.

[1] Rascal.

The permanent house at Far Lamorna was also taking shape. Robert moulded the bricks from local clay and burned them in a set of rounded, wood-fired kilns that glowed in the night. The big white bungalow formed three sides of a square, with a patio in the centre. It was built for coolness and light; the windows were huge and there were no ceilings, so we looked up through heavy dark beams at the thatched roof where geckos and fieldmice lived. The geckos clung to the walls with their tiny suckered feet and killed insects in the gable ends, while the fieldmice made nests and stole grain from the big kitchen where we stored the chicken food. Birds drank from the rock pool in the patio and flew cheerfully in and out of the windows, ignoring us. Each sunrise a mocking chat sat on the bedroom beams and sang, sweet and lemon shrill. When the early morning tray was brought in I crumbled the thin bread and butter and threw it on the floor for him. He hopped and pecked and fluttered, and took the crumbs away to feed his nestlings in the kopje.

Ordeal by Fire

One summer the rains were very late in breaking. The unremitting October heat stripped the skin from the land, in a pelt of scorched grass and withered vlei lilies. Day after day, ranks of sullen cumulus cloud built up above the northern horizon, without ever shedding their moisture, and we had to watch our land dying slowly in the sun. The water level in the earth dam fell by the hour, until in the end there was only a slimy puddle left. By now the forty-foot well itself held barely enough water to meet our most primitive needs, and we had to drive the thirty miles to Bulawayo and back every day to fill a truckload of forty-four-gallon petrol drums from the emergency standpipe outside the City Hall. We needed a hundred and thirty gallons to keep our stock alive, but our few cows grew bone thin and each day our small flock of sheep straggled higher up the kopjes in search of the meagre tufts of shrivelled grass and stunted bushes that remained. Even the eggs under the broody hens dried out, because there was not enough moisture in the atmosphere to hatch them.

And then came the veld fires. They raged down on us from all sides, leaving charred acres in their wake, and because the house was thatched we had to fight hard to save it. Without water, we were forced to fight the flames with buckets of sand, and by thrashing the leaping tongues of flame with the few tree branches that still had leaves on them. These were not the open-range fires that could be checked by burning safe islands, as Lance had taught me. This was Apocalypse-in-Africa, raging, blazing, setting whole trees alight and whirling huge spirals of molten embers into the air.

And worse was to follow. I went down to the grass-roofed outbuildings one evening, and was trying to clean a silk dress in a basinful of benzine, when Jenny, the children's nanny, wandered in with a lighted paraffin lamp in her hand. '*Madam!*' she screamed suddenly – and the next moment there was a tremendous explosion. With my hair and clothing on fire, I fled outside. Rodger grabbed me by the shoulders and flung me on the ground, rolling me over and over in the sand until he had smothered the last of the flames. The outbuildings continued to blaze, so I stumbled to my feet – and then Jenny screamed again and pointed at Robert.

He looked as if he'd been flayed. He had not known that there was benzine in the basin, so he picked it up and tried to fling it through the doorway. Instantly, he was drenched in flaming liquid. And the ambulance took four hours to arrive.

He spent six weeks in the Bulawayo General Hospital, with third-degree burns on his chest, arms and legs. Reginald Standish-White, whose own son Denis had been badly burned serving with the RAF, took charge of Robert and nursed him back to health, but although the injuries healed over, the mental scars stayed with him much longer. He was convinced that the bright purple cicatrices on his calves and upper arms made him look like a leper.

By late November the rains were still maliciously holding back. It was the ploughing season, but the seed could not sprout. We had to stall-feed the cattle and sheep, and when the bill for their fodder finally threatened to overwhelm us I took a job with an accountancy firm in Bulawayo to help tide us over. Lance heard about it and offered me my old job with his engineering firm, at a vastly increased salary.

My red cocker spaniel Dingo travelled to work with me every morning, and he took his rôle as Office Dog very seriously indeed. All visiting mine managers were meticulously scrutinized and then either granted a friendly wag of his stump tail if he knew and approved of them or warned off with a growl if he did not. Happily for the business, most of them passed the test and, after a while, some of his special cronies took to bringing him gifts, like good chewing bones or perhaps a couple of pounds of reeking duiker meat, wrapped in the bloodied pages of last month's issue of the local mining journal. Rhodesia was that kind of country, then.

Each day, when I heard five o'clock chiming from the clock tower in the market-place, I pulled the cover over my typewriter, drove furiously round to the nearest standpipe, filled the drums and then raced back to water the livestock. It eased me a little to see the great, velvety cows sink their muzzles gratefully into the cool buckets, drinking as if they would never stop, and I always gave an extra ration to the Jersey, who was due to calve before Christmas. The calf kicked and pushed inside of her, and I prayed that there would be sweet grass in the pastures and good, creamy milk by the time it was born.

There was a morning when the headman from the nearest kraal in the neighbouring Tribal Reserve came to see us. He scuffled his feet in the parched dust, wary of asking favours, and his eyes never left the great whale-backed dwala on the far side of the valley. Very early in the day Rodger and I had watched a pair of nesting crows dive-bombing a leopardess and her two cubs as they crossed the skyline of that long hill.

Rodger had grunted, and then spat over his left shoulder to ward off ill fortune. 'That is very bad,' he muttered. 'One *ingwe* is trouble enough. One with cubs is three times trouble. Soon, now, we will be needing that hill.'

'What for, Rodger?'

He hesitated. What he had to tell me was a tribal secret, one of those which were not normally shared with sceptical white folk. But, in a way, I was a friend, because I had given him work when he needed it and without asking any stupid questions.

'Chaminooka lives there,' he said at last. 'There, and in many other places, but mostly there. That is his mountain.' Chaminooka was the Rain God.

The headman was fidgeting. He sucked his breath in through his teeth and spoke to Robert.

'If the rain doesn't come this week our cattle will all die, and we ourselves will have to go into the towns to look for work. Please, *Inkose*, allow our women to cross your land and dance for rain. *Only* our women – *we* may not watch.'

'You are welcome to cross, *M'dala*, Father,' Robert answered. 'We also need rain. We cannot pay for any more fodder.'

'Father of the people, *Inkosiami!*' The old headman held out his cupped hands in the curious gesture of thanks that the 'Ndebele use; it was meant to show that the gift which Robert had given him was too great to be contained in one hand alone. 'Stay well, *Inkosiami!*'

I wondered, not for the first time, why Robert always contrived to relate so much more easily with Africans than he ever did with whites.

The drumming began that night. Hour after hour, the village drummers beat out the antique rhythms of Africa, that sounded like a giant heartbeat. They were drumming to please Chaminooka, drumming for rain, drumming very softly at first like the patter of raindrops falling on dry earth, and then loudly, crashing like thunder. The villagers would stamp their feet, turn, twist and sweat in the stifling night, chanting continuously in counter-harmony.

'*Tonight we drum to tell you that tomorrow we will drum for rain. Hear us, Chaminooka, and stay in thy mountain. Tomorrow we will send the fairest and fattest of our women to dance for rain. Be there, Chaminooka, when our women dance!*'

Leslie knew enough Sindebele to understand the words. She reached up and tugged imperiously at Rodger's tattered sleeve.

'Why only *fat* women?' she demanded.

Rodger looked down at her, bleakly. 'When did a thin cow ever get good calves?' he enquired. 'Be quiet now. I also wish to think about the rain.'

Drum for rain, the drums said. The drumming in the villages lasted the whole night through, until the sky turned jade green and another dry, hopeless, rainless dawn was with us.

Early that morning, the women came, shyly, like a herd of dark bushbuck ewes; they were painted all over with flecks of white, as symbols of the rain that had not fallen. Each of the women carried a calabash on her head, or a big cannister, or a clay pot, all full of native beer that smelled sweet as it foamed over the edges of the containers and trickled in frothy streaks down the brown skins. One woman carried a tin platter, sticky with a comb of last season's wild honey that was already turning black.

I asked if I might buy some of the honey for my children, but the woman laughed and shook her head.

'It is all for Chaminooka. It is to remind him that there is no water for the bees, so that they could make no honey this year. Because all the flowers died on the dombeya tree there is no honey now, no *nucé* for your son.'

Another woman carried a dead hare, grey and soft. I knew that the villagers badly needed all the meat they could find, but this, too, was for Chaminooka. If there was no rain there would be no more young hares.

Pitiful, shrivelled offerings. A dry branch of the dombeya tree, the mother of wild honey. Pink buds of vlei lilies that had died before they opened. Dried-out birds' eggs. The foetus of a duiker ewe, dropped because its parched mother could not hold it. This was the sympathetic magic of people who wanted to please the capricious god on his glass mountain.

The little file of women wound slowly across the scorched blackness of the long valley, walking where the veld fires had blazed, under a fevered sky that was still achingly bare of cloud. I watched as they climbed the hill – painfully, because the hot granite had blistered their bare feet. They vanished over the crest where the leopardess and her cubs had disappeared when Rodger and I had sat on the warm rocks. We had talked about Chaminooka, whom King Lobengula had killed in a sudden fit of jealousy a long, long time ago.

Rain God

When I first set down the legend thirty years ago, it was peopled with mystic Black heroes rising in wrathful godhead and smiting each other with magic wands. But putting all that aside, here is the story as I first learned it, slowly, from Rodger, from Tembo, and from old Kundachavey who had fought in Lobengula's impi.

In life, Chaminooka was a chief of the Manica tribe, whose territory lay in the cloudy highlands of Rhodesia, bordering on Portuguese East Africa, which we knew then as Moçambique. This chief was believed to possess supernatural powers over the weather; when the country needed rain, he pissed on a pumpkin patch to let the North Wind know that there was now no more water left for the crops. Since there was no point in leaving his reputation entirely in the hands of the gods, however, he usually timed the little ceremony to coincide with the first electric storms of the season. Predictably, the drought usually broke within the next few days.

Lobengula, who had succeeded M'zilikazi as ruler of the Matabele, became jealous of this enviable talent, so he ordered his impis to attack the Manicas, expropriate their lands and, if possible, find out if there really was anything in the rain-making voodoo. The Manicas, who were fighting on their own home ground, promptly routed the invaders, and Lobengula – who was nobody's fool – instantly sued for peace, while continuing secretly to boil up poison in his cauldrons. In what was intended to be seen as a conciliatory gesture he organized a great feast, which consisted mainly of oxen that his men had stolen and bubbling vats of home brew, which had been well laced with the vegetable poisons of the bush. But

Chaminooka, knowing his host, wisely stuck his fingers down his throat and vomited up the deadly beer before it had time to take effect, remarking, not without justice, that he saw 'blood in the eyes of the impi'.

Had Chaminooka been content to leave it at that the course of history – and perhaps the climate of Rhodesia? – might have been significantly changed. Instead, he was heard to boast about a fool-proof method of disposing of an enemy, which was to pierce him with a sharpened bullrush that had first been coated with the arrow poison made from the pupae of a venomous little beetle that burrowed in the sands of the Kalahari Desert. When news of the boast reached him, Lobengula acted swiftly, sending some of his henchmen to enlist the aid of the Kung Bushman, by force if need be, in collecting a goodly supply of the larvae, in case one wasn't potent enough. It was whispered that the penalty for failing in this quest would be death by slow castration, carried out *before* the victim was pushed over a cliff. It is a tribute to Lobengula's authority that most of his courtiers returned safely, except for a few who had stopped to experiment with the interesting beetles along the way.

In common with most Africans, Chaminooka was devoted to children, so he naturally embraced the little naked boy who came forward to show the chief his new spear, fashioned from a bullrush reed that he had found in the village that afternoon. Playfully, the child launched the spear at Chaminooka's chest. A single, small jab from the sharpened point was all that was needed, for there is no cure for the bushmen's arrow poison. Before he died, though, Chaminooka had the presence of mind to cry out to his gods and beseech them to divert all future rains to the north, to Mashona territory, leaving Matabeleland locked in a drought that could be ended only by lavish gifts of livestock to the Manica or, failing that, a full-blooded dance of appeasement, to be performed by the tribal belles. It was this dance that the women who were now stripping off their clothes behind the brow of the hill were about to offer the God.

Suddenly, I heard the song begin. 'Aie, Chaminooka! Aie, Chaminooka! Send the rain, send the rain, send the rain!' The low, monotonous chanting streamed down the slope of the hill.

I had learned very little about the ritual itself, except that the women danced naked to please the God. They poured beer from the gourds onto the rocks and it ran down in a brown stream that hissed, and then dried on the baking granite.

'Drink the beer, Chaminooka, and make water for us! Dance with us, Chaminooka, and drink the beer for rain!' And so on, and on. Finally, at sunset, the women returned, passing us in silence, too weary to utter a greeting.

64

★　★　★

That night I was sitting by an open window, reading a book and, as I read, the flame of the candle lighting my page shivered, danced and blew towards me. A small breath of fresh air crept into the stifling room and Robert, who was sitting at the table, raised his head.

'Wind's changed,' he said. 'It's beginning to blow from the north.'

He got up and stood next to me at the window. Dingo, his paws on the sill, sniffed the air. The fugitive hope that the candle flame had aroused was so fragile that we hardly dared speak of it.

We went outside. Overhead, the sky was clear and bright, but away to the north there was a solid block of charcoal that widened and climbed as we watched, slowly spreading out into mushroom heads of cumulus that broke and frayed at the edges and gave birth to yet more clouds, thunderheads that reached up and spilled over into the hot darkness where the drunken Rain God was sleeping, snoring like thunder.

Most Colonials manage to absorb some of the beliefs of the people among whom they live. Robert said, 'If the first rain falls at night it means a good season.' Then he remembered the correct magic and added, loudly, 'But it *won't* rain. These clouds will all be gone by morning.'

'No,' I agreed hastily. 'Of *course* it won't rain.'

I didn't think that a little European magic would hinder the spell, so I rapped my knuckles on the wooden frame of the door. 'Touch wood.' We went inside then, leaving all the doors and windows wide open. Then I remembered that leopards might not share our superstitions, so I picked Dingo up and locked him safely in the kitchen.

Chaminooka woke abruptly, at midnight. The curtains next to my bed billowed in suddenly, and something cold and sharp like a handful of tiny pebbles stung my face. This was followed almost immediately by a crash that shook the whole house. I scrambled out of bed. The brass wind-gong in the patio was ringing wildly, but the trees were deflecting the storm and I doubled back towards the courtyard. A roar came up through the bush, like a wall of water walking . . . and it *was* a wall of water. It caught me as I stood there out in the open, laughing, drenched, the cold deluge soaking through my pyjamas, the rain of Chaminooka, blessed god of the glass mountain. The driving storm spread over the house and leaped across the patio, raced through the garden and on, down over the rocks, hurrying like a horse going home, straight for the mountain, to wash away the dried rivulets of beer and hissing in the mahogany

65

trees, then widening far over the Matopos until the whole night was a white flood.

★ ★ ★

Influences of a more malign kind were at work further south that year. It was 1948, and the Nationalist party of Dr Daniel Malan, which had fervently supported the Nazi philosophy throughout the war, unexpectedly routed the marginally more liberal government of Field Marshal Jan Christiaan Smuts, and began to introduce apartheid. Rhodesians were shocked, but mainly because Rhodesian and South African soldiers had fought alongside each other through some of the most terrible campaigns of both wars. They despised the largely Afrikaner 'Nats', and the newsreel films of Belsen and Buchenwald reinforced their disgust. But, secretly, a substantial number still found it hard to disagree with the essence of racial division, and most whites were appalled at the thought that Africans might one day be granted political parity.

It was, after all, a long time before their tolerance would be put to the test.

The Freebooters

In 1951, someone – I forget who – decided to make a bid for international glory, and he chose Bulawayo as the unlikely setting for his enterprise. He somehow persuaded the city's civic and commercial leaders to mount the Central African Rhodes Centenary Exhibition.

As everybody should have known, it was not a good idea. An agricultural show, yes; an Empire Day parade of floats, perhaps. But not an international exhibition. However, a mixture of greed and folly won over the citizenry, and certainly, once the event had been formally announced, this dozing imperial backwater began to attract a remarkable assortment of adventurers, confidence tricksters, spurious aristocrats, and a selection of cads with cleft chins – all hoping to cash in on the simplicity of the locals. True, this unpromising mixture was leavened with a handful of people who had become bored with the narrowly provincial atmosphere – and the increasingly harsh political regime – of South Africa, and somehow felt that the exhibition might generate a little more cultural and intellectual excitement. Some hope. Most of them stayed until the last Royal Visitor had left, then swiftly vanished.

Among the first of the eager-eyed freebooters to arrive in the city was the Baroness Renada, of Romania, who was neither a baroness nor a Romanian, and who changed her titles and nationality with every new European crisis. When I first met her she was being devastatingly French, down to the last '*Zut, alors!*' This did not deceive the French consul, and in any case, during the next few years she became, successively, Italian, Spanish and, for a brief while, a White Russian refugee. By the time of the tragic revolution of 1956 she had metamorphosed into a heart-broken Hungarian, and she had the heavily hand-embroidered peasant blouses to prove it. Even so, she was a good-hearted, generous woman, and only very slightly lesbian.

Renada was closely followed by Barri, *aka* La Marquise le Juge de Segrais, who had been born in South Africa as Elizabeth Shaw. Barri had clear emerald eyes and a beautiful, haunting, slightly mad face. The calypso songs she sang to the guitar were also beautiful, haunting, and slightly mad, but nowhere near as crazed as her small evil son Jason. At the age of two, Jason was an infant Caligula. He never travelled anywhere without his personal bodyguard, a towering Nigerian who had once strangled a leopard with his bare hands – and who was often reduced to sobbing incoherence by the tantrums of his malign little master. Heaven knows how Barri had discovered this man, and it seemed tactless to ask. She had, she claimed, sailed single-handed through the Madagascar Channel, hunted on foot in Kenya, and learned her calypsos from an old brothel-keeper in Trinidad; but if ever she was pressed too closely on these or any other tales, the emerald eyes would slide away sideways and she would murmur, 'Do not speak to me any more. I am practising my yoga.'

Her lovers – and she had many – were always identified by the sticking plaster which decorated their inner wrists; the eerily beautiful drifter always insisted, apparently, on a mingling of blood as an infallible recipe for unbridled lubricity. Barri was also not a marquise, but unlike Renada she had at least taken the trouble to research the history of the Justice of Segrais, so that her claims retained a certain consistency.

At this time the hub of the brighter and less conventional society in Bulawayo was kept well greased by a local auctioneer who painted his fingernails pink and dyed his hair lamp-black. But he had also built himself a beautiful, multi-level stone house, overlooking the big reservoir from which the suburb of Hillside, where my parents lived, drew its water. With the water came generous quantities of bilharzia parasites and large lumps of jelly-like frog spawn, which clogged up the plumbing but which were considered a small price to pay for the privilege of living 'on the Hill'.

Jay, the auctioneer, was a great thrower of parties and he used to judge his success according to the behaviour of his guests; the wilder the better. He gathered together the more audacious spirits in the way a magnet attracts iron filings, and his prize catch in the exhibition season was a shatteringly handsome thirty-eight-year-old adventurer called Terrence Oliver, who had the manners of a duke and the morals of a used-car dealer at the shadier end of the trade. He had been forcibly ejected from South Africa at the end of a period when he had been detained at His Majesty's pleasure, because of a single-handed attempt to end the diamond monopoly of De Beers Consolidated Mines.

Looking for a less chancy livelihood, Terrence turned one of his most striking talents into a well-paid hobby. He became a semi-professional gigolo. Given his distinguished good looks and unflagging sexual stamina, even the women he subsequently swindled went on adoring him long after he'd departed with the fleece. When I met him in London several years later he was trying to disentangle himself from an Asian princess who had pawned her state's regalia without troubling to tell its custodians. Rubies, star-sapphires, emeralds, turquoise and peridot, both cut and uncut – all of them vanished into his wall safe, which was concealed behind an unconventional painting of Tristan and Isolde.

★　★　★

There was only one hotel of international standard in Bulawayo – the twelve-storey Victoria, which was completed just in time for the exhibition. It had been built for the sole purpose of crushing a supercilious hotelier who'd been crass enough to insult the wife of a millionaire who owned the last private gold mine in southern Africa.

The lady was a Mrs Little, and the Little family invariably spent their holidays in the bush, prospecting for gold. One afternoon they had driven into Bulawayo in a sagging old Land Rover, dusty, hot, tired, dressed in grimy khakis and accompanied by a fretful child. The Grand Hotel was full, so they checked in at the Royal, where Mrs Little asked for a glass of milk for the infant. The manager sniffed sourly and informed her that he was running a hotel, not a creche. Mrs Little then made the retort that disgruntled hotel guests the world over dream of making.

'Very well then,' she said smoothly, 'I'll just have to put you out of business.' Within the week she had commissioned an architect and soon, at a cost of several million pounds, the Victoria was built. It did not take long to extinguish the Royal.

We, the self-styled, self-satisfied *jeunesse dorée* of the early fifties, used to stop off at the Victoria bar after work in the evenings, and sometimes the Chef de Cuisine, Luis Corbis, sang to us, to the accompaniment of Barri's guitar. But the Grand Bar and Grill was where the group met at lunchtime on Saturdays. It was the best of the city's cocktail bars, a medium-chic establishment which had a cut-out picture above the bar of a bare-breasted brunette riding a startled-looking rooster; this was a daringly suggestive sexual conceit in what was a stonily strait-laced community. The bush sophisticates made any number of witless jokes about it.

I knew most of the regulars, but one day there was a newcomer. He was a tall man in his late thirties, with good shoulders, close-curled red-blond hair, a military moustache and incredibly blue eyes. Someone introduced us: Alex Munro, has an uncle who's a baronet, but watch him; never travels without his wife *and* his mistress, ha-ha. Joke over. Not a very good one at that.

Because Alex was so attractive he was speedily adopted by the Grand Bar and Grill set, but although he was easy company there were always a few unanswered questions about him. He was especially evasive about the past three years of his life. He claimed to have spent them as a trooper in the Palestine Police, but none of the many ex-PP men who now lived in Bulawayo – Robert included – had ever heard of him. His knowledge of the geography of the Middle East was hazy, and his Arabic was limited to a few fairly commonplace obscenities. Whenever anyone asked him what he did for a living he used to joke that he was unemployable – and unemployable he remained until the day the Department of Internal Revenue caught up with him over some unpaid tax and forced him to work for them as an accountant until the debt had been cleared.

Possibly because the tension between my husband and my father had by now reached a dangerous level, my marriage was showing clear signs of strain. I confided in no one, but Alex was quick to size up the situation. He made no overt passes, but he did take to spending a good deal of time at Far Lamorna. I distrusted him total-ly – but was glad of his friendship. Charming, sardonic, unreliable Alex, who laughed at everybody and, most of all, at himself.

Richard

That autumn a friend gave me a small white porcelain figurine which I innocently displayed on my dressing table, without first having the sense to ask who the lady was. I found out soon enough. She was Kuan Yin, ancient Chinese goddess of fertility, and a month later I realized to my dismay that I was once again pregnant. I flung Kuan Yin into the fishpond and sure enough the Japanese mosquito fish multiplied at such a rate that Rodger was able to develop a profitable sideline, bailing them out by the pailful and selling them to a pet shop.

That was where the comedy ended. The Permissive Society was a long way over the horizon, and since Rhodesia still clung tenaciously to the moral and social standards of 1930s England, there was no way that the pregnancy could be legally terminated. But another child at this juncture would almost certainly mean losing my job as secretary and accountant in Lance's engineering supplies company, and that pay packet was all that was keeping the farm, and us, afloat.

Angry, resentful, despairing, I had no one I could confide in; even though he had become a stern agnostic, Lance still considered that abortion was murder and nothing but. One day I headed for the Grand Bar and Grill to find some uncomplicated company.

A man I hadn't seen before was sitting on a stool at the service hatch end of the bar, singing in a rolling bass-baritone. This was not the sort of thing you heard all that often in the Grand, so I stopped in the doorway to listen. The words, acceptable then, unforgivable now, were:

> '*Darkies all work on the Mississippi,*
> *Darkies all work while the white folk play . . .*'

As the song ended I spotted Alex Munro at the other end of the bar and walked over to join him.

'What's up?' he asked, after he'd bought me a drink. 'Something is, isn't it?' Staring into my glass, I told him.

'Alex, if I have this child now I'll lose my job, we'll be broke and we'll have to sell Lamorna. What am I going to do?'

He thought for a minute or two, running his forefinger around the rim of his glass. 'Do one of two things,' he said at last. 'One, stop agonizing, and have it. Two, find one of the backstreet abortionists and pay him or her £100 for the privilege of killing you.'

A girl we'd known had died of septicaemia only a month before, and the woman who had wielded the knitting needle had fled the country just ahead of the law.

Robert was sitting by himself in one of the banquettes and he beckoned me over. 'You seem to be getting very chummy with Gingerwhiskers,' he remarked, not entirely affably. 'What were you talking about that was so interesting?'

'Sex.'

'Oh,' he shrugged. 'Is that all?'

The man who'd been singing ended his salute to *Show Boat*, graciously acknowledged a small round of applause, and raised a finger to call a waitress. In the process he caught my eye, held it for a while, grinned expansively, and then gave a courtly bow. Within minutes, and without actually issuing any invitations, we were sharing a table and he ordered the next round of drinks. He was about my own age, burly, unlined except for the sunspokes around his eyes. He was also utterly relaxed and, as I was to discover, this had nothing to do with the impressive bar check which the waitress brought with the order.

'Clark,' he said, introducing himself. 'Richard Clark, chief copy editor at the esteemed *Bulawayo Chronicle*. And I know who you are. You are June Kay, a worthy matron of this parish, and I'm delighted to meet you. I have a weakness for redheads.' For an hour he kept me giggling helplessly with a series of improbable stories about his life – which subsequently turned out to be mostly true – and then decided it was time for a tribute to rare Ben Jonson's *Celia*:

> 'Drink to me only with thine eyes,
> And I will pledge with mine . . .'

People stopped drinking to listen, and Mary behind the bar, her dyed red hair tortured into corrugated waves, snorted. But Richard was celebrating the fact that, as he put it, his One True Love had just renewed their broken engagement, so he refused to be discouraged. He then sang *Who Killed Cock Robin?*, but in Zulu.

A week later he was occupying the guest bedroom at Far Lamorna.

★ ★ ★

This development was triggered by an accident.

It was a fine Saturday evening and we had planned a big party, but Richard needed to work late and couldn't join the fun until well after dark. As soon as the ink was dry he dressed himself carefully in a white tuxedo and then roared out along the Old Antelope Mine road on his 350cc Norton motorbike. In those days most of the rural routes were only partly surfaced, with two

71

parallel strips of concrete, and a full covering of tarmac was almost unknown. It happened, though, that in honour of the coming visit of Queen Elizabeth the Queen Mother and the Princess Margaret, who were to grace the great exhibition, the local police post had somehow found the necessary resources to have a good quarter mile of roadway properly tarred, to smooth the royal passage along the route to a meeting with African chiefs.

The road at this particular point swooped sharply round a bend which was closely hedged with mopani trees on either side. As Richard accelerated out of the curve he saw a large animal lying across the road in front of him, warming its belly on the tar. As it turned its head to stare into the headlamp of his bike he saw that its eyes were a vivid emerald green. He also saw spots. It was a full-grown leopard.

Richard's alternatives were clear, and neither of them was attractive. He could steer in front of the beast and risk having it leap for his throat, or swerve behind it and chance having it whip round and rend him from the back. More by instinct than fieldcraft he chose the second option and, opening the throttle as wide as it would go, he hurtled past within inches of its tail. He was still looking back over his shoulder and yelling with triumph as he swung into the second bend, so he failed to see the cow that was ambling across it until it was only a matter of yards from his front wheel. He flung the machine into a sideways skid but it was far too late, and he hit the animal broadside on. The cow vanished in one direction and Richard cartwheeled in the other. When he finally spun to a halt in some bushes he staggered to his feet, his virgin sharkskin jacket was in shreds, his new patent leather shoes had lost their lustre, and chunks of skin had been gouged out of his hands, knees, elbows and right buttock. However, the Norton was still more or less intact and the headlight still worked. In the beam he saw that the cow had also survived – except that it was a bull and heading back fast in his direction. Sitting single-buttocked, he left the scene as swiftly as his wounds would allow.

The rest of the journey was slow and painful and when he finally reached Lamorna, some time after ten o'clock, even Robert was shocked by his language. I rushed Richard into the bathroom and bathed everything he allowed me to touch with warm water and disinfectant. His clothes, apart from those items which had been hopelessly torn, were thick with mud and grease. The only garment in the house that could be made to fit him was one of the sarongs in which I had chosen to see out my third pregnancy. It was short on me, and even shorter on Richard, but we managed to drape his shoulders with a paisley-patterned towel. Unfortunately the Baroness Renada was into a Girl Guide phase at the time and eager to practise on knots and how to untie them – particularly waist knots on sarongs. Finally I spiked her seventh gin with Cape brandy, after which she passed out.

★ ★ ★

The door of Richard's room would never close properly. Dingo had discovered this, and so had my other seven spaniels. To their credit, they always had the grace to wait until Richard had snuffed out his candles and was breathing regularly before they all sneaked in, led by the matriarch of the tribe, Bess. Dingo, Tony, Honey, Jasper, Susannah, Sherry and Spider would then arrange themselves carefully all over his body, while Bess exercised her right to sleep on the spare pillow.

'I will say this,' Richard conceded after one particularly sleepless night, when all eight cockers had suddenly become obsessed by the idea that there were mice in the wardrobe. 'I will say this, though . . . she does at least keep the others from sleeping on my face.'

There were other unsought diversions, too. Richard was woken one night by the glare of the big torch, shining directly into his face. It was held by Robert, who was totally naked and waving a shotgun. He was not wearing his dentures.

'Now look,' Richard pleaded, sweating coldly. 'I never touched her. I swear I didn't. I never as much as laid a finger on her.'

Robert continued to wave the gun. 'Thrs a fkg lpud fter th clvs,' he announced truculently. 'I wng y to cme n hlp me sht it.'

'I promise you, June and I really are just good friends!' Richard insisted. 'Can't we talk this whole thing over like gentlemen?'

'Thrs a fkg lpud fter th CLVS!' Robert yelled, even more clearly this time. 'I wng y to cme and hel me sht igs ballsoff!'

Dying cleanly was one thing. Life without balls was quite another. At this point, Richard told me later, he grabbed old Bess and tried to hold her up in front of his face.

'You wouldn't want to shoot an innocent little dog, would you?' he asked through her thick winter coat.

Robert swore, propped the gun against the wall and vanished.

Before Richard could jam the wardrobe against the door he was back, still naked but now with his teeth in.

'There's a fucking leopard after the calves!' he shouted. 'I want you to come out and help me shoot it!'

In the event the leopard kept its balls and lived to kill again.

The Darling Wilder Ones

Some time before the great exhibition was due to open, Richard suddenly came up with the idea that the embryonic Bulawayo Press Club should invite the Queen Mother and Princess Margaret to an informal party at Lamorna by way of a 'thank you' for the patience with which the royal pair invariably endured the attentions of swarms of reporters and photographers. If everything had gone according to plan I am sure that both their Royal Highnesses would have had much more fun than at any of the stuffy official functions.

Who first suggested that the party should be held on top of a rocky outcrop on the far side of our land which could only be reached after a fairly demanding hike through the undergrowth, followed by a climb up a notoriously slippery path, I do not now remember, but it was probably Richard. He was then, and still is, a romantic royalist – and he was then, and still is, apt to gloss over any little difficulties which might tend to get in the way of the Larger Concept.

At any rate, I did less than nothing at all to discourage him. Far from it. The more I thought about the idea, the more sensible it seemed. The royal visitors could not help but be bored witless by the endless rows of worthies lining up to meet them, and we were convinced they would be enchanted to spend an evening with the bush bohemians in a genuinely African setting – so different from anything they might encounter on Royal Deeside.

The intention was an entirely honourable one and although I might, every so often, toy with the idea of a Damehood, the main aim of everyone who had anything to do with the project was to give the two of them a rousingly enjoyable evening. And, to be fair, if only half of what has been written about them is true, then they would probably have accepted that it was all kindly meant and entered into the spirit of the thing.

How innocent we all were. If we had paused to think for even a fraction of a second we would have realized that, once the Authorities were told about our little plan, they would certainly fling us all down the steps of Government House, if not into the local jail. But the way Richard put it, the Royals and their entourage would be delighted at the invitation to drive the thirty miles from Bulawayo to Far Lamorna, and then bounce along on the rutted track to the

74

outcrop before tackling the last stages on foot. We would boil up great cauldrons of soup, roast buck whole over crackling fires and drink freely, while the stars wheeled overhead and the 'Ndebele drummers beat out their primal rhythms.

I still believe we might have had an outside chance of pulling it off if one or two of the more timid journalists had not suggested – insisted, actually – that we should have a dry run. If ever there was a misnomer, that was it.

There are two things to remember about the Bulawayo of that era. The first is that its social attitudes were about on a par with those of suburban England in the early 1920s. Women still wore hats and gloves and dreadnought knickers, and their mouths were permanently pursed; they married men who did as they were told and who played a lot of hearty games to purge themselves of impure thoughts. The other thing is that liquor was astonishingly cheap and a good many of the younger men were still celebrating the fact that they had survived the war, by getting drunk at every available opportunity.

Our mistake was to try and mix the two elements.

The younger newspaper men and women were a cheerfully anarchic crew, very hardworking and professional in a way that has now become unfashionable. They were also all first division drinkers. There were rumours of riotous battles fought up and down the sedate corridors of the *Chronicle* with water pistols and even firebuckets, which left the entire editorial floor of the building drenched. Thunderflash fireworks were used to enliven evenings when the news was dull and slow in coming. A senior member of the editorial staff was seen dancing alone on the roof of the building at two o'clock in the morning – stark naked.

The management and the editor knew nothing about this other life, or if they did they chose to ignore it so long as the editions came out on time. But they had to be invited to the trial party too. And so had their wives.

What really caused the trouble, though, was the number of people who were not invited but who came anyway. With jobs to lose, the Press people would probably have shown a modicum of restraint on the night; the gatecrashers, who included all the wildest of the town's professional drunks, had no such inhibitions. However, once the decision had been made, things moved far too fast for anyone to take the necessary corrective action.

The party was set for a Saturday night, and the outcrop which had been chosen was about half a mile from the house, and on the far side of the Old Antelope Mine road which bisected our land. Two long trestle tables, camp chairs and extra crockery had been hired from a catering firm in Bulawayo, but as the cargo lorry had dumped them unceremoniously by the side of the road, there was no way of transporting them to the site except by ox-drawn wagon. On the Wednesday before the festivities I began to organize the huge business of moving the furniture, cutlery, lanterns, tablecloths and skin rugs, plus all the cooking implements we were going to need, up onto the outcrop. Entering into the spirit of the thing, Robert went out and shot a couple of klipspringer to provide the main course, while Richard and his friend Luis from the Victoria between them composed the menu.

Came the Saturday, and Richard supervised the roasting of the klipspringers, basting them with a mixture of olive oil, chilli vinegar, herbs, spices and wine, as they rotated slowly over two carefully banked beds of glowing woodcoals. Luis kept himself busy mixing two giant tureensful of a silkily seductive cream sauce, loaded with garlic and perfect for the roast venison. There were potatoes nestling in the embers, bowls of snacks and salads, loaves and loaves of freshly baked bread flanked by dishes of butter that we'd churned the day before.

On the two biggest trestle tables we'd stacked up the hard liquor, the mixers and two tin tubs full of ice and bottles of wine. There were also three large barrels of beer, contributed by someone from a local brewery in return for his invitation to what the more raffish element in Bulawayo society had been predicting would be 'the piss-up of the year'. This was not precisely the image we had been striving for, but the tide was in flood and we could do nothing to turn it back.

It all started well enough. When the creeping dusk began to blur the outlines of kopje and boulder, we lit the paraffin storm lanterns and then touched a match to three huge piles of dry thornwood that had been dragged there during the day by Rodger's patient oxen. The flames from the brushwood leaped high, set the shadows dancing around the three giant, egg-shaped monoliths that towered sixty feet above us at one end of the main outcrop. In the firelight, the streaks of scarlet lichen on their flanks looked eerily like blood dripping from vast sacrificial altars. In the foreground, the 'Ndebele drummers, famous all over the southern half of Africa for their skill, turned the hollow bottoms of the wooden drums towards the fire and began to chafe the thin cowhide tops with their hands, tightening the skin.

The tribe were an offshoot of the Matabele, and the Zulus before them, but – somewhere – the warlike characteristics of those two nations had been bred out of them, leaving a jovial, hard-working people who laughed easily, drank with zest, and toiled willingly enough for the white farmers when they were not tilling their own patches of pumpkins, or playing an intricate gambling game with knuckle-bones in the sparse shade of the red-beaned mahogany trees. But they changed and became men obsessed when drums were to hand, hypnotized by the rhythms of an Africa that was older than living memory.

Tonight the drummers had stripped to the waist, and their bodies glistened with oil and sweat from the heat of the fires. The hide drumheads stretched taut, straining against the wooden pegs that kept them anchored to the pale yellow sounding boxes. Here and there a man began to tap, lightly at first, testing the sound for tension, sometimes stopping to chafe the skin again, stooping as if he listened for a message. The spatter of raindrops on parched earth. The feet of long dead impis pounding the dust. The sensuous, writhing heat of the fertility dance. The bellow of stolen cattle, driven by night from an enemy's kraal. Then, suddenly, they were all playing a wild, intricate, crashing beat, punctuated throughout by the heel-of-the-hand throb of the heartbeat on the tight, vibrating drumhead.

In spite of themselves, the first of the 'official' guests began to look decidedly impressed. Richard, although he had agonized over the wording of the invitations for hours, had neglected to mention anywhere that the event was strictly informal and the setting rugged, so that many unsuspecting souls had dressed for a normal, God-fearing and law-abiding dinner party. But they gritted their teeth and smiled forgivingly, and since the food was good and the drink fortifying, they began to unbend a little.

Then the riffraff, led by the Baroness Renada, came stumbling into the clearing. They fell on the provender with howls of delight. They snatched at the food and, between slavering gulps of wine, they made passes at all the most rigidly respectable guests. And Renada began to dance.

I had forgotten that her party speciality was to wrap herself in animal skins, worn over nothing, then gyrate wildly to the beat of the tom-toms as she shed each pelt with flourishing abandon. Just as the senior official in charge of the arrangements for entertaining the Royals arrived, with his wife, Renada whirled violently into the firelight's glow, and in a final paroxysm the leopardskin she'd been wearing slipped from her naked buttocks. She grabbed the two remaining jackal pelts that had been loosely fastened over her breasts, and flung them at him.

'Titties!' she yelled cheerfully. 'Look at my bouncing titties!'

Robert, who had been dozing comfortably with his back against a rock, suddenly opened his eyes wide, sensed that some acute social disaster was unfolding, snatched up a blanket and hustled Renada off stage.

77

At this point the company wives, acting as one, seized their enraptured husbands and hurried them off into the night, mostly without stopping to say thanks. The more career-minded journalists followed them, grinning apologetically as their equally offended spouses and girlfriends dragged them away. The girlfriends, most of whom had been keeping their swains faithful with promises of future carnality ('After we're married, dear'), were the most put out of all. As they made their way awkwardly down the rocky pathway the drummers broke gleefully into a fresh crescendo and began to sing an explicit little number about tribal fertility rites.

'Well, there goes a promising career,' observed Richard philosophically, as he watched the last of the invited guests vanish into the darkness. 'We might as well start enjoying ourselves.'

And then the party really did start to come unglued at the seams. Like souls possessed, the drummers stepped up the pace even further and the crashing cadences echoed off the rocks and reverberated through the crevices in the kopje. Flocks of bats, attracted by the prospect of an easy meal, came flittering in after the myriads of insects that shimmered in the firelight.

Renada, sensing somehow that the last restraining element had left us, emerged from her alcoholic trance and made erratically but unerringly for the most petrified bachelor in the company, a chartered accountant newly arrived from the London suburb of Isleworth. She enveloped him like a python twining itself around a hypnotized white rabbit, and dragged him off to her lair.

Somewhere in the background I could hear Barri's lilting voice raised in a Lorelei song that was steadily enticing a pair of young RAF pilots to their doom. The wife of one of them was asleep on the ground, her head resting on an ants' nest.

Shortly afterwards, the corps of drummers lapsed, quite suddenly, into a grumpy silence. Robert went to find out what had happened. 'Somebody,' he reported acidly, 'has been giving them neat gin.' The arrangement had been that we would keep them well topped up with food and beer, but we had warned everyone who would listen not to let them get anywhere near hard liquor, for which they had no head at all. Later, a good deal later, we persuaded the prime suspect to confess.

'But, dollinks, it vos just a few drops gin,' said Renada. 'Three bottles only, because they was so *hot* and there was plenty. I do *not* know who it was did give them the other two you did find.' We never did discover what she'd done with the white rabbit after she'd finished with him, but nobody ever saw him in Bulawayo again.

I did find Richard, though the next morning. After the drummers had dispersed, Luis fetched his guitar and he and Richard sang soulfully to a small group of sighing girls and unenchanted males for a while, until the lamps ran out of paraffin and the fires died down. It was beginning to rain anyway, so I fetched a torch and showed the stragglers back to their autos.

Well after sunrise, I led a small party of hired labourers back to the outcrop to clear up the débris. It was a dispiriting task and a wearying one, because my head felt twice its normal size and all the component parts of the party seemed to have been scattered over the surrounding terrain. I found a pile of carpets and hyrax karosses piled untidily in the mouth of a small cave, and it was only when I began to pull them away that I discovered Richard. He was seraphically asleep under the coverings, entwined with two of the girls, neither of whom was wearing a lot.

One, a South African brunette who worked as a secretary for a local solicitor and whom I had always regarded as insufferably prim, instantly disentangled herself and fled shrieking for the shelter of a convenient clump of thorn trees. The other, a much bolder spirit known as Big Babs for two very obvious reasons, was rather less disconcerted at being discovered in what was the most blatantly compromising situation, but then I knew she'd developed a *tendresse* for Richard and had been pursuing him with a single-minded diligence ever since her permanent boyfriend had taken off hurriedly for a spell in Johannesburg while one or two of his less orthodox business ventures were investigated. Richard did nothing to discourage her attentions either, until I happened to mention over the lunch-time drinks that the said boyfriend was a homicidally jealous maniac who always carried a .38 Smith and Wesson in the glove compartment of his car.

For all I knew it could well have been true.

★ ★ ★

The Queen Mother and Princess Margaret never did get to visit Far Lamorna. A pity. They might have enjoyed it.

Instead, they were escorted to a ceremony held outside the District Commissioner's offices on the flanks of the Matopos, where all the tribal chiefs were constrained to wrap themselves up in red flannel blankets and wear white pith helmets – all except one brave and venerable old man, who proudly wore the regal insignia of a leopardskin over the dreadful scarlet cloak which had been thoughtfully provided by an all-caring administration in order to cover his rags from royal eyes.

Moon Birds

'Why *Vendall* Clark?' I asked Richard one night, curious about the unusual name.

He laughed. 'Mother always maintained that it was a mistake on my birth certificate. Personally, I think it was a mistake in her love life.'

We were sitting in the moonlit drawing room, playing 78-speed records on an old hand-cranked gramophone, and I wasn't very happy, because he was leaving Bulawayo.

'Do you *have* to go?'

'I don't *have* to,' he said. 'I *want* to. Look, it's not much of a job. It's a fairly tatty little office, with a flatbed press, and the only way of making photographs is by pouring molten type-metal into a papier-mâché mould, and out in the back yard at that. But it's new. I'm not learning anything new here.'

'But why Northern Rhodesia?'

'First stop on the road to Fleet Street,' he said.

He left a month later. I watched him ride out of the front gate for the last time – and I didn't see him again for another four years.

*   *   *

That evening I took the .22 rifle and walked down to the edge of the long valley until I reached the boundary of Ted Sankey's land. The wire fence was slack where cattle had hoofed it down and I climbed through without difficulty. I was fond of the old Cornishman and he never minded my trespassing on his farm, because I shot nothing, upset no livestock and started no fires with carelessly discarded cigarette butts.

'I'm a terrible moon bird,' Ted had told me once. 'Never plant on a waning moon. The seeds don't like it. They get off to a bad start. I plant when the moon is waxing, and everything grows. The earth knows the law.'

Ted Sankey knew the law, too. He raised the best beef cattle and grew the best maize in the district.

The place for which I was heading was quite a long way down the valley, and it was my alternative refuge after the Rock. I couldn't go to the Rock by day, because its essence was secrecy, and I couldn't go to the Duiker Rock, which was my name for this second haven, by night. There were leopards in the shallow caves high up the kopje, but even they were less dangerous than the speckled night-adders which infested the foothills.

I tied the sling of the rifle to a length of coarse string and climbed the slope awkwardly, because I was now sure that I was more than nine months pregnant. The little wretch was taking its time. I drew the .22 up after me and sat cross-legged, watching the sunset flame and fade, cloaking the granite ridges in sheet gold before the long shadows fell for the last time that night. Go-'Way birds came. I waited for them to announce stridently that duiker were coming down to drink. The grey Go-'Way bird is a laurie, the drabbest member of a colourful clan, and it will screech a warning for anything that moves, from a snake to a buck to a leopard to a man – a nuisance when you're hunting and a blessing if the danger lies behind you.

I could see them jerking through the branches of a flat-topped thorn tree, moving in the ungainly way that parrots have, and at last they started calling. A duiker ram appeared, walking sedately, and then a ewe with a nervous fawn at foot. They drank from a small pool that never dried out, just below the rock. Mother and child broke away with a rush of hooves in response to some scare and then came anxiously back, the doe with frequent backward glances, her delicate ears spread to catch the slightest alien sound. The ram stepped away from the pool and staled, then they all left by the way they had come, up a shallow cutting between the rocks. I waited, hoping for more company, but none came.

Time to go. I put my hands palm-downwards, easing myself off the warm height of the rock, and a small ripple of pain ran across the top of my stomach. Yes? Yes. 'And about time, too,' I said aloud. 'You should have been born a fortnight ago.'

As I reached the centre of the valley a flock of birds whirred into a thicket, seed-eaters from the way they were flying. I had stayed out longer than I meant to and the moon was already rising, but I wanted to see what they were, because I needed some private sense of beauty to hold on to that night. I crept to the edge of the thicket, drew the leaves apart and peered in. They were tiny turquoise-breasted waxbills, huddled shoulder-to-shoulder together on a green branch, a row of small birds hiding from the moon.

Very early in the morning my second son, Oliver, was born.

★ ★ ★

In those days there was never any nonsense about mothers rushing home to Balmoral View with a day-old princeling in their arms. Ten days in hospital was the norm, particularly if the baby was a boy, who needed time to get over his eighth-day circumcision.

When I took my child home, Rodger was waiting on the front steps to greet us. He nodded briefly in my direction, then placed his hands together, palms inwards, and bent one knee.

'Inkosiami!' he said reverently to the small, squirming shrimp in my arms. 'Inkosiami! Great Master!'

I pulled the shawl away from Oliver's face.

'He's not very good-looking,' I said.

Rodger grunted.

'His *nose* is all right,' he said. 'Your other children are pretty, but this one looks like you. Never mind. Perhaps he'll be clever.' Men of Rodger's race had little time for small women. He looked at me critically, assessing my reaction, and then his face cracked into a wide grin. 'When he walks I, Rodger, will teach him to snare amaTendele (guinea fowl) on Inkos Sankey's farm. He has more birds than we have, and if I am with your child he cannot make too much trouble if we are caught. But tonight I give a party. For three days now we have been making the beer for this. I owe much money for the rapoko we have used. This party is to honour the new child. As you are his mother perhaps you, too, will wish to honour him by paying for the drink at my party.'

One Man in his Time

Rodger and his friends were, as things turned out, the only people to celebrate the infant's return. Robert had always rejected the traditional Proud Father routine: he certainly never paced nervously up and down outside the delivery room, handed out cigars, or got sentimentally drunk with his friends to Wet the Baby's Head. Because he was an atheist and I was still a defiantly lapsed Catholic there was no christening party, either.

Robert took a purely utilitarian view of births. They happened from time to time, and they interrupted the rhythm of the days, but since he was only briefly involved in their creation he considered that the baby's arrival was none of his affair. He would never have dreamed of rising during the night to soothe a fretful babe, and the very idea of changing a wet nappy would have nauseated him. Until the children were able to sit at table, their feeding time was something that took place well out of his sight and hearing, if they knew what was good for them.

At the time I believed that all husbands behaved like that and, to be fair, the phenomenon of the caring, sharing father who attends pre-natal sessions and holds his partner's hand during the contractions was a long way away. In 1952, any father who had tried to involve himself that closely in the preliminaries would have been regarded as a pervert or, at best, a freak of nature. Robert, though, took the attitude of lofty disinterest back to the primitive mode. It might have been different if his own childhood had been less unsettled, but he had grown up without any notion of ordinary family life, and nothing had happened subsequently to alter his blithe indifference to the sensibilities and needs of anyone else but himself.

Looking back, I think I've at last been able to fathom what made him so contrary, and the key word is 'rôle'. The abrupt move from drama school to a mere messenger's job had clearly blighted all his hopes for a career on the stage, and after that nothing had gone the way he expected it to.

Putting it simply, Robert had probably always yearned to be an actor, and nothing and nobody would ever be allowed to upstage him. He was, in turn, 'Robert the Soldier', 'Robert the Aviator', 'Robert the Roguish', 'Robert the Squire of Rocky Acres', 'Robert the Man of Action', 'Robert the Great White Hunter', and, always, 'Robert the Gay Lothario', centre stage and with every light in the house focused on him. They were mostly parts which, in truth, he filled quite well, and certainly to his own satisfaction. It was only in the final character that he lacked conviction.

And, where women were concerned, he was totally indiscreet.

★ ★ ★

The children's nanny, Jenny, was waiting for me in the hall when I brought Oliver home. I handed him to her and she carried him off to the spare bedroom that was to be his nursery. The bed where Richard had slept was still there, and Jenny was not quick enough to hide the scarf that had been draped across the headboard.

'Who does that belong to?'

Jenny was profoundly embarrassed, and for a few moments she couldn't bring herself to reply. Finally she said, in a whisper: 'Miss Carol. But Master told me not to tell you, and it was only for two nights, and . . . oh, Madam, please . . .'

My heart hit my feet. 'Miss Carol' was Mrs Venables, wife of a street-corner bookmaker. He was a voyeur, and she was a tramp who specialized in lively dinner parties for which dress was optional; she seldom wore more than a pair of slave bangles. She would also tell anyone who was prepared to listen that she needed to change her lover at least once a week, because if she didn't her face broke out in spots. She'd obviously been working on her complexion at Lamorna.

I could hear a recording of Handel's *Messiah* floating out from the bathroom, so I knew where to find Robert. It was his bath-time music. I don't know why.

He beamed up at me from the bath, toothlessly as usual. This was an idiosyncrasy of his that had always made me shudder. During his time with the RAF he'd contracted some form of trench mouth, and the station dentist had cured him by hauling out all his teeth and fitting him with a new set of ivories. Robert complained endlessly that they hurt, but he never thought to have a new pair made and he only ever wore them to the most important functions, or when he was involved with a new girl.

'Hullo,' he said, standing up and reaching for his towel. 'How's the brat?'

'He's fine. How's Carol?'

He scowled blackly, and turned his back on me as he dried himself. 'I suppose it was that stupid bitch Jenny who told you?' he asked, over his shoulder. 'I'm going to sack her, the second I'm dressed!'

'No you won't, because I hired her and I pay her! But what I want to know is why you didn't take that sweaty slut of yours to some hotel where they aren't fussy who they let rooms to?'

'Oh, for God's sake don't be so bloody immature!' he shouted. 'You don't expect me to live like a monk, do you? You know I don't sleep with you any more – you're not my type. I should never have married you in the first place, and Christ knows why I did.'

'Maybe you had a love affair with Lance's money,' I said bitterly. I stormed out of the bathroom and went back to the big bedroom which we still shared. For a long time I stood at the open window, looking out over the garden, which was shimmering with heat.

So – what to do? Without Robert to help with the rough manual work of the farm, I hadn't a hope of keeping Far Lamorna. And Lamorna was my life, as deeply embedded in my soul as the roots of the wild fig trees that snaked their tough roots down through the cracks in the granite. Whatever Robert did – however much he hurt me – I wasn't giving it up. Because it was impossible for a woman to operate entirely on her own in that patriarchal society, I had no option.

★   ★   ★

At length I felt Jenny's light hand on my arm.

'Madam? Please, Madam, don't cry like that. It sours the milk, and it's time to feed the baby.'

84

The Last of the Wine

Before Oliver was a month old I was back at work, but not for my father. I knew that I couldn't trust myself not to break down and cry on his shoulder, blurting out the whole unhappy story, and I still wanted him to believe that I was brave and self-reliant and well able to handle my own life.

But there were pressing, red-ink bills to be paid – over £300 to the builders' merchants covering cement and roofing beams for the small trading store that Robert had decided to build; some hundreds of pounds for livestock feed and a sizeable sum for Robert's new Hasselblad camera. I applied for a job in an advertising agency, although I'd never sold an inch of space in my life and knew less than nothing about the art. Doreen Mullins, who interviewed me, was a vital and immensely attractive woman with a plainly perverse sense of humour. She looked at me across the cluttered expanse of her desk.

'I've heard about you,' she said. 'They tell me that you can do anything you set your mind to. Can you?'

'No,' I confessed.

She laughed. 'In that case you've got the job. Let's hope we don't disappoint each other.'

I worked for Doreen for six happy weeks and then, out of the blue, I was offered a contract to sell all the advertising in all the brochures for the Centenary Exhibition. The terms were outrageously generous: 'You pay your own expenses, but you keep twenty-five per cent of the gross revenue,' said Norman Yule of the Exhibition Committee. In those days, few of even the biggest companies in Rhodesia ever worked through agencies, and space-selling had not progressed beyond the era of the travelling Brush Man; it was still very much a foot-in-the-door affair.

Sadly enough, the organizers of this bizarre undertaking were still hoping for knighthoods, or at the very least an Order of the British Empire. One of the reasons why the exhibition so signally failed to live up to anyone's expectations was that the event was scheduled for several of the coldest weeks of the winter, a time when the 'M'Kaza' blew constantly from the south-east, and the otherwise faultless climate was at its very worst. Billboards were toppled and the stands in the main complex of the exhibition were constantly rasped by dust. All the main pavilions had been constructed from prefabricated asbestos sections, and since no attempt was ever made to install proper heating systems, the audiences in the display halls and the vast main auditorium froze to the rapturous music of *Aïda*, performed by the Covent Garden opera company. It was the same story in the glamorous Carousel nightclub, where the multi-coloured glass floor, prettily lighted from below, turned into an ice-rink.

But the most disastrous sector of all was Centenary City, which had been heavily promoted as 'de luxe accommodation' in all the glossiest South African travel brochures, and had been designed to house the hordes of tourists who were confidently expected to flock into Rhodesia. Fortunately, just before the building contractors had put the final touches to the communal ablution blocks, one of the brighter members of the organizing committee decided to take a last-minute look at these exotic structures.

The site which had been selected for Centenary City had been an abandoned airfield which, when the war was over, had promptly been colonized by a thriving population of rats, voles, black beetles and centipedes. Newspapers had been stuffed into the twelve-inch gap which yawned between the top of the walls and the ceilings of the one-room prefabs, to keep out the worst of the cold.

'£250!' screamed Norman Yule. '£250 if you'll bring out a brochure which says that in view of the heavy advance bookings it's been decided to drop the "de luxe" tag so that Centenary City can be turned into a cosy home from home. Say anything you like, but get the replacement brochures out by next Tuesday, or we're done for.'

I was probably one of the very few people who ever had any real fun out of the exhibition: I got their brochure out on time, liberally illustrated with photographs of fat women wearing sling-backed shoes and perched awkwardly on high stools in Centenary City's one and only cocktail bar. Norman paid up promptly, with a special bonus for the pictures. On top of this, I cleared another £2,500 in commission from the sale of advertising space in the programmes. Sometimes these assignments took me as far away from home as the Copper Belt in what was then still Northern Rhodesia, Johannesburg, and the South African ports of Cape Town and Durban. I hired a cheerful African driver, David, who chauffeured me round the country and insisted that I should carry a gun in the glove compartment, in case we met up with 'bad peoples'. It was brutally hard work – but it paid for the completion of the house at Far Lamorna.

During the whole of this frantic period I saw my children only occasionally, my husband even less often. Leslie was boarding with my parents during the week and attending a Roman Catholic junior school a few steps away from their home in Hillside. The arrangement delighted Frances, and Lance shrugged his shoulders resignedly: he was only too aware that I could neither quit my advertising job nor leave the farm to run itself and move back to Bulawayo until my exigent brood reached high-school age.

I missed Tristram. He was five years old and still too young to be sent to the Rhodes Estate Preparatory School for Boys, an excellent and old-established institution that was set in the Matopos a scant twelve miles from Lamorna. He'd grown into a merry-hearted child, with a well-developed sense of adventure, a dawning talent for sketching animals, a vivid imagination – and no particular regard for the truth. I knew that he was terrified of his father, and as Robert and I began to drift further and further apart, my small son and I drew closer together. During my infrequent visits home, I was constantly on the alert to defend him from Robert's tyrannical rages, which could be triggered off by something as trivial as a trail of soap flakes spilled accidentally on the bathroom floor.

Oliver had started to walk and no longer looked like a peeled shrimp. Most of the news about him came from Jenny, who wrote to me frequently, ill-spelled letters laboriously penned in bright green ink on green-lined Croxley paper. She added a shy postscript to one of them: she herself was pregnant. 'And I tell you the truth, Madam, I can't think how it happened, because I only met him once.'

Even so, I was not unduly worried about my long absences from Lamorna. At least I was making sure that they all had a roof over their heads. Somebody had to.

When the exhibition finally closed its gates I went on diligently selling advertising space – this time for local agricultural shows and on restaurant menu cards. I also rented a room in an old sandstone building that had once been the headquarters of the buyer for the Consolidated Goldfields, and set up my own book-keeping business, which attracted a single client – a nice little Afrikaner bricklayer, who turned out to be too poor to pay me.

The rogues and renegades who had been drawn into Bulawayo by the lure of the exhibition were drifting away in search of new sheep to fleece, and the town had about it the smell of stale champagne. Barri, the self-styled Marquise le Juge de Segrais, cried when we said goodbye. A year later I came across a copy of her book, *Black Butterfly*. In it, the funereal bells were already tolling. 'I know I shall die young', she had written. 'I am cursed by the legend. The black moth came out of the sea and alighted on me.' I never saw her again, but she did die young, and smiling, in the arms of her fifth husband, the poet Phil Allen. He marked her grave with a piece of driftwood. I still mourn her.

The only one of the Robber Barons who stayed on beyond the death throes of the centenary venture was Alex Munro, and he was – in Robert's eyes, at least – still a too-frequent visitor to Lamorna.

★ ★ ★

For the most part, white Rhodesians ignored anything that happened too far from the country's boundaries, and they had accepted with equanimity the wave of independence which swept across the Middle and Far East in the 1940s. The Korean War at the outset of the fifties did have a direct effect, because it drove up the prices of commodities which the two Rhodesias produced – copper, coal, asbestos, chrome and iron ore, high-grade tin and gold – but the event that first began to disturb the even tenor of their ways was Kwame Nkrumah's election as the first Prime Minister of the Gold Coast in 1952, and again of the renamed Ghana in 1957.

It was the first country in Black Africa to gain full independence, and this made white Rhodesians nervous. I would like to be able to say that I wisely foresaw all that followed in the rest of Africa, but I didn't. Like many, I felt vaguely that we would somehow evolve a form of co-existence with the majority population. It was an illusion that was swiftly dispelled after the first parliament of the new Federation of Rhodesia and Nyasaland in 1954, where the prevailing note was acrimony.

The political winds of change barely stirred my consciousness as I watched Lamorna grow in beauty. Most of our furniture was antique, garnered from salerooms here and there, and the dressers gleamed with copper, silver and pewter, red Venetian crystal and creamy ivory. There were Persian rugs scattered on the polished floors, and some of the rooms were curtained with hyrax fur. The white-tiled kitchen smelled of gingerbread and herbs; the blue-tiled bathroom had a tankful of tropical fish instead of a window. The house was crammed with curios, guns, books, gramophone records, party guests, children and a tribe of cocker spaniels, led by the irrepressible red dog Dingo.

Bees flew back to the white hives above the dam, scarlet-trousered as guardsmen with the pollen of the wild aloe, and all day long the deep hum increased as they worked on the rich combs inside. Cows were bought, calves were born, hens clucked anxiously to clutches of chubby chicks. The wicked old Red Poll cow, Zenda, tried to kill Robert when he went too near her calf one day, and the brown mare Lulu's foal developed a dangerous habit of rearing up and striking with his forelegs.

Pretty Leslie learned to ride the chestnut filly, Julia. Dingo's mother Susannah had more pups, Rodger brought me an infant hyrax, a half-tame duiker, and yet another unwanted monkey. The white rabbit, Molly, unexpectedly produced a litter of apricot-coloured young, having dug her way out of the run and mated with a wild red rabbit.

One night Jenny suddenly went into labour, which lasted for all of half an hour from the first contraction, and I delivered her son by candle-light. The child was platinum-fair, sired by a young South African who had worked, briefly, for the Roads Department, patching up the concrete strips that ran past our front gate on their way down to the distant Limpopo River.

Tris very nearly blew himself and the house up by filling an iron watering can with some of his father's detonators, and then shaking it violently. Oliver ate his way through half a pound of birdseed and three cubes of washing-blue, and was sick on his new rompers. Robert put a fence round the farm to keep the cattle from straying, and installed a generator to give us electric light.

A pair of striped swallows built a retort-shaped mud nest under the thatch of the verandah, and one day a slender jackal bitch with two cubs at foot came to drink from the dam. The banana palms rustled in the wind and the peach trees broke their branches under the weight of fruit. And I was happy, happy, happy.

But Robert was not.

The Target

One evening in late November a crashing tropical storm roared in from the north and within minutes every gutter in the town was spouting torrents of water. I'd worked later than I'd meant to, so I was in a hurry to get back to Lamorna before any of our tiny local streams boiled over. I drove the little Morris across the flooded stormwater drains at top speed, soaking the distributor, and the car hesitated, coughed and spluttered to a halt. That was that. Every garage in Bulawayo closed promptly at five in the evening, so I hadn't a hope of getting home that night. I struggled out into the rain and headed dejectedly for the nearest telephone kiosk.

'Of course I'll collect you,' Frances assured me cheerfully, 'but, darling, do please try not to get wet.'

I looked like a drowned ferret. Frances arrived, eventually, driving her battered old Willys, and told me, with the air of someone offering sanctuary to an orphaned child, that I could have my old room back for the night, and she'd made some toffee.

I slept fitfully, disturbed by the *son et lumière* of the storm, and I had just drifted off into a light sleep when I was woken by a succession of sharp cracks that bore no relation to thunder. It was daylight, and I blinked my eyes against the sunlight that was shining in through the bedroom curtains. The cracks came again. They sounded like shots. Shots?

I didn't stop to look for a dressing gown. Lance's room led off mine, and as I ran through I took in the fact that the door of his wardrobe was open, and his Webley .45 service revolver was missing from its usual shelf. I paused for a brief moment to check, sick with apprehension. In the early days of my association with Robert there'd been times when I honestly feared that Lance, if he were driven too far, might shoot Robert and then take his own life. Later, the feeling receded because Robert seldom if ever joined me now on my own increasingly sporadic visits to my parents; but even so, I wanted no tragedies. Whenever I had the chance, I would slip alone into Lance's room to make sure that he'd left the pistol behind. Now it was no longer there, and my one hope was that, as he sometimes did, he'd taken it to shoot marauding dogs that savaged his cats.

He was standing at the bottom of the garden, still in his pyjamas, with the gun in his hand. In front of him was a sheet of tin, chopped roughly into the shape of a man, and nailed to a tree. He must have laboured for hours to make it.

He turned and stared at me, and his eyes were like cold blue stones.

'I'd have got him in the body every time,' he said, dispassionately. His voice was totally controlled, icy.

I knew who he was shooting at, whose outline that target represented. I walked back to the house, shivering, and halfway there I reached the solitary mimosa under which I had, when I was twelve, made one of my little private gardens. The ring of stones which I'd set around its border was still standing, overgrown with self-sown pink candytuft. I stepped inside the circle, leaned my cheek against the rough bark of the tree, and threw up.

The Lost Leader

'Fleet foot on the corrie,
Sage counsel in cumber,
Red hand in the foray,
How sound is thy slumber.'
SIR WALTER SCOTT, CORONACHE

I must have been mad, or blind, or both, because even after this sinister display I went on trying to ignore the corroding, total hatred between Lance and Robert. Their mutual loathing fed upon itself: essentially, Lance disliked people, and Robert could never imagine any situation in which he might be in the wrong.

One evening, when Robert was paying one of his very rare visits to my parents' Hillside house with me, a quarrel began between him and Lance. It started over something quite trivial to do with the training of horses, a subject about which Lance claimed Robert knew nothing at all. Before I could intervene, the argument had flared into a horrifically intense clash.

Lance ordered Robert to leave the house, and Robert refused to go. My father telephoned the local police. A deeply embarrassed young constable, hating what he was being asked to do, rode up on his motorbike, walked to the verandah and took his notebook from the breast pocket of his tunic. He then looked at me appealingly.

I tried to think clearly, found that I couldn't, and was too soul-weary even to attempt my usual rôle as conciliator. I was tired of being treated like a shock-absorber by both of them, with my own feelings shrugged aside as they acted out their venomous, primitive feuds. 'Let them fight it out,' I thought. 'Let them settle the issue their own way, for good or for ill.'

And it was for ill.

They stormed towards the front gate and I saw Robert raise his fist. His voice cracked with hatred.

'I curse you!' he shouted. 'I curse you in the name of God! May you die, and die alone!'

And Lance did die alone. That night. Of a massive heart attack.

★　★　★

We heard the news in the morning. Leslie cried, but not noisily, as most children cry. Great tears welled up in the olive-green eyes and ran silently down her cheeks.

'It's not fair!' she said at last. 'He was a good man. He always helped us. What will we do now?'

'I don't know, darling,' I answered. 'I simply don't know.'

She suddenly bent forward and kissed me, hard, on the cheek. As far as I remember, it was the last time she ever did that.

Leslie had never been a demonstrative child. She was courageous, self-reliant and seldom slow to turn events to her own advantage, horse-crazy and tender to tears about animals. The only person she truly loved was my mother. Over the years I had felt the child slipping away from me, but because Frances had so little joy in her life I had no intention of discouraging the relationship. Further, I was not going to beg for anyone's affection, least of all my daughter's.

I was once asked why I went on sharing a roof with Robert after the cold horrors of that night, and I could not answer. Three children? No. I'd have done better by them if I hadn't also had to keep Robert. Because Lance had told me that the bond was sacred? 'Marriage is for always, always, always . . .' Dead Lance was too easy an alibi. In the end, perhaps, it came down to that most destructive, scarifying and inescapable factor that wrecks so many lives. Habit.

Lance had detested Robert from the outset, but it is a measure of how deeply Robert reciprocated that loathing that he seemed driven to sustain it long after my father's death. It was as though he felt that Lance was somehow menacing him from the grave. I had sensed that he never entirely abandoned the old antagonism, but even so I was astonished by the final act in the tragedy. Years and years later, when Robert and I were at last winding up our joint financial affairs in Rhodesia, he wrote to me in England asking my formal permission to have Lance disinterred and cremated.

'I want my quittance from him,' he wrote. It was as though he needed the flames to wipe out the last traces of an antagonist he had feared as well as hated.

I replied, rejecting the whole ghastly idea out of hand, and I enclosed a separate letter to his lawyers confirming my opposition. I am not entirely sure that the letter the lawyers received was the one I had sent – Robert had always been able to do a fair imitation of my signature – so to this day I cannot be certain that Lance's body still lies in a quiet corner of the Bulawayo Cemetery, with the war medals I pinned to his shroud in place, and the wreath of red roses I dropped on the lid of his coffin mouldering gently into the earth above him.

Omen in the Sky

On the morning after Lance's funeral new difficulties began, and the first problem was a massive one. Under the terms of the will, his shareholding in the electrical engineering business passed to me. Ian, the office manager Lance had hired when Ronnie Napier left, was shocked at the very idea of working for a woman, and he said so in no very flattering terms. It was a blow that I hadn't foreseen, and a heavy one. Still, I did score one small, vicarious victory over the man. As he stalked out of the office he tripped over Dingo, who promptly bit him in the leg.

But Dingo's loyalty couldn't hide the fact that I was now in a pretty uncomfortable position. To begin with, I was not an engineer, and I didn't know an ampere from a volt. Yet I did have two assets in my favour. The years of working for my father had taught me his costing methods and how he kept his account books. I also knew what a set of sliderails looked like, which of the mines still used the old-fashioned stamp mills and where to buy the camshafts for them, who needed heavy-drive conveyor belt fasteners, that mines where dust levels were high used Totally-Enclosed Fan-Cooled (TEFC) Crompton Parkinson motors, and that the tin mine at Kamativi would take all the mild steel checker plate I could supply.

And most of Lance's clients knew me.

Robert? Robert had remarkable practical skills, but he too knew less than nothing about electrical engineering.

I needed time and solitude to sort things out, so that night I went back to the Rock. Moonlight silvered the granite and transformed the aloe leaves into shining spears. On Chaminooka's hill a hyrax trilled on a note of enquiry – for a snake, perhaps; not for a leopard. I heard the tiny susurrus of termite ants working in the dark. And I remembered the sound of Lance's footfalls, tramping up and down, up and down, on the verandah of 111 Jameson Street. He had pulled us out of far worse trouble than this.

I got some sort of answer from the Tabernacle. At least I had a choice. I could do a simple caretaking job and just sell off the stock, or I could make a real effort to hold on to the main agency – which meant looking for a qualified electrical engineer who didn't mind working for a woman, or being bitten by her dog.

As it happened, I arrived at the right conclusion fairly rapidly.

The next morning, ten minutes after I reached the office, the phone rang. The buyer from Kamativi wanted a 40–horsepower Crompton Parkinson motor, two sets of brushgear and fifteen 8' x 4' checker plates. I drove up to the warehouse in Lance's old Studebaker, spent three hours searching for what I needed, crated the motor with the help of the African staff, and had the whole lot loaded into the goods van of the passenger train because the mine wanted the order in a hurry. The telephone had been switched through from the office, and by midday I had sold two 15-hp motors, a ton and a half of angle iron, and twenty-five boxes of conveyor belt fasteners.

I had no option, now; I *had* to find an engineer the principals of the main agency would approve of. With the help of one of Lance's most respected friends, I found Hedley Duncan. He was also not all that enthusiastic about working for a woman, but – he needed a job that paid well as much as I needed the right man. But even then the battle was by no means over.

The Crompton Parkinson agency was the company's mainstay, and they were hesitating about renewing the contract. First of all, I must go to London and talk to CromPark, but there was no money in the bank to pay for my air ticket, because I had just invested every last cent of capital in a hundred tons of mild steel plates and sections that I knew I could sell.

I had to think fast. Ian had lost no time in setting up his own business, and was doing his damnedest to win CromPark's confidence. I had a beautiful diamond cluster ring that had belonged to my grandmother, but because Cecil John Rhodes had forbidden pawnbrokers to hang their signs anywhere in Rhodesia I hadn't a hope of hocking it. For a long time I sat at my dressing table, turning the ring over in my hand. The sunlight made small rainbows from the diamonds.

'I need an omen,' I said aloud, to nobody in particular. Then I looked up into the morning sky and there *was* an omen, a star – a star shining by day. It was the planet Venus, which is sometimes visible in the early light in the southern hemisphere, and I had been told that a sighting meant good luck. I put on my best dress, silvery-green wild silk modelled on a pattern created by Jacques Fath, and went to call on the manager of Allen, Wack and Shepherd, travel agents.

'My dear Mrs Kay,' he sighed, once he'd heard me through, 'we're *travel agents*, not jewellers, not pawnbrokers. I can't possibly meet the price of a return ticket to London on the security of a *ring*. I don't even know what it's worth!'

'You could keep the ring in your safe until I come back, and give me credit,' I insisted stubbornly. 'I promise to pay

– as soon as I can. And even if I can't, you can sell it to Forbes the jeweller. He is a Scot, but he'll give you a fair price for it.'

The manager of Allen, Wack and Shepherd was a Scot, too. Luckily, he laughed.

'I like your impertinence, young lady. But keep the ring. It's probably safer with you than it would be in our strongroom, because it was broken open last month. You can have your ticket. Good luck with the agency. If they've any sense at all they'll give it to you.'

Broken Bones

I knew and liked the men at the helm of Crompton Parkinson, Douglas Graham and J. B. Scott, but simple liking wasn't enough to hold a major agency; not if you are a girl who hasn't yet touched thirty, trying to keep your footing in an irredeemably masculine environment, and in a mineral-rich country where CromPark knew their machinery was already selling itself without much effort. But the CromPark agency was the life-blood, the heart and the arteries and veins of my new inheritance. And it was more than just a legacy: it was a memorial to all Lance's years of toil. I *had* to win.

At our first meeting in London, I told the two men my plans, and about the new engineer I'd hired, and how One-Stamp Wilson was switching from camshafts to electric motors, and Sam Bruton had hit the mother-lode near QueQue and was going to need 20-hp motors, quickly. They both listened politely, and wouldn't commit themselves. I left, feeling sick.

In the morning Douglas Graham telephoned. 'Lunch at the Café Royal?'

I can't remember what we ate, but the wine was superb. Before it took over completely, I stopped drinking and simply toyed with my glass, because I could sense that my host was weighing me up.

'Your father gave us splendid service over a good many years. But can you give me one good reason, just *one*, why we should trust *you* with our agency?'

'I'm my father's daughter.'

Two days later a registered letter arrived at my aunt's Holland Park house, where I was staying. In it was the contract for the agency. I sat on my unmade bed and sobbed with relief.

★ ★ ★

No need, now, to hurry back to Africa. Life had suddenly become exciting again, after too many downbeat years, but I had a feeling that I might need a good supply of happy and uncomplicated memories to tide me over the next few years.

'*Next stop Fleet Street,*' Richard had said, when he headed north. He had long since wiped the brick-red dust of Northern Rhodesia off his boots and taken a flight to London.

I sifted through all his old letters, checked various forwarding addresses where he no longer lived, made countless phone calls, and eventually ran him to earth at the *Daily Telegraph*, then the most assiduously polished newspaper in Britain, where he was a senior sub-editor. We spent all the time we could together, given his exacting job and my own crowded schedule. Once, when we were caught by a freakish mid-May rainstorm, we scorned the thought of shelter and walked through the streets of London hand in hand, soaked to the skin and laughing, remembering a hundred storms that we had shared in Africa. On another day, we took a pleasure boat from Westminster pier to the Royal Naval College and museum at Greenwich, to marvel at Nelson's tiny uniform. We went to Dr Johnson's favourite pub, the Old Cheshire Cheese, to eat the famous steak-and-kidney pie, washed down with ale. Then we graduated to small and suspect drinking clubs in Chelsea, or joined Terrence Oliver at the shimmeringly elegant Caprice. Like so many of the *condottieri* who had converged on Bulawayo for the exhibition, he had been washed back onto the shores of England.

I couldn't stay forever. I had contrived to pick up a useful second string to the business as a representative for heavy-drive conveyor belt fasteners, and I booked a flight back to Africa on the Wednesday after the long Whitsun weekend.

As a final treat, my cousin Michael suggested that we should drive down to Salisbury, in Wiltshire, to see the great cathedral. The stately Aston Martin in which we travelled was driven by a handsome, silver-haired former colonel, who still had the self-confident air and impeccable grooming acquired during a long career in the Indian Army. I don't know why I chanced to look out of the window when I did, but I saw the oncoming car seconds before it hit us. The impact was violent and the Aston Martin slewed sideways, began to turn over, and then slammed into a cast-iron London lamppost.

I don't recall how I got out, because both the back doors were jammed. I think somebody lifted me free. But I do remember saying 'I'll be all right, I'll be all right,' over and over again. 'You see,' I told the stranger who was sitting on the kerb and cradling me in his

96

Major Lancelot
Brassington-Burn

Douglas immediately
became my favourite uncle

Lance may have been the archetypical Rudolph Rassendale, but his Queen Flavia was something of a let-down

Myself when young

Rodger-alias-Mzenge... had
served six months for ivory
poaching

We camped at a place that
had no name

Far Lamorna

Leslie, Tristram and Oliver

Jack Chase and the dead cow
elephant
*(Photograph by John Monck-
Mason)*

...the blurred and shifting
quality of a macabre
dream...
*(Photograph by John Monck-
Mason)*

Galago Senegalensis: tiny, furry lemuroids that had made the mimosa thicket their home

The buffalo had begun to look restive

Top:
Cubby and Chink aboard the
DUKW

Shaka Zulu moored in the
Thamalakane

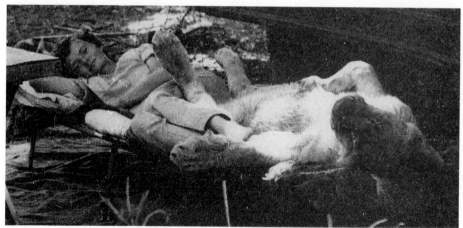

... the laziest animals on
earth (Chink and I)

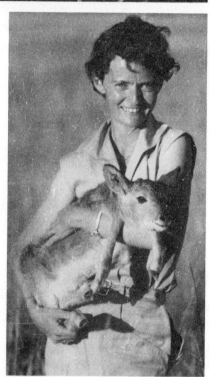

A bush orphan: my reed
buck fawn

Cubby

arms, 'I have to fly to Africa on Wednesday.' He looked at me and shifted my head slightly, so that it rested against his left forearm. He didn't seem to think I'd be going anywhere on Wednesday. I tried to stand up, and fainted from the pain of my splintered pelvis.

★ ★ ★

'Your friend's here,' the Staff Nurse said brightly. 'Mr Clark. Do you remember? You asked us to send for him.' Had I? There were blank, black places in my mind.

Richard came in. He somehow found one of my hands between the festooned drip-feed tubes and the sandbags which had been used to keep me immobile.

'I've telegraphed Robert,' he said. 'He ought to be here.'

'We can't afford another ticket,' I protested weakly, as I drifted off again into a limbo of pain and pethidine. It was years before he told me about my next, half-conscious remark: 'Why are you the only man I've ever known well who didn't make a pass at me?'

Once the crisis was over, I was moved to a private hospital run by Roman Catholic nuns. My first visitor there arrived during the rest hour, and announced himself by sounding several quavering blasts on a fake antique brass hunting horn. Robert also turned out to be wearing a second-hand bowler hat, which he'd bought at the same seedy curio shop as the horn. He did not endear himself to Sister.

It was mid-July before my pelvis had knitted and I was back in Africa, walking with wincing caution – but, at least, walking.

The atmosphere at Far Lamorna when I returned was uncomfortable. After the old house in Hillside had been put up for sale Frances moved into our spare room, where once Richard had slept with his quilt of spaniels. At around the same time, Robert's mother, Toby, had flown out from England. The arrangement did not make for tranquillity.

Toby regarded her son with a combination of irritated anxiety and deep suspicion. Having had to engineer his release from Wife Number One – the far-from-shrinking Violet – she was doubly infuriated by his marriage to me, and she took no pains to hide her dislike. She insisted on tasting his tea before she let him drink it, presumably on the assumption that it had been laced with extract of toadstool. Worse still, if he ever chanced to sleep past nine in the morning she did not hesitate to invade our bedroom, unannounced, to wake him up and make sure that he hadn't died in his sleep.

My own mother, too, was a great bedroom-invader. Although the last time that Robert and I had made love was the night when Oliver was conceived, nearly four years before, we still shared the huge L-shaped room that had been built in happier times, and I preferred not to advertise the fact that connubial bliss had for so long ceased to be a part of my life. After Frances had burst in on us on half a dozen occasions I took to bolting the door, but even that didn't deter her from rapping on the glass panels and shrieking that we had no right to shut her out. I don't know what she hoped to see – raw sex, perhaps. Well, whatever else might have kept Robert and me together, that wasn't it.

I examined my circumstances. The Crompton Parkinson agency was safe for the time being, but that on its own wasn't going to guarantee a reasonable living. I combed through Lance's stock records, to see where the best profits might lie. It became clear that the mines were clamouring for mild steel plates and sections, so I made friends with a quick-witted broker in the steel business and he began to forecast patterns of demand for me. His prices were fair and he never missed a delivery deadline. By mid-1956, my turnover in steel had doubled. Exultantly, I ordered more. Then, suddenly, the world's appetite for steel was satisfied. The ripples spreading out from the Suez débâcle began to wash away some of Rhodesia's post-war prosperity. Stockpiling came to an abrupt end and the market was swamped with surplus steel. I had to sell my stocks at less than they cost me.

In the run-up to the Anglo-French invasion that followed President Nasser's nationalization of the Suez Canal, industrialists everywhere had been buying up raw materials, just in case supplies were dislocated by having to be shipped on the long detour via the Cape of Good Hope. Once the immediate panic was over, and manufacturers discovered that the closure of the Canal didn't affect their exports all that much, normal trade resumed. But as far as I was concerned, the problem was that my customers now began to use their stockpiled supplies of steel, and there were no repeat orders. The bank manager stopped smiling.

Early in 1957, another blow fell. CromPark wrote to say that they had finally decided to set up their own office in Rhodesia. They thanked me for having handled their agency so well, and offered me a penny-pinching ten-per-cent discount on anything I bought from their new branch in the future. My engineering career had been snuffed out.

'Sell the firm now, while you can, before the price drops even further,' Robert advised grimly. 'A bigger company could absorb the loss and still show a profit. You can't.'

In the end I found a buyer for the firm. He paid me a miserably poor price and he sacked all the African staff, including some who had worked for Lance for twenty-five years. But there was no helping it: I had to accept the offer, because nobody else was interested. When the deal had been closed I sank the money into an apartment block. There was a shortage of accommodation in Bulawayo, so it seemed a sensible investment. But I was sore and sick at heart, unable to forget the haunted faces of poor old Charlie and Tom, who had believed that Lance's daughter would keep them on the payroll of a company they'd been with since they were young men.

Flight to Kenya

One night Robert was sitting directly under the pressure lamp, reading a back number of *The Surplus Register*, a curious journal, published in London and devoted to advertisements for such everyday commodities as ten-ton lots of metal hair grips, boxes of boxhooks (slight imperfections), and war-surplus gasmasks. In this particular edition the long War Surplus section offered for sale five amphibious DUKWs, built as lighterage craft for ferrying men and munitions between mother ships and the shore. Robert read the advertisement out loud.

' "£275 each. Spares available." What a marvellous idea. I'll cable your shippers and tell them to buy us one. We can have it properly overhauled in Britain, fitted out with a full set of spares and some extra tyres, and they can send it out to us early next year. Then we can equip it as a safari vehicle, sell the farm, and just wander around Africa for a bit. Later on, we could even drive up Africa, cross the Mediterranean, and finish up in England!'

I was struck speechless. There were the first signs of approaching political trouble in Rhodesia, because the white community had read the portents in the last, flickering afterglow of Empire, and had begun to worry about the future. The Africans, sensing the new uncertainty, began to agitate for an end to a separatist regime that was only marginally less restrictive than the South African model.

Now that there was less demand for Rhodesia's main export commodities, a general malaise set in and the property market began to sag. Farming property, in particular, was showing a slight greenness about the gills, although it still didn't look like a terminal condition.

'*Jesus!* I've never heard anything so absolutely bloody damned ridiculous in my entire life!' I said in blank disbelief. 'I want my farm, I want the cattle and the chickens and the sheep, and the new grove of gum trees. I do *not* want a sodding waterlogged caravan. I am *not* going to live like some sort of damp gipsy.'

Robert folded the *Surplus Register* with unnecessary care and laid it on the burnt-out grass beside his chair.

'Look,' he said . . .

I knew that tone of voice, and the real meaning of that coldly irritated 'Look'. I'd been wasting my breath. Whenever Robert wanted to do something he invariably just went ahead and did it. On this occasion, though, he did at least make some small attempt to conciliate me by pointing out, cunningly, that a few years spent on safari would provide me with all the material I could ever need for the travel book I wanted to write.

And just to sweeten the prospect, what was left of our marriage finally collapsed.

★ ★ ★

My house of cards was falling. The farm, which had for fourteen years provided my main reason for living, was put up for sale.

Richard had written to tell me he was married.

My husband was in love with another woman, and this time it was serious.

The girl's name was Beverly, and she was a hospital nurse. For some weeks she had been a frequent guest at our weekend parties at Lamorna, a new face in the mêlée of people who regularly descended on us for the sake of wonderful food and flowing wine. She was attractive, outspoken and well-bred, and I liked her – until, that is, she and Robert disappeared together for a weekend at the Victoria Falls Hotel. When he returned I asked him, bluntly, what the hell he meant by it and he replied, with equal bluntness, that he intended marrying her. This threatened not only the whole fabric of my life, but the lives of the children as well.

I could no longer fly to Lance for counsel, so I took the only other course I could think of: I went to the Rock. But my tabernacle was silent, empty. Perhaps the spirit of the place had left it, now that I was going.

After a while, I lay back on the warm slope, my hands clasped behind my head. It was a clear night and the sky was heavy with stars. The Milky Way was a luminous veil, and a nightjar was fluting in the bushes. Somewhere in the darkness of the long valley an owl hooted, and a star fell. Mine?

I stayed there for a long time, trying to rationalize the problems I couldn't solve. Sixteen years of marriage, however unhappy, couldn't be shrugged off as if they'd never existed, but I knew that implacably stubborn streak in Robert: it was something he himself liked to describe as 'singleness of purpose', and riding rough-shod over somebody else's feelings never seemed to bother him.

Far Lamorna never had been, never could be, a paying proposition. The only thing that had kept it going at all was the subsidy I had poured into it from the engineering business, and now that, too, had gone. Robert was always willing to work, and work hard, as long as it was at something he wanted to do in the first place and didn't involve accepting a monthly pay cheque.

I tried not to think about Richard's marriage. We had never been lovers, and he had never even kissed me, except happy birthday, happy Christmas, and then goodbye. Yet I was savagely, irrationally jealous.

By morning I had made up my mind. Tris was happily boarding at the Rhodes Estate Preparatory School and I didn't want to disturb his education, but I could take Oliver and go to Kenya. Given time, Robert might tire of Beverly. It wouldn't be the first time that he'd dropped one of his lights o' love after the first few expensive months.

I had friends in Kenya, people I adored: Annie and Louis van de Wiele. Louis was a yacht designer of considerable eminence and had invented the self-steering system of lashed twin staysails. He and Annie had sailed their own ketch round the world, after which she had written *The West in My Eyes*, the best book of the decade on small boat sailing. She was a cook of genius, the kind who could make an old shoe taste like roast pheasant. I wrote to her, and she cabled a reply: 'What are you waiting for? Come at once.'

Robert, who liked to keep his options open, drove Oliver and me to the airport.

★   ★   ★

The van de Wieles lived on the flanks of the Aberdare foothills, beyond Thompson's Falls. In the clear air, Mount Kenya brooded under its cape of snow. The house was built like a traditional log cabin, with a slatted, ceilingless roof and no internal doors, so that each room led directly into the next. The only independent unit was a guest room tacked onto the back; it had its own door, and Oliver and I shared it. There was a fiesta poster from Spain, with a picture on it of a woman in a swirling yellow flamenco dress, and a patchwork coverlet on the double bed. As I tucked the little boy in he squeezed his teddy bear to make it squeak, and I heard Annie laugh on the other side of the thin partition. The air was ice-clean and the night smelled of cedar, fresh grass and, curiously, of nasturtiums. A tree hyrax shrieked insolently from the forest and from somewhere high up on the ridge came the grunting undertones of a leopard.

That night I dreamed of Lance. It was a strange, almost supernatural experience that began with the sound of a disembodied voice that gradually became part of an image which was taking shape in the surrounding mist. I could now see Lance quite clearly and I held out my hands to him, but the figure made no attempt to take them. I felt hot tears running down my cheeks as I told him about my troubles. I know I spoke haltingly, but I was not afraid and I was certain he would understand. 'Will it be all right?' I asked, in the hope of reassurance. 'Yes,' he said, but he sounded hesitant. 'You are at the crossroads now, but you will go on . . . on, to a terrible glory.' The outline began to dissolve and I pleaded with it: 'Don't go. Please don't go. Please stay with me.' I woke then, and looked anxiously about the moonlit room, somehow expecting to find him still with me. Oliver slept on undisturbed, beside me in the big double bed, but the rest of the room was empty.

A terrible glory? It was not a phrase that would ever normally have occurred to me. I did not know what it meant then, nor do I know now. Perhaps it was only a single loose strand in the insubstantial fabric of a dream. Lance never came back to explain it.

Highland Hector

Annie and I were sitting on a neighbour's verandah one afternoon, waiting for her to return from a buffalo hunt that had started well before dawn. She had a house-guest, a Scot in his early thirties, and he was extremely attractive. He was also unattached – and so, virtually, was I. We danced together at a party one night, to a recording of *Blueberry Hill* played on a wind-up gramophone, and we fell, passingly, in love.

I think both Hector and I knew from the outset that marriage was not to be contemplated. Our lifestyles were too disparate and a daughter-in-law as wild and free as I was would never be tolerated by his sternly autocratic parents. But we loved each other enough to keep in touch across the world's oceans when he had returned to his native Scotland – and I was fool enough to keep the letters he sent me, which should have been burnt. In the incurably romantic way that some women have, I hid them under several layers of silk.lingerie in the drawer of my dressing table, and six years later Robert found them there. He waved the ribbon-tied bundle gleefully in my face and threatened to sell them to the London newspapers unless I made an appropriate financial settlement.

'How much do you want?' I asked, sick with apprehension and disgust. Hector was newly married, and I knew that I could never have brought myself to tarnish our brief and honest love affair by selling the story to one of the tabloids.

'Well, now, let's see . . . How about settling half the shareholding in your apartment block on me? Surely it's worth that much to keep your precious Hector out of the headlines? And just think what they'd do to his bride, with a name like hers.'

I knew what they'd do to Hector and his bride, so I paid. Without telling Hector – and if he ever reads these words, I would like him to know that the debt has long since been cancelled by time.

That, though, was still a long way ahead, and in the warmly realized present my life seemed to be reshaping itself. Hector's hostess was about to set off for a long vacation in Europe and there was no one to look after the farm while she was away. Her Kikuyu headman could be trusted to ensure that the land and livestock didn't run to ruin, because he hoped to inherit the place when the whites were finally thrown out of Africa. The memories of the Mau Mau atrocities were still bleeding raw in the minds of the European settlers, so she asked me to deputize for her at Wild Olive.

'If you're happy here, perhaps we can make some permanent arrangement when I get back,' she added.

The prospect seemed to open up a whole new set of opportunities, in a country which entranced me, with steadfast friends near at hand. More important, it would keep me clear of all the miseries of what looked like a certain divorce. I bought a second-hand Ford truck, with more rust than paint, and began to study Swahili: twenty words a lesson, memorized as I walked from Wild Olive to Annie's dining table early each evening. Everything seemed at last to be falling magically into place. Then the postal van brought me a cable from Robert.

It was imperative, he said, that I should return to Rhodesia at once, or – dismaying phrase – he would not be responsible for the consequences. There was no hint of what the 'consequences' might be. A day later there came a letter from my own lawyer, who had been a personal friend for a good many years, saying that he was worried, very worried, about the state of my affairs, and not just the domestic upheavals. It seemed that there was nothing for it: I had to go back. I sold the yellow Ford at a loss, packed our belongings, and took a plane south. I ruthlessly compelled myself to dismiss from my thoughts the cold fact that, by leaving so precipitately, I had let my kind benefactress down very badly indeed. In fact, she never did forgive me, and she was right not to. Not for the first time, I should have used my head and not my heart.

Robert was not at the airport to meet me, and later, when he went down to the South African port of Durban to collect the DUKW, which had been shipped out as deck-cargo, I did not go with him. The day after he left I collected our mail from the post office. One of the envelopes was stamped with a travel agent's address and I tore it open. It contained a return ticket from Bulawayo to Durban made out in Beverly's name, and charged to my account.

I drove straight to the hospital where she worked. She had been on the night-shift, but I found out the number of her room and woke her up. I handed her the ticket in silence, and left her to sweat it out.

A week later Robert drove the cumbersome vehicle back from the coast. Beverly was not with him, but her teddy bear was strapped to the windscreen as a mascot. I knew he would be travelling via Francistown and I met him there, still ludicrously hoping for a reprieve. He told me brusquely that he had no intention of coming back to Lamorna that night: he was going through to Bulawayo, where Beverly and her friends had laid on a welcoming party for him. He started up the engine and drove away.

But in the perverse way that the Fates have of arranging matters, there was no divorce that time, because Beverly suddenly and capriciously married the spindle-shanked little man with whom she'd been two-timing Robert right from the start. Robert was mortified to the point of dementia, and he vented his rage and humiliation on me. Not surprisingly, I developed a gastric ulcer which made me feel as though my diaphragm had been blasted with hot sand.

And the great emergency? Robert shrugged off my frantic enquiries when we eventually got together, and when I persisted he mumbled that the house had become haunted. Beyond hinting vaguely at various unspecified 'difficulties', he simply stonewalled. It was some time before I realized that, after the fiasco with Beverly, he had suddenly become afraid that I might withdraw my bankroll from his safari project. *That* was the sum and total of the crisis.

Leslie had no knowledge of her father's affair with Beverly, but day after day she saw him drive past the gates of her school on his way to the hospital. Her friends laughed at her, because he never once stopped to speak to his daughter, and she was sullen with hurt and anger. I didn't want to blacken her father any further in her eyes, so I didn't point out that few men on their way to a secret assignation with a mistress would have paused for half an hour's cosy chat on the school campus. Even when the love affair ended, Leslie was by no means mollified. She was now fifteen, and almost a woman. One night she packed all her belongings, kissed her dog goodbye and flounced out of the house. She hitched a lift on a passing truck and went straight to the parents of her best friend in Bulawayo. And there she remained for the next three years.

I don't believe that you can ever truly win with children, and some of the experts have at last got round to admitting that the human young actually need to be allowed to go their own way after puberty strikes. So, too, do lion cubs, hyena pups, foxes, young robins, salmon fry and slippery little elvers from the Sargasso Sea; certainly in almost every predatory species the young quit the parental territory as soon as the feeding range becomes too small to accommodate their rapidly expanding appetites and their egos.

But I had really lost Leslie when she was very young, long before this final rift. In fact, I don't think she had ever liked me. I had left the Roman Catholic church when the Bishop, the Most Reverend Father Ignatius, forbade the solemnization of my marriage to a divorced Robert. Frances, more fervent than ever in her faith since both her husband and her daughter had apostatized, was bent on saving, at least, her grand-daughter's soul from eternal damnation.

'Your parents are not married in the eyes of God,' she told the child in sly whispers. 'A civil marriage is unholy, so you are illegitimate. You will have to pray very hard, my poor lamb. Pray to God to free you from the stain of your birth.'

Leslie prayed, and very soon the hairline crack between us had widened into a canyon.

★   ★   ★

When the farm was put up for sale, both my mother and Toby went their separate ways.

Toby hurried back to Chester, near the Welsh border, and resumed a long-standing feud with her elder sister. Frances returned to London, intent upon marrying a childhood sweetheart she hadn't seen since she was fourteen. Alas, the marriage never took place: Oscar's boyish good looks had vanished with the years, and he now had all the elusive charm of a white rat. Added to this, he turned out to be a creep of the first water, with an all-too-obvious desire to get his hands on the widow's mite.

For our final month at Far Lamorna Alex Munro, the last of the golden young ones, came to stay. It was not a happy time. Robert had let the place run to seed while I was away. The walls needed repainting; drifts of cobweb hung from the ceiling. The little mottled gecko lizards still hunted flies in the misty shadows, but the Cape swallow's nest on the verandah had been broken down and the white rose on the patio no longer flowered.

On the evening before he left, Alex took me by the shoulders. 'I love you,' he said, 'but you don't want to marry me, I hope?'

'No,' I lied. I was so damned miserable that I'd have married Lucifer.

He looked relieved. 'I'm glad of that,' he said, honest for once. 'You do deserve something better than the regimental cad. But take my advice, Little Flower. Get out. Start again. Find a man who really cares whether you live or die.'

The Dusty Road

The sale of Lamorna had about it a foretaste of death. I was giving up more than just a home. The farm had been a way of life, complete in itself. It is now a quarter of a century since the DUKW swung out of the gate for the last time, but I can still close my eyes and see Rodger standing in the driveway, waving goodbye and crying.

It was the ploughing season, the time of the year which draws rural Africans back to the matrix of their country. They seem to smell the distant oxen in the home kraals, and remember where last year's ploughshare is hidden in the thatch of the hut. They run their fingers through the recollection of cool, pearly seed corn, they wait for the welcoming bark of the yellow lurcher dogs, and then they wait anxiously for their final week's wages. They sniff the air expectantly in the hope that the elephant rain will come soon, and in the morning they have gone and are striding down country roads or hitching lifts on cargo trucks if they are lucky; they have become as single-minded as horses which smell the stable.

I knew what had irked Rodger that morning. *We* were late in leaving, and he should have been gone a week since. But he had remained for loyalty's sake, and in the emotion of parting all his restraint had gone. He, who had never called us anything but Inkosi and Inkosikasi during all his long years of service, now stood beside the iron gate and, when the DUKW halted, he gripped Robert's hand.

'Goodbye, Kay,' he said huskily. 'Goodbye, Kay. Don't forget me. You are my father.' He was twenty years older than Robert.

Then he turned to me. 'Goodbye, darling. Goodbye, my darling. You must not cry.' He wiped his own streaming eyes with the back of his free hand. 'Old Rodger will come back to you one day. Goodbye, darling.'

He stood and watched us until the DUKW rounded the first bend in the road. Leaning out over the side I could still see him mouthing 'Goodbye, Kay! Goodbye, darling!' over and over again.

Was this paternalism? If it was, then I make no apologies for it. Let the post-Imperial hystericals shriek their loudest about Colonialist condescension. Maybe so, but I loved old Rodger, and I do not now intend to fudge my memories in order to mollify the Newly Righteous.

Shaka Zulu *the DUKW*

Robert never read anything except history and archaeology, and he had a special interest in the rise of Shaka, the 'Black Napoleon' who welded a collection of disparate tribes into the all-conquering Zulu nation towards the end of the eighteenth century. So he named the DUKW *Shaka Zulu*.

Shaka Zulu the DUKW was an unwieldy vehicle, just over thirty feet long by twelve feet wide, with a carrying capacity of two and a half tons of freight, or twenty-five men on land, fifty afloat, and he should rightly have been left to rust away in the Ministry of Defence's surplus storage yards after the war, instead of being hauled through alternate swamp and desert for over eight years. As a troop carrier, as an amphibious assault craft, he had played his part nobly; there was even a hint that he had served commendably in the Normandy landings. In Africa, he was an expensive white elephant.

For a start, his 104-horsepower, six-cylinder General Motors engine guzzled fuel at the rate of ten miles to the gallon on a dead-level surfaced road – of which there were few – and this fell to a grudging three miles a gallon in heavy sand – of which there was all too much. He was equipped with a Garwood power winch mounted aft, and carried 300 feet of steel cable with a breaking strength of five tons. He had a single-screw propeller which was engaged via a shift lever in the cockpit, a six-speed gearbox, and his own air compressor. Painted camouflage green, his net weight was just over seven tons.

Since we had set our sights on a journey into the deep interior, we must carry everything we might need: a full tool kit, a set of spare tyres, canned food, torch batteries, aspirin and a big FitzSimons Snake-Bite Outfit. The massive *Shaka* had to be tested thoroughly for both road- and water-worthiness before we put ourselves far beyond the reach of conventional repair facilities so, before attempting even the 300-mile journey to the comparative civilization of the Victoria Falls, we spent our first night camped in the bush a comfortingly short way from Far Lamorna.

The panelled walls of the eight-by-twelve cabin in the DUKW had been painted white, and there were rugs on the floor, one Persian, one a cheetah skin mounted on black felt. Two ship-style bunk beds covered with silver-grey karosses of hyrax fur. Acceptable, so far. Go on. Compare this with what you have just signed away; one marvellous, unusual, superbly well-run home standing on three hundred acres of pre-Cambrian granite – rock that was cast up out of the molten heart of a newly-settling planet over four and a half billion years ago, aeons before the first primitive lichens began to scrabble for a foothold on the rude grey surface.

A head, belonging to Kisi, appeared over the side of the tough, diamond-mesh steel grid that had been installed between the cabin and the driving cab. Kisi was my cook, a fresh-faced member of the 'Ndebele tribe who lived in the southern half of Rhodesia. He had replaced Tembo when the old man retired to his home kraal, to sit in the sun for a while, and then die. When I hired him he told me, proudly, that he had been born on 25 December and had been called Kisi because his mother couldn't pronounce 'Christmas'. He had been sent to a mission school and become semi-Christian, and he liked to practise his English whenever he could. He had a prodigious liking for the girls, and he had developed into a passable cook. I knew the danger signals, though. As he gazed at me across the breadth of the cabin I could see the whites of his eyes. He was not happy.

'Dinner?' he croaked, in the tones of one who hopes that his problems will go away if he doesn't think about them. Soft rain had begun to fall outside, and the firewood was probably wet.

The cook had only just returned from a month's kraal-leave, so he hadn't been around when the cabin of the DUKW was finally constituted. 'You'd better come aboard,' I said, nodding in the direction of the paraffin pressure stove, which had four burner rings and a guard rail around the top to stop the pots from falling off. It also had an oven, twelve inches square. 'This is your new kitchen. Big, isn't it?' He looked at me in blank despair, and I knew what ailed him, and I sympathized with him. We were both mourning the lost glory of our regal Aga cooker.

'*Hau!*' Mission-English failed him, so he took refuge in the Sindebele word that denotes everything from mild dismay to blazing anger. 'I cannot cook on *that thing*, Medem! It is too much small, too much . . .' he hesitated, looking for the precise words. 'It is too much trouble with bad fire.' His eyes rolled round, noted the tiny refrigerator that was driven by storage batteries, and the cupboard containing packets of dehydrated soup mix, dried peas, coffee, sugar, Heinz baked beans, bully beef, and several cans of an especially loathsome brand of pilchards in tomato sauce. He went on to inspect the rest of the cabin, opening cupboards at random: a wardrobe containing eight clothes hangers and a rifle rack; a second cupboard for folded shirts and underwear, on top of which was fitted a cutlery drawer and a portable enamel washbasin; a range of cuphooks for beer tankards, pewter wine jugs and bright red plastic coffee mugs. When he reached the after end he halted and clucked approvingly at the occupants of a wooden crate that had wire mesh covering one side. 'Twelve best hens!' he beamed. 'No madoda?'[1]

'We'll buy one later,' I promised, shifting my weight on the lower bunk and trying not to disturb Oliver, who had fallen asleep on it. 'But what we need now are eggs, not baby chicks!'

He nodded. 'What is under hens, in . . .?' He didn't know the words for cargo hold. I supplied them. 'One hundred and fifty gallons of petrol, and a smaller tank for drinking water. The generator for charging the big batteries is behind the chickens. Everything else goes in front.'

Camp beds, bucksails, camping gear, mosquito nets, spare blankets, coils of rope and several suitcases containing the residue of our civilized clothing had been dumped in the for'ard hold, through which the exhaust pipe ran. There had been nothing in the operating manual to warn us that the exhaust pipe of a DUKW rapidly becomes red-hot, but we found that out for ourselves. Later.

Kisi sighed again and poked his hand out of the side window, palm upwards. After a few moments he withdrew it and ostentatiously wiped raindrops away on the seat of his trousers. I couldn't understand the woebegone expression.

'Listen,' I promised, 'I'll light the damn stove for you, if you'll find the saucepans. They're in one of the cupboards, somewhere. I made a chicken risotto last night which I was saving for tomorrow, because that'll be our first full day on the road, but we might as well eat it now. You'll find it in the refrigerator. And, for God's sake, do feed the dogs and help me get them aboard. I don't like this camp too much. It's one of the bad places for leopards.' Far Lamorna was still only two miles away. I wondered, with

[1] Literally a male – in this case, a rooster.

sudden pain, whether my old Rodger was getting himself crying drunk.

Kisi scrambled down over the side of the vehicle, still clucking with disapproval, and came back clutching a box of matches. Oliver half woke, released his teddy bear. The fingers of his right hand uncurled, revealing a large red and black mahogany bean, a last-minute keepsake snatched from the tree that sheltered the beehives above the dam, at the home he had loved. He was six-and-a-half, rising seven, and I knew that he should be at school.

'Please God, not yet. Just let me have him for a little while longer. He's too young to be thrown into the maelstrom. I can teach him more than he'll ever learn in the first two years at boarding school anyway, and at least he won't be beaten and buggered.'

The top of the provisions cupboard had been stacked with the few books I had been able to salvage from the huge bookcase that lined half the drawing room at Lamorna. Steinbeck, Somerset Maugham, some of Hemingway, a collected James Thurber three inches thick, Saki, Damon Runyon, the definitive edition of Kipling's poetry, Flecker's *Hassan*, *Roget's Thesaurus*, three reference books on local African wildlife, an illustrated guide to edible mushrooms, the André Simon *Gastronomic Encyclopedia* and a battered copy of *Cyrano de Bergerac* in which Richard had inscribed my name, and his love, a long, long time ago.

The only free space left in the cabin was on the wooden lid that could be let down to cover the washbasin. Kisi set the makeshift table-top with knives and forks, and then took the knives away and substituted spoons for the risotto. He found Oliver's Beatrix Potter mug with the picture of Pigling Bland on it and poured cold milk into it, and then poured the milk back into a saucepan, dithering, taking time to settle down, and liking it all about as much as the priests at the Catholic mission had told him he'd enjoy Purgatory.

He yearned, ostentatiously again, at the dish of risotto.

'Are you all right for your own meal?' I inquired.

He hesitated for a brief spell and then began to rub the side of his nose, the inevitable prelude to a good, well-constructed lie. '*Hau!* Dog is stole all my meat, Medem!'

I knew the name of the 'dog' in question. It was Elizabeth Pakati, Kisi's current woman, whom he was leaving behind in Rodger's care. Still, I wasn't going to amplify his misery on a night like this. He accepted a large can of corned beef with grace.

One of the hens in the crate got its claw caught in the wire netting and squawked angrily, showering feathers. Outside, it began to rain steadily.

First Blood

It took us two days to reach the Victoria Falls, and on the way we drove *Shaka Zulu* through the Wankie Game Reserve, a journey that almost induced a coronary in the chief game warden and certainly unsettled his already ill-tempered elephants. I knew the area well and would have liked to linger for a while longer, but Robert was in a hurry now, cutting corners on time. He drove on past the Falls Hotel and made straight for the Zambesi. For three weeks we camped on one of the many islands which studded the course of the river, above the gorges where the water crashed down into the Devil's Cataract, boiled turbulently, tore at the rock walls and, almost incongruously, rose again in rainbows. Then, at the end of September we embarked on a punishing run up the banks of the Chobe River.

★ ★ ★

At its western end, the Chobe runs through a channel known as the Selinda Spillway before it merges with the southbound waters of the Okavango River. In the east, it joins the Zambesi through the twelve-mile stretch of the Kasaya Canal, and the mingled waters hurl themselves into the chasmal gorges of the Victoria Falls, where wild lobelia clings to the drenched cliff face, and you cannot hear yourself speak above the tumult of the waters.

The Kasaya is one of the few man-made waterways in the extraordinary complex which criss-crosses north-western Bechuanaland. It is also one of the most menacing stretches of water on the fringes of the Okavango Delta.

This narrow channel, which was forced through an area of malarial swamp, is fifteen feet deep on average and has a spongy bottom. It is kept clear by a three-knot current, and by travelling schools of the notoriously bloody-minded hippo, which hold all the records in Africa for biting chunks out of wooden canoes and killing the local fishermen. The water seethes through reeds, swamp grass, and a seventeen-foot-high growth of papyrus that closes overhead and shuts out all the sunlight. The air there is aswarm with mosquitos, the water choked with a tenacious weed that twists itself round propellers and can strangle an outboard motor in seconds. The bloated roots of the swamp grass are slimy with blood-sucking leeches. This is also crocodile territory.

True, the bird life is stupendous, but after two and a half hours and twelve miles of creeping laboriously upstream through the clogged channels, my face and arms stippled crimson with mosquito bites, I lost all interest in the tiny, jewelled kingfishers, iridescent violet gullinules, and whirring skeins of waterfowl. The Kasaya reeked of evil, and it didn't take us long to find out why.

As we emerged into open water a dugout canoe skimmed towards us, poled along by the African staff from the Barge Officer's department further up the river. The bottom of the vessel was awash with blood and water, and in it lay a man with horrifying injuries. One of his arms had been torn off at the shoulder, his ribs were crushed and his right thigh was a mass of mangled flesh.

'Hippo,' the steersman explained tersely. 'This man was standing in the river, mending his fishing nets. The hippo came from behind and bit him. I think he will die.' He dug his punt pole into the water and as his crew followed suit, he shouted back at us. 'The hippo is also dead. Our morena[1] shot him. The meat is good.'

And the meat *was* good, cooked with a handful of fresh vegetables from the Barge Officer's well-fenced garden. I had accepted his offer of a large and bloody hippo steak unhesitatingly. There was no butcher within fifty miles, and I had a family to feed. We had to accept what the land had to offer or go hungry.

★   ★   ★

Loxodonta Africana is not my favourite animal. The huge elephants of Africa are unpredictable and broodingly savage, and long before that first excursion to the Chobe I had heard, and seen, too much of their talent for wanton villainy ever to be at ease in their company. What took place on the hot afternoon of Friday, the ill-omened 13th of October, powerfully reinforced my instinct always to keep as much of Africa as possible between me and them.

We had winched the DUKW up out of the river and were driving along the old hunters' road to Kachikau. This was a meeting place for men like Selous and Gordon Cumming, who had travelled this route and taken not a few of the world's vanished species with them; the quagga, for one. It was ugly country, the colour of dull gunmetal, and the narrow dirt track was stitched in on either side by dense moselesele thorn scrub, tough enough to stop a Sherman tank in its tracks.

We crested a rise and began to idle downhill. Ahead of us, parked in the one place where the path passed on both sides of a tree, was a two-ton Bedford truck. The white driver and two of his African

[1] Tswana for 'master, sir'.

staff were standing to one side of the road. As a matter of bush courtesy we stopped to pass the time of day.

'Jack Chase,' said the man wearing the pith helmet, introducing himself. 'Came up here to look into a story about a rogue elephant. Better stay where you are for a while, until that lot has moved off. Take a look.'

The gully below us was a milling mass of elephant. I tried to count them and gave up when I reached two hundred.

Unexpectedly, the herd broke up and the main body began to move ponderously downstream, keeping close to the shallows. A small knot of cows with their calves stayed behind, squirting water into their mouths or tossing it in plumes up over their backs.

'You're OK now,' Jack said. 'They shouldn't give you any more trouble. Go on, and stop halfway up the rise if you want photographs. I'll catch you up. But remember that I can't drive my truck around you if anything *does* go wrong.' He looked at me. 'We might make camp together.'

Once we were clear of the gully, Oliver and I scrambled out on to the aft deck of the DUKW. Robert was sitting at the wheel, with the engine ticking over. Jack drew his truck up behind us and as he came to a halt the herd left the river and headed up the road, twenty yards away. Elephant cows which have calves at foot are notoriously dangerous, and as I watched them a small warning bell began chinking at the back of my mind. It should have been an air-raid siren.

The herd bunched, then milled forward – cows, calves and a lone bull. Some of the cows lifted their trunks in the air, and their wide flap-ears spread ominously. Then one of the cows screamed, and screamed again. She came out fast, angrily, with that magnificent elephant walk that looks like a series of stiff ballet kicks, and is a full charge almost before it is a movement at all.

She left the heaving ruck of the herd and charged straight down the track at speed, gathering such momentum that she could not have stopped before she hit the Bedford, even if she had wanted to.

Robert's gold-embossed Holland and Holland .465 double-barrelled hunting rifle was still in its sleek chestnut leather carrying case, tied in tape and sealed with a red wax government stamp, but somehow or other I found myself back in the cabin, tearing at the tough fastening. It was a futile gesture; even if the rifle had, by some miracle, been ready loaded I would still have been too late. I could see the rest of the herd pressing forward behind the enraged cow, and I knew that all hell would be let loose at any moment.

There was a sudden explosion, and a hard-nosed bullet from Jack's Gibbs .505 took the cow in the centre of the forehead at

113

almost point-blank range. It was a classic brain-pan shot and she fell twenty feet from him, sagging first to her knees then toppling slowly over onto her right side, just before her trunk hit the dust.

Somewhere between this frozen instant and the time when we'd first sighted the elephants on the road I'd yelled to Robert, who was still at the wheel, to drive on, but it seemed to take an eternity before he heard me above the racket of the engine. At last I felt the DUKW lurch forward and I braced myself against the wardrobe, as I stared aghast at the scene in the dust-cloud behind us, which had suddenly taken on the blurred and shifting horror of a macabre dream. Three of the dead cow's companions were trying to lift her back onto her feet, levering her body with all the huge power of their heads, trunks and tusks. Twice they raised her into a semi-sitting position and twice she flopped down again. Then, incredibly, she was on her feet, stone dead but wedged upright by the leaning force of her herd mates. I watched in stunned disbelief as they frog-marched her off the road.

But the drama was not over. Above the continuous trumpeting and squealing of the herd, I heard a man scream in terror. One of Jack's staff, a young African on his first safari, was out on the road and running desperately after the DUKW. The sight of the man had an instant effect on the elephants, already in a vicious temper over the shooting of the cow and frantic for the safety of their calves.

One huge animal that had been standing a little apart from the others suddenly wheeled round, shrilling with fury. He came looming up out of the haze and, although everything in me shrieked for speed, neither Jack nor Robert seemed to be at all aware of what was about to happen. Robert was driving as fast as the rudimentary track would allow, and as *Shaka Zulu* crashed and pounded over the broken surface, Jack's gunbearer, standing up in the back of the Bedford which was following behind us, began to hammer on the roof and point. The truck shot forward so abruptly that I thought it was going to collide with us, then two of the Africans leaned over the tail-board and hauled their terror-stricken comrade to safety. Back, way back now, I could just make out the tight knot of elephants with the dead cow still propped up between them, and then we were over the rise, and the trees and the high ground hid them from view.

The Hunters' Road glowed chalk-white in the last of the daylight, against a sky that was ink-blue with fast-approaching rain. As we set about making camp the storm broke over us like a shower of newly minted coins flashing in the headlamps. It was a warm, sluicing downpour that washed the veld clean – and rinsed out all the spoor as well. By morning the bush would be steaming with the piercing fragrance that only new rain could give it, and there would be fresh signs to read where the night-prowlers had printed the story of their passing in the wet soil. The trouble was that the imprints left by the elephants would also have been obliterated by the storm, so that if there was any tracking to be done it would be neither easy nor safe in the tangled scrub forest.

I loved everything about these bush camps: the smell of the newly lit pressure lamps; the bright beads of moisture on the sides of the canvas water bags and the always slightly smoky taste of the water itself; the dry, white, special smell of mosquito nets; the soft hiss of the big camp kettle swinging on its tripod above the log fire.

Oliver was in his pyjamas and dressing gown and he gave my hand a sudden squeeze. I looked at him to see how he'd taken the day, and he gave me a quick, shy smile, owl-eyed with excitement and fright. I realized again, and with a sharper pain, that the events of the afternoon had delivered an unanswerable argument against keeping him with us much longer. What I had first lightly imagined as a sort of long vacation under canvas was clearly going to be an altogether more hazardous undertaking. But, once more, I closed my mind to the prospect.

★ ★ ★

'I could use that DUKW of yours later on,' Jack remarked over the morning coffee. 'Got to winch that carcass off the track. They can't have moved her more than a yard or two.'

But they had. They'd carried her down to the edge of the river, more than a hundred yards from the spot where Jack had shot her, and she had fallen three more times before her companions had finally abandoned her for dead. Blood from the killing brain shot was still seeping from the tip of her trunk and, startlingly, a cluster of pink butterflies had settled on the top of her left foreleg. Jack bent down and brushed them away.

'There's a wound,' he said. 'That's why she charged.' He drew his knife from its sheath and began to cut deeply into the huge animal's flesh, probing for a bullet. He found it. 'A .303,' he said angrily as he finally levered it out. 'Too low for the heart, and probably been there for about three weeks. Bloody poachers! But why did they have to blaze off at a cow, in the name of God? She wasn't even carrying enough ivory to make a billiard ball.'

'Why did they move her?' I asked, although I half knew the answer.

'Work it out for yourself. They thought she still had some sort of a chance. If she wasn't actually dead then water might have revived her. Elephants are like that. The mistake most people make is in *not* believing everything that they hear about them.'

Later that day Jack drove off to Francistown and we continued on to Kasane. None of us knew it at the time, but the shooting of that wounded cow was to dog our fortunes for eight long years. The incident almost put an end to our endeavours to save the Protectorate's wildlife from annihilation – and, in the end, it cost Robert the safari licence that would have given him the only kind of steady livelihood he could ever have tolerated.

Calamity on the Front Page

I had wandered down the sand track which led to the Chobe, and halfway there I heard Kisi drumming thunderously on the roof of the DUKW, our usual signal for danger. Robert was a few yards ahead of me, busy trying to focus the long lens of his camera on a majestic bull elephant that was watering peaceably at the edge of the river. He looked round angrily, and began to say 'What the hell . . .?' when his expression changed abruptly and he shouted 'Oh, Christ!' as he started to run back up the hill. I followed as fast as I could.

There seemed to be dozens of elephants milling around in the bush on either side of *Shaka Zulu,* and to cap that there was a thin grey plume of smoke drifting up from the for'ard hatch of the vehicle. The DUKW was on fire, and it was carrying over a hundred gallons of petrol.

As I scrambled up the side, clawing for a handhold on the rail above the bridge, Robert turned the key in the ignition switch – and then abruptly switched the engine off again. Kisi was ashen-faced and trembling with anxiety, and he choked out something that sounded like 'Too much elephant is too much close!' He never babbled a truer word, yet the elephants were, in fact, the lesser of our perils. Even so, they were much too close for us to risk putting Oliver and the dogs down over the side of the DUKW.

When I reached the cabin the temperature inside was phenomenally high, and every surface was too hot to touch. Unforgiveably, none of us had bothered to check the fire extinguishers, and we now discovered that both of them had literally been cemented to their brackets by the mud nests of mason flies. By hacking at the thick encrustations with a monkey-wrench we managed eventually to free them, and Robert clambered up onto the front deck. But as soon as he lifted the hatch-cover, the flames boiled up at him. The two cylinders of Pyrene had pathetically little effect on the bonfire of camp beds, unironed laundry and cornmeal sacks, but what the little extinguisher jets *did* manage to do was to fill the driving cab with deadly clouds of carbon-tetrachloride gas. This meant that we couldn't get back inside to restart the engine, which might have helped to clear the fumes from the hold.

By this time Kisi had recovered his composure and was taking practical action by filling all the available buckets, and the two-gallon butter churn, from the water pump on the aft deck. He came running through the cabin, sloshing water about as he ran. There was an angry hiss as Robert poured the first bucket into the hold, and a mingled cloud of steam and fine ash billowed back, smelling strongly of charred rope. I grabbed the churn from Kisi and struggled forward with it, but the metal fittings on the deck melted the soles of my light sneakers. I passed the churn to Robert and then hauled myself up on to the canvas roof of the cockpit, choking from the smoke and dizzy from the pain of blistered feet.

There was a sudden, frightening, cessation of movement. Kisi sagged, breathing hard, his hands hanging limply by his sides.

'Water is finish,' he announced, wearily.

But if the water was finished, so was the fire. The steam was still rising, but there were no more flames.

Then I remembered Oliver. I plunged back into the cabin and at first there was no sign of him. Then I saw the grubby soles of two little feet poking out from under the hyrax coverlet on the top bunk. As for the dogs, they had made their way to the aft deck and were huddling next to the chicken coop, as far away from the fire as possible.

Elephants! Where were the elephants? We had forgotten all about them in our panic over the blaze; vaguely, I recollected that they were supposed to be afraid of fire. I leaned out of the window. A hundred yards away, right at the edge of the tree-belt, the back end of a cow with a calf in tow was disappearing at the tail of the herd as they ambled off to the river. The bush around us was curiously still, until a tinker barbet started up, tapping out the message of the hot weather with notes that sounded like a tiny, ringing anvil.

I eased off my ruined shoes and pulled on sandals, wincing as the blisters popped. Oliver reached down from his bunk and tugged at my hair, teasingly. No, I thought miserably, this simply is no life

117

for a child. He would have to go to join his brother. He could have been dead by now, killed horribly by his father's monstrous dreams of adventure. We could all of us have perished.

I limped forward to inspect the damage. The exhaust pipe that ran through the for'ard hold was still glowing in places, red-hot from too much low-gear driving through the clogging, hub-deep sand. I stared down into the charred interior. One of the camp beds had been bounced free by an especially violent jolt, and had fallen against the pipe, smouldered into flame, and set everything else alight. Our single consolation was that the vehicle's designers had located the fuel tanks well aft. In that desolate moment I would have been happy to see the wretched craft fed into a scrap-metal crusher.

However, the engine started sweetly enough and Robert drove the DUKW down to the edge of the Chobe, and we refilled the tanks with water that was still slightly muddy from the passage of the elephants through the shallows, but it was better than no water at all. When we finally reached Kasane it was dark, we were tired, and all of us were coated with a mixture of ashes, sweat and dust; but even then the day had saved one final misery for us. Robert removed the front hatchcover so we could clean out the hold, and while he was away trying to borrow a hose Oliver climbed up onto the hull and toppled head-first into the void. When I hauled him out he seemed to be covered in blood, with his nose spurting scarlet and his scalp laid open to the bone. We then discovered that our medical kit didn't include surgical gut, so Robert dusted the scalp wound with antibiotic powder and patched the skin together with strips of elastoplast. After that we wrapped the shivering child in blankets, and I took him on my lap and spoon-fed him with warm milk until his hands and feet began to feel warm again, and the colour returned to his cheeks. As I lifted him into his bunk he opened his eyes wide and demanded a story.

I felt we had lived through more than enough stories of our own in the past few days.

'Oh, for pity's sake, Oliver! Tonight? Well, what sort of story do you want?'

'About elephants,' he said.

★ ★ ★

Our first safari was ended, but along the way we had unwittingly picked up a potent bacillus, and the infection developed swiftly. Naturally enough, we attracted a lot of attention when we drove the DUKW back into Bulawayo, and immediately the local newsmen fell upon us for an impromptu press conference. Innocently enough,

I told them about the dead cow elephant's funeral cortege, and the *Bulawayo Chronicle* ran an excitable story on the front page, with pictures.

The article was read with distaste by a self-important little functionary in the Rhodesian Game Department and he decided, without checking any further, that we must deliberately have molested the unfortunate beast to provoke her into charging us. He took no official action against us, but he spread his story to all his colleagues throughout the government network of Northern and Southern Rhodesia and Bechuanaland. Because there was no formal complaint to reply to, we never, ever, lived the accusation down, and it was the beginning of a long campaign of official harassment which continued until Robert was forced to quit the Protectorate thirteen years later.

Venture to the Hinterland

'*Two months*,' Robert had promised when he first decided that we should take a farewell look at one of the last really remote and forgotten regions of Central Africa. 'Two months, just two, and then we'll drive the DUKW right up to Cairo, and then head for England. I promise!'

'Is that a politician's promise?'

'No, a proper one. We'll take a quick look at the Okavango Swamps and then I'll take you back to Britain. I promise.'

He was turning on the charm, a rare thing for Robert, and usually it meant that he wanted something so badly that he was ready to lie for it. The Chobe safari had now used up one of those two months, and I couldn't see how we could hope to cross the notorious thirstland of the Kalahari and still have time in hand to explore a largely unknown and uncharted delta, all in four short weeks. Still – a book?

The urge to write had developed almost as soon as I could join up my letters, and by the time I was six I was pouring out reams of poetry, mainly about blackbirds – a gesture to my growing interest in wild life – and reincarnation, which allowed me to escape into a world where children were allowed to play together. Two years later I was writing animal stories for the *Chronicle*. Eventually, this phase gave way to a fascination with African folklore when I sat and listened to tribesmen at Far Lamorna. They taught me about Tokoloshe, the fiendish dwarf who lived in the rivers and always got the blame for fathering any illegitimate child born in the riverside villages; the cat-eared *izizi* owl, whose melancholy cry foretold death; the cruel sorceress who forced her lover to drink his own blood as he lay dying, so that his soul would pass into Lekhututu, the great black Southern ground-hornbill, and immortalize the sound of his drum-note call for eternity.

On our second venture to the deep hinterland, travelling by day and writing at night, I began to keep a comprehensive safari log, not just recording the bare details of each day's journey, but describing the sights, sounds, colours, scents – and remembering the anonymous face of a fisherman who had cast his lines in the river and been mauled by a rogue hippo, for no apparent reason.

From these notes, my first book, *Okavango*, slowly began to take shape.

I comforted myself with the thought that unless the earth was destroyed in some sudden cataclysm, England would still be there when I'd finished writing it. Time enough, then, to head for the motherland, and friends, of my desire.

★ ★ ★

In 1958 very little was known about the top north-western edge of the Bechuanaland Protectorate, the place where the Okavango River, streaming down from its watershed in the cool, high cloudlands of Angola, spreads out to form an immense sweet-water delta on the arid flanks of the Kalahari Desert; it is water that never reaches the sea, and it is clear down to a depth of fifteen feet over a base of white salt sand. This was once a great inland sea, but the salt in it has long since seeped back, down into the earth's crust, so the water of the delta is sweet, with the freshness of rain, not brackish. The land was, still is, owned by the Batauana tribe, who had their administrative headquarters in the wattle-and-daub village of Maun, on the south-eastern rim of an extraordinary maze of waterways, lagoons, shallow pans and flood areas, within which are scattered islands heavily overgrown with riverine forest. This much we knew when we first set out, and very little else. Even an ordnance survey map we managed to find was pretty useless, since most of it was covered with little fleur-de-lys which, the legend told us baldly, simply meant 'swamp'.

Before we finally set out we spent four months completing our preparations and living aboard *Shaka Zulu*, which was incongruously parked in a friend's back garden. Then, on Saturday, 14 February 1959 – St Valentine's Day – Robert drove the massive

DUKW out onto the main road and I followed, at the wheel of a bulky Humber Super-Snipe station-wagon that had been custom-built for the Anglo-Iranian Oil Company and had somehow been diverted to Rhodesia, with a speedo reading of zero miles.

Oliver had now been settled at the Rhodes Estate Preparatory School with his elder brother, and I arranged with the excellent headmaster to shepherd them to our camp at the end of the school term.

But the Easter holiday was still weeks ahead on that bright February morning, and – Kisi apart – Robert and I were on our own again.

Our Lady of the Desert

'. . . a desert stretched and stricken, left and right, left and right,
Where the piled mirages thicken, under white hot light.'
RUDYARD KIPLING, 'JOBSON'S AMEN'

I sat on the edge of the camp bed and watched the small rain bouncing like silver globules of mercury off the taut canvas bucksail. The sky was white, washed with grey turbulence. Above me, a chameleon rocked laboriously along a branch in search of late insects. It reached a strip of bark and, pausing there, changed in colour from leaf green to mottled brown. I knew this camp of old. Soon galagos would come, light as air, furry and delicate, with vivid ruby eyes. These were *Senegalensis*, tiny lemuroids which had made the mimosa thicket their home.

It was near sunset and the little border post of Plumtree lay behind us. So, too, did any semblance of a hard road, because the tarmac ended abruptly on the Rhodesian side of the Ramaquabane River. Within a few yards the surface degenerated into a long sequence of potholes edged with jagged limestone rubble, leading on to corrugations – a 'tin-roof' road – and shifting sand. The canvas water bags hanging from the side mirrors of the DUKW were caked thickly with red dust, and fine sand plumed up from the tyres, filling the cabin with suffocating grit. After fifteen miles and three blow-outs we gave in to the agony, and set up camp for the night.

In the late 1950s, Bechuanaland was still a bone-poor country, and the professional prospectors from De Beers had not yet found

121

the diamond pipe that would eventually transform its economy. At the time, the soil had become too exhausted for successful crop raising, and cattle ranching was limited by unending droughts, the ravages of the ubiquitous tsetse fly and endemic foot-and-mouth disease. There were no significant industries and certainly no money to spare for road repair work, and the general poverty was further reflected in the run-down state of the Protectorate's towns, of which Francistown was the first, and last, along our route to the Okavango Delta over three hundred miles away.

Francistown was not an appealing place. The single street was an unsurfaced track, roughly compounded of stone chippings and sand. The two sagging hotels, heavily screened in mosquito mesh, both faced directly onto the railway line. A few rudimentary trading stores offered the great three-legged iron pots that are the standard cooking utensil throughout Africa, cornmeal, paraffin, bright coarse cloth, a slender range of basic canned or bottled luxuries, a slender range of basic groceries, and very little else, to an undemanding clientele. On the packed-earth sidewalks outside the stores African women hawked peanuts, sweet potatoes and a few locally woven baskets of poor workmanship. Ragged loafers thronged the streets, and balloon-bellied children whined endlessly for pennies. For eleven months of the year the heat was blinding – and there wasn't a shade tree from one end of the settlement to the other.

Yet for all the numbing boredom of this unmemorable little frontier town, I took away one sublimely beautiful memory which stayed with me for a long time after I'd shaken the last grains of Francistown sand out of my shoes. The name of the local school was 'Our Lady of the Desert'.

★ ★ ★

By the evening of our first day out of Francistown we had covered just sixty miles after seven punishing hours of driving. The road to Maun was in fact no more than two unadorned, parallel ruts which ran roughly north-west through 316 miles of semi-desert, and for the whole of that length it was anything up to two feet deep in sand. At best it was little more than a vague indication that here lay the quickest route away from anything approximating to civilization, to a place that nobody knew much about anyway, except perhaps that it lay on the edge of an endless malarial swamp and was the searing hot capital of an African hunting tribe. These were the Batauana, and in times past they had found a way through this same desert, to take control of the region from its original occupants, the Bayei, through a process of peaceful conquest.

122

Salt-white dust billowed up from the migrating dunes, shifting constantly across the track, dispersing in the hot winds, and then reforming further on with pitiless monotony. Even in the relative cool of sunset, the thermometer was registering 109°F in the shade.

'Game animals,' I reflected bitterly, remembering the glow of romantic enthusiasm that had so effectively blunted my first objections to this second venture into the wilderness. 'There will be game animals in abundance, and a human population of only one person to every two square miles of territory.'

We had been travelling for three grim days now, and so far I had seen neither hide nor hair of any animal, with the depressing exception of a long-dead, more or less mummified, cow. As far as I could see, I was on my way to dwell amongst half a person per square mile, and even that would have needed something of a miracle, given the barren emptiness of the country through which we were passing. Also, any animal foolhardy enough to live there would need to be specially adapted to eat sand dunes and drink the water out of the mirages.

At last we came to a solitary baobab tree, and pitched camp under it. Around us, the dazzling desert sand was parched, stark, fiercely compelling in utter desolation. Our small camp fire crackled in the empty night and overhead the stars hung brilliantly in a sky that was neither blue nor fully black, but possessed instead the colour and the depth of infinity.

A jackal – whatever did she find to eat here? – yelped somewhere in the distance, and a scorpion tacked its shining way across the bucksail at my feet, a small life in a lifeless land.

Aching, exhausted, I listened to the silence and tried to imagine what had happened along this bleached trail so long ago, when a disheartened and straggling column of men, women, children and animals had headed for the gamelands they hoped lay ahead. They were followers of Chief Tauana, fleeing from a family feud in the Bamangwato country to the south, and he led them out across this howling wilderness in search of a legendary delta. He must have known that this was the thirstland. How did his people carry water? In gourds, in the shells of ostrich eggs like the Kalahari Bushmen, in goat bladders? Did their meagre supplies last until they reached that unknown, enchanted swamp, the place their leader had dreamed about, and on which he had staked his future? And how many of the fugitives had survived to found the tribe of the Batauana, the Children of the Little Lion?

Wild geese crossed the moon, flying high and honking. They, too, were seeking swamp waters.

We came out of the desert two nights later and, with an instinct sharpened in the drought times, I smelled the water long before I saw it.

Shaka Zulu and his station-wagon escort headed down into a shallow valley, a place where the air was pure and cool. The silhouettes of trees slid by, and there were fleeting reflections from black water. It was too late to do anything but make camp and sag into our beds. I slept until the birds and a hooting monkey woke me. We were in the valley of the Thamalakane River at the eastern edge of the Okavango Delta, a place of wild blue water hissing through dense riverine forest, and still lagoons close-laced with the waxy flowers of waterlilies.

'Matlapanen,' a passing African saluted us. 'Morena Wilmot's camp. He is the one who kills crocodiles. This is a good camp. Many fish.' He spat into the dust and walked on without any further comment.

'He spits to kill bad luck,' Kisi explained. 'He has praised the fish, so now he must spit on them to show that they are nothing, or they will all go.'

★ ★ ★

Twenty-nine dogs and approximately five hundred inquisitive Africans arrived with the sun. If my calculations were correct, we were now being greeted by the entire human population of a thousand square miles. The crowd clustered round the DUKW, shouting, pointing, laughing, and clicking their tongues in disbelief. I dressed demurely under the blankets, to the delight of some forty-odd children who had been skirmishing inside the phalanx of their elders, all of them obviously wondering how I was going to make it into my clothes while holding the mosquito net to one side with my teeth.

At noon, Robert drove the Humber into Maun to make himself known to the District Commissioner, a functionary who, in those days, had wide and considerable powers. He took with him my shopping list: bread, butter, milk, some good fillet steak, potatoes, onions, oranges and any other fresh fruit that happened to be going. He was in a lethal mood when he got back to Matlapanen. The DC had learned by way of a discreet note from the Game Department that Robert was a molester of helpless elephants, a man who needed to be discouraged. The interview had not been cordial.

'What's the town itself like?' I enquired, trying hard to brush aside the fact that official hostility could make our sojourn in N'gamiland extremely unpleasant.

'A metropolis,' he snapped. 'Just your kind of town. You'll love it.' Then he handed me a cardboard box containing two cans of Nestlé's evaporated milk, one of lard, three of pickled mackerel, and a packet of dehydrated tomato soup.

'Is that all?' I asked, staring disbelievingly at the pitiful hoard. 'No bread?'

From his trouser pocket he drew a can of dried yeast. 'It's the last they had. You'll have to learn to bake. There's a recipe on the label.'

That afternoon I, too, drove into the village, to see for myself.

'Where's the main street?' I asked as we passed a stand of petrol pumps, and a small burial ground that was half hidden behind a straggle of poisonous milkweed hedge.

'We're on it,' Robert informed me. 'And what is more, this is where it ends. You probably didn't notice, but we have actually driven right through Maun. Riley's Hotel and Store. That's all there is. I only came this far because I thought you'd like to see it from the northern approach as well.' He swerved, and the Humber narrowly missed a pair of consenting donkeys. The jack was a big animal, with shadowy stripes on his flanks, the bastard progeny of one of the scores of mares that had mated with wild zebra. 'Take the truck if you want to explore any more. *I* am going to the hotel for a drink.'

Francistown may have been the utter pits, but I soon discovered that any resemblance between Maun and a normal human community was fleeting. The little settlement from which the Batauana Regent, Mohumagadi Elizabeth Pulane Moremi, holder of the Most Distinguished Order of the British Empire, ruled her fifty thousand subjects consisted mainly of dust, goats, milkweed hedges and flagrantly passionate donkeys. It was nothing more than a desert outpost, with no atmosphere to speak of and totally lacking in charm. The streets that meandered between the few modest bungalows leased by Europeans were inches deep in Kalahari sand, and skeletal dogs slept among swarms of evil blue flies.

There was no bank in Maun, no bakery, no dress shop, hairdresser or barber, no cinema, no florist – and no railway line. There was not even a telephone link with the rest of the world. A foolish pioneer had once attempted to install one, but the elephants used the poles as rubbing posts and broke them so often that the engineers eventually refused to put up any more; the new poles lay in the sand until the termites ate them. In a real emergency – say, when the beer truck didn't turn up – messages could be transmitted to Francistown on the police radio. Without this small link to civilization, Maun could have vanished and never been missed.

There was, of course, always Riley's Hotel, the hub of the village's social life. I'm told that the place has since been refurbished somewhat, but in 1959 the plaster peeled away from the arsenic-green walls in leprous flakes, the armchairs squeaked and puffed out clouds of dust and insects, and the edges of all the tables were charred with countless cigarette burns. A weathered cardboard notice nailed to a piece of wood next to the brick-bordered beds of amaryllis lilies that had never bloomed read, idiotically, 'Please Walk on the Garden'. The swimming pool contained a few inches of stagnant water, rotting leaves and drowned mice.

After an hour of depressing reconnaissance, I was startled to discover that the place actually contained two schoolrooms – one for white children, one for black. There was even a tiny post office, though the service it provided could easily have been surpassed by a carrier pigeon in moult. The small hospital was surprisingly well equipped, and never empty, for the staff had to cope with a range of savage, Old Testament diseases. Bubonic plague and rabies were both endemic; malaria, tuberculosis, sleeping sickness and all the venereal diseases were commoner than the common cold; so were ringworm, hook-worm, liver-fluke and ophthalmia. To complete the list of Biblical afflictions there was leprosy.

Set against all this, however, was the fact that the swamps were at least free of the usually pervasive African scourge of bilharzia.[1] The water from high Angola was sweet and clear, safe to drink unboiled, soft as rain, and left your skin and hair tinglingly clean to the touch. An African Ganges, miraculously pure.

Later I sat in what passed for the lounge in the hotel, sipping tepid beer and wondering what in God's name I was doing there when I could have returned to Kenya, friends and comfort. Someone had left a dog-eared copy of *Baby Doll* lying on the ledge under the table and I opened it at random. '*You promised my Daddy you'd look after me.*' No use trying that approach with Robert. He had never promised anything of the sort, and if he had Lance would not have believed him.

The Island

The glory of Maun was the Thamalakane River, and it was on the river that I chose to live. Our first base below the fishing shacks at Matlapanen was a charmless spot, made infinitely worse by the attentions of the local Africans who shuffled down to the camp in

---

[1] A disease produced by the parasitic trematode flatworm, found only in Africa and the Middle East. It occurs in rivers and still ponds and spends part of its lifecycle in a fresh-water snail.

droves both by day and by night, to stand around in circles, staring at us with unblinking curiosity. They might occasionally scramble after a discarded cigarette stub, but mostly they just stared. It would have been wholly unthinkable to live in Maun itself, so we cast around for a suitable island to retreat to, and at last we found one, eight miles upstream from the village. Whites were prohibited from owning land in N'gamiland, but Mohumagadi Moremi, the Queen Regent, cheerfully gave us permission to camp there and even waived the ground rent.

There was not a great deal of island, and for two months of the year, when the river ran low, we were joined to the mainland. But once the winter floods began to foam down from Angola it shrank visibly, until it was barely two miles long and a mile wide, and a belt of sparkling water lay over the one dry-weather road that led to the bridge which provided the sole link between Maun and the rest of the universe. Below us, the swift current of the Thamalakane tossed lilies against the bank. Behind, the forest sprawled, wet, green and tumbling to the water's edge.

There was a natural clearing in this forest, highly desirable because it was well shaded and not too far from the river. Here we set up the tents, but once *Shaka Zulu* had been beached beside them – a task completed only after hours of knuckle-scraping work on the winch and a lot of filthy language – we had to face up to the fact that we were effectively marooned. The only way of reaching Maun would be to swim down four hundred yards of water, through the crocodiles that had ridden down with the floods, collect the Humber, which we'd left at Matlapanen, then drive to Riley's store for the shopping, return to the river bank and swim back upstream with the groceries balanced on our heads. The first of many objections to this unattractive plan was that I had never learned to swim. (Frances had seen to that.) So we needed a boat. Robert went back to Bulawayo to get one.

He returned with an elegant white, glass-fibre fifteen-footer strapped to the roof of the Humber. I named her *Water Beetle* and I loved her, but she turned out to be one of the worst buys we ever made.

★   ★   ★

It takes time to create a home out of seven shade trees, a patch of sand, and nothing; but within three weeks the island camp was habitable. Kisi knew a girl (when did he not?) whose brother had this friend who had met a man whose father built good huts, and all of them wanted work. The men would cut bamboo for the walls and the women would fetch the tall grass for thatching.

Accustomed to the solid wattle-and-daub huts of the Matopos, I couldn't understand why we needed flimsy bamboo walls here. I asked Kisi.

He sighed. 'Because,' he explained patiently, 'this camp is *too much hot*. The wind cannot blow through mud, but it can blow through bamboo. Also, we cannot make mud from sand, and there is nothing else in this place.'

So Kisi's girlfriend's brothers and friends and fathers and uncles invaded the camp, which soon swirled with the fragrance of new-cut grass and the woodsmoke from the cooking fires. As soon as the first hut was complete Kisi promptly annexed it as his kitchen and thereafter became almost unbearably houseproud about the place. He would never let the children across the threshold, for which I could hardly blame him, but he kept a bowl of fresh water near the door so that *I* could wash my hands before I defiled his precious pots.

The second hut served as a store-room for the spare drums of petrol, sackfuls of chicken-feed, spare bucksails, a tool-kit for the vehicles, shovels, axes, pickaxes, a hefty garden rake to smooth the sand inside the tents, mousetraps and buckets, and a good supply of old magazines which were all full of advertisements for skiwear and delicate Italian shoes.

The third and last hut overlooked the river, and it was going to be my office. I had begun work on *Okavango*, and I pleaded forcefully that I needed uninterrupted privacy. This was only partly true. What I really needed was a substitute for the Rock, and this was as close as I could come to recreating it. So I moved my bed inside, filched a folding table and a canvas chair from the main tent, spread animal skins on the floor, tacked up my own pencil sketches of animals, and set out the few curios I had salvaged from Far Lamorna.

The first self-invited guest was my cherished bull-terrier bitch, Catherine, who answered to Cats. She scratched out a neat hollow in the carefully smoothed mud floor, curled herself in it, and swore vilely at Dingo when he ventured an enquiring nose round the door-post. Cats was soon joined by six hens, all cluckingly determined to lay their eggs in my waste-paper basket. In due course, Robert, the children and Kisi invaded my cell; Kisi came in carrying a trayful of cutlery and crockery and briskly ordered me out so that he could set my table for lunch.

Kisi sniffed. 'Master Robert and your children say they do not want to eat in front of the tent any more. Is *too much* nice here.'

'Look, would you shift out of that chair? I want to fix an electric light so we don't have to use candles at dinnertime.' Robert dumped a bagful of handyman's tools on the desk and snarled at Kisi to run the wires across to the storage batteries on the DUKW

Oliver's small, clammy hand insinuated itself into mine. 'I *like* it here,' he breathed, with all the beguiling innocence of a fallen seraph. 'Can I sleep on your divan?' He paused, and looked up at me to see what effect he was having. When he realized the syrup wasn't working he switched to blackmail. 'If I *have* to go on sleeping in the tent then snakes will come,' he said firmly, 'and you'll be sorry!'

'*You'll* be the sorry one if you don't get out of here double quick,' I warned. 'Snakes have come in here already. Look, there's a python in the thatch just above your head.'

He backed out, howling with fright.

'All right if I move your books and things, Mother? I need to make a place for my genet cat in that corner.' Tris always seemed to have a supply of half-tame animals stuffed down the front of his shirt.

Situation normal, I reflected ruefully. In no time at all my retreat is going to be littered with guns, gramophone records, cardboard boxes full of birds' eggs, and Oliver's discarded socks. I might as well surrender the place to them now, and go back to typing in the DUKW. To be fair, they did at least allow me unrestricted use of the place when they were taking baths, or going to the loo, or fishing. By day, red birds flew in under the thatch, squirrels came to investigate the typewriter, and geckos hunted flies overhead. At night, the moon shone through the chinks in the bamboo walls and made a shadow-chequered pattern on the floor. Fireflies drifted in from the cool grass by the river, and congregated there in their thousands.

We hadn't the plumbers' stores to install running water, so our bath – a tiny canvas tub stretched over a wooden frame and resting on the ground – was filled from galvanized buckets heated over open fires. The loo, set thirty or so yards further into the forest, was simply a deep circular pit crowned by a seat improvised out of planks, with a hole cut roughly in the top two. It was a great place for informal meetings with sickeningly large spiders and several species of venomous snakes, especially at night when the torch batteries had faded to a glow-worm dimness.

We built a run for the chickens. Those hens with the sense to stay inside it were – more or less – safe, except when the resident gang of punk vervet monkeys broke into the enclosure and began to throw eggs at the fowls, and at each other. Those birds which flew up over the chicken mesh wire to nest in the bush became the immediate prey of every roving genet, night hawk, owl, and leguaan (monitor lizard) on the island.

New Hampshire hens are indifferent parents and seldom go broody, so I kept two old African *shenzis*[1] as foster mothers. Tondelayo, the brown *shenzi*, was a veteran from Lamorna and so old that she should have been using a zimmer frame. But she sat faithfully and well and brought out thirteen chubby New Hampshire chicks from each setting. The pullets she fostered were reserved to increase the flock, but the young roosters were fattened for the table.

★ ★ ★

Kisi made me a garden and fenced it with poles and chicken netting against the bush buck. In those hothouse conditions the seeds usually germinated within three days and then shot up like beanstalks until they were four or five inches high. Then they turned bright yellow and died back to the roots. I calculated that there was not enough nitrogen in the thin soil, so I poured on sulphate of ammonia, imported from Bulawayo at hideous cost. The tomato plants reared ten feet into the sky and then produced two pea-sized tomatoes each. What the monkeys didn't get, the birds ate; they had to be starving to bother.

I asked Kisi how *he* managed for vegetables. 'I use yours,' he confessed disarmingly. 'Those dry ones you buy in packets from the store. Also, Maritsasi is *too much clever*. She bring leaves.' He hesitated, not quite sure how to describe wild spinach to anyone as stupid as I obviously was for ignoring what had been so readily available, and for so long. 'Leaves . . .' he gestured vaguely '. . . for cooking.'

Maritsasi, she who had so many hut-building friends and relatives, was Kisi's steady girl. In exchange for a pound of sugar and a big bar of Sunlight soap she initiated me, with many giggles, into the simple mysteries of boiling waterlily roots, and showed me where to find tiny, acid wild plums, and river dates that tasted like slightly sweetened sawdust. After less than a week on this Spartan diet I yearned, with all my being, for a two-pound can of Cape peaches in heavy syrup.

In two respects we were lucky. Except during the breeding season, when the female river bream tend to take their younglings in their mouths and refuse all bait, the fishing was stupendous. And superb game birds – green pigeon, wild ducks and geese, guinea fowl, teal and francolin – cost next to nothing.

The *makoros*, dugout canoes, came skimming down the river from Lagxana (which is pronounced La-gunner) Sasunda, loaded

[1] A scruffy, tough, bush-bred hen.

almost gunwale-deep with bundles of reed, but also carrying buffalo and impala biltong, otter pelts, lion, leopard and lechwe skins, karosses fashioned from the purple-tinted hides of tsessebe, as well as barbel and bream taken from the fish traps and threaded together through the gills on strips of bark.

The river men were profoundly superstitious. Our camp was the first stop on their way to Maun, and they were prepared to sell almost anything for a small price, just to set their luck rolling for the rest of the day. It could be an impala skin, a fly-whisk made from the tail of a giraffe, or a hippo-hide whip; once this initial deal had been struck, they brought out what they knew we *really* needed: the feathery carcasses of the game birds, and the strings of fish. The going rate was five pence for a guineafowl, four for black duck, teal and francolin, three pence for four bream – if they were good ones.

But our living conditions on the island fell some way short of ideal. For one thing, the climate was against us, with violent swings in temperature. In summer the thermometer could go as high as 120°F, and in winter a bitter wind harried in from the desert with sand in its teeth. Every morning the sedge would be white with frost crystals and we would huddle near to the camp fire, shivering in pullovers. Then, abruptly, the cold would lift and the heat would blast down on us once more. And this was a heat that shimmered in living waves over the countryside, and billowed up into burning-glass clouds, the accursed fair-weather cumulus of Africa that never breaks as rain.

The land became as dry as old parchment, and the clay at the edges of the receding waterholes twisted up in tight brown curls. Beneath that hard crust there were live fish, barbel that had dug themselves in before the last of the treacherous water evaporated. They survived in the baked mud in a curious state of half-hibernation until the pools filled again.

October was known as 'suicide month', when nothing mattered except the next swim in the river and the next cold drink. The khakis we wore were permanently stained black with sweat, our eyes ached from the unremitting glare, and we were cursed with the knowledge that there was no escaping the torment. Tempers frayed, and trivial incidents provoked unforgiving rows.

Then, one morning, we would hear the high, clear, triple-noted whistling of a bird. The copper-coloured Paradise flycatcher had arrived, heralding the elephant rain. The first, early storms broke. These were not the steady, pounding rain of the true wet season, but hard rods of water driving down out of a sky that was riven by cobalt lightning. By Christmas we would be trapped in a steamy torrent that swiftly transformed the dried-out island into rank green jungle. In an explosion of new growth, the forest moved relentlessly in on us. Creepers insinuated sinuous tendrils through the windows of my little office, pink-striped vlei lilies thrust their way up through the mud floor of Kisi's kitchen, and snakes lay across the paths, full of venom and always ready to strike. The soil burst with mushrooms, ranging from the tiny, conical ones that the early Cape settlers boiled up to make ink, to monsters measuring two feet across which grew singly on anthills and tasted like slightly sweetened cabbage. This was one area in which the monkeys performed a useful service. They were experts at distinguishing between the deadly and the edible. What they ate, we ate too, and that included the shaggy ink-cap, which sounds vile and is in fact very good to eat.

There was, at least, plenty of shade in the camp, all the firewood we needed, and abundant water. The worst rigours of our self-imposed isolation were lifted for a while by moments of piercing beauty. One sunset, when I was spinning for bream at the place where the narrow little Boro River poured its clear waters into the Thamalakane, a pair of wild otter came to sport round the boat, fishing the evening rise just as ardently as I was. I loved, too, the scent and crackle of the log fire at night, the sight of the sullen, coppery moon that rose just across the river, flooding the swamps with light, and, rising before the sun, the vultures trailing ragged wings across the orange dawn sky. But most of all, I loved the wild animals of the island; by this time, they were the only things that were keeping me there.

At dusk, tiny, fragile galagos floated down from the trees, looking eagerly for insects. A cane rat that was the size of a spaniel lived in the damp reeds below my office and the trees were always filled by a chattering horde of small yellow squirrels. They were noisy fruit-thieves, and living alarms against snakes. Sometimes, walking the island at night with a torch in my hand, I would see reflected the red eyes of spring hares, strange ground-dwelling rodents that looked like kangaroo rats. Once, a porcupine shuffled importantly away from me. On another night, I surprised a whole family of aardvarks busily raiding what the monkeys had left of the mushroom beds.

I used to lie awake at night, listening to the intricate point and counterpoint of the swamps, compounded of the high chirruping of a million delicate white sedge frogs, fruit bats, cicadas, and the thin, violin whine of mosquitoes. Sometimes, there was the liquid warble of a nightjar, the flutter of soft brown owlets in the forest, or the slow whisper of the reeds as barbel rose to feed in amongst them. But the sound I really listened for, and longed to hear, was the barking of the Chobe bushbuck.

132

This is the most beautiful of all the African antelope. It is not especially big, about the size of an alsatian, and it looks as though it has been modelled in the purest porcelain. The rich russet coat is flecked with white, like the hide of the Indian chital.

Bushbuck are near solitaries, living in small family groups in the forest, shy and rarely seen. When I first arrived on the island there were three of them, a ram, his ewe and their young one. I tracked the infant's small slotmarks in the wet earth at the river's edge, and watched with delight as he grew from a long-legged fawn no bigger than a rabbit on stilts to a dream of dark copper and snowflakes, with his sharp horns just beginning to show. For me, he embodied the spirit of all that was wild and most beautiful on the island.

And I wish that I had never, ever, told anybody about him.

Crocodile Hunters

I was working aboard the DUKW one night when I heard the stutter of an outboard motor and the sound of a dinghy coming up the river at speed. The wash set *Shaka Zulu* rocking and decanted a packet of paperclips onto the floor. I swore. Visitors, at this time of night? It must have been close to eleven o'clock and I wasn't even halfway through writing up the day's log.

The dinghy swirled round and someone flung a mooring rope aboard. A hand grasped the gunwale, and a stranger heaved himself up over the side. He was white, though his skin had been tanned to a pale copper by the sun. He was a little under medium height, wiry, with curly brown hair and eyes of an indeterminate colour that was somewhere between light blue and hazel, and he wore the regulation swamp garb of khaki shorts and shirt. He held out his hand.

'Wilmot,' he announced, in the clipped vowels of South Africa. 'Bobbie Wilmot. You've seen my crocodile camp down at Matlapanen. Dad and I just got back from a trip up the Gomoti and I thought I'd come and pay my respects. Sorry it's so late, but I saw your light was on.' He laughed, a shade apologetically. 'It's easy to lose track of time out here.'

And from the sound of him, he hadn't spoken to a white woman in quite a long time, I thought. But I'd heard about *him*, and even more about his father. Cronje Wilmot had survived countless bouts of malaria, an attack of bubonic plague which he fought off alone in a remote and deserted hut, and a savage mauling by a wounded lion that he had followed into long grass. He was a gifted naturalist, and had somehow tracked down the venomous little beetle whose pupae provide the Kalahari Bushmen with their deadly arrow poison, used so effectively against Chaminooka. Cronje must have been well into his sixties, but he was still hunting as unflaggingly as his son. The Africans compared him to a marabou stork, because of his stiff-legged gait and white hair. He and Bobbie ran the crocodile-hunting concession for the whole of the Swamps.

Eventually we teamed up with them in a desultory sort of fashion, insofar as that if we both happened to be heading for the same place we would travel together. Our first joint safari took us up to a hazardous waterway called the Savuti Channel, which was staked like a game-pit with the fire-hardened and sword-sharp stubs of mopani trees which had been burnt down in a bush fire and then submerged when the fickle river changed its course.

Crocodile hunting is all night work, and both the weather and the phase of the moon play a significant part in it. Ideally, the night must be dark, because crocodiles have sharp eyes and are liable to sink out of sight long before an approaching craft gets anywhere near them. Niloticus, to give the creatures their proper scientific name, have double-lidded eyes, and the inner membrane closes the instant that they submerge: once under water, there is no way of detecting their presence. And the weather has to be calm, because if the surface of the water has been ruffled by the wind they tend to keep to the bottom anyway.

If the moon is down and the air is still, the technique is to sweep the water with the prow lamp and, once you spot the sinister red reflection from their eyes, you aim the boat at them as fast as the outboard motor can drive it and try to shoot them in the brain-pan before they have a chance to submerge. It sounds straightforward, and isn't. The drawback is that you have to be within a few feet of your prey – a few inches would be better – to have any real chance of success, and the shot has to be absolutely accurate, because that one vulnerable spot in the top of the skull is a tiny target. If you are lucky and your aim has been true, you then gaff the crocodile before it sinks and drag it aboard. The final, and vital, step is to sever the spine with an axe.

The trouble is that Niloticus have stupendous powers of recuperation, even from a bullet fired at close range from a heavy rifle, and unless the brain-pan is entirely shot away they have a dismaying habit of coming back to life hours after having been theoretically killed. On a more mundane level, precision shooting is essential to avoid spoiling the belly skin, which is the only saleable part of the entire hide.

It was an occupation which I regarded with fear and sick loathing – and one from which I could see no escape. For one thing, I was not going to allow Robert the opportunity of accusing me of cowardice. For another, we needed an extra source of revenue to supplement the income from my freelance writing: safaris are an expensive diversion, and our capital was being steadily eaten away. In truth, though, my main problem was that the post of hunter's mate required someone with the build of a Soviet shot-putter, and I was small and slight. I just didn't have the necessary muscle-power. But I gritted my teeth, breathed deeply, and got on with it.

The Wilmot flotilla of boats were all sturdily constructed in timber and metal. Bobbing next to them, *Water Beetle* looked what she really was – a Sunday afternoon pleasure craft, which should never have been committed to the tough conditions of the swamps. Anyway, we clambered aboard her at nightfall, and just before midnight we reached what looked like our first stretch of really open water, free of those dangerous mopani stumps and well clear of the banks. At this point, Robert loaded the Mannlicher 40/06 and one of the Wilmots' spare drivers took the helm. He twisted the throttle wide, and we shot straight ahead. An instant later there was a violent jar, followed by a splintering crash. Bobbie vanished in an arc over the bow, with his rifle in his hand, and I found myself sprawled in the bottom of the boat with a torrent of ice-cold water pouring in over me.

While I fumbled about for my own rifle, with thoughts of hippos filling my mind, Robert clambered over me and, imaginatively, plugged the rent in *Water Beetle*'s side with a cushion. Even so, the boat continued to fill and our situation was becoming more perilous by the second; to our right there were dense reed beds, a shoreless shore of unstable, floating vegetation where it would be impossible to find a foothold. To our left, but further off, the splendid forest swept down to the water's edge.

Bobbie Wilmot had swum back to the boat, and he flung his rifle in as he prepared to haul himself aboard. He was halfway in when our driver twisted the throttle again, in what could have been a reflex action, and we roared off towards the forest. The prow nudged the margin and just three seconds later *Water Beetle* sank gently down onto the silt of the shallows.

Somebody reached out a hand and I scrambled ashore. Bobbie pointed out sourly that glass-fibre was worse than useless in this environment, and that our only hope was to shoot a buffalo and wrap its hide round the hull to make it watertight again. Against this was the fact that our rifles were mud-caked and useless; we were a long way away from our base, in heavy game country that even the Masarwa Bushmen never reached;

we were cold and sodden wet; our blankets had drifted away; we had very little food because we had not planned to stay out for long.

We did have one resource, though. I had picked up Bobbie's trick of carrying matches and part of the striking strip from the box in a tightly corked bottle. Bobbie's own emergency supply was at the bottom, but mine were in my shirt pocket and once we'd dragged up a pile of driftwood we were able to light an enormous fire. By great good fortune we were able to retrieve the blankets and in a couple of hours they were dry enough to sleep in.

Twice during the night I woke, to see the African crocodile crew stoking the fire and sending sparks up into the inky sky, where they seemed to merge with the stars for an instant. Even at that hour, when scents lie dormant, the bush around us smelled as sweet as a farmyard. I drifted back to sleep, dreamed that I was back at Far Lamorna and woke, just before dawn, to hear cattle lowing.

Cattle? We had pitched our makeshift camp right on the edge of a game trail, and the lowing came from a breeding herd of buffalo which were now heading down to the river for a morning drink. I rolled myself out of my blanket and clambered to my feet. Luckily, we weren't directly in their path, but I could hear the frail tearing sound as the nearest animal peaceably cropped the grass, and the insistent bleating of calves whose mothers had moved away from them. It was as innocent as the dawn of time. All my surroundings seemed to have taken on a sudden strange clarity, like the air after rain, as if every sight, every sound, was being recorded for ever in my consciousness. In the bushes beyond us, a dove cooed, monotonous and plaintive, and a beetle scraped its way over the dry leaves at my feet. Then, abruptly, the small, familiar sounds were obliterated by the whiplash crack of a rifle. The herd thundered away, but one animal belled twice, despairingly, and was then still.

Bobbie had obviously cleaned out his gun. He came back into camp carrying his own Mannlicher, shouting orders in Tswana, the language of the Batauana. The crocodile gang cast off thin grey blankets, heaved themselves up, searched for their knives and then disappeared into the forest. Bobbie filled a tin kettle from the river, set it on what was left of the fire, dragged a log over and sat down. 'Christ,' he said. 'I need coffee. What a bloody, bloody night. They'll skin that beast out and we'll patch the hull. Buffalo liver for breakfast, June? There's some salt in the grub-box, but we'll have to eat with our fingers . . . the plates and things was washed away.'

The crocodile gang returned, laughing among themselves. One of them carried the hide of a half-grown calf draped over his shoulder, while the others lugged bleeding haunches, side meat, kidneys, liver, tongue. The blood dripped down onto their bare feet and there were splashes of red along the game trail. But there was food for three days, too.

Bobbie and Robert between them patched up the dinghy with the raw hide, and we puttered gently back to camp, sadder, but not a lot wiser. *Water Beetle* would remain a floating calamity to the end.

The Delta

Gradually, under Bobbie Wilmot's patient guidance, the little fleur-de-lys on our survey map of the Okavango Delta were transformed into reality: 7,000 square miles of strange, watery fastness.

To get some idea of the shape, put your hand palm downwards on a table with the fingers spread wide. From elbow to wrist is the Okavango River streaming down from the Angolan highlands, where up to 240 inches of rain fall every year. The swamp itself begins at the point where the river enters the Protectorate at Mohembo and then pours in torrents through a tight-knit mesh of papyrus – a wild, uncomfortable, incredible channel that no boat can penetrate. (In Mohembo most of the wild life has been exterminated, and only roving hippo and the crocodiles survive there.)

When it reaches level ground at the wrist, where Mohembo is, the huge volume of water spreads out over the surrounding semi-desert, where it divides into fingers, rivers which are finally reunited at the base of the triangle and then turned aside by a limestone ridge on their final course down towards Lake Dow. What complicates the picture is the fact that the Angolan water can take up to half a year to reach the eastern edge of the swamps, so that the rivers actually rise in the dry season. Then, by the time the rains break over the delta in November, and the forests have sloughed off their winter garb of yellow and brown in favour of a million different shades of green, the rivers have begun to fall again and the small rains of the desert can do little to restore the levels.

Then, although the main channels generally flow steadily south-east, any one of the interconnecting waterways can decide to flow in either direction, or simply dry up altogether. Of such ilk is the

Mokhokhelo. For most of the year it is a river of dry sand, strewn with the pearly shells of freshwater mussels, and linking Chitabe with the Kwaai. If by any chance the reeds have built up sufficiently to cause a blockage in the headwaters of the Kwaai, holding back and diverting the Angolan flow, then Chitabe fills first and the draining channel of the Mokhokhelo takes the overflow and starts to run north-west. A month later, though, it can be flowing contrarily in completely the opposite direction if hippo have chanced to break through the blockage to release the weight of water pressing for the Kwaai.

One evening, Robert and I found ourselves in an isolated lagoon that had five channels flowing out of it, and no discernible stream coming in. At that point we decided that whoever finally mapped the swamp channel, it was not going to be us.

Of course, no two rivers can ever be wholly alike in mood and feature, but during our first two years in the delta we came to possess a more than passing knowledge of most of them.

The Monachira is surpassingly lovely. Red fireball lilies[1] carpet its lonely islands; the wood ibis comes to breed and the carmine bee-eater pauses there in its long southern migration. One of those islands has a special significance for me, too.

On the open plains of Kunaragha, to the west of Maun, the river runs through a sea of shocking-pink lilies every autumn, and I have seen zebra cantering through them, followed by a bat-eared fox. No painter ever had a palette that could catch those tints. I have also seen a leopard, standing on an anthill with the early morning sun behind him, his chest still drenched with the blood of a fresh kill. But, for all its beauty, I never liked the place.

Elephant come to pluck the ripening nuts from the palm trees that grow on the banks of the sparkling Gomoti, and tiny, pale sedge frogs with vermilion legs live among the whispering reeds of the Boro.

The Savuti murmurs to itself, between the waterlogged trunks of a forest that drowned there; Zibaleanga – 'Little Fingers of Water' – is noisy with hippo.

The Thamalakane, river of lilies, swept past our island to run under a derelict wooden bridge of surprising loveliness, and then under another, of equally surprising ugliness; we never said as much, though, because the residents of Maun were proud of their modern bridge, built solidy of concrete. Also, the clean white sand below the bridge was an excellent place to dump garbage.

The Botletle is really only an extension of the Thamalakane, but the whole character of the river changed radically once its course

[1] *Hermanthus.*

turned eastward. It was an evil place, running through dark dolomite outcrops and dun-coloured desert on its way to Lake Dow, and it was home to immense crocodiles. In the thorn scrub on the sandy banks, the crimson-breasted shrike methodically impaled live insects to serve as a larder. Here, the brown hyena pack-hunted, dragging down their terrified prey. And the Botletle damn nearly killed both of us, when we went to hunt its waters in 1960.

But the Kwaai is the river of this story. The Kwaai is Africa undiluted, and it took eight years of my life and all my capital, and in the end it destroyed my marriage for a second, and final, time.

The Young Lions

Jack Chase lived a long way down the railway line from Francistown, in the village of Mahalapwe, where he owned a pleasant little country hotel, unforgivably named the Chase Me Inn. I hadn't seen him since he'd shot the cow elephant on the Chobe, but snippets of gossip about his roaringly unconventional approach to life had reached me along the news grapevine. He had a line in stunningly bad jokes, and I cherished the report of one encounter with a gullible tourist.

'Sir,' said the tourist, wanting to make conversation, 'that's a very fine lion's head that you've got up there above the bar!'

'So it is,' Jack replied smoothly. 'But you should see its arse on the other side of the wall in the dining room. That's even bigger.'

When he got back to Mahalapwe after the fated Chobe safari, Jack discovered that a pair of lions had trailed the migrating wildebeest into the area he was responsible for, and it was in this period that the lioness conceived. The gestation period is 108 days, which is short for so large an animal, and when the wildebeest moved off one night in search of fresh grazing, the lioness was heavily in cub. The pair stayed on, and because their normal prey had left the area, they took to killing cattle.

After three weeks in which they had killed seventeen beasts, the African owners sent a delegation to Jack, asking for help, and he took up the trail from the site of the most recent kill. He followed the pugmarks left in the fine Kalahari sand for fifteen miles without catching a glimpse of the pair or, even more strange, the smallest trace of their lair.

The lions were ranging for miles in their nightly forays, and not once had they returned to an old kill. When the shooting light failed

139

with the last of the sunset, Jack turned for home, without realizing that he could have found the solution to the riddle just fifty yards from where he broke off his search.

But the next day he returned to the site before dawn, and this time he could *smell* lions. He knew enough about the species to anticipate a charge, and when it duly came the big, black-maned lion crumpled in its tracks from a head shot. At this moment Jack caught sight of the lioness sliding away among the trees, and he wondered why she had failed to follow her mate's attack. However, he squatted down on his haunches to examine the dead beast and was surprised to find that the huge animal was in extraordinarily poor condition. There were no old wounds, no sign of tooth decay, so why had the cattle carcasses been abandoned, barely touched? Was there something wrong with the lioness? Cubs? Cubs.

In the thickets he found the four of them, a male and three females huddled together in a small clearing behind the scrub. As Jack approached they tottered unsteadily down the anthill where they had been lying, and stopped at his feet.

'They weren't much more than skin and bone,' he told me as we stood together at the rails of the showgrounds in Francistown. 'The only thing I could do was bundle them into the Land Rover and take them home with me.'

'What do you think had happened?' I asked, trying to unhook the male cub's claws from my newly pressed slacks.

The lioness, Jack said, would have known that her milk was failing, and therefore knew that her cubs were doomed. The area had been cleared of game by the Tsetse Fly Control teams, so because there were no cattle grazing near to the spot where she had cubbed, she and her mate had been compelled to raid kraals anything up to twenty miles away. At this stage the pair had become frantic with anxiety, too worried to fully satisfy their own hunger before hurrying back to the lair. But they had not been able to drag meat with them over such long distances, and they regurgitated none.

'And this one was the runt of the litter,' he added, cupping his hand under the smallest cub's chin and turning her face upwards. She had beautiful, tip-tilted eyes, dark gold with brown flecks in them. 'I sold the other two females, but this one still needed care.' He saw my expression, and laughed aloud. 'God, but you are a sucker for a sob story, June! What are you going to call her?'

'Chink,' I said.

I bought Chink and her brother Cubby for £25, because Jack told me that they were devoted to each other and he wanted them to go to a good home. I was staying at the Tati Hotel in the town, so I took them back there and locked them into my bedroom. The next morning the manager threw me out, even though I had paid him for

140

the shredded blankets and the bandages to bind the scratches on the head waiter's legs; I even offered to buy new sheets as well, because I had an uneasy suspicion that the stain made by lion's pee would never wash out. Restraining himself, he told me icily not to bother about the sheets because he was planning to have them framed as a memento, and would I just get those two out of here at once. And would I inform Mr Chase that he could settle his bar bill by cheque and then do his drinking somewhere else in future.

'It will be hyenas next time!' he hissed. 'I'm trying to run a hotel here, not bloody Regent's Park zoo!'

As my luggage was carried out Chink hooked her forepaw round his ankle and deftly unravelled part of his sock.

The Weak Must Die

'Any fool can tame a lion – only a fool will.'
CARL FISCHER, CIRCUS OWNER

The arrival of the cubs started me on my long career as foster-mother to a succession of bush orphans, all of which either died or bit people.

It may well – no, it *will* – infuriate all the thousands of kindly souls who have sobbed over too many wildlife films, but I do believe that it is foolish, selfish, and in the end cruel to try and hand-rear young wild animals in an artificial environment and so prolong lives that would have been forfeit in nature. Bush orphans invariably carry the seeds of death within them. In the wild, the weak die, *must* die, in order to preserve the strength of the species.

That being said, if I had to face the same situation again, seeing a young and vulnerable creature dying for lack of care, I would do precisely what I did then – try to raise it and then hope that, just for once, the Fates would be sympathetic. This does not alter the fact that I would still be wrong to try, but there is no logic in love.

★   ★   ★

So the cubs were given the run of the camp, never chained up or kept in cages, which was as near as I could get to reproducing their natural circumstances. By simply watching their behaviour I learned a good deal about lions.

141

When they are not actually hunting, which they tend to do as little as possible, lions are stone idle. They feed lying down, they drink lying down, and if you take them out for a walk they will flop into every patch of shade along the way, limbs sprawling. Provided that the hunting is good, the average lion is more than content to spend eighteen hours out of every twenty-four asleep on its back with its paws in the air.

Wet lions are something else again. Wet lions are a pain in the fundament. That beguiling little cub that has just been for a swim will then roll over and over in a patch of burnt grass until it is deeply, sootily black and then romp through the camp like a furry tornado, drag the laundry off the drying line, knock over the lunch table, rip the feathers from three bolsters, and then finally prove its overflowing love for you by trying to claw the shirt off your back. The cub is now quite dry, so it goes to sleep.

To their credit, though, they are at least entirely predictable. The leopard is oblique and slant and all cat, but a lion is unable to lie because it cannot veil its eyes. Leopards are solitaries; the gregarious lion is closer to a dog in character – and for some curious reason lions seem to hate other species of cats, and will go out of their way to kill them.

This much, and a lot more, we learned about lions. But the mistake we made right from the outset was to disregard the rule laid down by the great circus man Carl Fischer. He shook his head over my acquisition, and he especially warned me to get rid of Chink. 'She'll spoil her brother's temper if you don't. Give her to a zoo before it's too late.'

Alas for the plans of cubs and men. In the end it was Chink that we had to keep.

'Maritsasi is somehow getting a baby . . .'

'Madam.' Kisi rubbed the side of his nose with a forefinger and traced a pattern in the dust with his big toe. 'I wish to go home to Rhodesia. Tomorrow.'

'*Tomorrow!*' I was aghast. Without Kisi there would be no child-proof kitchen, no organized meals, no crisp and fragrant loaves. I had far too many other duties to cope with to be able to do the cooking as well. We would all starve. I told him so.

He remained unmoved, his eyes focused on the top branches of a tree. Obviously, I was not getting through to him.

Did he want more money? Was he ill? Was somebody making trouble for him? That went home.

Trouble. Yes, much trouble. The Queen Regent had let it be known that she wanted a word with him, and he suspected that she might be planning to send him to prison.

This was appalling. What had he done?

He had done nothing at all. At least, not by himself. It was the fault of his girl. 'Maritsasi is somehow getting a baby,' he said evasively, and because he was not a Batauana the Queen Regent had said that he must be made to pay for its upkeep *for ever*, even until he died! The thought was too much for him. He broke down and cried.

I told him that I would intercede with the Queen Regent on his behalf, and he cheered up enough to brew himself a mug of tea. While he was consoling himself with it, the latest batch of bread burned.

★ ★ ★

I had met the Queen Regent – who preferred to be called, simply, Mrs Moremi – very early in our stay in N'gamiland. She was a small woman, perhaps a little on the plump side, who dressed in simple cotton print frocks and wore a headscarf. But there the simplicity ended. Behind that sweet smile and the soft voice were an iron resolve and a mind sharp as a scalpel.

She knew about everything that went on in the Province, both above and between the sheets, and if anything drew down her wrath she was swift to bring the offender to justice. It was all done quietly and with as little fuss as possible, and she always channelled her actions through the body of elected elders who made up the Kgotla, the tribal parliament. Her deputy was a good, grey, grizzled giant of a man named Badirwān Sekao. He was the power behind the Kgotla, but the power behind *him* was the woman with dimpled cheeks and sherry-brown eyes.

One morning Elizabeth had asked me to take tea with her. It was served by her parlourmaid, and the Regent offered me biscuits, first apologizing because there was no cake.

'I would have made one,' she said, smiling, 'but I have so little time these days, with Letsholathebe away in England.' Letsholathebe was her eldest son, the Heir Apparent, and he was at the time studying social science at Southend-on-Sea in Essex, writing letters home that ached for the sun and for freedom from the dank grey weather of eastern England. 'And you do not have much time either, June, I hear, with all your writing and all those young animals. Now, tell me – do you like my house?'

The neat white bungalow was comfortable and unpretentious, as unfussy as Mohumagadi Elizabeth Pulane Moremi OBE herself.

'Two things,' she said, as we parted at her wooden front gate. 'I believe that you are something of an artist, and I have no pictures. Please make me one. The second thing is that I have no tomatoes. Could you spare some of yours, or have the monkeys eaten them again?'

I take your point, ma'am, but how exactly did you find out about *that*? Only Kisi and I knew about the gang of vervets which had ravaged my tomato patch. In any case, he was from the south of Rhodesia and spoke Sindebele, and the few words of Tswana that Maritsasi had taught him had nothing whatever to do with tomatoes.

She laughed at the expression on my face.

'I have many ears,' she said. 'Goodbye, June. We must meet again when we are both less busy. I like you.'

I liked her, too. She was a black Victoria.

★　★　★

Now, at our second meeting, I hoped that she liked me enough to forgive my cook.

She sat bolt upright at the desk in her little office and listened patiently as I made excuses for Kisi. There was a slight pucker between her eyebrows.

'But June,' she said, when I had ground to a breathless halt, 'we are not talking about Maritsasi's baby. I do not even *know* about Maritsasi's baby. Not yet. We are talking about Gutwano's baby. Gutwano is your laundrygirl, is she not?'

I nodded, baffled. 'Yes, ma'am, but Gutwano isn't Kisi's girl. Maritsasi . . .'

'Perhaps Kisi has more than one girl?' the Queen Regent enquired drily. 'Perhaps, too, his desire to return to Rhodesia in such a hurry is not because I might put him in prison, but because,' and a ghost of a smile lifted the corners of her mouth, 'he does not wish Maritsasi – or any of her male relatives – to find out that he has made love to Gutwano. I know Maritsasi's family well. They do not like outsiders to mistreat their women, and they can be very rough at times. Now, regarding Gutwano, Badirwān has told me that there is some doubt about the number of her child's fathers. I will not put Kisi in

144

prison, but he must make some contribution towards his possible share in fathering Gutwano's baby. I think £15 would be fair? You may keep your cook, June.' She chuckled suddenly. 'I also think it would be a good idea if you sent him to the veterinary officer for certain alterations.'

★ ★ ★

It must have been about eighteen months later that it suddenly occurred to me one day that Maritsasi had still not been delivered of that inconvenient babe, but I didn't think Kisi would want to discuss the matter, and it was never mentioned again.

Black River Bushman

That summer we took on a slim, unpredictable, hawk-nosed Black River Bushman as a part-time guide. His name was Kweri, and he worked when he chose to, which was not necessarily when we wanted him.

Kweri was the headman of the Zankuio village, a small hunting encampment that lay far off in the deep mopani between Maun and the Kwaai valley. These remote regions of the Protectorate were always light on real news and heavy on rumours, so reputations were generally fairly heavily embellished to add to the interest. The overall verdict on Kweri was that he was a species of black Robin Hood: brave, but a rogue who would steal ammunition from you so that he could go and poach giraffe – which were classed as royal game – and then save your life, unobtrusively, at the risk of his own, and modestly refuse to be rewarded for his gallantry.

Kweri himself did little to dull this luminous image. He assured me, with every sign of sincerity, that his mother had been killed by a lion, a man-eater – which would have made it the only one ever recorded in Bechuanaland. However. He described how he had then tracked the lion down and stabbed it through the heart *while it was still lying across the remains of his mother's corpse!* I have reported that lions are idle – but *that* idle? Kweri was an accomplished raconteur and his eyes never wavered for a second as he unfolded his tale, but his right big toe had a life all of its own, and it was tracing an intricate pattern in the sand.

In the late autumn Bobbie Wilmot asked us to join him on a hunting trip to the Mababe Flats. We usually picked Kweri up on his home ground at Zankuio, but on the morning we set out we came across him waiting for us at the point where the road that ran past the fishing shacks at Matlapanen turned inland, towards the distant valley of the Kwaai. He had come to Maun to sell skins, he said, to buy sugar, to have his best ploughshare mended . . . Kweri's village lay well within the tsetse belt and there were no oxen there; there was, therefore, also no plough. I waited.

'A man is sick,' he muttered, after an interminable pause. 'He took a leopardess in a trap, but before he could kill her she mauled him. He will die if he is not helped.'

'But, for God's sake, Kweri,' I protested, 'I'm not a doctor! Go to the hospital. Get Dr King.'

Kweri shook his head vigorously. 'I was there already. Before sunlight. The doctor is not there. Only a white nurse, who will not come. Zankuio is very far.'

Too damn far, I thought, as the shooting-brake lumbered through the sand. It was midday and desperately hot, but I had wound the windows up to keep out the swarms of tsetse. Kweri had sat in silence for an hour, deeply preoccupied, but at last he coughed, to signal that he was about to speak. 'The boy's father has sent for the witchdoctor,' he said. 'Perhaps he is already there. There was no reason for the leopardess to attack like that, because the boy was very careful when he went near her. This badness was wished upon him by an enemy! Now, only the right magic will make him well again.'

'So why do you need me, then?'

Kweri coughed again. 'I like to be sure,' he shrugged.

Hedging his bets. Fair enough. But I was puzzled why he should imagine that an animal which had spent the night in hideous pain, one foot clamped in the teeth of a steel-jaw trap, had no reason to attack.

* * *

The young man's hands had been badly torn but Robert, who was travelling ahead of me, had done a reasonable job of patching them up by the time Kweri and I arrived. But apart from the wounds, the boy was also pitifully emaciated and coughing up blood. It was tuberculosis, the scourge that strikes down so many of those who sleep in windowless huts in the smoke of smouldering fires.

I liked Zankuio. The village huts stood well apart, were neatly thatched and shaded by tall mopani, still wearing full summer foliage. Twig marks showed that the sand had been newly swept, and a few scrawny, brightly plumaged chickens fussed around a cooking pot still encrusted with cornmeal porridge. A yellow dog scratched

146

itself, yawned and then went back to sleep, and a bare-breasted girl shyly offered me an unripe watermelon.

I paid her what she asked, a shilling, though it was twice the going rate, and she suddenly and unexpectedly caught my hand and held it against her face. It was not in any way a gesture of simple affection, surely? Kisi spoke to her in Sasarwa, and I caught the word 'Tau', my only word in the whole of that click-and-grunt vocabulary, and even then it had been borrowed from Tswana. Tau, lion.

'What is her name?'

Kisi giggled. '*Hau!* I cannot say it. These people speak with the tongue high in the mouth. Her name is – almost – Ix. She wishes to tell you about the time when she was nearly taken by a lion.'

Kisi translated. She had been a very little girl, only *so* high, and she was sleeping by her father's fire one night in this very village, here in Zankuio, when a lion had crept out of the darkness and seized her by the head. Her agonized screams had woken her brother, a boy who himself had seen only ten dry seasons.

'But he was brave,' she assured Kisi solemnly. 'He snatched up a burning log from the fire and pushed it into the lion's face. Even now, I can remember the smell of burnt fur. The lion let me go and ran away into the night. See, I still have the scars.'

She did indeed have the scars, deep cicatrices on her temple and cheeks.

'And then?'

'Then I was ill for a very long time, and my father thought that I was going to die. The witchdoctor came, but his magic did not make me better. It was only when the white Morena doctor came from Maun with strong medicine that I became well again.'

I looked at Kweri, who chose to gaze at one of the chickens.

'The District Commissioner says that there are no man-eaters in the Protectorate,' I reminded Kisi.

'But the lion did not *eat* her,' he explained patiently, in the tones of one instructing an irredeemably stupid child. 'It only *wished* to.'

A child ran up to Ix and clung to the skin kilt that was her only garment. Ix pointed to her stomach. 'Mine!'

It was a year before I saw either Ix or the child again. By then that safari to the Mababe Flats had set the fuse to a series of extraordinary, dangerous, and deeply disturbing events.

A Taste for Danger

Years ago, in the United States, there was a circus trainer named Ruben Castang who claimed that he could communicate directly with his animals. His ability to read the thoughts of the beasts, to sense what they were saying and make them understand what he wanted them to hear, was not unique, but the extent of his skills was exceptional. In a mixed cage, things got out of hand one night when a tiger and a bear suddenly started a fight to the death. Castang backed away a little and yelled to one of the keepers to bring a slab of raw liver. Then he put his head as near as he could to the tiger's ear and roared the challenge to fight. As the infuriated beast slewed round to rend him he slapped the bloody meat across its gaping jaws – and the battle was over.

I pass on this bizarre incident only to show what can happen, in extreme cases, when human beings become too deeply involved with wild creatures, either because they want to hunt or train them, or just because they have a driving need to identify with them. A more recent, tragic example was Dian Fossey, whose obsession with the gentle mountain gorillas of Rwanda blinded her to the need for making contact with fallible humans, and led directly to her murder. When it comes to a species so surpassingly, nobly beautiful as the lion, even a passing interest in observing their social behaviour can lead to odd and unnerving consequences.

The thrill of danger has always been one of the primal stimulants, and I had realized for some time that Robert derived a special pleasure from taking unnecessary chances. He took to calling up wild lions, and the first time it happened was on the safari to the Mababe Flats.

★ ★ ★

After leaving Zankuio we turned off the bush track that led to the Kwaai valley and headed north, towards the Mababe Depression. It took us a long time to find water, and we finally made a scratch camp, late in the evening, next to a mud puddle that passed for a freshwater spring.

During the night I woke unexpectedly, filled with an inexplicable sense of unease. There was a low moon in the western sky, coppery through the haze of dust and smoke. Somewhere, out in the darkness of the Mababe Flats, I could hear wildebeest stamping and snorting, and the demented heckling of black-backed jackals.

Kweri got up, threw more logs on the fire, and lay down on his blanket again.

I called a question.

'Tau,' he replied. Lion.

For a while longer I lay on my back, savouring the living darkness around me. On nights like this, when the moon was in its last quarter, you could actually smell lion, and it didn't take the frustrated wailing of hyena to tell me that the prides were on the move. An instant later there was a new sound – the frantic, agonized bellowing of a wildebeest calf.

'Hyena.' Bobbie Wilmot was on his feet before I'd had time to take in what was happening. 'They're tearing that calf to shreds.'

He and Robert and I scrambled into the cab of the Wilmots' big cargo truck. The ground had been rucked up and pleated by rooting warthog, and as the vehicle crashed over the uneven surface the big headlamps picked out a galaxy of wildebeest eyes, strung like a sparkling bracelet of blue and green along the edge of the distant thickets. There was no sign of the calf, but four hyena darted away.

'Wait,' said Bobbie grimly. 'Those bastards'll tell us where to look. They won't leave it for long.' He pulled the handbrake on, but left the engine of the truck ticking over.

The hyena bunched, turned, and glared at us, and then one of them made a quick dash forward. Within seconds they were all head-down in the grass, tearing at something, and snickering hideously. Bobbie let out the clutch and the truck jolted forward. The hyena backed off. We could see the calf now – and it was still breathing. Bobbie swore crudely, dropped to the ground and ran over to the little beast. I saw him slide his long hunting knife cleanly into the base of its skull. Then he stabbed the knife into the earth and wiped his hands on the grass, cleansing them of blood.

'Poor little sod had a gunshot wound in one hind leg,' he told us as he climbed back up into the cab. 'Couldn't keep up with the rest of the herd. I just won't tell you what the hyena had done to it. But anyway, let's wait here for a while. See what happens. I've got a feeling this party isn't over yet. Look.' The bracelet of wildebeest eyes was tossing up and down. The beasts were anxious, getting ready to run. Then a pair of vivid emerald eyes flashed once, quickly, and shut off again. Lion? A lioness, on her own. She bounded away into the tree belt.

We drove back to the camp to change over into the Humber station-wagon, which had a high-powered spotlight fitted to the roof. While we were away the lioness returned, and she was crouched over the kill when we arrived. She froze when she heard the shooting-brake, and in the bright beam of the spotlight we were able to see her clearly for the first time. She was a beautiful creature, big for a lioness, and her coat gleamed like golden silk.

She seemed uncertain, puzzled. This was not her kill, and she knew it. She had filched it from the hyena and they were still skirmishing about, resentfully, at the edge of the circle of light. However, she was hungry enough not to care.

The Humber had a canvas-covered roof opening, and I stood up in the back to manipulate the spotlight. Then I heard the passenger door click. Robert was getting out.

'No!' I hissed, but he shook his head impatiently and began to walk slowly towards the lioness. He was unarmed.

'Please!' I whispered to Bobbie. 'Please cover him with the shotgun!'

He did not answer for a moment and then he said, quietly, 'I'm sorry, June. It isn't here. We left all the guns back in the camp.' The steel tyre lever was lying on top of the tool box. He picked it up and threw it down onto the grass.

'Take that with you.'

Robert nodded, picked it up.

For three-quarters of an hour I watched in frozen, horrified fascination the quiet and deadly game that was being played out in the arena formed by the pool of light cast by the spotlamp. Robert and the lioness were stalking each other. When he advanced towards the carcass, she edged away from it. Then her courage returned. She flicked round, and padded quickly back.

So far, Robert had been silent, but after a while he began to 'talk' to her in the low, crooning notes he used when he was speaking to our own cubs. Sometimes the big lioness growled softly, answering him, and twice she gave the peculiar, high-pitched scream of irritation that Chink used when she was being thwarted. Once, she began to walk away and then turned unexpectedly. Robert backed off, not hurrying, though, and feeling behind him for level ground with his feet. She sniffed at the wildebeest calf, raised her head again and stared full at him. Instantly, he froze, throwing a long shadow in the light from the spot like a streak of charcoal on the grass. For a moment, neither moved, then she twitched her tail, grunted, and drew off. Robert walked towards the carcass, and when he was about six feet from it the lioness began to advance on him again. This time he stood his ground.

A hyena wailed hysterically and trotted across the circle of light.

The lioness twitched her tail a second time and I saw her head begin to tilt slightly to one side. I knew that danger signal: her patience had finally run out. So had mine. I groped for the rail that supported the canopy of the Humber and I was going to get back into the driving cab and hit the hooter as hard as I could before Robert joined the calf as so much carrion. Bobbie grabbed my shoulder and as he did so the lioness resolved the situation. She straightened up and began to move quietly away, up a shallow depression on the far side of the kill.

Robert cupped his hands round his mouth, and roared.

He was answered immediately from the darkness by the bass grunting of a lion. A second animal joined the chorus, then a third, a fourth, a fifth. The rest of the pride were closing in fast. Robert returned to the Humber and sat down on the front bumper. The lioness watched him go, then she returned to the wildebeest, seized what was left of it and dragged it off into the deep grass.

I cannot now remember what I said or did that made Bobbie Wilmot suddenly prise my fingers loose from the spotlight and propel me gently towards the edge of the vehicle.

'Don't worry,' he said as he helped me down. 'He isn't the only one. I like to flirt with death, too. It adds a spice to living.'

'Or dying?' I snapped.

He laughed. 'Don't try to stop him. You can't. Nobody can. He's made that way.'

So was Bobbie Wilmot. Well, in the end he flirted once too often.

13 October

13 October was an anniversary marked out for ill-fortune. It was a year to the day since Jack Chase had shot the wounded cow elephant on the Chobe and, in the process, inadvertently blackened Robert's name for ever in the eyes of the Game Department; and we were back in the island camp between safaris.

Cubby had taken to killing chickens, despite all our efforts to discourage the habit, and round about midnight I was woken by the frightened clucking of the birds as he scooped them off their perches. Normally either Robert or I would have dealt with him, but on this night we were both deadly tired after spending the whole day trying to repair a major fault in the engine of the DUKW. Robert called out to Kisi and told him to chain Cubby up until morning.

It was never clear exactly what went wrong. Perhaps Kisi was still half asleep, perhaps Cubby decided to grapple him in the dark, but whichever way it was, Kisi hit out at the little lion with a heavy stick which caught the cub across the kidneys and ruptured them. When Kisi failed to bring the customary early morning tray of coffee I got up and went to look for him. I didn't have far to go. He was sitting on the river bank, crying, and Cubby was stretched out beside him, barely breathing. Even if we'd been equipped to do it, not even an immediate operation would have saved the poor little creature, and there was nothing we could do except watch impotently as his life ebbed. By noon, he was clearly reaching the end. He raised his head slightly and looked up at me, then stretched out his paws and somehow managed to stagger painfully down to the river's edge. He lay down thankfully beside the water, and died.

We buried him in the forest, near the place where he and Chink used to sleep during the day. Then we packed up the camp and moved across the river to Bobbie Wilmot's fishing shacks at Matlapanen.

It was a month before I could bear the thought of going back to the island.

Foxy

Of all the young wild animals I tried to rear during the eight years I spent in the delta, only three ultimately escaped tragedy. One was an infant vervet monkey, another was a lion cub called Oberon who remained intractably savage and returned eventually to his own kind, and the third was a black-backed jackal. She was a shy, red, foxy creature who always belonged far more to the night and the dark forest than she ever did to me.

Her mother had been caught in a steel-jaw trap and been bludgeoned to death for the sake of her skin, which would have fetched all of two shillings from a fur trader in Maun. Of the two cubs that the hunter dug out of their earth only one survived the journey to the village: a fine-boned female with a tiny pointed face and a thick pelt of russet fur on which the characteristic black saddle was already beginning to darken. I bought her for pence, and took her back with me to the island.

Although I was the only person she didn't try to attack, Foxy and I never became really close because she was a little too old to tame when I got her. Just occasionally, after I had fed her, she would leap into my lap and thrust her nose into my hair, but even

152

these small gestures of affection were rare. Still, she did teach me some of the more obscure facts about her kind, particularly in the matter of diet.

A lot of people believe, and not without reason, that all the carnivores live solely on meat, but in fact very few of them are that exclusive. There was a civet cat who used to visit the camp at night to eat cold cornmeal porridge from the cooking pots. The bat-eared foxes thrive on fruit, and the honey ratel supplements his diet of honey and bee grubs with meat, snakes, insects and fruit. My genet kitten adored cheese and grapes. Our lions ate grass – really ate it, and the greener it was the better they liked it. Foxy outgorged them all. She dug up and ate tree roots, and enjoyed wild plums, sweetcorn cobs, grasshoppers, stale bread, sweetmeats and, to my fury, most of my fowls.

She had been with me for about six months and was still a young vixen when I noticed that she was becoming increasingly restive. She had always tended to wander away a little at night, but now she stayed out longer and longer. The wild was calling her and because she had always had her liberty I made no effort to keep her in camp. When she was ready to fend for herself she would leave me, but until that day came I was content to act as foster-mother in return for her rather grudging affection.

I was walking her back through the woods one evening when she quickened her pace and trotted on ahead. We had wandered further afield than usual, but I guessed that her midnight excursions had often taken her to this particular stretch of country because she obviously knew it very well. I lost sight of her in the long grass, and although the path held the light prints of her paws for a while I was unable to follow her very far, because she turned off and disappeared down a little runnel that led into dense thorn thickets. I called after her repeatedly, but when she failed to respond I went back to camp without her.

She was still not back in time to feed with the dogs, as she usually did before setting off for the night, but just before dawn I felt her leap softly onto my bed. Her small body was soaked with dew, and she stretched herself out across my throat. She smelled strange, sickly-sweet. I put my hand up to her muzzle. There was blood on it. Chickens again? No, chickens all fine, Kisi reported resentfully. Foxy was not his favourite animal. I checked her over carefully to see if there might be any wounds, but there were none. Her stomach seemed full and she was drowsily content. She had made her first wild kill.

We had reached the cusp, the changeover time, from the freedom of the camp which I had offered her, to the far tougher other life that she was choosing for herself. Foxy understood this as well as

I did. When she woke after sleeping off her feed she was disturbed and nervous. Instead of spending the day curled up under my bed the way she had always done, she kept padding anxiously after me wherever I went, springing into my lap when I sat down, and pushing her face into my hair. When I took her with me down to the river at sunset for her nightly root-digging game her restlessness increased, and she kept glancing back over her shoulder towards the thickets where we had walked the night before. I landed a bream with the light fishing tackle I was using and as it flapped about at my feet Foxy sniffed at it incuriously, and then nudged my arm, her eyes anxious.

I knew what she wanted. Together, we took the woodland path again. She kept close by me until we came out onto the open molapos on the far side of the fig forest, and then she cantered swiftly past me, with her ears pricked forward and her brush held low. I called her name and she hesitated, looked back, and then came straight for me.

She came at a gallop, like a dog racing the wind, and sprang into the air when she was a few feet away. I caught her and she reared up in my arms, her paws on my shoulders, nuzzling my hair in the old, endearing puppy trick.

'Goodbye, Foxy,' I whispered. For it was goodbye. That last, fond gesture had been her farewell, to the past and to the person who had rescued her from starvation as a cub. Foxy paid off what remained of the debt with a single swipe of her rough little tongue across my cheek, wriggled free, and was gone, streaking for the distant edge of the molapo and the wild world beyond it.

I never saw her again, although later that night I heard a jackal yelping somewhere far off in the darkness. I knew Foxy's eager soprano and I called back, hoping, against all reasonable hope, that she might hear and return. But I had reckoned without the power of instinct. From further away came a deeper note, a dog's voice, and the next time Foxy called she was nearer to him than she was to me. He yelped again, demanding now, and she answered. For a while there was silence, and then a symphony broke out, the voices of a dozen jackals, all calling together, so that I could no longer distinguish one note from another. Foxy was at home, with her own kind.

Later that season Kisi told me that he had seen a jackal stalking the hens at the back of the camp and in the morning, sure enough, there was a pullet missing. I guessed who the marauder was, and I did not grudge her a meal. When three more fowls disappeared within the same week I began to have second thoughts – until I came across tell-tale evidence beside the thicket. There was a handful of well-gnawed bones lying scattered about, a handful of

New Hampshire feathers and, in a patch of fine sand, the prints of two sets of unbelievably tiny feet. Overprinting them was the larger spoor of a fully grown jackal bitch. Foxy, my bright savage, had cubs and was killing to feed them.

I walked back to the camp and gave instructions to the staff that they must never set snare wires near the chicken run, and that a chunk of meat should be set out every night on the low branch that had once been one of her favourite lying-up places.

A week later, I saw her cubs playing outside the thicket. Foxy was nowhere to be seen – probably away on some illicit poaching expedition – but I left a token gift of a guinea fowl out for her. In the morning it had gone, and that night a jackal called, very close to the tent. Foxy's voice? There was no way of telling. The pitch was a shade deeper than the soprano I had once known. A shadow slipped away from me in the starlight.

When the dry weather came, Foxy moved the cubs to fresh hunting grounds, beyond my ken.

Wild Eden

Time seemed to be slithering away between my fingers. That optimistic limit of a single month in the delta had now been stretched to half a year, but neither of us felt any inclination to leave. The Okavango basin held an apparently limitless population of game, rich not only in variety but in the sheer numbers of the species. It was like much of Africa must have seemed, before the rifles.

One afternoon, in search of water, we had to drive through a press of buffalo. They were lumbering steadily along, shoulder to shoulder in an immense black crescent that stretched between the fringes of the forest. I tried to count them, but you can't count the numbers in a herd that is three miles long and a mile deep; even then, I still could not see those on the outer perimeter of the crescent, on either horizon. Three thousand head, maybe four thousand? They were also seeking water, led by instinct to the far-off Savuti Channel, which never dried out. Though there were so many of them they were eerily silent: apart from the thudding of ponderous hooves on the hot sand, the only sound was the occasional location bleat from calves that had somehow fallen behind their mothers.

Once, coming into a molapo where the new season's grass was just beginning to show through the burnt crust left by the

August fires that the nomadic Masarwa Bushmen started every year in order to limit the available grazing and so force the game to concentrate in what green areas were left, we found ourselves in a crush that made our senses reel with awe. There were sable and roan antelope, the purple tsessebe, scores of buffalo and blue wildebeest, spiral-horned kudu, impala, families of warthog, browsing giraffe that looked for all the world like giant spotted orchids and, unexpectedly, three little bat-eared foxes scampering between the hooves of a troop of varnished zebra.

Years later the memory of that day, and that scene, gave me the title for my second book, *Wild Eden*.

Later, we came across the dogs. They were not dogs *canidae*, which covers domestic dogs, wolves, jackals and foxes. They were *Lycaon pictus lupinus*, the implacable Cape hunting dog, which is in fact not a dog at all and cannot interbreed with the dog species. Its only living relative is the equally terrible dhole of the Indian Deccan, described immortally by Kipling in his story of the Red Dog. *Lycaon* is certainly a handsome beast, but he is also the most relentless and cold-blooded killer in the world, a pack-hunter moving across a roving territory and destroying every animal that chances to cross his path. The Cape hunting dogs' method is fast, bloody, and highly efficient. They stalk, watching every move that the herds make, often crouching belly-down to disarm the suspicious antelope. Then the lead dog stretches, moves slowly to his feet, and breaks into a run. He will mark one animal, for choice the weakest and slowest in the herd. He is almost as fast as a cheetah, and the pack streams out behind him. The antelope snorts, doubles back in its own tracks, swerves, tries to throw off the pack – and is lost. The lead dog leaps to grab at its flank, at its testicles, tears away living flesh, then drops back and eats it on the run while the second dog in the pack speeds up, rushes the antelope and seizes another ragged mouthful of flesh. He, too, will then drop back, and then the rest of the dogs close in. There is nothing left of the antelope, not even for the vultures.

But . . . I have seen these self-same dogs hurrying their pups out of harm's way while the sentinels stood up on their hind legs and pranced to distract our attention from the young. I have seen the brood bitches of the pack sharing the care of their whelps, which have been hidden down aardvark burrows during the day to escape the heat, and regurgitating food for them impartially.

The Cape hunting dog is on the vanishing list, and that is another of Africa's tragedies. *Lycaon*[1] is the main enemy of the impala antelope. If the dogs are shot out the natural culling process is halted, the impala over-breed, over-graze, and eat out the specialized plant food that the bull sable antelope needs in order to attain fertility. So the following year no sable calves are dropped – and yet one more species faces the axe of evolution.

★   ★   ★

Living as we did then, almost continuously on the move, eating and sleeping in the open without putting up a tent for months on end, we saw a great deal that we would certainly have missed on a conventional safari. We were constantly surrounded by animals, too many to record now. Only the highlights remain, still etched deeply in my memory.

One night, walking back from a brief excursion outside the camp, I saw a black-maned lion standing on a termite hill, his silhouette ink-blocked against an enormous copper moon that was just rising. He turned his head to stare at me, coughed softly, and then turned away again to gaze out over the swamps, a guardian of the night. I have seen a pair of cheetah, their chests dappled with blood, stand watch over a fresh kill in the early morning sunlight. The cheetah relies on speed rather than cunning. It kills swiftly, gorges until it can swallow no more and then moves on again, leaving the remains for the little, hungry, yellow, yapping jackals who will tussle and tug at the carcass until only the skeleton is left. Even the bones aren't wasted, though. The laughing hyena will pick up the scent on the light dawn wind and crack even the biggest of them for the marrow, which is something that even the lions can't manage.

★   ★   ★

Then, without warning, almost overnight, the spell was broken, and all I could think about was how I could escape from the delta. It was mid-December, and the temperature had risen to 98 degrees of lung-scorching heat. The rain and the rising waters had brought with them a writhing tangle of snakes and the air was choked

---

[1] In his excellent book *Origins*, the world-renowned anthropologist Richard E. Leakey writes: '. . . the only daytime hunters [other than man] among today's carnivores are the wild dogs, whose forays are taken at dawn and dusk.' This is true for the reserved areas in East Africa, where there has long been a measure of protection for the species, but before the creation of the Moremi Wildlife Reserve in the delta *Lycaon* was hunted unmercifully, for the sake of the government bounty-money on the tails. The packs, which range over a huge area, were driven to seek the cover of darkness for their hunting excursions.

The other side of this coin is that the Okavango lions, which were strictly nocturnal when I first arrived in the swamps, rapidly reverted to making their kills by day once the hunters and trappers had been barred from the valley of the Kwaai.

157

with flying, stinging insects: the malarial mosquitoes, tsetse fly, and a shiny, scarab-like beetle that contrived to drown itself, in lemming-thousands, in every available dish of water. My lovely golden cocker spaniel bitch, Honey, had succumbed to *nagana*, the animal form of sleeping sickness, which we had failed to diagnose until it was too late to save her, and one of the other dogs was beginning to sicken. Worse, my sons were about to be consigned to us for the school holidays, on the cargo truck that plied between Rhodesia and Maun, and I did not think that a malarial Christmas would cheer them up much.

I wanted to spend Christmas back at the Victoria Falls. With extreme reluctance, Robert agreed, but my dreams of a restful, civilized holiday were doomed long before we reached the Falls. The story of the Chobe cow elephant, grotesquely distorted by now, had gone on ahead of us, and the Chief Game Ranger was quick to strike. He served a prohibition notice, banning us from keeping Chink anywhere in the area, and even from returning to our old camp on what we had christened Long Island.

Why?

Oh, because the DUKW's mooring ropes might chafe the trees. Because we might frighten the hippo. Because Chink, who was not yet nine months old and was still being bottle-fed on patent baby food, might maul one of the elephants.

'*Balls!*' shouted Robert, scarlet with anger. The expletive did nothing to soothe the game warden, and it didn't win us a camping site either.

Nonetheless, we stayed at the Zambesi until the middle of January, when the new school term began. Tristram and Oliver went back to school on the flanks of the Matopos, and Robert and I prepared to drive back to the delta. Just before leaving we hired a young Lozi tribesman called Leonard.

'This man calls the crocodile . . .'

In theory, Leonard was Robert's gun-bearer; in practice, he turned his hand to almost everything. He manned the dinghy, skinned the crocodile that we shot, cut firewood and fetched water, and he always lent a hand when I had problems with any of my young animals. He was also a spinner of wonderful tales, an African Aesop, and we got on well together.

'Wait until we return to the Zambesi,' he remarked one day as he gripped the head of an orphaned buffalo calf, while I tried ineffectively to force milk between its lips from the spout of an old tin teapot. 'There I will show you a man who calls the crocodile together and commands them as though they were his children. He will send them away from his dog when it swims in the river, and order them to catch another animal that has come down to drink. When he himself enters the water the crocodile are afraid to touch him, and he swims about between them, using a hollow reed for his breath. This is *true*, Ma Tau. I have seen it with these eyes.' He had taken to calling me by my Tswana nickname, which meant Mother of Lions.

'And what else have you seen?' I enquired, trying hard not to show my disbelief. I liked Leonard, and I wanted to leave his ego unbruised, but I had forgotten that not all of his tales were pure fable.

He looked away. 'I know something very bad,' he sighed, gloomily. 'It is about a friend of yours.'

'Do you wish to tell me?'

He nodded. 'It is better that you should hear it from me and not from a policeman. That way you will at least have the truth. You know Mog?'

Of course. Mog was a tribesman of middle years, a Roman Catholic, devoted to his young wife and their infant son, mild-mannered, kind to my dogs, altogether a darling man. I said so.

'He has other things in his heart as well. He has stolen cattle. Not one, but a great many.'

N'gamiland is semi-desert and no use for large-scale cultivation, with all the wealth of the tribe locked into a monoculture of cattle on a thin sand soil, so that with the enthusiastic aid of a thuggery of nomadic goats the desert spreads further every season. But so entrenched was this custom that under tribal law stock theft was often held to be more criminal than homicide.

'Do the police know this?'

'The police know,' Leonard affirmed gloomily. 'You cannot hide a cow under the floor of your hut as if it was a piece of money.' He paused then, perhaps hesitating because he was afraid that by talking openly of evil, some bad luck might rub off on us. 'He was to be brought before the Kgotla last week to be judged for his crime.'

'*Was?*'

'Mog has been to see Tagaan.'

'Oh, my God!'

Tagaan was the most powerful witchdoctor in the whole Protectorate, a man who routinely practised necromancy in its vilest forms; the police suspected that he was behind every ritual murder in Bechuanaland. He was neither Batauana nor Bayei, nor Masarwa, Mambukushu, or Herero. Some people said that he was of mixed stock and could speak every known language in Africa. Certainly, nobody knew where he came from, because he had simply arrived out of a late summer storm one night, and had remained to cast a web of supernatural fear over everyone in the region. But although his crimes might be suspected, he was never, could never be, brought to justice, because no one would ever dare to testify against him.

'What price did he ask, to clear Mog of the charges?'

'Kidney fat, from the body of his enemy's son. That small boy who used to herd his father's cattle in the sweet grazing between the river and the mopani forest. Mog and a friend waited until the child had driven the calves into their kraal for the night, away from the cows so that there would be milk for the family in the morning, then seized him and tied a gag across his mouth. They took him to Mog's house, but the table in the hut was too small for such an operation, so they took the door of the chicken coop off its hinges and used that. So, the child is dead, but Mog will go free, because the man whose cattle he stole was warned by Tagaan not to speak against Mog – and no one will disobey Tagaan. Ever.'

And Mog did indeed go free, and no one did disobey Tagaan, ever. The next time Mog came to our camp he brought me a gift of dark wild honey for my children, and a small holy card with a picture of the Infant Jesus on it.

★ ★ ★

Leonard turned his attention back to Belinda, the buffalo calf. She was the sole survivor of a mass slaughter at Kunaragha, where the loutish boyos from Maun – white, South African – had entertained themselves hugely by shooting from the backs of pick-up trucks at everything that moved. What the guns failed to kill outright the hyenas finished off, before moving on to tear three orphaned calves – which the gang of 'hunters' had somehow overlooked – limb from limb. Belinda had escaped because in her terror she had headed for the hunting camp instead of the open molapo. Leonard caught her for me, and tethered her to a tree.

I kept on trying to feed her, but she twisted away and lashed out at us with her sharp little hooves. Her nose was like damp velvet, her eyes the colour of dark violets. She smelled sweetly of dairy parlours and fresh grass.

In the end I stood back, defeated, with an empty teapot in my hand. All the precious milk had dribbled out of her mouth and

160

soaked away in the sand. But Leonard stroked her reassuringly. 'She will not drink yet,' he explained shyly, 'because she is still very frightened and she thinks we wish to kill her. But soon she will see, and she will think "These people do not wish me harm. They only wish to feed me, so I will stay." '

He was a rare man, Leonard, sensitive, with a special touch of tenderness. I looked at him and he said, angrily, 'When our Morena hunts he kills one animal only, and he does not leave it until he knows it is dead. He does not leave wounded creatures in the bush, and he does not shoot cows that have calves. Now, you should not go too far from this camp by yourself, because there are many wounded buffalo. They wait to kill people.'

★ ★ ★

There were mountains of discarded meat piled everywhere, and all night long the hyenas shrieked jubilantly as they scouted round the edge of the camp. I could not sleep, so I sat on the side of my bed and then watched as a young jackal bitch, drawn by the smell of the carcasses, crept into the glow thrown by the fire. She was so like my lost Foxy; I held my breath and watched her with delight. But somebody else had seen her. There was a spurt of flame from a rifle, and the little jackal crumpled where she stood. I heard the marksman laugh delightedly.

'What did you do that for, you stupid sod!' I screamed.

'*Agh*, missis, it was jus' fun!' And he laughed again.

You bastard! I thought. You bloody, degenerate, heartless bastard! And who are you, anyway? It turned out to be Jack Ramsden, son of a white father and a Herero mother (and they were married, as he kept telling everyone). In fact, he had a fine reputation as a hunter who would shoot any beast he clapped eyes on, whether he needed the meat or not. It was not a propitious meeting. Even so, he would one day spearhead the campaign to save the country's wild-life from extinction, though if anyone had predicted that on that bloody night at Kunaragha Jack would have hooted in derision.

With dawn came the vultures. Almost before it was fully light I heard them planing in from the sky, settling in the tree tops so that in the end they formed a black frieze against the yellowing east in an unbroken line; the wheeling sky held thousands more.

The buffalo calf, when I went to tend her, seemed weak from hunger, and this time I poured well-diluted evaporated milk – which was the only milk we had – into the big red washing-up bowl from the galley. I put my hand into the mixture, with my fingers crooked upwards. Interested, she finally lowered her muzzle, stamped her diminutive hooves and began to suck greedily at

161

my fingers, just as domestic calves will do. She sneezed as the milk bubbled into her nostrils and blew most of it over the ground, but at least it was a start. I was anxious to get her back to the sanctuary of the island as soon as possible, so we packed the DUKW and left Kunaragha the same afternoon.

Chink had been left behind in our base camp with Kisi in charge, and she had just one ambition as far as the buffalo calf was concerned, which was to reduce it to veal chops as soon as possible. It was time to limit her freedom a little, so I chained her up in the shade and in the evening I tethered Belinda to the front bumper of the Humber to stop her from wandering off into more danger.

I was jolted awake shortly after midnight by something hard and sharp hitting my face. I reached out and my hand closed on the soggy, frayed end of a rope. Then a soft muzzle butted my hand. Belinda had chewed through her tether, carefully skirted the lioness, and come looking for me. Somehow she had located my bed in the dark, and in her wobbly attempt to climb into it with me a hoof grazed my cheek. I reached over and helped her up. She gave a soft moo of contentment and settled down, curled up with her back pressed companionably against mine.

By morning, I was fully established as Belinda's mother, and she gave me no peace. She trotted after me everywhere I went, like Mary's persistent little lamb: to the kitchen, to the bathroom, to the loo. It was only when I climbed up into the DUKW that I had any privacy at all, and even then she would prance about, bleating piteously until I came back down again.

I located Chink's old bottle and used it to feed Belinda on her evaporated milk mixture, but she became obsessed with the idea that she was getting her milk from the wrong place; with her iron-hard head she butted me insistently in the groin, which was where any sensible buffalo calf would expect to find udders. Sometimes she actually butted me off my feet and then continued to butt me as I struggled to get up.

Of course I should have known that I couldn't win. At the end of a week she began to scour. Nobody in Maun knew the composition of buffalo milk, and I only discovered years later that it has the highest butter-fat content of any milk. Worse, I then made the mistake of actually diluting the evaporated milk even further, in the belief that it was too rich for her. The thin mixture killed her in two days.

East of the Sun

I should have foreseen that the slow-paced delight of life on the island could never last. In the late autumn of 1961 Robert decided that it was time for us to explore the valley of the Kwaai. Tris and Oliver had joined us from Bulawayo; so had old Cronje Wilmot, who had decided against accompanying his son on a crocodile-trapping spree for South African zoos which wanted live exhibits.

When we paused for a while at Zankuio to collect Kweri, Ix came running over to the shooting-brake and gabbled something to me in Sasarwa, and rubbed her stomach enthusiastically. Hungry, I thought, and rummaged in the glove compartment for half a packet of Scottish shortbread, the only food I had with me. Ix looked surprised.

Kisi grinned broadly. 'She not *hungry*,' he explained. 'She getting one more baby, that is all, and when it comes she want you to give it a name.'

I never had the chance to give it a name, but I saw the baby just over a year later, in extraordinary and tragic circumstances.

★   ★   ★

Late that afternoon we parked the DUKW and the shooting-brake in the shade of a clump of camel thorns. A small herd of giraffe that had been feeding among them rocked away, and a startled mongoose scuttered for cover. Robert decided to leave Kisi in charge of the camp, while he, Cronje and the children and I proceeded upstream by boat. I knew that this would mean man-handling the dinghy through the champagne-cold waters of the Kwaai, because the levels would not rise again until the winter floods came roaring down from Angola, and I wasn't happy about making a second, scratch camp away from the reassuring presence of *Shaka Zulu*, because the sun had already set and there was little light left. But Robert was in a bad temper, determined to press on to reach hunting water, for we had now begun to hunt crocodile in earnest. It was the old, old story – once again we were running out of money and the only way we could meet the crippling costs of keeping our safari on the road was by killing crocodiles and selling their skins.

We were short of fresh meat, so Robert waded ashore with a lightweight rifle and disappeared into the sand-coloured landscape.

163

Two hundred yards further on I beached the dinghy, just too weary to go any further. Cronje, Kisi and tall N'goma, who was Maritsasi's brother, stayed behind to unload the boat, which was harder work than finding twigs for the fire. Then, from somewhere beyond the narrow belt of forest came the nasal twanging of wildebeest, followed by three shots fired in quick succession. A spiral of dust whirled up as the herd broke cover and thundered off down the molapo. Robert came trudging back.

'Second and third shots miles high. Something's knocked the sodding foresight out of true and I'll have to zero it in again. There's a wildebeest there, down but not out and still kicking, so I need some more ammo.' The 30.06 was the faithful friend from our farming years, a good baboon-blaster, but something upwards of 2,000 rounds through the barrel hadn't done much for the rifling and the gun now threw high-right anywhere above a distance of about seventy-five yards. 'Anybody else coming? It's not far.'

Kweri wanted to; so did Tris.

'Do you have to? Oh, all right, but do be careful. *And don't tread on snakes!*' He was twelve years old, after all. I supposed that I'd have to stop mollycoddling him now.

Tris gave me a fleeting smile, not all that friendly – damn mothers – and he was gone before I had time to change my mind. But within minutes he came running back, with an open knife in his hand.

'Dad's in *big* trouble!' He looked to see how I was reacting, revelling in the drama of it all. 'Maybe I'd better not tell you . . .'

'You tell me right now, and tell me fast!'

'There's a lion on the kill. He told me to run back and keep my knife out in case of accidents.'

Tris had told me his first real lie when he was only five, and it had been a good, imaginative lie about a cobra that spat in his mouth when he was yawning. 'Oh, rubbish!' I snapped back. 'He's only been away from the kill for at most eight minutes, and lion couldn't have moved in that fast.'

'Did! They did! There's a whole lot of them. Three. Honestly!'

Kweri padded past me in the darkness.

'Morena wants the big battery, and the lamp.' He ran on down to the boat.

Morena is going to need the Holland and Holland too, I thought. I clicked open the lock of the leather carrying case, but the rifle was too heavy for me to handle and it seemed to be ages before I'd got the barrels, the stock and the fore-end properly assembled. N'goma and Kweri hoisted the ponderous battery on an oar, and I gave them the .465 together with a boxful of soft-nosed bullets. Cronje went with them, carrying the big spotlight.

164

The campfire was crackling cheerfully and the first faint stars were out, a lovely evening. Tris and I were silent, both fighting panic.

'Oh, come on,' he said eventually. 'Let's get the beds made while we wait.' But neither of us could drag our eyes away from the tree belt, straining for a sight of the brilliant beam that would tell us that Robert had connected the battery to the lamp.

I prayed silently. 'Dear God, please don't let him start talking to lions again. Anything, but just not that.' God must have had other things on His mind that night.

Time passed, but slowly, and at last the light did blaze up in the sky. Tris reached for my hand and began nervously to twist my rings round. We listened for the sound of a shot, but then N'goma came back with the message that the Morena wanted me. There were three lions on the kill and he thought I might like to see them.

'Go and tell the Morena that I can't just leave the children alone here.' Which was the best excuse I could think of for not going out to inspect three lions, on a kill, at close range, in the dark.

N'goma went, and came back with Kweri, and then announced with lofty unconcern that he was prepared to stay with the children. It was almost comforting to realize that someone else was also scared witless. The big Masarwa did his best to hide his fear by stroking the barrel of his antique Martini-Henry, lovingly, and with the confident air of a natural protector. 'One day,' I reflected, looking at the battered gun, 'that damn thing is going to explode in his face, or the brass wire he's wound round to keep the barrel in place is going to break just as the lion charges, and then – goodbye, N'goma!'

Wordlessly, Tris held out his Boy Scout knife to me and solemnly patted my shoulder. Oliver unfastened his holiday-present torch from his belt and pressed it into my other hand. I left the two little figures standing forlornly by the campfire, N'goma towering over them.

Kweri and I walked quickly. Even from some distance away I could recognize the now-red-now-green flash of the lions' eyes as the beam of light caught them. And Robert was 'talking' to the pride. I felt again the gut-twisting horror of the confrontation on the Mababe Flats. As I got near to Robert, Cronje handed the lamp to Kweri, one of the terminals somehow came loose, and we were in total darkness. When the light shone out again the lions were out of sight.

Robert said 'Easy now! Just stay where you are,' and clutched my shoulder, just in time to stop me from bolting. 'It's absolutely charming . . . a whole family, lion, lioness and their half-grown cub. I couldn't bring myself to shoot any of them.'

Cronje looked at him, frowning.

The male lion stalked back. He was black-maned, heavy-shouldered, running true to type, one of the powerful buffalo-killing lions of N'gamiland. The lioness came after him, and the two of them settled on the wildebeest carcass.

In a flash, Robert's mood changed. 'That's *my* bloody kill!' he shouted, 'and they know it! I'm going to get that meat.'

I tried to cry out, to yell 'No!', but my throat had constricted and I couldn't utter a sound. Cronje could. 'You can go by yourself, boy, and I'm not holding that lamp for you.'

Kweri spat, and shook his head. Robert looked sulky. I found my voice.

'What exactly happened when you got back here with Tris and Kweri?' I demanded. His reply dumbfounded me.

'We nearly walked onto them. When I'd left the wildebeest was down – lung shot – and coughing and grunting. You could still hear it when we got back, but by then it was too dark to see anything. Kweri said that some lions had moved in and I just laughed at him, but he went on insisting so I stopped to listen. When I heard a bone crack I knew lions were in fact there. So I stayed and talked to them while Kweri went for the lamp.'

'You stood . . . here?' We were at most twenty-five yards from the pride.

'Good Lord, no. No – much closer. I only moved back here when I heard you coming.' He chuckled. 'I thought you'd be scared if we went any nearer, but we can move in if you like.'

I could have throttled him.

'Such hairy chest . . .'

The rock-ribbed road that led to the creation of the Moremi Wildlife Reserve might have been a good deal smoother if we had taken the trouble, at the outset, to woo the white residents of Maun a little. For sure, we did nothing at all to endear ourselves to any of them: Robert exercised to the full his almost supernatural ability to whip up hostility by ridiculing people to their faces, and I – I did something even more unforgivable. I blew the whistle to the press, shrill and clear, on one of the most sensitive subjects of all, the matter of poaching.

166

When we first arrived in the delta there were no more than a hundred Europeans living in Maun, setting aside whole batches of free-range children. The officers of the British Colonial Service were a breed entirely apart, living in standard-pattern, English-suburban bungalows, and they decorated their spartan quarters with little touches of Home: cut-glass ashtrays fashioned in the shape of swans, china ducks in flight across the walls, mementoes of parents who had served before in India, and a great many framed photographs of their distant Dear Ones. Most of the traders were Afrikaners, from South Africa, and there was a leavening of totally displaced persons like the absolutely last of the White Russian refugees, and a vet from Denmark who cooked, even in Maun, according to the precepts of André Simon. Lastly there was the enchanting Chief of Police, who deserved better than to have been exiled to this rather grim little outpost of the fast-dwindling Empire.

Before the explosive burst of publicity about the Okavango Swamps began to attract the big, professional safari organizers – firms like Kenya's famous Kerr, Downey and Selby – the most able of all the white men who hunted there was Lionel Palmer. He was tall, with broad shoulders and an accent that announced his origins as South African English. He was a superlative marksman and a tracker of genius. I knew that what he wanted more than anything else was international fame as a White Hunter. I saw him prove his talents by picking up fading ghosts of evidence from rock-hard earth that was far too dry to hold a spoor.

'Dust is spiralling up on the far side of the molapo. Buffalo dust, not elephant . . . elephant dust has a different drift to buff. And this grass, here, has been flattened by lion, not antelope.'

He was never wrong.

'How can you possibly be so sure?' Robert demanded once, irritated by an achievement he could never hope to match.

Lionel simply stared at him, and did not answer. It was not, in any case, a skill that was easily explained because it lay in that foggy territory between inborn instinct and hard-learned skills of deduction. There was never any great love lost between the two men but in the end even Robert was moved to admit that what Lionel possessed above all other bush talents was the extraordinary ability to think himself inside the skin of any animal he was hunting.

Lionel and I got along together well enough, always provided that I was not writing angry articles for the newspapers about the reckless over-shooting in the area and, worse, pointing an accusing finger at the local lads. At least we shared an ability to read the signs that even the most elusive creatures left behind them in the sand.

There was another facility that Lionel possessed to a legendary degree and that earned him the sometimes sour respect of other men. The word *macho* wasn't generally in use in those days, but 'Egotesticle – that's what he is!' a bar-room wag exclaimed one day. 'Just plain egotesticle!'

★ ★ ★

Spring came to the delta, bearing on its sap-scented breezes the Baroness Renada, making an uninvited pilgrimage to The Wilderness. She had somehow slipped back into being Italian, without ever quite managing to shed the German accent that she'd acquired for her previous rôle, and she kept shunting serenely between the two.

'*Madonna mia*!' She loffed us! Ve vos lovely beobles, and she vanted to be mit us alvays. She also loffed Chink, *che bella*!, so beautiful too, and one day she's a-going buy for her a donkey to eat, from the Society for the Prevention of Cruelty to Animals, or, as she always put it in her inimitable way, the Society for Preservation of Cruelty to Animals. I suggested that slaughtering a blameless donkey to feed an already roly-poly lioness might not come all that high on the SPCA's list of priorities, but she tossed her head impatiently.

'It is not I mean for dem to kill donkeys!' she protested, deeply offended. 'Only to give vun vich had been already killed by some cars, or something. Surely dey do not mind? Such beautiful a lioness!'

She meant well. It seemed unkind to remind her that the nearest SPCA offices were some 700 miles away. That apart, the cargo truck contractor would probably draw the line at transporting dead donkeys, especially in warm weather. She saw my expression and changed tack, twining herself around me.

'You haff such loffly tits!' she crooned. 'Like wirchin. You like me, yes? You like that I loff you?'

It was only when a stream of still more unexpected guests began to arrive on the island that she ceased her frantic attempts to unbutton my shirt.

At any time, new faces were rare in Maun, and the news of Renada's arrival had flamed through the village. Lionel's brothers-in-law, Ronnie and Kennie Kays, led the rush, hefting a crate of beer between them as a lure. Ronnie was a stocky young man, with a shiny skin and a high colour. He was a brilliant mechanic, and without him every car and truck in the area would soon have ground to a grating halt, with sand lodged in every moving part. Kennie was Maun's darling, and his regular engagements to a different girl every summer were the highlights of the hot season gossip. Eventually, the daughter of one of Kenya's most renowned hunters managed to manoeuvre him into saying 'I do' in front of the District Commissioner, and for a while all the zest went out of Maun's social life; there was no longer anything to look forward to.

Lionel, naturally, was right behind them, generously proffering a bottle of Scotch. It took him less than no time at all to get Renada's measure. Within minutes she was leaning on his shoulder, her straight brown hair streaming over his bare chest and her wide, scarlet mouth curled up provocatively at the corners. And Lionel the Stud was whispering into her nearside ear, 'You come dudu-byes . . . you come dudu-byes wiv me.'

'So strong,' Renada murmured, bosom heaving theatrically. 'Such hairy chest. So big . . .!'

'Ouch!' yelped Lionel.

And still more guests followed: small, wiry Dougie Wright who had once been mauled by a lion and cherished an unending vendetta against them as a consequence; the girl who was known locally as 'The Floating Trophy', anxiously keeping a proprietorial eye on her corps of gentlemen callers; a laughing couple from the veterinary department; the beautiful young livestock officer, who had blue eyes and played the guitar. I rather fancied him myself for a while, and he was the only person who ever bothered to call at the island to see how I was faring, during Robert's now increasingly prolonged absences.

The welcoming party finally ran out of energy at five in the morning. Renada had gone to sleep, with her head in Lionel's lap and her shoes close to the fire. The acrid stench of burning rubber soles finally drifted across to Kennie, who staggered over to Renada and poured beer on to her smouldering footwear then shook the empty bottle disconsolately before hurling it into the bushes.

The Gauntlet

Because the whole of N'gamiland was tribal territory there was, so far as the tribesmen were concerned, no closed season for hunting. They were generally entitled to shoot whatever they wanted to, when they wanted to, and only hippo, giraffe, roan and sable antelope, and elephant were excepted. But on balance the tribal hunters killed only what they wanted for their immediate needs, and though they often used villainously barbaric methods they very seldom wasted anything. It was a simple, informal arrangement, but it might have worked well enough if the tribes alone had been involved. Instead, it came up against the sharply conflicting interests of the white traders in Maun and the contemptuously cynical over-shooting by European safari parties from South Africa, Rhodesia and the Protectorate itself, who knew that nobody was going to check that they hadn't exceeded their licences.

There was also a curious kink in the law that prohibited Europeans from using steel-jaw traps but omitted to ban imports of these vile implements, so every store in Maun carried a stock of them. The Africans used them constantly, together with snare wires and rope nooses, because in the main the only other weapons they possessed were hand-forged, iron spears. Only the wealthiest of them owned guns, mostly the long-obsolete Martini-Henrys and the even more antique Tower muskets with barrels that had to be heavily bound with brass wire to stop them from bursting. The muskets were, of course, muzzle loaders and they fired home-made lead balls which were usually prised out of animal carcasses and hammered back into shape to be used again. They were not often used, because powder was expensive and as often as not the guns inflicted more damage on the hunter than the hunted.

What threatened the ecological stability of the delta most was the massive trade in the pelts of the carnivores. In the early to mid-sixties the white traders were paying up to £40 for good leopard skins. For the nomadic Masarwa Bushmen, a sum like that meant the difference between bare survival and a marginally more easeful life, because it would buy them a few luxuries: a handful of salt, some sugar, a bar of soap, a new blanket, a skinning knife . . . even, perhaps, a necklace of blue glass beads for a much-desired girl.

In 1961, N'gamiland alone exported 2,000 leopard skins, and as the predators were steadily shot out, so the numbers of the species on which they normally preyed began to rise uncontrolled. By the end of the year, for instance, there were troops of up to 200 baboons, with the inevitable knock-on result that flocks of ground-nesting birds were alarmingly reduced as the baboons raided their nests. More threatening still, constant trapping of the smaller carnivora allowed the numbers of plague-carrying rats to explode. Four thousand genet skins were exported from a single village in 1961, baled up together with uncounted pelts of serval cat, civet and black-backed jackal.

* * *

Then there were the whites, who often didn't even bother to buy hunting licences. Seven Afrikaners from South Africa organized a safari in the swamps. It lasted for a day and a half, and in those thirty-six hours – allowing time for food, sleep and drink – they shot seventeen buffalo dead and left considerably more to die of wounds in the bush. Of the buffalo which were actually brought down, eleven were cows, six of them heavily pregnant and five with very young calves at foot. One of the calves was riddled with bullets as he stood guarding his mother's body, and the rest were, inevitably, left to wander until the hyena got them as well.

Five blue wildebeest, three impala and a warthog also fell to the guns. The sportsmen gralloched them all and then dragged the gutted carcasses behind their trucks, to lay a blood trail and so attract lion close to the perimeter of the camp during the night. After dark, as the first wild bursts of hyena music rose from the molapo, the heroic hunters scrambled into their Land Rovers and, with the spotlights all focused on the bait carcasses, waited happily with loaded rifles to blast any predators that might be tempted to feed. By morning their humour had vanished somewhat, however, because all they'd managed to bag was a half-grown lioness and a jackal bitch puppy. Obviously, they left them to rot, without bothering to skin them.

Later in the day, as the fun began to pall, they loaded the hindquarters of four of the buffalo onto a five-ton truck and left the remaining carcasses for the vultures. Then, on the way back to Maun, a lone tsessebe bull leaped the track. A young man standing in the back of the truck thumped the roof of the cab.

'Listen!' I heard him yell as the driver slowed down, 'I'm really tired as hell of bleddy buff. Let's make a change, hey?'

I counted the shots. One, two, three . . . eleven, twelve . . . sixteen! Each shot had been carefully aimed, to strike a different place on the stricken beast, so that it would be maimed by degrees, rather than killed outright. I simply could not believe what I was seeing. The tsessebe was standing, its head lowered and its feet set wide, blood streaming from its nostrils, dying slowly. The youth jumped down from the truck and walked up to the animal, and I thought that he intended to finish it off at last. Instead, he took his hat off and fanned it in front of the animal's eyes, laughing and looking back at his companions to see how they were enjoying the joke.

'This is how they play the bulls in Madrid!' he shouted exultantly. 'Let's see if I can make this bugger charge me!'

But the tsessebe didn't charge. Instead, it coughed up frothy blood from its perforated lungs and crumpled slowly to the ground, at its tormentor's feet. And even then it took another twenty terrible minutes to die. Only then did they slit its belly.

Sitting in the Land Rover which had been second vehicle in the little convoy, all I could do in that bloody company was to stare out of the window so they wouldn't see my tears, and wish them all in purgatory.

★ ★ ★

Three Europeans made their way into the swamps carrying steel-jaw traps as well as their rifles. They set and baited the traps with great care, hoping for a leopard, since this was 'the cheapest way to get a decent skin'. But the traps can't distinguish between species and, one after the other, they were triggered by hyena which then gnawed frantically at their mangled limbs until they could be dispatched with a bullet in the skull. Their tails were cut off, though, because they qualified for a government bounty. These men regarded the bounty as just so much beer money, because they all had well-paid jobs; at least the African hunters really needed the cash.

Their last victim in that area was a lioness. They were too frightened to go near her during the early part of the night, when her agonized roars first alerted them to their good fortune, so they left her to twist and tug in unbelievable pain until the sun was well up, and at ten o'clock they went in and drilled her full of bullets from a decently safe distance. They noticed that there was milk oozing from her teats, but they made no effort to find her cubs, which were left to starve to death.

After this sortie the party moved downstream to our old camp in the Kwaai valley. Here, using spotlights, they managed to kill three lions which had been attracted to the bait; one of the three was a part-grown lioness, little more than a cub. Night shooting was illegal in Bechuanaland, but there was no one to see that the law was observed, so the confident, careless, easy-to-find lion was the best and easiest target; a powerful spotlight to dazzle the eyes, a quiet stalk towards the feeding lions, a telescopic sight – and there was another trophy to bundle into the back of the truck.

Between July and October in 1962 I know of eleven lions that were shot on forty miles of river frontage in the Kwaai area, and these did not include the beasts that were trapped by Africans. I had to watch, once, while licensed hunters practised their sadistic rites on an elephant bull. As he came down to drink in the late afternoon they carefully shot him in the left foreleg, so that he wouldn't be able to move too far. At about noon the following day they returned to finish him off. One by one, they placed eighteen .303 bullets in the crippled bull, again deliberately avoiding the heart or head shots that might have killed him outright. He simply stood there, unable to move, and I thought he was never going to die. But, at last, he

172

toppled over, almost gently, finally at peace and beyond the little mercy of men. And the tally went on and on.

One day Robert and I came upon the heavily poisoned carcass of a wildebeest and, around it, the vulture-torn remains of two lions that had been skinned, seven hyena, eleven jackal – and twenty-nine of the vultures that had also fed on the bait. It was known that there was a South African hunter in the region at the time, who was after skins he could sell, and he had obviously decided to save himself trouble by using strychnine instead of bullets. By the time we had reported our find, of course, the man was safely back in the Cape, so nobody ever took action against him, either. There was one tiny consolation: it was unlikely that he would ever get repeat orders, because the hides of poisoned animals soon shed all the fur.

Then there were the two Maun residents who bought themselves new rifles that they needed to sight in. They took themselves off to Lake N'gami, and zeroed in the weapons with a little live target practice on grazing springbuck. By the time they were satisfied that the guns were throwing true there were fourteen of the graceful little antelope lying along the shores of the lake, either dead or mortally disabled by the shots.

But that little escapade was dwarfed by the infamous Maun safari, when three morally lobotomized goons took out eighteen game licences between them and then went on to shoot eighteen each; a total of fifty-four antelope. By then they were enjoying themselves so much that they next killed a zebra and dragged it behind their Land Rover to lay the blood trail. That night they had wonderful sport, shooting inquisitive hyena in the beam of the headlamps whenever they came in sight. By midnight, they had a total bag of thirteen hyena, a kudu cow, a tsessebe, a reedbuck, three porcupine, a bat-eared fox and a honey badger.

With all the wonderful certainty that hindsight brings, I accept now that there were times when I should have intervened directly, made my protests then and there. But remember, at that time this sort of behaviour was often considered perfectly normal, and anyone who objected was automatically written off as a freak and a wimp, not to be taken seriously. Probably this attitude explains why those good and simple souls wanted to lynch me for trying to undermine their pleasant pastime.

I don't remember now what it was that finally drove Robert and me to change from being passive, if angry, critics of the slaughter. It might have been an accumulation of outrages, or some small but especially brutal incident. Probably it was that hideous Maun safari. We had joined it as guests, and that inhibited us from protesting. The best we could manage was at least to withhold our applause. At any rate, there came an evening when our thoughts coincided, when we both recognized the stark truth that not even the huge game population of the Kwaai could sustain killing on this scale for long. We decided that, come what may and cost what it might, we had to stay on in the delta until we'd seen a game reserve created.

It was then, knowing precisely what local white reaction would be, and how angry the idea would make the Colonial Office's minions, that we turned to the tribesmen for support. But they were just as hostile as the rest – until the doctor, Don King, suggested that we should try talking to Isaac Tudor.

Isaac Tudor

Isaac Tudor had skin the colour of honey, a quicksilver mind and the tongue of a striking viper. He was a Kung Bushman on his mother's side and white on his father's, and he wielded enormous influence among the Batauana.

We needed a strong and resolute ally, someone who had brains as well as political clout. Robert sounded him out circumspectly, and after that I invited him down to the island for a business lunch. He accepted at once, partly because he had a natural curiosity and partly because he somehow sensed that it might provide him with ideas to harry and discredit the local British administration. He wasted no time on small talk.

'Your husband and I have already discussed the thought of setting up a tribal game reserve,' he began. ' "Kill the cow that bears the calf and tomorrow you'll have no meat" was how he put it. Well, it sounds like good sense, but you do realize, don't you, that all the tribes in N'gamiland are hunting people by tradition? They grow miserable crops, the tsetse stop them from cattle-ranching, and all that's left for them to live on is game. They eat the meat and they sell the hides to the traders for ready money. It could take another ice age to convince them that they're destroying their greatest natural asset by killing off their *dipholoholo*, their wild cattle. So what do you want me to do about it?'

'Talk to people. The elders will listen to you. Maybe you could begin by getting them to set up a – what could you call it? – a fauna conservation society. We have to start somewhere.'

'*We* have to start somewhere? Yes indeed, Mrs June. And what is in it for you?'

174

'Damn all,' I replied, honestly if inelegantly, 'except that I've always loved animals.'

He grinned. 'I also get the feeling that you do not care too much for your fellow whites in Maun, especially the ones who are in authority. Well, come to that, neither do I. So maybe I'll help. Do you know Michael Dithapo?' We didn't. 'Tribal nobility,' Isaac explained. 'What is more, because of that he is a big and very sharp thorn in the DC's side. His people, the Dithapo clan, have a lot of power. Michael himself is anti-white, anti-Administration – an all-round troublemaker. Our beloved DC describes him officially as "a spreader of disaffection", and that makes me think you should meet him. He is a marvellous person, and I am sure you are going to like him. He has a very – flexible – mind. Almost as flexible as mine.'

Two days later, Isaac brought Michael Dithapo to the island, and I did like him, immediately. He was in his mid-twenties, and in spite of his rather ferocious reputation he was a sensitive man, with an attractive, open face, and beautiful hands with long, tapering fingers.

Kisi brought cans of beer that had been cooling in the river, and we sat outside in the shade of the tent to drink it. I repeated my arguments for creating a game reserve.

'Yes, and what are my people going to live on if they stop hunting?' Michael asked, coolly. 'Game are the main source of protein. So you are asking us to nobly give up our supply of food and start a policy of polite starvation? Of course, that would indeed make the conservationists in the *First* World very happy indeed, but for us it is a crazy idea.'

I hadn't expected so swift and conclusive a brush-off, but I bit off the acid retort that first sprang to mind and persevered as calmly as I could, although I could feel my smile beginning to ice up. 'I wasn't suggesting that at all,' I said. 'All I'm saying is that not only are you eating your seedcorn' – I was in no mood to mind my metaphors – 'but you're letting the Europeans help you finish it. Forget calling it a reserve or a sanctuary and just say that it's a game farm, if that helps. What I'd thought of was to have an ecologically viable area at the heart of the region, then set up a buffer zone around it, and let the tribesmen hunt the overspill in the third zone. That way they'll still have meat in plenty, without killing off the breeding stock.'

' "Ecologically viable",' murmured Isaac happily. 'Really, Lady June, you will have to stop using long words like that, which only very clever people like Michael and myself can understand. What you really mean is "Ban all hunting in the Kwaai valley", isn't it? Because it is the best, the richest game area that we have, the cream.' His metaphors were also faltering. 'And you love it,' he continued. 'Without self-interest,' he added.

Unexpectedly, Michael laughed. 'Well – there might be something in the idea, but it'll never work. To start with, you'd be up against people like Jack Ramsden, because he's a hunter first, second and last. You know what people say about him, "He cut his teeth on the stock of a rifle"? But even if you could somehow win him over, what about the Bayei?'

The who?

'Ah yes, the Bayei!' Isaac leaned back in his chair. 'But surely you know the beautiful Bayei? They love the Batauana like a mouse loves cats, so anything that we – and I count myself a Batauana – anything that we want is going to get a turned-down thumb from them.'

'But aren't they subjects of the Batauana?'

'Oh yes, but don't forget that there are twice as many of them as there are of us. No, you need to brush up on your tribal history before you get yourselves into a fix. But I charge for giving lessons.' He held up his empty beer bottle and then turned it upside down. Kisi took the hint and hurried over with a fresh bottle.

N'gamiland was not one people, not one tribe. Driven from their original homelands by the 'Ndebele, the Bayei trekked north-west, to settle in the exotic, sub-tropical country round the Chobe River, where they remained until the original Chief Tauana crossed the desert with his band of followers and annexed the delta. By the time this happened, some of the Bayei had also moved off under the leadership of their chief's eldest son, and migrated to Lake N'gami. The two tribes got along with each other well enough until Letsholathebe the First mounted the throne, after which the Batauana embarked on a more or less bloodless takeover campaign of conquest against the Bayei, and robbed them of most of their cattle.

'All this happened in the mid-1880s,' Isaac continued, 'and ever since then the Bayei have been cunningly stealing their cattle back from us, which is very dishonest of them. I must tell you that the only thing which stops a war between the Batauana and the Bayei is that the Bayei refuse to fight. They always have. They believe in – how shall I put it? – secret erosion.'

'And you forgot to say that their national sport is ritual murder,' Michael interrupted tartly. 'And don't forget to mention the 5,000 Hereros and the 15,000 Masarwas, and all the other little tribes in N'gamiland. They'd all have to be converted, because even the smallest of them has a voice in the tribal Kgotla. Try telling Kweri that he and his precious Masarwas will not be permitted to hunt in the Kwaai valley and you'll hear that voice, very loudly.'

It was clear that this was no time for a stately game of hints and half-suggested queries. 'Are you going to help me or not, Michael?' I asked bluntly. 'Just so that I know, and we don't waste each other's

176

time.' He did not answer immediately, and for some of the longest seconds in recorded time I suspected that my question had been a little too abrupt.

But, 'Oh yes, I'll help you,' he said eventually. 'It will not be because I share your progressive ideals, though. The fact is that I have heard privately that the DC hates the thought of a tribal game reserve because, number one, he thinks that it would mean more problems for his department and, two, because if the idea succeeds then we would not be quite so ready to do what he tells us is good for us. Also, I would really enjoy being in at the kill if, by some fluke, the tribesmen overruled the administration and the DC got the sack.' That seemed fair enough.

Just before the two men left, Isaac took me aside and enquired sweetly, 'Is it true that you have been teaching Kweri about *ecological viability*?'

'Yes,' I said resentfully. 'And he called me Mohumagadi, Great Queen.'

'And then he laughed?' asked Isaac. I ignored the question.

That discussion on the island was probably the most significant of all the innumerable meetings that we were to have with the tribal elders, various power brokers, mischief makers and a long and knotted string of officials. But Michael and Isaac made a special point of introducing us – as friends – to all those elders, because they were the men who would, in the end, tip the balance one way or the other.

★ ★ ★

Robert had taken to staying away from the island for longer and longer periods, and for months on end my sole companions were Kisi, Leonard and an ancient Black River Bushman who sat patiently repairing his worn-out mokoro on the bank. In an effort to shake off the depression that loneliness brought, I turned to my typewriter and began to fire off sheaves of warnings to the Secretariat in Mafeking that the game laws in N'gamiland had become a standing joke.

The British administration was profoundly indifferent. Few of its officials had ever ventured as far as the delta, and by the time they had skimmed disdainfully through my first seventeen letters on the subject, none of them wanted to. Their survey maps showed them clearly that the fleur-de-lys area was nothing but unproductive swampland, barren of promise, devoid of opportunities for personal advancement in the Service. In an attempt to divert the swelling tide of correspondence, one of them did suggest reviving a long-abandoned scheme for draining the swamps, which would have solved both his problems and mine in one fell gurgle. The drainage plan had been conceived in distant Whitehall, but after a brief initial period of enthusiasm someone checked the costings and three years of paperwork were swiftly buried in the basement filing system.

As my pile of letters continued to mount, so did the temperature. Encouraged by rumours that the tribesmen were beginning to come round to our way of thinking, the British administration began to regard us as dangerous *agents provocateurs* who might well succeed in setting local government against the central African authority in Gaberones. The thought of the administrative headaches involved in managing a tribal game reserve filled them with dismay; and if we blew the whistle to the press on the random killing methods employed by the tribesmen themselves, they would have to deal with a hornets' nest of antagonism – the last thing they wanted.

The Hunting Party

'Do you know, Ma Tau, that they have not come here just to shoot? They have brought steel traps with them.' Leonard looked worried. He squatted down beside my chair, his signal for a formal *palaver*.

A South African hunting party had invaded our camp: three whites with six camp servants. They drove their overloaded Jeep furiously up and down the valley, yelling exultantly that they were going to kill every single animal that was listed on their hunting licences – and any others they felt they could get away with. I watched them start out, my whole body jagged with apprehension and loathing.

It was not long before they had fully justified my fears. Their first two victims were hyena which they trapped and then shot – all for the sake of the ten shilling bounty money on the tails. When we came across them they were standing over the carcass of a big, light-coloured bitch that they had lured to her death with a zebra bait. That in itself held a special horror. The carcass was that of a lone zebra mare we had earlier seen drinking with a herd of sable antelope. She had been heavily in foal, and what was left of the half-devoured embryo lay beside her.

They had been hoping to trap lion, one of the men explained earnestly, but just as the lions were approaching the hyena had sprung the steel jaws. They had found her there in the morning,

178

shrieking with pain, and they were impressed by how ferocious she still was.

'Man, it was jus' crazy!' said one. 'That animal was crazy. It kept trying to get at us! I didn't know hyena was like that. I thought they was cowards!'

Leonard, looking furious, was standing next to me and he whispered in Sindebele: 'He would be crazy, too, if he had been caught in a steel trap all night, with two lions feeding a few feet away from him.'

The hunters came back to the camp before first light the next morning. They had caught a third hyena, but it was still alive. They said we could have it if we were prepared to take it out of the trap – and pay them the ten shilling bounty. They dug each other in the ribs, and smiled, pleased by our anger. We gave them the money, and in the shivering dawn wind we set out in the shooting-brake to find the hapless beast.

I stood in the open back of the brake, with the wind ruffling my hair, knowing all too well what we were likely to find. As a distraction, I tried to switch my mind to the strangely unphotogenic nature of the country. It looked over-exposed even before you started filming, because the harsh, arid colours shaded imperceptibly into each other with little contrast; it was a landscape with no fat on it, and not much meat either once you left the narrow forest belts. The sun was a sliver of red above the horizon, and soon the live air would be shimmering with heat.

We found the location of the trap easily enough and Robert and Leonard and I fought through the barrier of thick scrub and backward-hooking wait-a-bit thorn bushes, guided by the pitiful whimpering of the hyena. It turned out to be a young male, and his right forepaw was clamped fast in the steel jaws. He was tugging frantically, sometimes lunging forward to tear at his mangled foot with his teeth. I saw a small triangle of metal push its way up through the exposed bones and then disappear again in bubbles of blood.

Our problem then was that in order to release him we would somehow have to get a sack over his head, but every time Leonard tried to drop a loop of rope round his neck he snapped through the cord. An anaesthetic dart would have solved the problem, but the nearest dart gun was 700 miles away, in Bulawayo.

At the end of an hour we were still trying to rope him. The sun rose clear of the trees, turning the Kwaai into a river of mica. I could smell the heat coming and the camel-thorn pods set up a dry, castanet-rattling as a breath of warm air shook them. The hyena's eyes were beginning to glaze over with shock. Unless we could free him soon it would be kinder to shoot him.

'Men who do things like this do not understand pain,' Leonard hissed. 'It is a pity that they cannot be taught.' He looked up at me, rivulets of sweat on his face mingling with something that looked suspiciously like tears. 'Do they not know that God made these also?' The hyena, in its torment, gave a long, low call of distress and bit again at its trapped foot. At that moment Leonard suddenly straightened up and lunged with a forked stick. He caught the hyena's neck and pinioned it to the ground, leaning his full weight on it, panting. Robert grabbed a sack, tugged it over the animal's head and roped it on securely.

Once the animal could no longer see, all the fight seemed to go out of him and he lay quietly while Leonard operated the keys of the trap and prised the jaws apart. The razor-sharp teeth unclenched, slimy with blood and hair. We tied the hind legs together and then carried it to the shooting-brake and rushed it back to our camp.

I bathed the lacerated foot gently with a strong solution of permanganate, borrowed from the snakebite outfit, then dripped an antibiotic emulsion onto it. The pads on the injured limb were enormously swollen, and it would be weeks before the hyena would be able to fend for himself again. We stretched a steel rope on a swivel between two trees, and tethered him to it with one of Chink's spare chains.

'Do you have a name for him yet?' Leonard asked, as he removed the sack and the hyena struggled to its feet.

'Shauri,' I said. 'Swahili. It has several meanings: in this case it means "trouble".'

Hyenas are said to be easy to tame, but Shauri loathed us from the very beginning, and I could do nothing with him. I was not really surprised. For the rest of his life he would associate all humans with unendurable pain, and nothing else. At the end of a fortnight he was still wholly intractable, but at least the wound in his foot had healed surprisingly well and he no longer limped. We decided to release him.

I say 'him' because we'd taken it for granted that Shauri was a male and he could well have been, but hyenas are notoriously difficult to sex. The bitches are usually bigger than the dogs and, rather creepily, they carry sham male genitals.

On freedom day we had to rope him again and then slip the sack back over his head, with a loose fastening that could be freed by a light jerk with a forked pole.

Chink was sitting beside me, watching the proceedings, and I was curious to see how she would react once Shauri was loose. But it was his reaction, not hers, that startled me.

When the sack was pulled away the hyena stood stockstill for a moment, bewildered, his sides heaving, and then his plum-purple eyes flicked quickly over the group of humans. I didn't like that look, and I was ready to run for cover, but in the end it was at Chink that he stared. He knew about lions. He had followed them, fed with them, snatched scraps of meat from their kills. In that moment of fear and uncertainty, Chink was the one creature that was not wholly alien, a focal point of familiarity, perhaps even of safety. They were both creatures of the wild. Chink noted his interest and dropped her head forward, and the hair on her spine was rising. Shauri ran to her. He came quickly, no longer looking at us, seeking sanctuary with her. He crouched down on his belly, cringing, cowering to her for protection. For an instant they remained poised, the lioness standing frozen with her eyes fixed on him, the hyena lying at her feet, looking up as though pleading. Then Chink backed away, nervously, still with a young lion's inbred suspicion of hyenas. Shauri got to his feet, and for a moment he looked as if he was going to follow her. Then he was suddenly aware again of the silent ring of humans. He spun round and sped down towards the river, splashed across the channel and plunged into the welcoming forests on the opposite bank.

That was the last we saw of him.

Lion Cub Curfew

On the same day that we released Shauri the South Africans set another of their spring traps, and during the night two lions were drawn to the bait. The lioness stepped onto the trigger plate and the jaws snapped shut, driving the triangular metal teeth deep into her forepaw. The sportsmen, hungover from the night's beer-and-brandy session, went out to check their traps rather later than usual the next morning, adding a few more hours of agony to her struggle. Their aim was not especially steady, so it took nine shots to kill her.

'Her mate is still calling for her,' Leonard told us moodily. 'Maybe he will come back. If you need pictures, perhaps we can feed him at that place.'

So Robert shot a wildebeest and we dragged it to the edge of the clearing near which the trap had been set. In the morning we found that a small amount of meat had been eaten from the carcass, but in a way which didn't seem to make sense. The paunch had been dragged a few feet away, clumsily; the skin of the beast had been licked clean and, most puzzling of all, one of the ears had been nibbled. Lions always leave the head of their prey untouched until they have eaten the rest of the body. That evening, we drove the DUKW downriver to this new location and settled down to watch.

As it grew dark, Robert put the binoculars up. 'There's a little lion in the grass,' he said, and I laughed, because this was a stock joke of ours. 'The little lion close behind you' had always been Chink.

'It's not Chink,' he said softly, 'and there are three of them.'

Then, out of the thicket where they had lain hidden during the day, crept the three cubs of the dead lioness. They were about five months old, alone, and helpless without their mother. Until they had stumbled on the dead wildebeest they had been without food and without hope of finding any. We watched them trying to tug small shreds of flesh from the bait, and when it became too dark to see we switched the spotlight on once or twice, to make sure that they were indeed on their own. Each time the beam struck, three little pansy faces bobbed up above the kill and they scampered away, peered at us from the fringe of woodland for a while and then, when nothing more happened, stole quietly back to continue feeding.

They had now become our personal problem.

To leave them there to starve to death or to be killed by hyenas was unthinkable, but nor could we park on the west bank of the Kwaai for another two years, watching over them until they were fully grown. They needed to be captured without being harmed, but we had none of the necessary equipment for live-trapping. A covered pitfall seemed to be the only answer, so for the next three days Robert and Leonard hacked away at the iron soil with a firewood axe, shovels, a tyre lever and a crowbar. What we really needed was a pickaxe and dynamite, but we had neither. We wired a spade to the winch cable on the DUKW and tried to use it like a dam scraper, but it was chaingang work and not terribly effective.

But, gradually, the pit deepened. We based our estimates of a lion cub's jumping abilities on Chink's usual clumsy performance, but what we forgot to feed into our calculations was that although she was four times older than these cubs she was also disgracefully overweight, under-exercised and bone idle. These cubs were wild lions, born to a harder heritage.

We imposed a strict curfew. By half past five at the latest, all work had to cease and we boarded the DUKW, to sit in the winter darkness, gauging each step against the chance of creaking floorboards or the clang of the metal grids on the bridge. We spoke seldom, and only in whispers.

There was no moon, and when the cubs returned on the second night it was already too dark to see much of them; we had to rely on our ears to tell us that they were about.

I woke just before dawn, aware of small, muted noises outside. Two of the cubs were sitting on the kill but the third was down at the river, drinking. He was about to lap, but then sat back and glared at his reflection in the still water, swatted angrily at it, wrinkled his nose and shook a wet forepaw in disgust. As he turned and ambled back up the path the largest of the litter took a fat, uncontrolled, teddy-bear swipe at his companion and sent her flying backwards into the grass. She landed with a thump, bounced back and charged him, and within seconds all three of them were rolling over and over, in the carefree play of the fully fed.

A thin, blinding pencil of light appeared above the horizon and as the first shaft of sunlight fell across the carcass the cubs stopped their game abruptly, staring towards the east. Without a sound they turned and slunk back into the protection of the quiet forest. Their own curfew had come with the sun.

We made a swift breakfast and for the rest of the day we redoubled our efforts at digging. As the pit grew deeper, it became harder to lift the soil out and then scatter it, so as not to betray the location of the trap. In the end I walked back to the camp upstream, fetched the shooting-brake and used it as a dump truck to carry the earth away. It was a necessary precaution: the cubs were growing wary, and they showed it by postponing their meal for a little longer each night.

After thirty hours of bone-breaking toil we felt that the pit was deep enough, so we began to construct a wooden cover for it, based on the medieval French *oubliette*. This cover had to be supported on a wooden centre-pole which had been sawn very nearly through, so that – in theory – a sharp tug on a rope leading back to an observation hide would collapse the whole superstructure of poles, branches, twigs, earth, scattered leaves, bits of wildebeest meat, and the cubs, into the pit below. Even so, the pole had to be strong enough to stand on without appreciable 'give', because even the slightest tremble under their feet would have alerted the young lions instantly.

We completed the trap just before sunset. The last spadeful of earth had been carted away from the site, the last dry leaf and moulted guinea fowl feather laid cunningly in place. Not even the most critical eye, we felt sure, could detect that the surface had ever been disturbed. To kill any human scent I soaked a bucket of dry elephant dung in water and sprinkled it round. We cut the decomposing remains of the wildebeest in half, so that the cubs would be forced to feed in a tight group. We dragged the frayed hindquarters across the river and left them there for the morning horde of vultures and marabou storks.

The cubs came very late that night, but as they approached the kill I heard Robert whisper to Leonard: 'Stand by.' In the seemingly endless silence that followed I strained my eyes into the moonless darkness. Then, suddenly, the word of command came.

'*Donsa!* Pull!'

I suppose it was inevitable that the whole thing would go wrong. The support pole resisted Leonard's frantic tugging and the lid stayed in place. I heard a startled 'woof!' of fright from one of the cubs as they raced back into the forest. And that, for the night, was that.

In the morning we carefully dismantled the trap, removing the entire camouflage, down to the last dried-out beetle. Robert wearily changed the position of the centre pole, sawed through a few more fibres, rebuilt the top and made Leonard stand on it to test its strength. It collapsed instantly. I gave Leonard a bottle of disinfectant and some lint to cleanse the deep scratches on his backside, and he was man enough to laugh about it. He and Robert then rebuilt the whole contraption, with even greater attention to the fine detail.

By the time it was fully dark the cubs had still not shown up. We agreed that I should take my bed up onto the roof of the DUKW, and would tap lightly with my fingers if I heard them feeding.

The night was full of small, secret noises. Birds called briefly, and the occasional splashes from the river told me that antelope were coming down to drink. With my head pillowed on my hands I watched a meteorite trail a shower of sparks across the frozen sky, and as the last ember burnt into oblivion there was the soft, almost imperceptible sound of a lion cub moving stealthily through the grass. A moment later I heard breathy little grunts and barely audible snuffling, but the sound was intermittent, so I waited, hardly daring to breathe, until I was certain that they had settled down. Then I tapped, very gently. Five minutes dragged by and all I could hear were the night birds and the antelope splashing from the shallows again. But at last came the unmistakable sound of a bone being crunched. Robert, also listening, and standing in the lee of the DUKW below me, hissed '*Donsa!*' and together he and Leonard hauled on the rope.

There was a crash as the pole broke and the cover collapsed, followed by an angry outburst of woofs and grunts. Leonard shouted 'Light! Light!' and the spotlight revealed him furiously tugging at the camouflage branches that had tumbled into the pit, trying to get them out before the cubs used them to climb free. In the light from the spot I watched the cubs leaping upwards, clawing for a foothold. But there were only two of them. The third had obviously sensed danger and sprung clear as the trap started to go, and within minutes the female cub managed to scramble up the vertical sides of the pit and disappear into the night. It would have been dangerous to climb down, because the remaining cub was spitting furiously. We pulled the rest of the branches out and went to bed, fairly certain that he would be gone by morning.

But, miraculously, he was still there; my wretched little Oberon, the runt of that ill-starred litter, with his wild, burnt-orange eyes, and a heart that harboured an implacable hatred for all the human race.

There was nothing we could do for his siblings, except to place a parting gift of meat, well away from the trap. The following day we left for the headwaters of the Kwaai, taking the savage little waif from the lion cub curfew with us.

The 'Lion Leaves'

We camped at a place that had no name, not even in Sasarwa, the language of the nomadic Black River Bushmen. There had once been a village there, and the foundation rings of huts still showed through the stubby grass. Africans avoided it, if they could. I once asked Kweri why its inhabitants had deserted it, but he turned his eyes away and would not answer. Leonard was rather less reticent.

'Spook-spook,' he told me. 'It's a bad place. There were a great many deaths, that had something to do with the Masarwa. The local people say that the spirits still walk, and that on certain nights you can still smell blood. I do not like to come here myself.' But whether it was a massacre, an outbreak of plague, or a mass witchcraft killing he didn't, or wouldn't, say.

Whatever it was, it certainly filled me with a deep unease, foreboding. A grove of knob-thorn trees had taken root, and the grey and leafless trunks towered like the pillars of a ruined cathedral, below the high canopy of foliage. Giant lianas twisted down from the arching branches, where hundreds of small, unseen birds kept up a constant twittering.

In this unwelcoming setting our dinghy, *Water Beetle*, burnt at her moorings. A party of indigent Masarwa had carried out their usual August ritual of burning back the long grass on both sides of the forest, to stimulate new green growth. Unchecked, the flames first raced round us and then swept inwards, threatening the camp; while we were fighting to save the DUKW, the tent and the rest of our belongings, the oily sedge caught alight and ignited a carpet-fire of dry leaves, which crept unseen until the flames touched the dinghy's hull. *Water Beetle* blazed like a torch.

She was not insured. Of course.

★ ★ ★

For a while we lingered disconsolately in the tsetse-infested knob-thorn camp, uncertain about our next move. The wind came to blow the moon up, and the lions roared it back down. Because we were more than two hundred miles away from the nearest butcher shop our only meat was what Robert could shoot. After every hunt, Kisi would imperiously commandeer all the prize cuts – the fillets, liver, kidneys, and sometimes the tongue – before the remainder of the carcasses went to feed the dogs. The few scraps that were left over were dumped near the forest to serve as flash-camera bait for carrion-eaters.

Very early one morning Leonard woke me by tapping gently on *Shaka Zulu*'s hull.

'Trouble,' he said. 'Ix is here.'

'*Ix?* But Zankuio village is over a hundred miles away!'

'Yes, I know, but she is here,' he insisted. 'Ix and her man and the child that we know, as well as a new one, very small. There is also an old *salughas.*' Salughas, grandmother. 'They need food. You had better come now.'

Kisi had brought a pot of thin, sugared gruel and, still half asleep, I took it from him without quite knowing why, and followed Leonard.

I hardly recognized Ix. The plump and cheerful girl of a year ago, who had been so proud of her new pregnancy, had dwindled into an old woman. Her empty breasts hung like flaps, and although her stomach was still distended, this time it was from starvation. Her skin had a terrible ashen tinge, her face was a shrunken death's head, dominated by haunted, despairing eyes. She did not cry, but her bony shoulders began to shake.

The summer rains had failed and the thin crops in the Zankuio fields had shrivelled without bearing a single head of maize. Everybody had been hungry, and children had begun to die. So, very early one morning, her man woke her and told her to pack up all she could carry, and when she had done so they had started walking

186

towards the Kwaai valley, where all the animals were. They took the narrow bush paths, and they rested only for a brief while each night. For three days they had no food, no drink.

'He' – she nodded at the man – 'has no gun. We are too poor. But he has his spear and we hoped that we would find a lion on its kill and drive it away, to take its food for ourselves. Then I found that I had no more milk in my breasts for the baby, and he cried all the time, but we had to go on. My mother kept falling down.' The elder child, naked and covered with dust, looked wonderingly up at me, but the babe simply lolled against its mother's shoulder. The old woman, her knees raw and bleeding, stared blankly down at the ground, exhausted beyond hope. The man sat a little apart, saying nothing, dumb with misery and an odd, painful shame.

'We smelled the meat that you had put out for the lions,' Ix continued, and by now she was crying. 'We had no way of lighting a fire, but we ate the meat that was left without cooking it. I had seen the big boat-car and I knew that it was you, and that you would not mind. When we had eaten, we went to sleep beside the bones. So now you see me.' She looked wistfully at the bowl I was still grasping. 'Is that,' she asked hesitantly, 'food for my children, perhaps? I have been chewing wildebeest for them.'

The children had the first spoonfuls of the sweet gruel, then the grandmother had a little and the man took his share. Ix had hers last of all, and by that time Kisi had brought what was left of yesterday's bread and a canful of diluted condensed milk. But they ate slowly, careful not to induce stomach cramps by gulping.

Later. 'What the hell are you crying for?' asked Robert, who had wandered over. 'We can feed them, and the old man can lend a hand round the camp.'

The 'old man' was probably in his late twenties.

We moved camp the same day, ten miles on into the complex of lagoons and riverine forest, driven as much by the sense of depression that the ghost village engendered as by the painful onslaught of clouds of tsetse. At the new location, Ix and her family set up their belongings in a clearing that was far enough away from our campsite for privacy and yet close enough to provide protection, for the area showed signs of being infested by lion. Nor were the lion tardy in letting us know that they were out in force. Again and again during the night we were woken by a succession of exasperated roars, and they had some reason to be annoyed because their protests were interspersed by the shrieking invective of the old salughas, Ix's mother, who was defending her share of zebra meat against a resentful pride of seven young lions. She won, too, by dint of decibel power, and long before sun-up the last of the seven had slunk off into the relative peace of the mopani forest.

★ ★ ★

Ever since we had sold the Bulawayo engineering business, money had been something of a problem, but we were now getting close to the stage where a shortage of ready cash was likely to prove more than just a passing inconvenience. Without some sort of revenue we could be forced to cut short our private crusade. Although the cheques from magazines and newspapers were a big help, what we really needed was a project that would bring in enough to clear the more pressing debts. That was the spur for my first book, *Okavango*, and by this time I had reached the halfway stage. I guessed that the book would need some good lion photographs, and since Ix's husband seemed to have a fair working knowledge of their habits, I put the problem to him. He nodded courteously, and later Leonard helped him to drag a fresh bait to a place near the forest where the earth was heavily stippled with pug marks.

That was when I first heard about the 'lion leaves'.

A party of Masarwas had drifted in from nowhere in particular, and settled themselves comfortably beside our fire. They exchanged news with Ix's husband, and swapped hunting yarns with Leonard. But the stories soon shaded into the supernatural: reports of were-lion, were-hyena and were-crocodile, chilling tales of witchcraft and ritual murders. Leonard told again his story of the man who could call up the crocodile in the Zambesi, and the Bushmen nodded emphatically. In Zankuio, they said, in Zankuio there is a man who can transform himself into a lion. 'This is true. We have seen it.'

Kisi had been translating, but before he could continue the narrative, Ix's husband interrupted.

There was a leaf, he said, that would drive off lion. But it was a terribly powerful medicine, so you could only burn a very little at a time and on a small fire, because if the smoke was too strong it could kill a man. If you got it exactly right, though, no lion would ever come near you.

There was an uncomfortable silence, and then the Masarwas began to mutter uneasily among themselves. One of them spat over his left shoulder and moved further away.

Something was very much amiss. The conversation had died out completely, and Kisi was looking downcast. Leonard sauntered over, and Kisi asked him something in a language I did not know. I called him across to where I was sitting, a little way away from the fire, and asked him, as obliquely as I could, what was wrong. He looked embarrassed, and he took his time before answering.

'*Aie!*' He kicked idly against a tussock of dry grass, disturbing a nest of ants, then squatted down next to my chair. 'Everybody knows,' he said finally, '*everybody* knows that no man can change

188

himself into a lion at night. That is only fire-talk, a fable. But that part about a leaf that can drive away lions and kill a man is evil. It is Bayei-medicine.'

'Tagaan?' I asked, recalling the frightening story about the ghastly price that the witchdoctor had demanded from Mog.

'No, no!' Leonard answered impatiently. 'Tagaan is not Bayei and he doesn't play with leaves. This has come from Tamai, the Bayei headman. You know the man . . . he wears a collar and tie even when it's hot. He brought you that wooden dish with some dried beans last month.'

To be sure I knew him. He was a friend. We were on hand-clasping terms, and he no more resembled my idea of a traditional witchdoctor who could kill a man with burning leaves than I looked like the Serpent of Old Nile. Another illusion lay shattered, in sad fragments.

I lay awake for a long time that night, listening for lion, but none came. Nor did any come the following night, or the night after that, although I could just hear them calling from further off, in the deep mopani. Our enticing bait was ignored, except by a pair of jackal which flitted past like little grey ghosts in the moonlight.

In the morning I found Ix's husband standing poised on one leg, supporting himself on his spear, warming himself in front of the early fire. He pointed at the cameras, still in their protective canvas hoods, outside the tent, and made an enquiring nod.

'No, nothing,' I admitted ruefully. 'No lions. No pictures. We haven't sighted one since the Masarwas were here. They must have frightened them all away.'

It was the first and only time I ever saw him smile.

'It is not the Masarwas! It is me that made them leave you in peace. Every night now, for three nights, I have burned the lion leaves we spoke about, and I can promise you that as long as I am here no lion will come near this place!'

I never found out what the 'lion leaves' were, nor would Ix's husband show me where he had picked them. The African bush is full of poisons, the best known of which is Strychnos Spinosa, 'the strychnine-bearing spiky one', known colloquially as the 'Kaffir orange'. The hard-shelled fruit taste like custard-apples and are beloved by men and baboons alike, but the bark and leaves of the tree contain a virulent alkaloid poison. But Strychnos is a highveld tree, and does not grow in the delta. Whatever deadly plant the solitary hunter had used in his garnerings not even his fellow Masarwas were ever prepared to discuss.

★ ★ ★

Oberon's temper was not improving, and the fact that we felt it necessary to keep him on his running chain didn't do anything to sweeten his disposition. He remained unapproachably fierce, so that every time we moved camp we had first to lasso him and truss his legs before it was safe to lift him into the truck. It was a dispiriting business and probably cruel, but the alternatives all seemed even more heartless: we could shoot him outright or we could turn him loose to starve. Innocently I hoped that, somehow or other, we could keep him with us until he was old enough to fend for himself in the wild. I had a lot to learn, and the whole idea was unbelievably naïve. By the time he was two years old he would weigh upwards of 400 pounds and be capable of killing any of us with a single swipe of a paw.

As things turned out, Oberon didn't wait to grow up. One day, as we were struggling to rope him, he doubled back and then leaped forward with all his strength, snapping his chain. Chink, who had never liked him, skipped sideways as the enraged cub streaked past her, to vanish in the forest. There was no hope of recapturing him, but I still nourished a tiny hope that he might – just might – be capable of feeding himself by catching ground-nesting birds and small, slow animals. I need not have worried. Two months later I almost tripped over him.

I was following the pugmarks of a pride of lions which lived near the KuBu lagoon when Chink came skidding past me, grumbling anxiously, only to stop abruptly as another lion emerged onto the path ahead of her. It was a young male, about seven or eight months old, who paused and then turned to stare coldly at us. There was no mistaking Oberon's bandit-hard eyes, almost the colour of carnelians, but even more distinctive was the band of white fur around his neck where the running chain had galled him. He drew back his lips and hissed resentfully, and then moved off into the long grass. From some distance ahead a lioness called, and Oberon answered her. The KuBu pride had accepted him.

The Man-eater of Matopi

About a mile below the Matopi Rapids in the Botletle River there is a deep pool of black water, half enclosed by a curve in the bank and held still and sombrely stagnant by the roots of a wild fig tree. In this pool lives, or lived, a fourteen-foot crocodile. All crocodiles are, by their nature, potential man-eaters, but it is only when they attain the courage that great size and strength bestow that they will attack humans. The man-eater of Matopi weighed nearly three-quarters of a ton, and he was strong enough to drag a buffalo under. However, it was only after he had taken his sixth victim – a foolish girl who was washing clothes in the river and hanging them to dry on the lower branches of the fig tree – that the villagers who lived near the rapids sent a delegation to ask us for help. We were there to shoot crocodile anyway, so Robert went after the man-eater.

The Botletle drains out of the Thamalakane near the south-western rim of the delta and sweeps eastward towards Lake Dow, near the Magadikgadi salt pans. It is snagged along its length with sandbars, shallow rapids and cataracts, and when the levels are low it splits up into a series of lagoons, each divided by a reef of jagged dolomite that will tear the bottom out of any river craft. Spike-leaved cacti grow thickly along the sandy banks, together with desert succulents and low-growing thorn scrub that offers no shade, and there is a hot wind that mischievously twists the dust up into whirling spirals which circle the sky and then fall back to earth in a chaos of fine, sharp particles.

It is an unwelcoming environment, but the crimson-breasted butcher-bird spikes it victims on the thorn bushes, and the scrub shelters the brown hyena, which is now on its way to joining the long and shameful list of endangered species as its habitat is remorse-lessly destroyed. What has happened is that the endless veterinary cordon fences which were built to preserve grazing for domestic cattle have crudely cut across the old migration routes that the vast herds of antelope and zebra once followed across the desert. It might have seemed a good idea to some dim and remote agro-economist, trained in the tame English farming counties, but the trails brought food to all the Kalahari lions, the leopards, and their retinues of small predators and scavengers, and as the wild grazers were corralled off, so the hunters declined.

There is only one predator that has, so far, escaped the malign consequences of civilization, and that is the terrible crocodile of the Botletle.

★   ★   ★

In spite of, or perhaps because of, our experiences with the Wilmots, we had never seriously considered taking up crocodile hunting as a permanent way of earning a living. Now, though, we were driven by the absolute necessity of generating enough revenue to pay expenses until publishers' cheques came through to keep the bank at bay.

The technique required is not an easy one to learn, and mistakes can be unpleasantly terminal. Another encouragement to precision

191

shooting is that a misplaced shot might emerge through the belly skin, which is the only part the traders are interested in. A botched blow with the axe or a slip with the flensing knife can have the same effect, and on top of all this there is scale-slip to worry about. To guard against this the carcasses have to be left submerged in water until the following dawn and then towed back to camp for the skinning to start. If there is the slightest trace of decomposition the transparent, film-like shield which protects the scales begins to slough away, leaving white blotches on the hide. If all goes well, the hides are scraped free of fat and flesh, covered with coarse salt and rolled up in wet sacks, to be sent to the dealers. And after that they are made into boots, belts, purses and expensive luggage.

When Robert and I first took *Shaka Zulu* down to the Botletle in the late spring of 1960 the river had not been hunted before, and it harboured crocodile that had grown undisturbed through many long-lived generations: the yelping young that had emerged from soft-shelled eggs buried in the sun-warmed nests along the banks had achieved nightmare size. They were man-eaters, cattle-killers, anything up to eighteen feet of implacable death, the sole survivors from the age of the great reptiles.

Water Beetle had now been replaced by a new dinghy, *Fleur-de-Lys*. This craft was, as it happened, the product of one of Robert's convictions, that he had natural and sole rights to any resources that might come our way. Some months earlier I had written a short article about lion cubs and posted it off to a women's magazine in Britain. Surprisingly, and flatteringly quickly, I had a letter of acceptance with a cheque for £500 attached. It was fabulous money, the single biggest amount I had ever earned from my writing. Almost choking with pride, I hastened to show it to Robert. He looked at it, and then said as he put it in his breast pocket 'Yes, well, there are a few things I need to get in Bulawayo.' And that was his only comment.

He took himself off a week later, spent some of the money on a little high living – 'For God's sake, you don't grudge me a decent meal, do you?' – and used the rest to buy the boat. *Fleur* was an aluminium-hulled twelve-footer, a lot lighter than her predecessor but also a lot smaller. She was dangerously frail for the task to which we put her, but at least she was extremely manoeuvrable and she also planed beautifully. With a 10-horsepower outboard motor she could carry me over open water at an exhilarating speed, up to fifteen knots. But what we hadn't bargained for was that the Botletle was a very different proposition from the rock-free swamp waterways that we'd worked with Bobbie Wilmot the previous year.

The Botletle is a river that rises in Hell.

Top:
Kisi and the carcass of a
twelve-foot crocodile

Cape hunting dogs (*Lycaon
pictus lupinus*) are the
bloodiest killers in all Africa

At nine months old, Chink
was still being bottle-fed on
patent baby food
(Robert, Chink and I,
Victoria Falls, Christmas
1959)
(Photograph by Eric Woods)

We tethered Shauri by
Chink's spare chain

My wretched little Oberon, the runt of an ill-starred litter

Leonard and the eighteen-footer man-eater from the Botletle river. This gigantic female had blue beads and fragments of a girl's copper bangle in her stomach, as well as the bones of cattle, goats, antelope and the remains of another crocodile

Timber – both sides of the
coin

Isis, my serval kitten

Poachers' work. I found my young Bushbuck ram lying in the sedge where he had dragged himself to die...

The hunting camp of the Masarwa Bushmen was razed by their headman Kweri in order to make way for the newly created Moremi Wildlife Reserve in the heart of the tribe's traditional hunting territory

Richard
(Photograph by A.J.E. Pike)

Myself
*(Photograph by Richard
Vendall Clark)*

We drove the DUKW down onto the north bank of the river, parked in the thin shade of a lone acacia tree, pitched a temporary base camp, then launched *Fleur* and set out to explore the channel. We had to go slowly, to avoid the rocks, and we found soon enough that even where the water seemed deepest it often concealed sharp ridges of black basalt. We had travelled about two miles downstream when we encountered the Matopi Drift, our first cataract. Nobody knew much about the stretch of water below the rapids, because the dirt road turned away from the river at that point and ran upwards towards Bushman Pits. There was white water in the cataract, and because we dared not risk our frail craft on the underlying rocks we turned for home. The next day we moved *Shaka Zulu* down to a spot just above the drift. In the afternoon Robert and Kisi manhandled the boat past the broken water, to a point where the Botletle widened out once more. Then we waited until it was dark.

The heat had been almost unendurable for days, and from the look of the sky we were in for an early downpour of elephant rain, which came in enormous drops and also set the herds moving on the migratory trail each year. On this day, the wind was blowing in gusts from the south, driving hard and with a cargo of sand, and rank after rank of bud cumulus had been building up since dawn. We battened down the hatches of the DUKW and left camp after an early dinner.

The night was black as jet, because there was no moon and the low cloudbanks shut out even the feeble starlight. There was a quarter-mile of rough ground to cover, interspersed with little tongues of water of the sort where crocodile like to lie up at night. We almost fell over one of them, close to the rapids, and Robert fired twice at it in quick succession. The water churned violently at his feet and a tail thrashed up in the dim light of our forehead lamps. Kisi, who had been press-ganged into acting as gaff-boy and skinner, stumbled forward across the rocks and the two of them hauled it up onto dry land. It was a six-footer, cleanly shot, and between us we carried it to the boat.

I had almost forgotten the sinister magic of nights in the crocodile boats, but two hours in the icy darkness, shivering on the stern seat of the little silver boat, retrieved the memories. I recalled Bobbie Wilmot's words, spoken when he and Robert and I came home from that ill-starred expedition up the Savuti Channel. 'It's always new, June,' he had said. 'However tired I get, however lonely, frightened or desperate I become its always new. Nothing is ever repeated, no two nights are ever the same. It takes you like a fever.'

Robert had now switched on the powerful prow lamp and

was sweeping the river with it. After a while he whispered 'There are a couple of croc on the shore, there. I'm going after them on foot.' Reluctantly, Kisi and I did as we were told and made for the opposite bank.

I watched Robert's headlamp dip and sway as he picked his way through the boulders and sedge, working slowly upstream until he reached the rapids, where he stopped and looked about him. It seemed an eternity before he fired.

Kisi clambered over the side of the boat and started off to help him, while I reconnected the prow lamp to the battery to give him light. Then 'Put that out!' Robert bellowed from across the water. If his shout hadn't sent any surviving crocodile to the bottom, it was a certainty that the searchlight would, and I cursed my own lack of forethought. By now Kisi had joined him and the headlamps showed dimly that they were dragging something heavy. At that moment I heard a tiny, scraping sound from the reeds a few feet away. I held my breath, and the ominous wet slithering began again.

'Only the very big crocodile move like that,' I thought. I had no rifle with me, and Robert had forbidden me to use the main light. All I could do was to edge over as far as I could on the stern seat, away from whatever was coming towards me through the shallows.

Robert called softly, 'Bring the boat. This one weighs a ton.'

Anything to get away from that threatening rustle in the osiers; I stood up and thrust the dinghy away from the bank with one of the oars, and as I did so there was a splash and a mighty swirl nearby. So my silent companion had been a crocodile after all. Thankfully, I rowed away, but I would not have been quite as relieved if I'd known that the river had more and even greater horrors in store for us.

As *Fleur* nudged the bank next to them, Robert and Kisi began heaving the second carcass into her – a nine-footer, with half its upper jaw shot away. 'Are you sure it's really dead?' I asked apprehensively. Part of the brain-pan still seemed to be intact. 'The shot didn't kill him outright, so I stuck my hunting knife in his head,' Robert answered dismissively. 'But you didn't use the axe?' 'Wasn't necessary.'

The wind was becoming more ill-tempered, the sky was a tumbling mass of charcoal cloud occasionally ripped by lightning, and as I put the boat into midstream she was buffeted by the combined force of wind and current. She kept straying off course, but Robert shouted to open the throttle fully, and as I did so she shot forward, her bows rising up over the spray. He was watching the river ahead, but I could barely make out his hand signals and

194

the roar of the outboard combined with the peals of thunder to drown out his shouted instructions. We were in a bleakly unhappy situation, because if *Fleur* hit a reef at that speed she would simply split open, and the odds against any of us reaching either bank alive would have been minimal.

Then, as a crackling sheet of lightning lit the river with a blue incandescence I saw Robert signalling frantically with his left arm. I swerved obediently, and the next instant there was a second huge lightning flash followed by a powerful gust of wind. *Fleur* was buffeted by the gale-whipped waves, but I managed somehow to keep her on course, steering straight into the slant of the storm and wincing as the driven rain hit my face like a shower of buckshot. Concentrating as I was on keeping our croc-laden boat afloat, I did not know precisely where we were heading, or why, until Kisi yelled 'Look!' and pointed.

Unblinking in the beam of the prow lamp, two huge, flat rubies stared back at me, from the black and bottomless pool that was held in the curve of the bank. I stared back, and shuddered. It was, I *knew* it was, the man-eater of Matopi.

Another surge of wind almost wrenched the tiller from my hand, but Robert continued to point straight, straight ahead. Ten yards, five . . . ten feet. There was a tiny spurt of flame as Robert drew on the trigger of the heavy Mannlicher Schoeneur, and the giant crocodile slid down the mud bank into the pool, flailing the water into a bloodied foam with his vast tail, and slashing convulsively with his jaws.

'Go for him!' Robert shouted, his voice shrill with excitement. 'Go on, go for him or he'll get into deep water! He's there, there, *there*! For God's sake, go for him!'

I spun the boat round until I could see the crocodile more clearly. He was a little further off shore now and still whipping up the water with his mighty tail. Kisi leaned over and hooked at him with the gaff, but the croc writhed away, and Kisi leaned further yet. Almost instantly the dinghy tilted over and water poured in over the gunwale.

'She is gone!' shrieked Kisi. 'The boat is gone!' I flung myself to one side as hard as I could and as the man-eater wrenched free *Fleur* righted herself, wallowing low in the water.

Robert was beside himself with fury. 'Why didn't you damn well put her to the left?' he stormed. 'Left! You know, *left*! Port! Red! The hand with ruddy rubies on it! We've lost him now, we've bloody lost him!' I'd had about enough of being shouted at and I was about to yell back at him when, straight ahead of us, a tremendous head reared out of the river in a plume of spray. Instinctively, I drove directly at it.

Robert clutched at it and missed, then he and Kisi together tried to grab its tail as the boat slid alongside the monster. 'They aren't supposed to do that,' I thought, stupidly. 'It's not dead.' I could see the full length of the crocodile now and I noted absently that it was two feet longer than our boat: fourteen feet of wounded, half-demented death. The two men hauled again, and once more *Fleur-de-Lys* heeled over dangerously. More water rushed in and lifted the keel clear of the river, so that the propeller was out of the water.

Kisi suddenly left Robert's side and scrambled back to join me. There were tears on his cheeks and he was half out of his mind with fright. 'Tell Maritsasi –' His words were whipped away by the wind but I knew what he wanted to say. 'Tell Maritsasi that if I never come back she can have my chickens, and my new blanket, and my money in the old cocoa tin.' Poor, brave Kisi. I wanted to put my arm across his shoulders and cry with him, because I too was petrified, but such gestures were not acceptable in the Colonies. In any case, there was a wounded crocodile in the river and we had to do something about it, fast.

The croc had drifted a little way from the dinghy, and somehow *Fleur* contrived to stay afloat, thanks to Kisi's efforts with the baling bucket. The drama seemed to have been lost on Robert, who was still scanning the river with the light. And 'There he is! Right behind you!' he bellowed. 'Quick, go for him!' We closed on the brute once more, and again Robert grabbed its tail. 'Head for the shore! We've got the bastard this time!' he exulted.

We didn't get him, though, because when we were within a few feet of the shore I heard a long-drawn hiss from the bottom of the boat, looked down, and screamed in mortal fear. The nine-footer that had lain 'dead' on the duckboards for an hour had resurrected itself and was viciously alive.

Its head was nearest to Kisi and it scrabbled towards him as he and Robert tried to find the axe. Kisi gave up the search and jabbed furiously at the oncoming croc with the gaff hook, just enough to deflect it and turn it back towards me. I drew my legs up onto the narrow stern seat and pulled at the motor's starter cord over and over again as the crocodile came weaving towards me like something out of a horror movie. I gave one more mighty tug, the overheated outboard caught at last and drove the dinghy over the tree roots and hard up against the bank.

But that didn't turn the crocodile. In my struggle to evade it I balanced myself on the after gunwale, but not securely enough. I toppled backwards into the river and as I surfaced, spluttering, there was an immense splash just behind me. It was the man-eater.

Most people know those horrendous dreams, when you are trying to flee someone, or something, but you can't get away, no matter how hard you struggle. On that night, the universal night-mare became my reality as I stumbled through the mud and reed to make dry land, my mind blanked out against the menace in the river. I know now how animals must feel when the predators are at their heels.

But I did somehow reach the shore, covered in slime and cling-ing weed, sobbing, but unscathed. When I had caught my breath I heard the thud of an axe, but not from the boat. It was Kisi, who had somehow wrestled the nine-footer ashore and was hacking through its spine. There was blood, thick and heavy, seeping from its mouth.

Robert was standing beside him on the bank, staring at the partly submerged hull of *Fleur-de-Lys*. 'How did it get like that?' he asked, mildly curious.

'We nearly capsized,' I replied tersely. 'Twice. Remember?'

'No, did we? I must have been concentrating on the big croc. Let's bale her out and go and look for him.'

When I protested, fighting the tears I was determined not to show, he scowled, and when I still held back he lost patience. 'Just get back into that fucking boat! That, or you can bloody walk back to the camp!'

I had no option, then. The camp was many dark and dangerous miles away. Much as I hated and feared the hideous business of crocodile hunting, I was not going to entertain Robert by confessing my feelings, then or ever. There had been little enough cordiality between us for some time, and nights like this one didn't help, but I was too deeply involved in the game reserve project to back out of the partnership now. And Robert knew it.

The dinghy slid back into deep water, and the prow light fondled the river once more, picking up the straggling flotsam of reeds and dark bubbles rising from the slippery black barbel, mud-nosing at the bottom. Of the Matopi man-eater there was no sign, no sound, no movement.

Fever Heat

October almost killed us. The shade temperature in the cabin of the DUKW often stood at 117°F, and our troubles began to tread on each others' heels.

They began with Chink, who had developed a taste for chasing cattle. There had been no African-owned livestock on the island, and the fleet-footed impala in the valley of the Kwaai had left her drinking their dust. But the Botletle was crowded with village cattle, inquisitive and slack-witted goats, and ambling donkeys, and Chink wanted to play tag with all of them. I worked out the amount of compensation we were going to have to pay for each 'best ox in the kraal, medem', and when the sums I totted up on the back of my cigarette box reached four figures I regretfully decided that she would have to be put on a running chain for most of the day. The theory was sound.

I was fishing just above the rapids one afternoon when a file of ranch cows straggled out of the scrub and began to swim across the river. Chink, who had been snoozing the hot hours away under a tree, woke with a start and tore after them, but instead of being pulled up sharply, the force of her charge broke the collar staple and she launched herself into the river and struck out strongly in pursuit of the herd. The current was strong enough to sweep her almost a hundred yards downstream and by the time she made the bank the cattle, steaming as the sun dried them off, were close to their home kraal.

Robert set off after her in *Fleur-de-Lys*, and he managed to coax her into the boat before she had done any harm. Even so, the villagers had signalled their grave disapproval from the opposite bank by shrieking, wailing, beating drums and empty paraffin tins and recklessly discharging their equivocally lethal old Martini-Henrys into the air.

Chink's escapades apart, our domestic circumstances had become far from fragrant. Because of the intense heat, and the generally discouraging conditions in the Botletle camps, it became extremely important to maintain civilized standards if we were to keep our morale from plummeting. It was not easy, and it took a lot of effort.

There was now no shade at all in the leafless wilderness of stunted acacia thorn. After the one wild storm that carried the elephant rains there were no more showers to bring relief from the dehydrating heat. The dry sand seeped and filtered into everything, creeping up over the canvas groundsheets, getting into all the food, the drinking water, our clothes, hair, eyes, ears and nostrils. The nights were almost as hot as the days, and when we crawled into our beds on the DUKW the sheets were covered in a fine and gritty dusting of still more sand.

We were also beset by a constant swarm of fat and loathsome blue-green flies that came buzzing over in squadrons from the kraals across the river. Faithfully we set out the Tugon Fly-Killer plates and within an hour they would be black with disgusting little corpses, while a carpet of dying insects crunched beneath our feet on the floor of the cabin. In keeping with the spirit of the times, the sturdy JAP generator that charged the big batteries for our refrigerator and the electric lights suffered a ruptured oil seal and seized solid. Within hours the meat would begin to stink, so I left the fridge door open and hung a wet cloth across it, in the hope that the process of evaporation would keep our supplies at least edible if not cold for a little while longer.

I also rigged a primitive form of cooler with some well-soaked cornmeal sacks and a canvas-seated camp stool, and there was just enough movement in the air to keep the butter from liquefying and the beer from boiling. It was no use as a meat safe, though, and within twenty-four hours of killing the goats on which we fed Chink – and sometimes, if they were young goats, ourselves – the carcasses had invariably become hosts to hundreds of squiggling maggots.

In fact, for most of the time the only bearable place in the camp was the 'crocodile cooler', where we stored the hides to keep them from spoiling. This was a simple box structure, made from four tall uprights and four cross-members, over which we had draped our biggest canvas sheet; water was poured into the sagging roof and dripped steadily down inside. We used to sit there for hours at a time on the worst days, reading by candle light and trying to ignore the pungent odour of coarse salt and the clinging, musty stench of crocodile.

Leonard and Kisi had more than enough to do, skinning and preparing the hides from each night's hunt, so I took over all the cooking. I spent hours being semi-kippered in the heat and smoke of the open kitchen fire, swallowing aspirins to keep the constant hot-weather headaches at bay, seething tough old chickens and guinea fowl in a variety of elaborate sauces to try to exorcize the dismals. Maritsasi helped by bringing buckets of water to fill the collapsible bath so that we could at least soak our dusty bodies clean twice a day. We changed our clothes constantly, too, but although they dried soon enough after they'd been washed, we could always sense the dust that had dried on them. For the first time in my life I even left off my light cotton briefs and bra, and dressed simply in shorts, a loose shirt, sandals and nothing else.

When I was not attending to some specific task, though, I found myself becoming overwhelmed by a terrible, hopeless lethargy, unable to sleep and nauseated by the very thought of the food I had cooked. Never especially well covered, I began to lose weight, and in the end I had to prevail on Robert to limit the hunting to two nights in every three. But even on the 'off' nights we were unable to rest in the smothering darkness of the cabin. We lay there, on top of our gritty sheets, tormented by mosquitoes, and with sweat caking the powdery dust that settled on our naked bodies.

Then one day the thermometer registered 120°F. It can't go on, we thought. But it did, and the Botletle began to feel like the original Fiery Furnace. I began to question the whole purpose of our crocodile hunting, although common sense reminded me sharply that we needed the hide money. For one thing, we had to lay out £120 for two new tyres for the DUKW, since the originals had been torn by the endless sharp stumps of mopani and finally burst, beyond repair. The JAP engine needed to be replaced and, on top of this, our property agent in Bulawayo had written to tell us that the latest financial slump had cut back on demand for apartments and, as a consequence, half of ours had no tenants. The same post brought a curt letter from the bank, pointing out that we'd reached the limit of our overdraft.

So we went on shooting crocodile. All shapes, all sizes. There were sometimes small ones that allowed Kisi and me to row right up next to them, and shoot at almost point-blank range; at other times we shot and gaffed eight-, nine- and ten-footers in the long rapids below the camp. But a middling seven-footer that had been lying in wait for our dogs took five bullets and repeated blows from the axe before it succumbed. One of our best kills was a twelve-footer with an almost perfect skin, with small, finely-graded, blue-tinged scales, which we tracked down after it had emerged threateningly from the reeds at the river margin and given Maritsasi the fright of her life when she went to draw water one evening.

We were trying to locate a well-known killer one night when a pair of urchins wandered into the camp and watched silently as we built the fire and set the kettle on it to make coffee. The elder of the two, dressed in ragged khaki shorts, stood idly rubbing one foot against the other while he chewed a piece of bark as we warmed ourselves; contrarily, the river itself was always freezing cold at night, in spite of the oppressive heat ashore, and we might have considered submerging ourselves in it, had it not been for all the unpleasant things lurking there.

The larger urchin finally found his tongue, spat out the bark and said, contemptuously; 'You people really don't want to find crocodile at all, or you would go to Ramowtu.'

'Where?'

'Ra-*mow*-tu,' the child repeated, syllable by syllable. 'Down-stream. There are big ones there. There's one – I know her – who lays her eggs in the same place every year, and every time, when she has gone, I dig them up and destroy them. But it does not matter, because she has no mate and the eggs would never hatch anyway. She is like a chicken who lays even when there is no rooster. There are many crocodile at Ramowtu and they kill the cattle, so if you want to see them that is where you must go.'

'Will you guide us?'

He spat angrily at the ground. 'My father will not permit it,' he said sourly, and then spat again. 'He says I have to stay here and watch over the goats, because it is not time yet for me to be given a man's work.' Then he looked up obliquely from the fire, and slyly conceded, 'If you give me five shillings I will tell you where to go.'

It was an absolutely outrageous demand, but because we were amused by his shrewdness, and also because we appreciated a bush-reared boy's happy facility for discovering the secrets in every burrow and stream, and under every rock, we paid up. He pocketed the money, and then pointed, with a flourish. 'You go down there, straight down the river. Then you cross over one shallow place where all the birds are. Go on then, past the lands where the women are ploughing. Then the big reeds, where the river curls like so.' He indicated a curve with his hand. 'Big pools, no more rocks. That is Ramowtu.'

I thought of Peter Pan. First turn to the right and then straight on 'til morning.

We had to undertake a daylight reconnaissance of the downstream route so that we would know what we would be up against in the dark, and the experience was not reassuring. We encountered length after length of tumbling rapids and sudden shallows where the water fanned out into a series of mazed pans, each much like all the others, and with no obvious channel through them. Further down still there were rock-built fish traps spanning the river, put there ages since by villagers and then abandoned. In order to get the boat through we had to dismantle them, standing waist deep in the chilly water to manhandle the slippery rocks, constantly aware that at any moment a crocodile might decide to come and investigate.

A woman, ploughing near the bank with a pair of oxen, waved and shouted something. 'She says we should hurry, because it will soon be dark,' Kisi translated. 'She also says that there are many crocodiles here,' he added. We hurried.

As we reached the first stretch of open water, the sun set, with the extraordinary brilliance that the clean desert air sometimes lends it. The tossing river behind us created a shifting kaleidoscope of gold and shimmering turquoise, transmuting into flame and shot-silk Nile green, then drawing out into ribbons of rose madder, emerald, orange and green again, as the light slowly changed. It was like sailing into the heart of a rainbow. Then we rounded a bend, and the riverine forest held back the sunlight. Abruptly, we were gliding through inky water, sinister with dark black pools, as the night came rushing down on us from both banks.

Our black Peter Pan had told nothing less than the truth about Ramowtu. There were scores of crocodile lining the banks, those characteristic eyes mirroring our lamp in a hellish red garland. We swung towards a twelve-footer and Robert snapped off a shot.

In its death throes the monster flung itself high into the air, lifting the full length of its body clear of the river in an incredible final spasm, trailing weed from its jaws and slashing convulsively from side to side. For an instant it hung motionless, suspended right above me, and then it toppled back in what seemed like slow motion, plunging into the water a few feet from the boat. Then it floated back and Kisi prepared to gaff it. But above the acrid, unsettling smell of the crocodile, I now detected the pungent note of hot oil, and when I touched the cover of the outboard I discovered painfully that it was almost red-hot. The water pump had been choked by weed, but before I could cut the engine, the cylinder had jammed.

We were fourteen miles from our camp by this time, and the only way we were going to get back there was by physically dragging the dinghy over all those interminable rapids.

This epic of porterage took us twelve painful hours, and after the first two we encountered the buffalo, a herd of around 150, spread out along both sides of the river, drinking. The huge horn bosses stood out like opaque crescents of charcoal in the vague and watery night, and their hides glistened as they splashed across the channel ahead. Some of them stopped and turned to look at us, for buffalo have an insensate curiosity about anything unfamiliar. The sight of that galaxy of hostile eyes, like dull rubies, made me shake with horror. There was plenty to be afraid of.

We could not row away from them because the dinghy was stuck in one of the shallows, and as we heaved and shoved at the hull I was appalled to see that they were drawing closer, moving with their heads raised as they tightened the semi-circle around us. The leading animals splashed forward with the rest of the herd pressing close behind them, and by now they were not being merely inquisitive. They did not like humans; the local hunters were abysmally poor shots, and although buffalo cows with calves at foot were notoriously dangerous, a wounded buffalo was the undertaker's best friend. This herd clearly had long memories, into the bargain.

All I could do was shut my mind to the menace, and turn my back on them as we continued to bully *Fleur-de-Lys* over sandbars, mud, reeds and rock, cut off from both banks and fast approaching a state of helpless exhaustion.

Then the resistance ended and, miraculously, the boat was floating in deeper water. But we were not altogether clear of danger. The water was ugly, difficult, and it tore like a mill-race between the jagged rocks sunk in the river bed. But at least we could row, and we were still rowing at dawn. I cannot remember much of our last hour on the journey back from Ramowtu, but I do recall somehow that the dawn brought a cold stillness to the river, turning the drifting veils of mist a rosy pink. An Egyptian goose with a convoy of fussing goslings swam ahead of us, leaving their own small, silver wakes.

When at last we came within sight of the camp I saw Leonard sitting on a log beside the fire, and an aroma distilled by the gods told me that he was brewing coffee. Appositely, I thought, he happened to be singing to himself about the evil ways of M'goba, the legendary crested serpent that is Africa's version of the Mayan plumed snake, Quetzlcoatl. I would have liked to hear the full version, but all I could manage was a hoarse plea for some of the coffee, before I crashed into my bunk in the DUKW without bothering to undress.

In November we loaded our cargo of crocodile hides into the DUKW and returned to Maun to camp beside the river for a couple of weeks. The heat was still intense and the air swarmed with mosquitoes. Unable to bear it any longer, we drove back to Bulawayo and rented a cottage on the Figtree Road on the flanks of the Matopos.

I got myself a job with a firm of plate-glass factors, and Robert went off looking for excitement in the unpaid ranks of the white Colonials who were busily trying to organize a final break between Rhodesia and Britain. The leader of this angry group was a man who had served with some distinction in the Royal Air Force during the Second World War, and had a disfiguring facial scar to show for it. But his loyalty to the Crown didn't stretch to giving blacks the vote, and his name was Ian Smith.

The Crippled Lion

There is a clipping from a lion's mane in the bottom drawer of my desk
and I haven't the heart to throw it away, because it came from Timber.

★   ★   ★

After two years of living rough in the greatest game country
left on earth, I should have known better than to take on a
maladjusted lion.

Timber was a cripple. He'd been born in a zoo, with five
generations of cage-breeding behind him; he had also been stunted
by a serious vitamin deficiency that had turned him into a Toulouse-
Lautrec among lions, a glorious head attached to a twisted body and
grotesquely stumpy legs. He'd been bought by a circus proprietor
in South Africa as part of a job-lot of cubs, and it was soon obvious
that he'd never be any use in the ring, even as a clown. He was too
weak to jump up on the barrels, and although his cage-mates stole
most of his share of the meat his new owners still calculated that he
was costing them money. They prescribed a bullet.

The Figtree Cottage, named after the nearest village, had grounds
big enough to accommodate a tribe of dogs, a dozen chickens – and
Chink, who was now in disgrace. She had not been cured of her
gleeful interest in chasing cattle, and after two narrowly averted
homicides we attached her to a twenty-foot trek chain and confined
her to the garden. The Polish lion-tamer from the circus came up
to visit her, and stayed to talk about Timber.

'Why don't you come and see him?' he asked. 'It would be good
if he could see that he had even one other human friend, in the little
time he's got left.'

It was innocently said, perhaps, but I should have shunned
the circus grounds as if they had harboured all the seven plagues
of Egypt, and done my crying safely at home. Instead, I went to
watch Alex Sanesky let the young lions out of the cub-cage for their
morning exercise. He called their names as they came tumbling past
him down the wire tunnel that led to the ring. Eventually, after a
pause, the last cub crept past me, shuffling on his hocks because
he was too weak to use the pads of his hind feet. While the others
gambolled in the ring, he edged himself painfully towards a corner

of the big cage, asking to be left there, alone. I slid my hand between the bars and scratched his back. He turned his head and looked up at me with clear, honest eyes of a very deep gold, set wide apart and brimming with a gentle sadness. I had seen other runts who were noisy, quick-tempered, quarrelsome, but this one was different. He seemed humbly grateful that he was still alive.

'How long has he left?'

'They told me to shoot him tonight, after the show.' The trainer looked down at his big hands, suddenly shy and embarrassed. 'I do not know how I will be able to put a bullet in his head,' he sighed. 'He is the nicest lion I ever met.'

'Will the manager take a cheque?' I asked.

Timber's hind feet and hocks were covered in callouses, and he had never in his life been able to walk on all four feet. He had a cough, and I guessed that the deformities were a form of rickets, so I put him on a course of antibiotics and fed him a high-vitamin diet. Wary at first, when he found that he was being fed regularly and no longer had to forage among the straw for the scraps that his cage-mates had left, he stopped growling anxiously over his meat, and after a while he even allowed my bull-terrier bitch to feed from the same bowl.

She was Pandora, one of a too-short line of beloved but accident-prone white bull terriers, and she would have tried to mother a full-grown tiger if one had happened her way. Timber endured her effusive face-washing with quiet dignity, but Kisi disapproved: Pandora was a favourite of his; Timber, who once hooked a paw around his ankle when he was carrying a trayful of glasses, was not.

Perhaps I should have thought more dispassionately about the risks involved in allowing Timber the full freedom of the house and garden. Maybe what clouded my judgement was the fact that although he was close on two years old he was no bigger than a normal nine-month-old cub, and weighed only about 90 pounds. Chink, the same age, was four times his size. I also failed to realize just how deeply Chink loathed him; it was an oversight that nearly cost me my life.

It happened one evening when Robert was out at yet another political meeting, and I was getting ready for a cocktail party. The dogs and the lions had been fed, and I had left Timber curled up contentedly with Pandora on the kitchen floor. Unexpectedly, there was a sudden cough of anger from Chink, followed by a furious, full-throated snarling, and I rushed to the bedroom window. I saw to my dismay that Timber had hobbled out-side, pulled aside the thorny barricade that we had built across the verandah to keep the two lions apart, and was sitting well within the danger circle of Chink's chain. The lioness herself was standing on the low wall just above him, and her eyes were blood red.

She was going to kill him.

I called softly to him, but instead of responding he edged closer to Chink and reached out tentatively with one of his paws to pat her. She lashed out furiously at him, snarling, and he toppled over onto his back. Then her ears flattened ominously, and just as I reached for his collar she struck out again and her dew claw, which didn't retract, raked my arm. In the greatest emergency of his life Timber saw in me only another threat, and he must have felt that he was being cornered, for he flung himself straight at me. It had been raining and the verandah planking was wet. As I dodged away from the line of charge I slipped and fell heavily, between the two animals.

Chink was now standing statue-still on the wall, glaring down at me as Timber trembled across my body and gave the lion call for protection, the strange, questioning 'Ah-ow?' that all lions use when they are afraid. Then, painfully, he struggled to his feet and as I eased myself out from under him he moved aside to let me pass. But Chink had not moved and her eyes never left my face. Her lips slowly drew back to show her teeth, her eyes narrowed in anger, and her shoulder muscles began to bunch. She was waiting for me to get out of the way before she launched her full attack on Timber. As I reached the verandah door she sprang, and Timber retaliated with unsheathed claws. As they grappled, I slipped out of a side door onto the lawn and located the only weapon available.

For ten minutes I blasted the pair of them with the full force of a jet of water from the garden hose, and finally they spluttered apart, shame-faced and sneezing.

It was only after I'd dragged Timber back into the kitchen and restored the thorn barrier that I began to appreciate just how close I had come to a brutal death. Either of them could have killed me with ease. Chink was a powerful beast, and even though Timber's body was small he had the head of a normal adult male lion, and a set of enormous canines had replaced his milk teeth.

The thought left me shaking, and I went through to the drawing room to pour myself a large neat Scotch. As I slumped on to the divan, Timber limped in from the kitchen and clumsily pulled himself up beside me. He dropped his rough, frilled head across my knees and I dug my fingers into the sandy mane that was beginning to thicken round his shoulders. He endured the rough play for a while, then climbed down and wandered over to the fireplace. It was a cold evening, and there was a cheerful log fire blazing, but he wasn't looking for warmth. Instead, he contemplated the pile of logs that Kisi had stacked by the hearth. With the utmost care he selected a chunk of firewood, shook it free from the others and came back to chew it on the rug at my feet.

While he was still at the circus his cage-name had been 'Simba'. I had changed it to Timber when I discovered that he always chose a piece of rough wood as his comforter, a security blanket in moments of misery.

Change for the Worse

Early in 1954, the parliament of the newly created Central African Federation met for the first time, and in London the Colonial Office congratulated itself on a masterly solution to a potentially intractable problem. In their well-intentioned but muddled way they thought they had found a cheap and simple method for counterbalancing the power of South Africa with a new, strong and harmonious union, and on paper it must have seemed a good idea. Unhappily it was based on the widespread misconception that all Africans are part of an homogeneous whole rather than members of individual nations as different as, say, the British and the Greeks. It also credited the white Rhodesians with more altruism than they actually possessed. In reality, of course, the whole idea stood as much chance as a joint venture between the Montagues and the Capulets or a Hatfield-McCoy armistice.

Seven years later, by 1961, few people even pretended that the great experiment had much life left in it, and the situation was not improved by events across the border. In March, a tribal revolt in Angola had been brutally put down by the Portuguese army and in May the South African government finally avenged the Boer defeat of 1901 by quitting the Commonwealth and beginning the process of wiping out all traces of the detested British connection.

Those whites whose commitment to Rhodesia didn't extend beyond their monthly pay-cheque began quitting for more congenial havens, while they could still take their money with them. Those who remained had mostly convinced themselves that, somehow or other, they would be able to maintain their comfortable status. But half my apartments remained unlet, and although my salary from the plate glass company kept us in meat and potatoes, we were still spending more than we were earning.

★ ★ ★

I knew that primarily Robert wanted money to put *Shaka Zulu* back on the road, although I did nothing to encourage this ambition. I still ached to be in Europe, where the insects didn't carry fatal diseases, the water didn't poison you and the forests were free of snakes and elephants. I wanted to be able to wear my golden sandals, a long Thai silk dress, jewels and good perfume. I wanted to be able to eat in restaurants, with people whose conversation was not confined to the price of crocodile hides. Most of all, I wanted to be some place where I wasn't always having to watch animals die.

I was, in short, well overdue for a little civilized excitement.

In the meantime, while I struggled to scrape up some capital, Robert had found himself a new crusade, a fence-straddling campaign to win strong representation by the conservative tribal chiefs in the Smith regime. Every government minister he approached with the idea dismissed it out of hand, and in the end he got bored with the whole affair and began one of his customary financial exercises.

Precisely how he did it I never found out, but somehow he managed to raise a final bond on my apartments – without my consent – and then announced, curtly, that we were going back to Bechuanaland, and that we would stay there until the Batauana agreed to establish a game reserve in the valley of the Kwaai. This was far more important, he said loftily, than my wistful longing to get away from Africa before my brain turned to grease.

Quitting Rhodesia also meant that I would once again be out of touch with the children for long periods: at the Figtree Cottage, I was at least within easy reach if anything did go wrong.

Oliver was still my blue-eyed owl, and would have agreed to go and live on the dark side of the moon as long as he still had my hand to hold, but Tris was a different matter. He was now fourteen and the school's reports about his academic achievements were not encouraging, although he was already showing signs of a talent for writing. More of an athlete than a scholar, he was an excellent horseman and had an intuitive ability as a tracker, which later – much later – earned him the rôle of guide with the Rhodesian armed forces during the bush war in the Zambesi valley. But I was less happy about the changes in his personality. The old closeness between us had gone, and I knew why. He had sensed the tension and unspoken hostility between his father and myself, and wasn't sure on which side his loyalties lay.

★ ★ ★

When the rainy season came, we loaded the vehicles again and headed back to the bloody Protectorate, with two lions, five dogs, twenty-three chickens and Kisi. Once more we set up a home of sorts on the island. During our brief stay at the Thamalakane base camp there was no noticeable change in Timber's temperament. He tolerated the chickens when they roosted contentedly on him as he lay in the shade, and he was on mutual face-washing terms with the dogs. It was when we took him into the deep bush that the trouble began. It was almost as though the sights, sounds and smells of his wild heritage had somehow revived an instinct that five generations of cage-breeding had failed to eradicate. The first sign was that, almost overnight, his eyes changed from the placid gaze of a cub to the wary glare of a hunter. Within hours of making our first camp in the Kwaai valley he became aggressive, and much harder to handle.

I didn't think of it then, but it stands to reason that the special diet that had straightened his limbs must eventually have begun to stimulate hormonal activity. In human terms, he was changing from a boy into a post-pubescent teenager; as part of a pride, he would have been disciplined by the dominant males and the fully grown females, but we were in no position to cope with his more assertive nature.

The next day he made his first kill. There was a freak hailstorm and the air was full of tumbling lumps of ice the size of pullets' eggs. I grabbed Timber's collar and hauled him into shelter under the DUKW. He peered out, snarling at the hail, then, as the storm rumbled away over the swamps, he came out to sniff tentatively at the strange new landscape, transformed by glittering ice which the sun was breaking up into rainbows. I watched him patting a large hailstone along the ground and then went back into my tent, giving no thought to the chickens that had also taken refuge under the DUKW. Later, when I came back, he had killed three of them. He had eaten everything except the wingbones and the feathers from two, and when I tried to take the third carcass from him he closed his jaws tightly on it and backed away, growling menacingly.

That night he killed again.

There was more rain threatening and I tethered him to the back of the DUKW, so he could shelter. My golden cocker bitch,

Gillie-Anne, had a litter of pups who were just beginning to walk, but they never wandered far away from her – except for one especially adventurous pup that we'd nicknamed Howler. During the night I woke, with the hazy suspicion that something was wrong. I moment later I heard a sharp yelp. I woke Robert, who grabbed a torch and disappeared into the darkness. When he came back his hands were covered with blood and he laid something gently down on the bucksail. It was Howler, and she was dead. Timber had bitten her through the heart.

We should have shot him then. We didn't, because we loved him, and he depended on us, and it would have seemed like shooting a child. We watched him carefully, though, and he still seemed outwardly to be on friendly terms with the adult dogs, so we managed to delude ourselves into thinking that he'd only wanted to play. Just like poor, big, simple-minded Lenny in *Of Mice and Men*. But we did at least move him well away from the DUKW, and we tethered him even more securely to a tree by the water.

The boys came to join us for the school holidays and we set up a new camp near the beautiful log bridge that once spanned the Thamalakane on the road to Maun. Timber was still on his long chain, but I didn't much care for the way that he sometimes looked at Oliver, so I warned the boy to keep well clear of him.

It was five days before Christmas, and the afternoon was hot. Timber was safely chained to his tree, and Oliver was playing with Gillie-Anne's pups by the tent flap. Chink's travelling cage needed cleaning, so I drove down to the water's edge, where Leonard was cutting grass for her.

Fish eagles were quartering the river and I stopped work to watch them. One came down in a superb power dive, rose with a squirming bream clutched in his talons and his wings cascading bright water, away into a tree, screaming in triumph.

Then other, human, screams reached me.

'*Mummy!*'

I yelled that I was coming, picked up the crocodile gaff and ran towards the sound. By the time I got to Timber's tree Robert and Tristram were already there. Tristram's shirt was bright with blood, and he was cradling Oliver in his arms. Robert took the child from him. *So much blood!* Oliver's shorts, and his legs, were covered in it.

Robert carried him back to the tent, and when we'd stripped off his clothes we saw that he was bleeding profusely from a wound below his knee. We turned him over and discovered deep fang punctures in his back, just fractionally higher than his kidneys. I washed out the two long rents that Timber's teeth had made, syringing them again and again before packing the wounds with the veterinary tetramycin that we normally used on injured animals, which was the strongest antibiotic I had.

A little of the colour came back to Oliver's face and he managed a wavering smile. 'It wasn't Timber's fault, Mummy,' he said. 'I knew he didn't like me, and I went too close. If people look at my leg I'll tell them I fell on a stump, or they'll make us shoot him.'

I couldn't answer him. I couldn't speak at all. He stared at my face, suddenly aware of what was likely to happen. 'If you shoot him, I know that I'll die!' he sobbed. Then his hand turned cold in mine, and for the next two hours I sat beside him as he fought off his second terrible shock. At last he grew calmer and I spoonfed him with a little soup and scrambled eggs. Then he said he was sleepy, and I kissed him goodnight.

Robert and Tris and I sat and talked for a long time.

'What actually happened, Tris?'

'When I got there Timber had Oliver by the back. I tugged his jaws apart, but then he shifted his grip to Oliver's leg. I hit him on the nose as hard as I could, and then on the ear, but it didn't make any difference, so I pulled his mouth open again and sort of picked him up and slammed him against a tree. Oliver was screaming so much that I didn't really have time to think properly, but after that Timber let me carry him away.'

It was well past midnight when we finally decided. 'But make no mistake,' Robert said as he stood up, 'this is his last chance, his very last. The next time he does anything even a little wrong he'll get the bullet. The only reason I'm not shooting that damned animal now is that it might make Oliver worse.'

Oliver was sleeping, one arm flung over his head on the pillow, relaxed, his breathing regular. In the morning I injected him with penicillin. He was cheerful, and his temperature was normal. But my own nervous reaction had finally struck. For many nights I couldn't sleep properly and I was plagued by recurrent nightmares. I would wake, screaming, from a vision of Oliver sleep-walking towards Timber's tree, and the lion was about to kill him. This happened so often that, in the end, I moved Oliver's bed next to mine and tied our wrists together with string. It wore off in time, but I was left with a sense of dread that I had never felt before, and that I was now never to lose.

★ ★ ★

Before Oliver had fully recovered, there was yet another tragedy. I was walking back from the river one night, carrying a torch, when I saw something white lying on the path. It was my bull-terrier bitch Pandora, and she was dead. There wasn't a mark on her. Oliver kept asking for her, and I had to tell him the truth. The little boy put his head down on my lap and sobbed and sobbed. At last he raised a tear-stained face to mine.

'I'll always remember Pandy,' he said. 'And I'll always love her – even when I'm a grown man, and a soldier.'

The Safari Lion

Lionel Palmer and his brothers-in-law, Ronnie and Kennie Kays, decided to set up their own White Hunter Company, which they called Safari South. The local Batauana didn't much like it, and they tended to refer to it as 'the Safari Lion, that is eating our wild cattle', but they tolerated it because it also brought increased revenue for the tribal coffers from the sale of hunting licences.

From time to time, Robert was asked to help entertain the firm's clients. Partly this was because *Shaka Zulu* had unique attractions as swampland transport, but mostly because Chink allowed the short-stay visitors to take close-up photographs of her – without her collar – and she posed like a professional.

In time, we began to acquire a few private clients of our own, usually as a result of the pieces I'd been writing for newspapers in Rhodesia, South Africa, South-West Africa and Moçambique. I had managed to accumulate about £500 from the payments, and we sank the money in extra tents, a termite-proof steel eight-seater table, some comfortable chairs, a really big paraffin-powered deep-freeze and an adult-size canvas bath.

Our own flock of chickens provided fresh eggs every morning, and poor layers ended up as table birds. Kisi still baked wonderful bread, and venison and game birds were there for the shooting. In the season, there were also freshly caught bream. I adapted an André Simon recipe to make a delectable wild pâté: a pound of sweet butter for every antelope liver, big Spanish onions, peppercorns and lemon juice. Canned cream, powdered soups and dehydrated vegetables still had to be brought from Bulawayo, and so did the little luxuries like cans of black Leicestershire field mushrooms, quail-in-aspic, asparagus spears from the United States, and bottles of exotic fruits. Because Rhodesians mostly restricted their tipling to beer-and-Scotch, with beer-and-brandy as an alternative, we couldn't offer good wines; the South African wines are good now, but in those days they were thin and feeble, and the Moçambiquan varieties were best left stoppered. We overcame this deficiency, however, by increasing the amount of gin we served by the camp-fire when the day's hunting was over.

Safari mornings started early, with freshly brewed coffee and a light breakfast served at around four a.m., so that the clients could reach the chosen locale before the sun had driven the game back into the shelter of the forests. At this hour of the day, the veld smelled as sweet as a farmyard, and the tracks made by buffalo and wildebeest were easy to follow in the dew-drenched grass. The warthogs paraded their sounders of piglets in the long molapos. Even the night creatures – genet, civet, serval cat and aardvark – were still out and about, nosing hopefully for unwary rodents, sleepy ground-roosting birds and, in the case of the aardvark, the seething nests of termites which are their sole source of food. Lions, too indolent to move until the heat became intolerable, were still lounging about on the cool sand round the waterholes. And when the sun was fully up and the light was filtering down through the canopy of mopani leaves, the swift and elusive cheetah came out to hunt. Cheetahs kill only by day, and they never return to a kill. Unlike most cats, their claws aren't fully retractable and their main weapons are sharp eyes and speed. A quick stalk, a blur of black and yellow – they can outrun horses – and the hunt is over. Unless, that is, the quarry is sharp-witted enough to dodge the pursuer, in which case the cheetah will simply lose interest and go and try its luck elsewhere.

As soon as Robert had left with his guests, Kisi and I would rush about the camp, making beds, knotting the mosquito nets back into place, sweeping the drift of dead leaves and the charred remains of lamp-fixated beetles and moths off the tent floors, collecting piles of yesterday's sweat-stained khaki clothes to dump in the washtub, lighting the fires under the big forty-four-gallon steel drums so that there would be hot bathwater for the party when they returned.

If we'd camped near a river, I would take the dinghy out and fish the morning rise, while Kisi rolled his sleeves up to the elbow and began pummelling flour and yeast into bread dough. When we'd reached that stage the morning was usually half over, and the two of us would get together in his kitchen, which was often not much more than a single shade tree, a wood fire and a long table improvised by balancing scaffolding planks across two of the ubiquitous petrol drums, and plan the day's menu. If it was game pie then I made it, using layers of bacon, venison, guinea fowl, onions and canned mushrooms, dried herbs and grated lemon rind, all covered in a rich espagnol sauce and topped with shortcrust pastry.

The safari party would usually get back by noon, hot and dusty and yelling for cold beer, hot baths, clean clothes. Then they'd sit around complaining that they couldn't find their cigarettes and that they'd read everything in the book bag, and magnifying their achievements . . . 'Did you just *see* that incredible shot when I got the waterbuck; just wait until I show them that trophy back in Manchester, Milan, Düsseldorf, Pittsburgh, Lyons.'

The afternoon heat smote the camp, and even inside the double-fly tents it felt as though you were trying to breathe through a thick blanket. The clients read paperbacks, dozed, drank long glasses of chilled limejuice. Some of the bolder ones went down to the river, stripped, and lay in the shallows with hats pulled down over their eyes to keep out the glare. Once, though, one of them was woken by the chilling sounds of a pack of seven wild dogs crashing through the reeds about ten yards away from him and he watched in horror as they caught a fleeing impala and dragged it down. He was back in camp within seconds, shaking; the fact that he was naked had made him feel especially vulnerable, and he was afraid that when the pack had finished off the impala they might turn in search of other, pinker prey.

By four-thirty the sun was usually beginning to lose a little of its vigour. Kisi filled vacuum flasks with tea and Robert loaded his charges into a Land Rover to go off in search of new excitements. The swamps were always unpredictable. Sometimes, driving along the rough sand paths through the mopani forest the guests would come across big, heart-shaped tracks in the mud by the inland pans, and follow them until they found kudu browsing sedately on the crisp green foliage. At times, sable and roan antelope mingled with the mixed herds of wildebeest and impala in the long molapos, or there would be buffalo and zebra drinking together at the river verges. But on other days there would be nothing to see except wood doves and, perhaps, a solitary warthog backing into his burrow amid a swarm of flies.

Kisi and I could always judge what sort of foray it had been the instant the party clambered out of the Land Rover. If the game had been elusive they would be frozen-faced with disappointment, looking for faults so that they could relieve their resentment by criticizing someone, anyone. If it had been a good day they'd be waving and shouting, all of them trying to tell us at one and the same time about their unprecedented encounter – 'You know that long, whatsit, the long meadow place, well, there were fourteen lions lying out by the tree belt, seven big ones with seven cubs, so all the gang leaned out of the windows and waved their hats and the lions beat it into the trees except for this little one, this cub that turned round to see what was after him and tripped so he fell flat on his face.' Robert, on the other hand, was usually looking sour. What he wanted was full-frontal photographs, not close-ups of fourteen furry backsides.

But the clients paid and we needed the money, so if they wanted to practise skeet-shooting by aiming at the moon then we'd just have to let them get on with it. In many ways the fact that they were, in effect, subsidizing our own wild idyll should have been compensation enough, but it didn't seem so at the time.

Catch 'em Alive

Chink had become an increasingly intractable problem.

She was just two years old, and the civil administration in Bechuanaland had decreed that we must henceforth keep her in a cage. It was not specifically Chink that they objected to, they assured us; they felt that the whole principle was wrong. A lioness who had lost her fear of humans could all too easily progress to hunting them.

At the time, all the unforeseen dangers that had been created by Joy Adamson's famous lioness, Elsa, and her cubs were still being carefully concealed from the outside world. A major share of the royalties from *Born Free* were being channelled into conservation projects, and everyone involved was feverishly denying the smallest hint that there might be anything amiss.

In Bechuanaland we knew nothing about all this, so the governmental *diktat* looked to us suspiciously like a combination of personal animosity and simple bureaucratic bloody-mindedness. We hinted as much. 'Either take her outside Bechuanaland or shoot her, then,' came the explicit retort.

We would have taken her out, too, but by the time the prohibition was handed down we were once more deeply involved with the tribes in their campaign to set up a wildlife reserve, and the fate of thousands of animals depended on their success. Nor was there ever the slightest chance that we were going to shoot Chink. Official letters began to take on an increasingly peremptory tone as we suggested one alternative after the other in our efforts to stall the process while we looked for someone, *anyone*, who might give her sanctuary until we'd accomplished our mission. We were at the point of despair when Gerald Durrell, author, naturalist and – more to the point – owner of a small but very well-regarded zoo on Jersey, in the Channel Islands, answered our *cri de coeur* and agreed to take her. In his letter he wrote that Jerry Mallinson, his deputy director, was coming out to Africa on a collecting trip and, if we cared to look after him while he was in the swamps, then Chink could fly back to Jersey with him at the end of the safari.

Jerry was very tall and very fair, almost ash-blond, with humorous light blue eyes. He also turned out to be warm-hearted, cultivated, intelligent and possessed of infinite patience. These excellent qualities are not often encountered in the wilderness, and they made him doubly welcome.

He'd brought with him a fine selection of carefully designed trapping gear, ranging from expensive mist nets for snaring small birds to tough animal-mesh for capturing everything from spring hares to cheetah.

Trapping began at our island base, where an awe-struck Jerry was impressed to discover that the chittering hordes of little sand-coloured squirrels that Kisi kept shouting at when they tried to invade his kitchen were, in fact, a rare sub-species (*peraxerus cepapi Maunensis*), found only near the Thamalakane. We set squirrel traps in every likely tree, baited with bread, maize seeds, wild figs and raw eggs, and then Jerry fidgeted us all into a state of nervous exhaustion as we sat staring at the traps, waiting for the springs to snap shut. None of them did, except one at the foot of a tree, and that was because Gillie-Anne happened to sit on it. Tris watched us with ill-concealed amusement, and after a while he simply climbed a tree and took an infant squirrel out of a drey. The mother bit him, but Jerry was delighted.

On one unseasonably warm day a python cast off its winter lethargy and crawled out to warm itself in a splash of sunlight that fell across our main driveway. The cockers, being sensible as well as cowards, at once clustered round Kisi's ankles for protection; at least, those that managed to climb onto the kitchen table with him did. But the bull-terrier bitch, Cats, with all the inherent intelligence of the breed, ambled over with the friendly intention of washing the reptile's face. I grabbed her collar, just in time.

Jerry was ecstatic. Python were what he wanted *most*, he enthused – after aardwolf, ant-bear, black serval, cheetah, palm civet, zorilla, and a white lion that someone had once told him about.

As it happens, the mechanics of catching a python are really quite uncomplicated. You fling yourself in one direction and the snake hurls itself in another. The cook screams. You then grab your host's sports jacket (which is also the only one he has) from the back seat of the car, and throw it over the snake's tail if it is still where you last saw it. Irritated, the python comes zipping towards you, but you manage to free yourself from the jacket which has somehow twisted itself round your feet and then grab the reptile's scaly head in one hand and its tail in the other. The snake is now immobilized and you are perfectly safe. Provided that you do not let go of either end.

You stand there, quite still, while the snake coils its body around your arm and stops the flow of blood in your veins, until some fool woman has finished taking your photograph with a camera that she had forgotten to load. Any really world-class zoologist then bundles the catch into a netted cage from which a resentful broody hen has just been hastily evicted, and gives it five live mice which have earned the death penalty by eating the bait in the squirrel traps. Finally, his juvenile assistant labels the cage 'Python' with the lettering facing inwards, so that the snake can see what its name is.

★   ★   ★

When the possibilities of live-trapping on the island had been exhausted, we headed for the Kwaai. This time our convoy included a borrowed Dodge vanette, which had been converted into a travelling cage for Chink. Bringing up the rear was a Masarwa tracker, Mrewa, riding an old grey gelding named Whisky, which Robert had bought in the curiously naïve belief that he could shoot good game pictures from the back of a horse in lion country.

Just as we reached the junction of the sand track leading off to the Kwaai, the transport truck which slogged between Francistown and Maun pulled over to one side with a screech of brakes in a spray of dust and disgorged a weary, travel-stained and very drunk African. At first I didn't recognize him, but as his face cracked into a wide smile my heart leaped. He lurched forward, holding out both hands in greeting.

'Hullo, Kay,' he said hoarsely. 'Hullo, darling. Hullo, my darling. It's me. It's old Rodger. I've come back to you. Hullo, Kay! Hullo, darling!' All I could do was to hold on to his outstretched hands, while Robert pounded him on the back in greeting.

'Get up into the DUKW, you old rogue, and come with us.' But Rodger was looking hard at the pony.

'This horse yours, Inkosiami?' When Rodger used the affectionate diminutive, 'My own master', it always meant that he particularly wanted something. Robert nodded.

'Then why you let that black man ride him?' he spat. Rodger-alias-Mzenge-alias-Jackson Sibanda might seem old and poor and ragged, but he came of proud Zulu stock and everyone, most

217

whites included, was therefore his social inferior. 'Old Rodger rode the horses on the farm, and old Rodger will ride this one, right through the heart of this lion country.' He bundled Mrewa off unceremoniously, and as he hiccuped into the saddle Whisky whickered softly and approvingly. Drunk or sober, Rodger could still ride any pony ever foaled. But the aged horse held us back, and it was not until the afternoon of the third day that we reached the valley of the Kwaai. Our old camp was green and lush and thickly overgrown, and a pervasive feeling of doom still hung over it.

Sticks and String

All our attempts to trap vultures and marabou storks failed lamentably. We strung the catch-nets between trees in the flight-paths where the birds normally came down to water and, as an added inducement, set out piles of wildebeest entrails as bait, but the big birds simply flew straight through the nets, leaving them in tatters. The Masarwa tracker watched us with growing irritation and in the end, unable to tolerate our stupidity any longer, he intervened. If Morena Jerry was serious about wanting such ugly, evil-smelling birds, he announced loftily, then he, Mrewa, would catch the things by the dozen. The price, he added, would be £2 per bird. Since Mrewa's normal income was around £12 a year, fees on this scale would have elevated him into the local millionaire class. Given our own feeble record to date, however, we decided to leave him to it.

Sure enough, the next morning he trailed into camp carrying a young white-necked vulture as big as a turkey. Shrugging off our respectful praise, he helped Jerry to install the reeking bird in yet another of my precious chicken coops.

'How you catch him, black man?' Even Rodger was curious.

Mrewa spat into the dust. 'Sticks and string,' he said contemptuously. 'These birds are not big fools just to fly into a net and stay there.'

Mrewa's traps were crude, simple – and deadly effective. They consisted of a noose anchored to a stout stick, and a small circle of green twigs grouped round a wooden trigger, which was baited with meat. Confused marabou storks and bewildered vultures were

218

hauled in quicker than we could cage them. Mrewa became a very rich man by the standards of his tribe. He began to walk with a bragging swagger, and took to smoking a store-bought pipe.

But when it came to feeding our new acquisitions we ran into trouble right away. For the first three days the birds mournfully rejected even the choicest cuts of meat and began to look like badly worn feather dusters. In the end I persuaded Jerry to let me try my hand as a dietician and I fed them on what they always ate first in the wild – eyes, udders and testicles. It was the perfect menu, and they bolted down the disgusting fare as fast as we could dish it up.

It was autumn, April, and the impala were in rut. So, to judge by the sounds that came echoing out of the valley, was everything else. Hyena shrieked their love lyrics from dusk to dawn. The baboons roosting in the fig trees scratched themselves, coupled compulsively, and hit their inquisitive children. Below one of the trees a pair of leopards patrolled, waiting hopefully for a careless infant to miss its footing and fall off a branch. And we acquired our own resident pride of lions – he, she and 'it', who was half-grown, playfully pretty and female.

By now we had rather more birds than we could comfortably accommodate, and the big trap was set up to catch mammals for the Jersey Zoo. We baited it lavishly with offal and set it on a game trail that was heavily stippled with the pug marks of lion, leopard, cheetah, spotted hyena, jackal and genet. In theory it was an ideal location and we lay awake night after night, waiting for the crash of the gate to signal that we'd caught something. But for hours on end all we heard was the sound of hyenas – laughing.

Then came a night when every living thing seemed to be on the move, and the chorus of sound coming up from the game trail was almost deafening. Above the startled barking of bushbuck and the lunatic gibbering of hyena we could hear the female cub screaming with frustration while her sire roared his lungs out. Then, as if someone had flipped the 'off' switch, the whole caterwauling concert ceased and there was a startling void in the night, where a moment before there had been pandemonium. Nobody spoke, and the pony put his ears forward.

Luminous hands on my wristwatch said that it was midnight, precisely on the hour.

Somewhere off to the left there was a deep cough of fright, a quick tumult of stampeding zebra in the molapo as lions broke through the tree belt, and then the resounding clang of metal as the trap slammed shut. At last we had caught something – but what?

I was halfway down the path when I felt Jerry's restraining hand on my arm. 'Please, June! The trap's five hundred yards away and we can't possibly try to handle a frightened animal out of the cage in the darkness. Whatever we've got there is going to be quite safe till the morning.'

At least the darkness concealed my blushes, so I muttered a good night and went off to bed. A tongue rasped across the sole of my right foot and I muffled a shriek. As usual, in the face of the remotest danger, good and noble red dog Dingo was yellow all the way through.

The Africans were talking among themselves, and I caught the same word over and over again. '*Piri*.'

'What makes you thing it's a hyena, Rodger?' I asked, as lightly as I could manage.

Because – it was a long explanation: because, the old lion was too wise to get caught and if it had been the cub the lioness would be waking God Almighty by now, and you could hear a trapped leopard cursing from five miles away, almost, and no cheetah would eat meat that it hadn't caught and killed for itself. But *piri* was such a scavenger that he would make a meal of almost anything, including the corned beef cans in the rubbish pit. He bet me five shillings that it was a hyena, and I drifted off back to sleep listening to Chink's usual pre-dawn lullaby and the endearing sound of the vultures as they vomited in sympathy.

'What is it, Jerry?'

He must have risen with the Morning Star, because when I met him he was walking back into camp from the direction of the trap.

'You owe Rodger five bob.'

★ ★ ★

The neighbourhood baboon troop which always roosted just behind the camp contained at least two young ones who should rightfully have been doing time in a monkey jail. They were ugly, greedy, quarrelsome and given to hysterical midnight screaming fits that brought every hunting leopard within earshot streaking straight for the tree. One night, after the baboons had kept us awake until the small hours with their brawling, Robert and Jerry set off vengefully with catch-nets and a powerful torch.

Within minutes Jerry returned to the camp at the gallop, yelling for hot water. Rodger filled the canvas washbasin for him and the silver-blond head disappeared into a foam of soapsuds. He was still spluttering with rage when I handed him a towel.

'They were flinging *shit* at us! Shit! Mrewa took a direct hit in the face, and your husband's plastered in it from head to foot. I'm *never* going to get the stink out of my hair!'

He crammed a hat on and returned doggedly to the attack, but within the hour he and Robert were back in camp, reeking to the high heavens and trailing empty nets. The females and young, they explained bitterly as I edged away from them, had all fled to the safety of the topmost branches, while the militant dog monkeys bombarded the men with handsful of hot dung, voided expressly for the purpose. As a defensive strategy it lacked elegance, but it worked: Jerry, Robert and Mrewa never mentioned the matter again.

★   ★   ★

Our time on the Kwaai was at an end. It had certainly not been Jerry's most rewarding catch-'em-alive expedition, or our most profitable safari, but it had nevertheless been a curiously happy time. Chink was coaxed without much difficulty into the Big Trap for the long journey to Gerald Durrell's zoo.

'She's fallen head-over-paws in love with our lion, Leo,' Jerry wrote enthusiastically from Jersey. 'Would you like one of her cubs? They're due in about three weeks.'

A month later we had a letter from Gerry Durrell, with a postmark dated two weeks previously.

'It is my unhappy lot to have to tell you . . .'

Chink was dead. Somehow, she had picked up a stray virus infection and she had died giving birth to three cubs, all stillborn.

'This is William!'

I hadn't heard from Leslie for three years, not since the afternoon she'd stormed away from Far Lamorna with a suitcase in one hand and her pony saddle slung across her shoulder. I did hear, though, from her brothers, who saw her from time to time, that she had got herself a job, was doing well, and was living with the parents of the girl who'd been her closest friend at school. They also said that she was bounding with health and looked happy. Then I received a letter addressed in a vaguely familiar handwriting.

She was married.

Of course she'd had to lie about her age to poor, credulous Father Andrew, but then she was – well, she almost was, if not quite – eighteen, and I really wasn't to worry. William was a young Afrikaner from the Cape Province, and she loved him, and she was absolutely certain that their marriage would be a lasting one.

'Like yours, mother,' she concluded.

A few months later Leslie and her young husband took the long passage to Maun in the cargo truck. They had no idea where to find us, so they headed for Riley's Hotel. Ronnie Kays came across them there, looking forlorn and sharing a single glass of beer because they hadn't the money for two. Ronnie bought them a glass apiece, drove them down to Bobbie Wilmot's camp at Matlapanen and tipped two of the crocodile gang to punt them across the river to our island base. It was dark by the time they arrived and as Leslie emerged into the light of the kerosene lamp her eyes were shining and she was clutching her husband's hand.

'Mum!' she said ecstatically, 'this is WILLIAM!'

If this was a true attempt at a rapprochement, after the years of silence and misunderstanding, then I was more than willing to meet her halfway. I turned half a dozen disgruntled cocker spaniels off their favourite camp chairs, and Kisi came scuttling up, dead on cue, with a trayful of drinks. As Leslie was blowing a line of white beer froth from her top lip, and still holding William's hand as though she would never let him go, Robert, who had been cleaning his rifles, stalked across to the tent.

'Oh, it's you, is it?' he said coldly.

I sensed instantly that we were on the brink of a violent and wholly unnecessary clash of two strong personalities. William stood up, as politeness demanded, but a small muscle at the back of his neck began to twitch. Just as Lance and Robert had hated each other on sight twenty years earlier, so Robert and William glared at each other with all the latent savagery of two hostile dogs.

William was a formidable young man, a semi-professional boxer who could have flattened even a powerful man like Robert in the first round, yet he seemed to be making a real effort to hold his temper in check. It was an inauspicious beginning, chillingly familiar, but I still believe that, in spite of the instinctive antipathy that had sprung up between them, William would have tried to come to terms with Robert, if only for Leslie's sake. But he was never given the chance. On the pretext that William sprang from humble Afrikaner peasant stock, Robert refused to accept that the marriage had ever taken place. He continued to introduce Leslie as 'Miss Kay' to callers, and when he could bring himself to mention William at all he referred to him as 'Barnard'.

He never relented, either. Even when Leslie produced two enchanting children, Slade and Sharon, his attitude failed to soften

222

in the smallest degree. Only many years later, after William's hideously mangled body had been extracted from the wreckage of two cars which had met head-on, at speed, did Robert consent to acknowledge his grandchildren and grudgingly allow them to visit him.

Of course, the reconciliation could never have lasted. I should have known. I was still trapped by my residual loyalty to Robert, and Leslie by her feelings for her own husband and children. Inevitably, the gap between us finally became as wide and unbridgeable as the Grand Canyon.

The September Kgotla

'*Killer Jack Ramsden,*' Michael Dithapo had called him in 1960. '*Cut his teeth on a rifle stock.*'

By 1962 the trigger-happy hunter had undergone a remarkable transformation. Jack was, after all, nobody's fool, and for two years he had listened carefully, weighed the evidence, and meticulously sifted out the opinions of every major and minor tribe in the delta, and then he finally accepted that the continued killing of breeding stock didn't make any kind of economic sense. The deep-dyed leopard had changed its spots, and Jack took to conservation with all the bright-eyed fervour of a born-again Christian.

He had heard from Isaac Tudor that I was determined to expose the atrocities of the poachers in the swamps, and he brought me new evidence. Did I know that the Masarwa Bushmen in some areas routinely surrounded herds of red letchwe antelope and then deliberately broke the legs of as many of them as they could so that the flesh of the still-living beasts would stay fresh for longer? That the Bayei were only clearing their snare lines every three days, leaving the trapped animals to die by slow strangulation? That lion cubs and other small carnivores were being clubbed to death, so as not to devalue the skins with bullet holes?

'I know that you want us to set up a game sanctuary,' he said earnestly, 'but we must to do this thing carefully. If you try to prohibit all trapping throughout the whole region then the tribes will never sanction it. Remember that we have hunted here for two hundred years, and the Bayei and the Masarwas were here before us – all of us hunters. It is the only livelihood that we know, apart from the small herds of cattle. We have to keep our hunting rights outside of any reserve area, but before we start thinking so far ahead we have to teach the people that conservation is a good idea. Your husband's words will be my text: "Kill the cow that bears the calf, and tomorrow you will have no meat." '

And he did use them as a text, intoning them with all the passion of a revivalist preacher at all of the meetings he held with every elder and all the headmen of any consequence in Maun village.

Montso Mogalakwe – Mog – was another early convert. He was an elderly man and devoted, in his quiet way, to his young and pretty wife, their small son, and the gin bottle – not necessarily always in that order. He belonged to the scant handful of Batauana who had been converted to Christianity by the early Dominican missionary fathers. I was fond of him, but I honestly did not think he would be much use to us in the rough-and-tumble of the campaign. I underestimated him. Considerably.

The next man to join Jack's crusade was the village schoolmaster, 'Rocks' Ledimo. I had seen him shepherding his flock of solemn children in and out of the school playground, for when the heat became unbearable classes were held out of doors. I heard him one day reading to the children from a tattered copy of Jack London's *White Fang* which he often carried in his jacket pocket. The children themselves sat, round-eyed, in a long line on the low brick wall, wondering what wolves were.

Dave Monwela and Gas Segadimo also followed the lead of their peers. Dave was deputy chairman of the Batauana Tribal Council, second only in rank to Badirwãn Sekao. Good, steady, intelligent Dave, a wholly reliable friend and one of the extremely rare politicians to respect the value of understatement.

Gas Segadimo was something else again; tribal aristocracy, and a man whose temper blazed easily at real or fancied slights. It was said that he made a very bad enemy indeed and was almost impossible to handle in his difficult moments – even Jack had problems in trying to calm him down. But he also had the reputation of being the staunchest of allies once he'd committed himself, and hundreds of thousands of animals in N'gamiland remain for ever in his debt.

These seven men – Jack Ramsden, Isaac Tudor, Michael Dithapo, Mog, Rocks, Dave Monwela and Gas – constituted the influential hard core of the Batauana elders, and they were backed by the bellowing strength of the Deputy Regent, Badirwãn Sekao, and the quietly sagacious tribal Member of Parliament for N'gamiland, the Honourable Tsheko Tsheko MBE. It was they who forged the spearhead.

224

Late that year they made a formal application to Mohumagadi Moremi for permission to discuss the conservation project at the 'small' Kgotla in September. This was the first tentative step on the long road we still had to travel before the creatures of the Kwaai valley would be safe. Elizabeth Moremi agreed to the request.

★ ★ ★

By tradition, all Kgotla meetings were held in the open air, under the tall, gum-scented acacia trees outside the Batauana Administrative offices, a whitewashed bungalow with a tin roof and mosquito-gauze screens, close to the Regent's own neat home. These gatherings were always formal, in an informal sort of way. The tribesmen, who came in from all quarters of the swamps, sat on the ground. They were there to settle the future policies of half-a-dozen divergent tribes, and to weld all of them into a single, law-abiding union, under the suzerainty of the Batauana, formulating a new and binding political structure for the land they shared, and somehow tying together all the disparate strands of tribal law and custom.

On this warm September day, goats and donkeys criss-crossed the sand between the sweltering ranks of tribesmen, and at one moment a majestic Battaleur eagle swooped down to tear at the body of a dead *pi* dog that nobody had bothered to bury.

I will not pretend now that the meeting went strictly according to the book, because in Africa *indabas* like this one almost never do. The trick is to begin by talking about something that has nothing whatever to do with the matter in hand for at least the first five hours, then to switch abruptly back to the main issue and cry 'Yes' or 'No' several times, very loudly. After that, there is usually a brief interlude for enthusiastically discussing even more irrelevant topics, before it becomes proper to move to the real business of the meeting, when the questions can be put and debated in earnest.

Once the engrossing matter of Sub-Chief Morapedi's aunt's five stolen cows had been satisfactorily disposed of, a tall and gangling Bayei shambled to his feet and recited a long list of wrongs and misdemeanours which he laid squarely at the door of the Protectorate's British administrators. The District Commissioner, Ambrose, was present as the sole representative of the Crown, and he fiddled nervously with his tie. His thoughts must have been unhappy ones; back in London, the mandarins of Whitehall did not look with favour on distant officials who rubbed up against tribal prejudices.

The Bayei sat down to clucks and murmurs of approval, and for a while the meeting reverted to the usual pattern, with a lively wrangle about the unsanctioned presence in the delta of unlicensed safari operations and the insatiable greed of the government, 'which is taking all the revenue for themselves, and doing nothing to help save our *dipholoholo*, our wild cattle.'

That gave Jack Ramsden the cue he needed to wrench the discussion back to the need for a game preservation plan, and he began to read from a paper that Robert had prepared for him.

'We don't want the whole country turned into a game sanctuary. If we did that it would deprive people of their only source of income. All we ask is that one special area – very small in relation to the rest of N'gamiland – should be set aside for our *dipholoholo*, so that we who live from our hunting will leave enough game for our children. The Tsetse Fly Control must also respect our game areas, and we must help them to find other ways of controlling the fly.' The standard method of controlling tsetse consisted mainly of wiping out the buffalo and antelope which were hosts to the parasite, before the fly could cross-infect horses, cattle – and people.

'Every man wishes to pass on a legacy to his sons,' Jack continued sonorously. 'I ask you now to remember that the wild creatures are not only *our* heritage; they also belong to our children, and we do not want them to know what a giraffe looks like only from a picture in a book.'

The oration splintered against a stony wall of dissent.

'We in N'gamiland live on our domestic animals and the wild creatures, and we respect our own livestock more than the game animals, because cattle meat is easier to obtain. We know that the buffalo and the antelopes bring the nagana disease, so it is not clever to keep them alive. Instead, we must kill them to protect our own stock. We can easily sell a cow – but how do you sell a buffalo?'

'And who will travel to N'gamiland just to see a *cow*? We have animals here that can be seen nowhere else on earth. In Europe there are now only a few deer, rabbits and foxes, and some wild pigs left. In India the only lions live in one small piece of forest. In America, there were so many bison – like our buffalo – that they covered the plains, and now they count them only in thousands. People from these countries will come to see our *dipholoholo*, and they will spend a lot of money here, so that we can buy more cattle. We cannot dig for wealth, like they do in South Africa,[1] so let us make sure that we protect what we still have. If we destroy our wildlife, then we will also have destroyed our future, and our children will all have to go and work in the coal mines.'

---

[1] They can now, because Botswana has been found to have rich diamond deposits.

The argument rolled on and on, and just when Jack appeared finally to have drawn the teeth of his suspicious audience, one of the elders raised another – and altogether more awkward – point. How was it possible, he asked with terrible simplicity, even to discuss so momentous a proposal when the Chief Designate of the Batauana, Crown Prince Letsholathebe, was at that moment away studying social sciences in England? Jack cursed under his breath, Michael Dithapo examined his hands minutely and Dave Monwela avoided my eyes. Only Isaac seemed relaxed, leaning against a tree with a half-smile on his face and gazing reflectively at the dissenters. I began to feel that nothing could, would, be done until Letsholathebe returned, and that could be years away.

Mohumagadi Elizabeth Moremi had been sitting, listening gravely as what had now become a constitutional issue assumed even greater importance. At last, when the sun was well past its zenith and the first of the evening flight of sandgrouse were whirring in to drink from the river, she broke the stalemate.

'My people still need time to consider this whole matter,' she said firmly. 'The Kgotla is dismissed.'

And we still didn't know the answer.

★ ★ ★

Three days later Robert received two letters, both signed in the firm, legible hand of the Regent. The first one gave her approval to the formation of a Fauna Conservation Society in Maun, and the second concluded: 'The question [of a game reserve] will be discussed at the full Annual Tribal Meeting in March.'

That was six months away. In the meantime, our money was running out once more, and the game was still running the hunters' gauntlet.

The Innocence of Cain

Acting before the momentum was lost, the founding members of the impressively named Fauna Conservation Society of N'gamiland unanimously elected Jack Ramsden as chairman. As well as Michael Dithapo and Isaac Tudor, the society now gained other, formidable support, most notably from the Chairman of the Tribal Council, Badirwăn Sekao. He was a middle-aged man, old by African standards, but he had the vigour of a young warrior and a voice that could break boulders. He dispensed justice fairly and with unshakeable rectitude, and one of his full-throated denunciations was usually enough to turn cattle thieves and chicken-snatchers back to the paths of righteousness. He had a soft side, though; once, finding me sad, he drove a truck 300 miles across rough country to bring me a beautifully made orange clay water jug that he thought might cheer me.

Cadet members of the Moremi royal family, leaders of the aristocratic ruling clans made up the bulk of the steering committee, and at first only four of the local Europeans were elected: the doctor, Don King; the newly converted Ronnie Kays; Robert; me. On a day when, for some reason or the other, I had to stay in camp, they elected me as secretary, fund-raiser and public relations gofer.

I was furious when they told me. I did not *need* any extra work. My first book, *Okavango*, had just been published to consistently good reviews, and I was halfway through writing the sequel, *Wild Eden*. I was firmly in the grip of whatever demon it is that battens on writers, and I wanted to be left alone with it while I finished the book. And when it was done, I still wanted to go back to England, to live like an ordinary, reasonably civilized woman for a while.

But in fact I was trapped. I knew that I could not now just walk out on the Batauana, and with something close to despair I finally accepted the hand I'd been dealt. England would have to wait.

Isaac Tudor, who had brought me the news, rubbed his hands together and gave me a silky smile.

'The society has no money, June,' he reminded me, unnecessarily.

'Yes, I know!' I snapped, 'but I suppose I'm stuck with it. I'd better do something for the newspapers.'

I wrote a moderately savage article about the poaching and all the illicit over-shooting that had led to the formation of the FCS, and sent it off to Chris Kavanagh, editor of the *Cape Argus*. The headline it was given was not as restrained as I had been.

'KILLERS OF THE OKAVANGO!' it screeched.

Normally, letters addressed to Maun arrived at tortoise-speed, but somebody in Cape Town must have sent a copy of the newspaper by special delivery. Within five days a great storm was raging over my unrepentant head.

The District Commissioner was magenta with rage. He shrilled, through clenched dentures, that 'KILLERS' seemed to suggest that the British administration had been worse than limp-wristed in its response to 'these *alleged* atrocities', and, even more unforgivably, that the Game Department had not been doing its job properly. Why, he demanded, had I not consulted the members of the society before dispatching this inflammatory material? I pointed out that not all of them could read. Then why hadn't I consulted *him*?

'Oh, but I did!' I replied maliciously. 'There's a copy of the article in your official file. Didn't you read it, then?'

At the hotel I walked into the bar and, for a moment, the whites who had gathered there were ominously silent. Then they, too, exploded with anger. Here was I, a comparative newcomer, whom they'd occasionally invited on safari out of the pure kindness of their hearts, and this was how I repaid their hospitality, by ratting to the newspapers just because they might sometimes have shot one or two more buff than they were entitled to. Why hadn't I at least made it clear that it was *outsiders* who were doing the damage, and not the patently blameless local lads?

One large lady, slightly fuddled by Cape brandy, tottered over to me and pointed an accusing finger. '*Why?*' she beseeched me in quavering tones. 'Why did you make out that it was our boys that done it? Why didn't you say that they was all as innocent as . . . as innocent as . . .'

'Cain?' suggested Isaac Tudor, who had been listening.

There was an appalled hush. 'Anyway,' he continued, beginning to enjoy himself hugely, 'I think it was rather touching, the way that *our secretary* wrote about the animals. It was especially nicely put, the bit about the buffalo hunt and the orphan calf that she took home and bottle-fed. I myself remember that calf very well. I even remember who caught it for her, and who it was that shot its mother – *and seven others* – when he only had a permit for two. I also remember where that hunt took place. It was very pretty in Kunaragha, that April.'

The silence was almost visible. Lionel Palmer and Kennie Kays turned away from me, their backs bristling with hostility. I had been careful not to name names in the *Argus* story, but both of them knew only too well who I'd been getting at. By this time the bar was beginning to fill up with the usual Saturday evening crowd of tribesmen, and old Mog Mogalakwe was loudly translating a copy of the story for their benefit. It was well received. They slapped their thighs gleefully, rocking with laughter, and then began pointing derisive fingers at individual Europeans, who did not seem to share the joke.

Ronnie Kays, too, was angry because some of his friends had been implicated, but he was also the first to simmer down and offer me a token goodwill drink. Later still an uneasy peace was somehow cobbled together, but I knew that the secretariat in Mafeking had inked a permanent black mark on the cover of my file.

I waited, then, for the next round of trouble to come rolling in. It wasn't long in arriving either, and this time it was serious.

A slightly amended version of the article had, in the way that these things do, found its way on to a desk in London, and from London it trickled down to Rome. The United Nations Food and Agriculture Organization was needled into action and hastily dispatched a team from their Special Report Section to review the situation. I knew that their report would be likely to carry a lot of weight with those international organizations who held the purse strings for conservation projects like ours. We were going to need all the cooperation they could offer.

As the official representative of the British Crown it was the DC's privilege to take the visitors under his wing, and he swept them up as soon as they arrived, making sure that they would not be contaminated by any member of the society, and once he had them safely inside the Residency he pulled up the drawbridge. I knew well enough that he didn't like me, but I never suspected that I would have to fight for an interview with the FAO men. But short of physically throwing me off the Residency verandah he did everything in his power to keep me from speaking to them. Finally I wrote a brief note to the officials, and Jack Ramsden persuaded one of the DC's house servants to smuggle it through the *cordon sanitaire* that had been drawn round the place.

It worked, but only to the extent that the two officials permitted me a grudging twenty minutes of their time. But the DC had, naturally, nobbled them pretty effectively.

The Messrs Hill and Rhiney were quiet, untypically sour Americans; but against that I felt sure that most international bureaucrats hadn't much to laugh about at the best of times. So, sitting in the hideous cut-glass-and-lustreware living room of the Residency, I put my all into winning their support. The charm was wasted, and after ten minutes of blank hostility I began to feel as though I was trying to scale a wall of ice. As quasi-diplomats they were not rude, of course, but they both had an aura of dislike that flamed like a beacon.

A few minutes before my allotted twenty minutes expired the DC cut in, adding another layer of permafrost.

'I really don't think you need bother these gentlemen with all this speculation. There isn't going to be a game reserve. I have it, on the most *respected* authority, that the project will not be approved by the Kgotla.' He smirked triumphantly. 'I don't think that you have quite grasped the point, Mrs Kay, but there are far more Bayei than there are Batauana, and the Bayei are totally opposed to the whole idea. I have, of course, consulted with the elders and the headmen, and they did not attempt to conceal their position. And now I do believe there's a committee meeting tonight, so shouldn't you be there taking notes?'

I took my dismissal like a man. As far as he was concerned, the whole matter was clearly – and very satisfactorily – at an end.

Isaac was waiting in the bar when I arrived at the hotel. Hill and Rhiney were to attend the committee meeting in one of the hotel's public rooms in five minutes, but I badly needed to talk to my friend and ally, so I dragged him round to the back of the building, where we could talk in private among the scented frangipani trees.

'I wouldn't worry,' he said laconically. He half closed his eyes and drew deeply on a cigarette. 'Of course there were Bayei at the small Kgotla when we set up the society. Of course they supported – and they will support the reserve, too . . . when we have finished talking quietly to them. There are many ways of persuading people, and your friend Tamai knows all of them.'

We went back, laughing, into the deadly, dusty lounge where we held all our meetings. The room had been pretty dismal to start with, and it had decayed even further over the years. There was a long tear in one of the curtains that someone had tacked together with safety pins. A broken leg on one of the tables was propped up on several bricks, and there was a waste-basket full of empty beer bottles and crumpled cigarette packages.

When the DC arrived with his two awesome guests, Jack Ramsden briskly opened the meeting and the Commissioner rose to introduce the men from the FAO. With an even more emphatic smirk he told the committee that Hill and Rhiney had an important dinner engagement, with *him*, so they would only be able to read out their prepared papers. There would be no time for questions. Since everyone knew that the sole purpose of the visit had been to enable the two to report on N'gamiland's wildlife, which belonged in law to the tribe, this did not go down at all well.

Hill delivered a paper of insulting simplicity, explaining in carefully dislocated syllables to the poor, uneducated Africans that it was a ve-ry good thing to pre-serve an-i-mals, and that nat-u-ral re-source-es must be pro-tec-ted. Michael Dithapo was staring fixedly at the ceiling and biting his upper lip, but the rest of the committee was looking angry and embarrassed. The DC imperiously waved down several attempts to ask questions, and then Rhiney rose majestically to his feet. He admitted cautiously that he had indeed noticed quite a lot of game in the Okavango, and he agreed, *in principle*, that the organisation for which he worked would support efforts to conserve it. Science, he declared grandly, describing parabolas with his hand, had no boundaries. Then the DC nudged him and the three of them made ready to leave. But Chairman Jack held up a restraining hand.

'One moment, please. A member of our executive committee wishes to bring a further point to your attention, gentlemen.'

Isaac Tudor lounged to his feet, with the deceptive slowness of an uncoiling python. He was delighted, he told them, *delighted* to assure them that the Bayei, having hitherto been at odds with the Batauana, were now wholly in favour of the project, and many of their elders had joined the society.

This good news left the DC mottled with anger. Hill and Rhiney said nothing. All three left.

'Bloody clowns!' observed Michael dismissively, as we walked out into the stormy night. The air smelled of rain, and lightning flickered above the horizon. 'Who did they think they were talking to? Bloody children?'

★ ★ ★

The *Cape Argus* article had whipped up a fair old storm, but it had also established the Okavango firmly in the consciousness of a good many sympathetic people. A week after the story appeared, Maun's postmaster personally delivered a bulging sackful of mail because it wouldn't fit into our box at the post office. There were letters from children, lawyers, lorry drivers, doctors, farmers, housewives, accountants, railway workers, preachers and publicans, lonely souls and old age pensioners . . . all of them wanting to join the society. Better still, most of the envelopes contained money. It didn't add up to a great deal, because most of the gifts came in small amounts: £5 from a man whose pet monkey had just died; £1 from a woman who cherished a tame meerkat (yellow mongoose); twelve shillings and sixpence enclosed in an envelope with a teddy bear printed on it from a small boy, who wrote that he had cried a lot when he heard how cruelly the animals in the Okavango were being treated, and here was the contents of his money box. One of the very last letters, though, was from a generous friend in Illinois, who had once hunted with us. His cheque, for a magnificent $1,000, bought the society's first, second-hand patrol Land Rover.

I sent to Bulawayo for reams of paper, had dozens of glossy wildlife photographs printed, and set to work typing yet more appeals on my antique ex-army Imperial portable.

Then Kennie Kays arrived at the camp, carrying something on a rose-coloured velvet cushion.

232

Cat from an Egyptian Frieze

It was the usual randomly cruel story. One of the tribal hunters, clearing his fish traps, had discovered two serval kittens in an unguarded lair in the reed bed and bundled them into a skin pouch. By the time he reached Maun, the smaller and weaker of the two was dead. Kennie Kays paid two shillings and sixpence for the survivor and rushed her down to me at the camp.

She was extraordinarily beautiful: black spots on a maize-coloured ground, black paint-stripes down her spine and clear, clear emerald eyes set in a tiny, piquant face, surmounted by enormous ears. When she sat, she elongated herself into a telescope of a cat. She looked like a painting from an Egyptian frieze. And I named her Isis.

But she would neither eat nor drink. For two days I tempted her with every delicacy I could think of, using every trick I had ever learned in coaxing orphaned bush infants to eat. I ran my tongue over her lips and nostrils, so that she would learn my smell and the taste of my saliva. I sucked the teat of the feeding-bottle before I presented it to her. I offered her eggs, fish, raw minced meat and newly shot doves, but Isis steadily averted her head from all of them. By the evening of the second day she had become very weak, and I knew that if I couldn't get some food into that tiny, fragile body, she would be dead before the night was out.

She lay in my lap, tried to stand up, collapsed, and reached out with one small paw to touch my hand. And at that moment I suddenly knew what I should have been doing from the outset. In the wild, her mother would have pre-digested the meat and then regurgitated it for her litter. Without her smell on it the food would have been wholly unacceptable to the kittens.

I tucked Isis down inside my shirt, picked up the latest batch of doves and took them to the kitchen. I sliced the breasts off the plump little birds and ground them up with the mincer, feathers and all. Kisi sighed theatrically and stood on one leg, the attitude he always adopted when he disapproved really deeply of whatever it was I happened to be doing.

The African dove has a pungent, gamey flavour. It is unpleasant cooked, and unimaginably worse when raw. I discovered this fact when I began to chew the first mouthful, but I had no sooner spat the glutinous mess into the palm of my hand than the kitten wriggled eagerly over and began to feed. She ate ravenously, licked the last particles from my fingers and then looked hopefully around for more. During the night I chewed up three more doves, with undiminished loathing, and Isis ate them all. By the morning my stomach was heaving, but Isis was blissfully asleep on my pillow with her paws curled over her nose.

Once she had started to eat I hoped that she would be ready to accept minced beef. She turned up her short nose contemptuously, then reached over and coolly raked her claws down my cheek. It was raw doves or nothing, and I had better chew them all *plus* the feathers, or she'd go back on hunger strike.

Kisi said sulkily that he wished to return to Rhodesia, *tomorrow*, and this time it wasn't a question of Maritsasi's baby, it was a question of feathers in his mincing machine.

I tried the kitten on fish.

'You chew it first,' said Isis.

So I chewed tiddlers, which at least tasted only of raw sardines in a river mud sauce, and Isis wolfed them down. After a while, she took it into her head to try and catch them for herself. I retrieved a wet, subdued and half-drowned kitten from the Thamalakane one afternoon, when the strong current caught her and swept her into the reeds. After that she was content to settle for her tiddlers served *au naturel*, in a pint-size glass beer tankard. The doomed fish darted round and round in the water, and she spent contented hours hooking for them. When at last she outgrew the tankard I took to putting her fish in the canvas bathtub. It was a game which fascinated Isis, but it shocked my rather prim children, who complained that the smell stuck to the canvas so much that they came out of the water stinking of kippers.

At night she slept curled up in the crook of my knees, but during the day I carried her about with me, inside my shirt. For a long time she was on three-hour feeds, which was socially awkward. She came on shopping trips to Maun, to all the committee meetings, and even to parties. It was difficult, sometimes, having to explain to my hosts that I needed to go outside to chew raw doves.

I didn't care. Isis was thriving, and one day would inherit her wild freedom again. Or so I hoped.

Ten Hours until Morning

Weary alike of endless committee meetings and the unrelenting antagonism of officials, we decided to take Tris on a final safari before he had to go back to his boarding school for the summer term. Oliver had other and more important things on his mind. He had recently acquired a South African girlfriend; she was nine years old, her name was Tabitha, and she had a tumbling profusion of red-gold curls, a snub nose and freckles. Even better, she owned a dun-coloured donkey that she occasionally permitted him to ride from her home to the post office. Obviously, nothing that we could offer equalled these attractions: we committed him to the indulgent care of the Van Zantens and left without him.

Kisi and Leonard stayed behind, too, in charge of the lions and the DUKW, but we loaded *Fleur-de-Lys* onto the roof of the shooting-brake and headed straight for the reed-shawled lagoons of Txatxanyika.[1] Txatxanyika lay beyond the vast mopani forest which I had named the Ariadne, for no better reason than that it had as few landmarks as the Minotaur's labyrinth in ancient Crete, and even Theseus would have lost his way there without the princess's thread to guide him. The small islands flanking the lagoon were clamorous with breeding colonies of marabou stork, herons and the rare wood ibis. We spent a single mosquito-infested night there, then launched the dinghy and followed the main channel of the Kwaai until it lost itself at the junction with the Monachira, to become just one more indistinguishable waterway in the complex of the delta.

The confluence was marked by an island, known as the Ruby Island from the red hermanthus lilies that carpeted the forest floor every summer. Walls of forest rose like a shield against the ever-present sun and the swift glitter of the water, and the turf in the open spaces was short and green, streaked with white patches where salt had leached through the sand, granulating around the roots of the sharp Kalahariensis grass. There were no monkeys, because the current at the junction was fast and treacherous, too deep for them to cross. Only winged creatures came here, or those which had no fear of water – the sitatunga, the red lechwe, basking hippo, cane rats, otter and occasional herds of buffalo, swimming across from

[1] The spelling has been updated to Xakanaxa, but the pronunciation remains the same: Ka-ka-ni-ka.

the mainland in search of fresh grazing. A twisted palm tree here and there bore witness to the sporadic presence of elephant, and a honey badger – who must have lived a hermit's life for years – had left blunt prints in the loose earth at the entrance to his set.

We arrived at noon, and here the men left me with camp kit and enough supplies to last me through the night. *Back tomorrow. Keep the shotgun, although you should be safe enough here. Stay and write.* A last-minute unloading of tsessebe meat, which was not improving in the heat of the unshaded dinghy.

Stay here and write, and sketch, and be alone and think and plan the articles you should have written long ago, and the books that you may never write at all, I thought. There was nothing new in this situation, and over the years I had built up a defence mechanism to counter loneliness.

For the first two hours, I neither wrote nor sketched. I merely dragged a camp bed into the shade of a giant mochaba tree and went to sleep on it, drugged with sunlight after two days in the open boat. I dreamed steadily, of lions in a red, rocky place, lying along the banks above a road that ran away into nowhere. The dream, a recurring one, always ended just as the first lion jumped down into a gully and turned its head towards me. On this day there was a variation, for there was a sound of wind-song between the rocks, muffled at first and then shrill and whining, like a jet passing over-head. I stared into the hard eyes of the big lioness that had been the first to jump, and woke as the wind fanned past me.

It was a vulture, coming in to land.

For a moment I was bewildered, not fully awake. The second vulture brought reality with it.

Why vultures? I propped myself up on my elbows, aware that my shirt was damp with sweat and clinging to my back in the heat. The big birds were coming in thick and fast, settling contemplatively in the trees on the far side of the water meadow. A hundred vultures? Probably more. There were none on the ground, and that in itself was odd. A kill, with the killer still on the carcass? A wounded animal that still breathed? Vultures did not gorge on the living.

Eventually, thirst drove me to the river. I carried a pail back, half full of the cold, clear swamp water, then returned to fill the big safari kettle, enough for my cooking and washing. There was plenty of dead wood lying about and I spent an hour collecting it. The logs made deep gouges in the soil, ant-roads to my fire. I built a pyramid of twigs, lit it with a cigarette lighter, and bent to blow on the flame. Smoke stung my eyes and filled my nostrils, beloved scent, signature smell of all Africa to me. The pressure lamp needed pumping then and I hung my mosquito net – necessary, in those latitudes – from a branch above my bed. That done, I went to look through the cold box, not enthusiastic about cooking but aware that I should eat. There was a bream there, caught by fisherman Tristram on the way up, and two tiger fish, uneatable without elaborate preparation. The tsessebe, an old bull that Robert had shot on the fringes of the Ariadne, was probably tough, so I rejected the idea of a steak. The haunches were awkward to handle and instead of hanging them in a tree I left them propped against the side of the cooler, unaware that before the moon rose I would owe my life to that decision.

I filleted the bream inexpertly, cold glittery scales sticking to my fingers, set oil to heat for the potatoes, ate my solitary meal.

So, what now? Now I can write.

I set up the folding table, typewriter in place, and found a canvas fishing stool. The light was going fast, but because I was interested in the story I lost track of time. When I looked up, the horizon had turned to orange and the vultures were leaving, flying off to some distant roost on a larger island. Whatever they had been watching earlier in the day had either sought cover itself, or been mercifully veiled by the first screen of darkness. I went on typing, grateful for the friendly glow being cast by lamp and fire as I told the story of the dog, a companion in the days of Far Lamorna. *Tonight, I have no companion at all, on this wild and lonely island where the silence is oppressing me.*

I raised my head, and found my companion.

He sat hunched on the other side of the fire and stared at me, gaunt, almost unbelievably emaciated, the tawny coat hanging loose on his once great frame, and the black hairs of his lower mane matted above a shoulder that had been laid open to the bone in some awful encounter. There was a half-healed gash across his forehead, and another gaping wound in his nearside flank at which I did not care to look. Hunting territory – both north and south – but these were not gunshot wounds. Bloody testimony to the scimitar horns of a sable? A buffalo would have inflicted similar injuries. This was the wild avenging the wild, where only the fit survive. The vultures had said that he was not surviving, but dying instead of slow starvation because he was unfit to hunt.

For a moment I sat petrified, incapable of action, as my conjectures chased themselves for those first, frozen seconds. I knew lions. I had lived among them, kept them in domesticity, and learnt love, respect and fear. I knew enough to predict their moods from those candid, undissembling eyes. I looked, and predicted.

'*Coming,*' the baleful yellow eyes said, attenuating to slits. He drew back his lips, exposing enormous canines, and as the muscles on his shoulders flexed I reached instinctively for one of the tsessebe haunches that I'd propped against the cold box. I hurled it towards him with the adrenalin strength of panic, and he caught it as it hit the ground, good shot, just in front of him. As he pawed at it I turned and sprang for the mochaba tree under which I'd slept away the earlier afternoon heat. The camp bed, set on uneven ground, crumpled as I stepped on it, and as I grabbed for the nearest of the lower branches I felt a searing pain behind my left armpit as a muscle tore.

Mercifully, the tree was easy to climb, because the trunk had bifurcated a few feet from the ground, but it was difficult to see the best handholds in the half-darkness above the glow cast by the pressure lamp. I groped blindly, using my sense of touch. My right arm was still sound, but I needed both hands if I was to drag myself clear of the lion's reach, and every time I was compelled to use the left I felt a new and brutal shaft of pain. My heart was labouring, and I breathed in short, hard sobs.

The bark tore my fingers and there was a red-hot burning on the inner side of my left thigh, where I had scraped away the skin at some stage. But by this time my mind had begun to shut out all feelings, all thoughts that were not concentrated on the absolute need to find a safe refuge. I was thirty feet above ground now, and there were no more branches within reach on that side of the tree. I edged out towards the tapered end where the leaves began, and as I did so I heard the lion leap for the tree, not scrambling up the trunk as I had done but springing for the first of the lateral branches. His hunched shoulders rose above the circle of light, and he grunted as his forepaws gripped.

Lions can climb. I remembered, too vividly now, the games that I used to play with Chink, competing to see which of us could get highest. Young lions can get up trees quite easily, but 'this lion is not young,' I reassured myself. 'This lion is also wounded, odds in my favour. But this lion is starving, reduce the odds, and because of his hunger he has lost any remnants of the fear he might once have felt for human beings.' As I reached the end of my branch, I twisted round to see what was happening below. He had gained a foothold, and was standing with his hind paws on the lower branch, rearing up for the next rung in the ladder.

The tree shook, and I clung with both hands to stop myself from falling. I anticipated rather than saw the gathering of muscles that launched him on his second leap, and heard his claws rasping through bark, two branches below my own. But either he misjudged his spring, or he slipped, or the wounded shoulder would not sustain his weight, for he crashed back through twigs and leaves, ten feet, a broken fall, then an almighty cracking of wood as the branch he had hit gave way, and he fell another ten feet to hit the ground, the breath driven out of him in a long sigh.

238

For a few moments he lay still, winded, then he swayed to his feet, dazed, his head hanging, facing away from me now, and I could see again the terrible wound in his flank. Small leaves drifted down, glinting where the lamplight hit them, spiralling gracefully down in a tunnel of light. Small, inconsequential impressions. The lion, standing head-down by the fire. The wreckage of the camp bed. The overturned table, and the typewriter on the ground. Every detail now indelibly etched on my mind.

For a while, he ignored my tree. Instead, he walked over to sniff at the remains of the tsessebe bone and then turned to inspect the second haunch, which had fallen into the embers. He hooked it out, picked it up in his teeth and shook it free from charcoal.

He ate the meat and when he had finished it he washed himself, chest and forepaws first, then the wounds in flank and shoulder, snarling with pain. When he had completed his toilet he lay down, dropped his head on his outstretched forepaws and went to sleep.

I looked up into the sky, trying to gauge time by the stars and wishing that I could see my watch, a new one and set expensively with garnets, but damn-all use in the dark. Ten o'clock? Eight hours to go until morning, and two more hours after that before the sun would be hot enough to drive him to cover. Ten hours in all. Far away across the swamps there was a luminous glow at the edge of the world. Moonrise. How long between one moonrise and the next? I longed for it to bring light to my tree, where the darkness was almost worse than the waiting.

I moved slightly, easing cramps, and the lion raised his head, his jaws open in a soundless snarl.

An hour later, the ants found me; a swarming, unstoppable horde of midget stormtroopers that worked their way into my ears, hair and nostrils, and clustered eagerly round the blood on my grazed thigh. They squirmed into my shirt and I peeled it off – dangerous on the insubstantial branch – and tried to rub them away soundlessly, because the lion was back on his feet. He looked up once and then away, staring out over the swamps, his ears forward in response to some sound that had eluded me. I heard it the second time, the rallying cry of a wild dog pack on the mainland across the channel, perhaps a mile away, the sharp, half-musical 'Coo-eee, coooo-eeee?' carrying over water. A momentary diversion, nothing more. The lion lay down again.

The fire burnt itself out but there was moonlight now, a white radiance outside the glow still cast by the kerosene pressure lamp – nothing quite in shadow except for the forest itself, which the shadows never left, even by day. The ants increased and a few of them, the bigger ones, began to bite in earnest. I knew about lions, but I didn't know how to deal with an onslaught of ants, and

239

certainly I was beginning to understand this particular lion. He was playing the patient game, the waiting game, the stare-it-out game, and it would last until he grew tired of waiting. I wondered how long it would be before he picked me off my branch as cleanly as a monkey picking a ripe fig.

He was beginning to grow restless again, perhaps because his wounds had made him feverish. Suddenly he stood up, grunted twice, and walked abruptly off into the darkness between the deserted camp and the river.

If there was to be any chance of surviving the rest of the night I had to act now and, at last, I knew what I had to do. The shotgun was down on the ground, next to the wrecked bed. I had needed both hands in order to scale the tree unencumbered, and I could not, even if time allowed, climb it again with the gun. But I could tie the long bedding rope round the trigger guard and haul the weapon up after me.

Shaking, I edged back into the sheltering darkness until I could feel the reassuring bulk of the trunk against my back. I cannot now remember precisely, even vaguely, how I managed it, because my movements were executed at panic speed, and only two things stand out clearly in my recollections of that scrambling descent. One was putting my hand into yet another nest of ants, which did not sting but squelched messily, almost making me lose my grip. The other was a fruit bat, flying out of the night straight for my face and turning when it was only a fraction of a second away. I screamed, but soundlessly.

Lechwe stampeded near the river as I dropped to earth. I moved speedily, ripping the canvas cover off the gun, shoving four cartridges into the pocket of my shorts and then threading the slippery nylon rope through the trigger guard before tying the other end to my wrist. I now knew roughly the route I needed to take back up to my refuge, but I was hampered by the uncoiling rope and the bulk of the shells in my pocket. By the time I reached my branch I was choking with pain and fear. I straddled the bough, breathed deeply, and then threw up, violently.

When the nervous retching finally subsided the cold of the swamp night hit me. I shook most of the ants out of my shirt and put it on again, but it was far too thin to give much protection. Shivering, I began to draw the gun up through the lower branches, terrified each time that it snagged, and dizzy when it spun giddily at the end of the line. At last it was within reach of my hand and I grabbed at it, missed, and grabbed again, successfully. I looped the rope through a fork in the branches, leaving enough slack to make the gun manoeuvrable if I needed it in a hurry, but then doubts began to take over. 'Look,' I thought, 'if I do fire this gun, the recoil is

240

going to knock me out of the tree, and that will be that, with or without the lion.' I felt for my cigarette lighter, flipped it open and burnt through the rope, made the shorter end holding the Bonehill fast and then lashed myself round the waist to the vertical column of the trunk behind me. Even if the recoil dislodged me, I couldn't fall far now. Then I loaded the 12-bore and held it crosswise on the infinity of branch before me, still on its improvised lead.

The lion had not reappeared but the sentinels of night said that he was on the move: alarmed snorting of lechwe, chicker of what I took to be a cane rat foraging in the reeds, unexpected clinkings from guinea fowl disturbed in the bushes near the river; a sound-track of lion movement, marking the progress of the hunter.

Two o'clock by the moon. Ten minutes later the pressure lamp wheezed, faded and then died as the paraffin ran out, and although the meadows beyond were still white with moonlight, the darkness beneath the tree was absolute. Five minutes later the lion returned, and this time he did not hesitate. The waiting time was over and he began to climb purposefully, working out each move in advance. First branch up, easy, turn to the right from the bifurcation, pausing to draw breath before reaching for the second branch, less easy now, but making it after some slipping and scrambling. There was a strong liony smell coming up to me now, three branches above him, and perhaps this was my last real chance of life.

The metal of the long-barrelled Bonehill was cold to the touch. I made sure that the knot was clear of the trigger, drew the smooth wooden stock against my cheek. There was a rasping of claws on bark as the lion began to scrabble upwards once more, and the smell was stronger, more immediate, a nauseating compound of blood and urine. In my insecure position it was impossible for me to aim at all accurately, pointing the gun straight downwards and slightly off centre. I had four shells – two to frighten, two to kill.

I used the first one.

The night exploded and the hammer-blow punch of the stock against my injured shoulder made me yell with pain, repeated when the force of the recoil knocked me backwards and the rope around my waist jerked tight. Automatically, my fingers snatched at the second trigger and there was a dull click. Misfire. I did not think I had hit him the first time but he crashed back to the ground, roar and crash and roar again, and was gone in an immensity of sound that left the night shocked and still and quiet behind him.

For the second time that night my stomach rebelled and I threw up again, pain, the cold and fear taking an acrid toll that left me limp and shaken. After ten minutes I broke open the gun, ejecting the one spent shell and the one dud one, but not reloading, simply because my hands would no longer work. I did not think the lion would come again in the dead hours before dawn and I closed my eyes, trying to blank out the memory of that contorted, vengeful face and the gaping shoulder.

I dozed, but sporadically, waking every time I slipped forward and the rope bit into me. Three o'clock, four o'clock, dead quiet, moon well over to the west now. Lions calling, a long way off, the hunting hour and time for vigilance. But I was too tired for vigilance, and the gun dangled at the end of the rope, unattended.

Dawn came, a milky thinning of the moonlight at first and then a greyness sliding into soft sulphur. Birds arrived with it, not vultures but plump red-headed barbet birds that pecked at the fig fruit. There was a fresh vividness of sunlight now in the outer meadows but no lightening in the forest as yet. What was that? Flecked black and white, cheerful porcupine making for home.

I do not remember precisely how long I stayed up the tree, but I do recall vividly that I never considered making a second descent. I was too fatigued, too vulnerable, and above all I knew that once I was back on the ground I wouldn't have the power to climb back a third time. So I waited. Towards noon the shadows pooled under bushes, as if they too were trying to escape the heat, and my thirst became almost unendurable. My tongue rasped drily against the roof of my mouth. The ants made another sortie, and then the flies came. Peering down, I noted absently that the tree was oozing droplets of sap round claw marks and small splintered holes where shotgun pellets had punched into it. No blood, so at least I hadn't hit him, or at least not mortally. And there were no vultures circling the island. Had he gone for good? I hoped he had gone, but I couldn't be certain. Lechwe passed, walking sedately on their way to water, and a green pigeon called in successive ricochets of notes.

By three in the afternoon I was, I suppose, approaching delirium, tortured by thirst and beginning to see strange, vivid whorls and zigzags about behind my eyelids.

At three o'clock I heard the roar of the outboard coming downstream, but I did not see *Fleur-de-Lys* arrive, because I fainted.

★   ★   ★

Confusion. Incomprehension. Shouting. More pain, and a sensation of swinging in a halter, rope around my chest cutting into my armpits. Somebody saying something urgent, hands guiding my feet from foothold to foothold. A sense of overwhelming relief as I was lowered gently to the ground, and sobbing gratitude for the wet cloth being wiped round my lips, and the first taste of water trickling into my mouth from a mug that someone was holding.

242

Tris? I think it was Tris who sponged the coagulated blood from my thigh, and later held half a cup of brandy to my lips. I gagged at the raw unpleasantness of the spirit, and found the strength to protest.

'I don't want . . .!'

'Oh, for Chrissake, mother! Just drink it. Dad's gone off with the rifle, looking for your friend.' I didn't remember saying anything about the lion, or why I'd been up the tree, but I suppose I must have. Tris lifted me gently on to the reassembled camp bed and then squatted on the ground, holding my hand.

Had I told them what had happened, I mumbled, presently. No. Then how . . .?

'Shit,' he said. 'I've seen enough lion shit over the last four years to be able to recognize it without a lot of trouble. Or do you think it was a *mouse* that left that pile of crap under the tree?'

When I woke, the kettle was spitting on the fire, and fish were frying in the pan. 'Small-mouthed bream,' observed Tris. 'Caught them on the way down. River's stiff with them.' Then he added, as an afterthought, 'Pity you weren't with us, really.'

When Robert returned he was soaked in sweat, and his trousers were wet to the knees, as if he'd been wading. I hadn't been able to eat, but I was taking gulps of scalding hot, sweet coffee.

'Did you see him?'

'No, not a sign of him, but I did find pug marks leading down to the water on the far side. There's an easier crossing there, to one of the bigger islands. But we're not going to spend another night here. Tris – let's start packing up. We haven't much time.'

Time, again. How to define it? It was purely relative, and it could only be measured by the events that took place within each span of minutes. They could add up to ten hours until morning, or the few moments that it took to leave the Ruby Island diminishing in the wake astern of the boat until it became just another island-outline in the many outlines of the lonely delta.

Seven Fingers of Gin

'*The District Commissioner intends taking Gwai [Kwai] as hunting grounds for Safari South and other hunting parties from outside N'gamiland. He intends building hotels, bars and cafes entirely for whites and non-whites will not be permitted to hunt there.*

'*I deeply feel that this injustice can only be remedied by having the*

Batuana and the other people in this land keep and preserve the animals against this intrusion.'

K. OAKENG, CHIEF'S REPRESENTATIVE AT
SHAKAWE, AS REPORTED BY MONTSO MOGALAKWE

'Ma Tau, would there be just one small drink in that bottle for an old man who has travelled many miles to spread the preservation gospel?'

We were sitting outside the tent on the island. Montso Mogalakwe had a heroic passion for gin. He poured himself a modest five fingers of Gilbey's London Dry, puffed contentedly at his pipe and settled back into his chair while I continued to read his report on the tribal reaction to the game reserve idea.

It was an astonishing document. Mog was the society's local propaganda officer, and he had coursed through the villages like a bloodhound, rounding up all the elders and forcing them to listen to an exhaustive translation of the entire eight pages of the society's constitution. No one was spared the ordeal: Batauana, Herero, Mambukushu, Barotse, Mbadi and Masarwa – all had been endlessly harangued about the purpose and plans of the FCS, and all the audiences had responded with their own voluble comments, spiced with several bitterly libellous remarks about certain British officials.

African thinking can be curiously oblique at times. Begin a debate on a single, isolated issue, and the discussion will soon drift off to something which – to the Western mind – has nothing at all to do with the matter in hand, and yet will eventually prove to be wholly germane to the subject. By the time I'd finished trying to unravel all the subtleties in Mog's report, something that had seemed, on the face of it, a clear-cut issue about preserving the threatened fauna had somehow resolved itself into three separate disputes, each of which now had its own enthusiastic following.

First of all, the government was resonantly castigated for a whole series of unrelated disasters, including an outbreak of foot-and-mouth disease and the failure of the rains, and only as an afterthought condemned for gross incompetence in the matter of game conservation.

Next, and much more disturbingly, a group of elders unearthed the details of a plan by the British administration to lease out the Kwaai valley to safari firms – without troubling to consult the tribe which actually owned the land.

At least that did lead to the final point, when all the contending voices declared that, rather than accept the government's leasing plan, the entire area should be declared a tribal game reserve, where nobody at all was allowed to hunt.

But in traditional Africa there were never any short cuts to the ultimate destination.

★ ★ ★

I lay awake for a long time that night, pondering the implications of Mog's report. So far, he'd achieved an outstanding success, but – he had not yet approached the Bayei. They were a huge tribe, as numerous as fireflies in November and, scattered throughout the delta, just as elusive. If they could not be won over, then there would be no reserve – whatever anyone else wanted, and however deftly Isaac juggled with the truth. The facts of the matter were that the tribe was not only large and widely spread, they were also cruelly poor, and revenue from the hunting parties would help to finance the impoverished Protectorate.

It would also – and this was by far the most important factor for the Administration – Save the British Taxpayer Money. As for the animals, they could fend for themselves.

I had another sleepless night after Jack Ramsden managed (and I never asked how) to obtain a copy of a letter the DC had written to his masters in Mafeking. In it, he reported sourly that the Kays gave indecorous parties and 'held drunken orgies on the island for the tribesmen.' I was so incensed by all this that I poured Mog an extra slug of gin the next time he visited the camp. He fell into the river when the boat arrived to take him home.

'I am one of those people who says very little . . .'

Ploughing time was over. The corn was beginning to tassel in the home fields of the men who had returned to the grimy factories or the gold mines. The yellow dogs were masterless again, and bright-necked gamecocks pecked and strutted in the dust around the old women who sat listlessly weaving grass baskets in the shade of the empty huts at Zankuio. The hunters had taken their spears, and the younger women, and gone back to the game country, where the restlessness of the autumn rut was building up in the red impala herds of the Kwaai valley. The rams were sparring for territory, and the sand was churned up by the incessant slither of fighting hooves.

The date was the tenth of March 1963, and in five days the Kgotla was due to sit. There were five months of exhaustive toil behind us – and the Bayei had returned to Maun.

Eight of them strolled into camp that night, with an excitable little Herero in tow, and flanked by Jack, Isaac, Michael and Mog.

At that time, Africans used to pass on the tribal histories and traditions from generation to generation by word of mouth and, like the minstrels of medieval Europe, the tribal bards were men of status. So, until the early missionaries determined, in their iconoclastic zeal, to smash the old gods and replace them with a pitiful sacrifice nailed to a cross, there was no written language. For millennia, peoples north of the Equator had been recording the events of the day on stone, clay tablets or papyrus, but until the middle of the nineteenth century, when they were introduced to the Written Word, Africans in the south and east of the continent learned of their past from the spoken sagas.

The Bayei, especially, were renowned as inexhaustible talkers, but even so I was in no way prepared for the spate of richly embroidered arguments that were tossed back and forth over the orange flicker of the campfire.

'I am one of those people who says very little,' announced the first speaker modestly, rolling each syllable around his tongue in happy articulation, 'and I have not much to speak. But it is in my head that . . .'

It was still in his head *that* a full two hours later, but he eventually yielded the floor and sat down to a burst of applause from everyone except the second speaker, who had been clearing his throat in anticipation for the past hour and fifty minutes.

He, too, turned out to be a man who said very little. At the end of *his* second hour he still hadn't got beyond the point where his aunt's favourite cow, which had died of malnutrition in 1925, would have been alive and mooing still if the game reserve had been created, or there had been a different District Commissioner in charge.

By this time, speaker number three was snoring, so speaker number four seized the heaven-ordained opportunity to tell us at length how his sleeping friend had once served a term in jail for shooting a giraffe on Crown lands. He then went on to extol the ideals of conservation in a crisp ninety-minute speech, during which speaker number five succumbed to the drink and had to be carried away, and speaker number six, coming back from a call to water the forest, tripped and fell full-length over Dingo, who bit him in the leg.

Speaker number seven was lying quietly on the ground. He appeared to be dead. And then the real drama began.

I had spent most of my time among the Christianized Batauana, so I had forgotten just how deeply the Bayei were still involved with the practice of sorcery. After the customary applause there was a sudden, inexplicable pause.

As if they'd been dragged round by a powerful magnet, the remaining speakers turned to stare intently at the eighth man, the quiet one who had simply sat gazing into the fire, with his hands folded in his lap, throughout this interminable night, never once showing the slightest reaction to what was being said. Now, abruptly, he got to his feet, and a small knot of ice formed around my heart. It was Tamai, whom Isaac had once described lightly as 'the understudy witchdoctor'. It was Tamai, who had – indirectly, through Tagaan – counselled Mog to cut the kidney fat from the little herd-boy, the son of their enemy. It was Tamai who now spoke softly and compellingly.

'Look at me,' he said. He made a small gesture with his hands, the long, expressive fingers weaving patterns like the slow coils of a viper marking a trail in the dust. The Bayei were mesmerized. Jack, Isaac and Michael avoided his glance, and I wondered whether they also feared being drawn into that serpent's embrace.

'You know me,' the speaker continued, 'and his audience nodded apprehensively. 'You know my power. I am Tamai. Listen to me carefully, now, so you will know what I wish.' Then he turned to Robert, with a small, rare smile. 'Although you have a white skin, Ra Tau, you have African blood in your heart, so it is the African in you who urges us to preserve the game.'

He cupped his hands together. 'Look at me,' he said and, twitching nervously, the group round the fire obeyed. 'I have all my porridge in my hands. If I eat it all now, then there will be none left tomorrow. It is better to have ten shillings every day for ever than to have ten pounds now and nothing more when it has been spent. So, it is better to care for the game, instead of selling it for a big price to the Safari Lion at the Kgotla.' He gazed for a brief moment at each of the group in turn, and then concluded: 'I am Tamai, and I have said all that I came here to say.'

'Eh-*hey*!' they all chorused, and there was a shivering terror in the cry.

Jack Ramsden stood up. He was shaking a little, and his skin had turned the colour of milky chocolate. 'The Bayei have spoken,' he said, in the necessary, formal acknowledgement, and then added with deep feeling: 'This is the first time in many years that the Batauana and the Bayei have been able to agree on a common issue. The feuds are behind us. The Bayei will support the reserve.'

The Tribal Council

One afternoon, as I sat sketching in the dappled shade outside my reed-built office, I heard a swish of leaves and an animal broke out of the forest on the far side of the clearing. It was a young Chobe bushbuck ram. For a moment he stood frozen, russet body incandescent with sunlight. Then Leonard, who had been setting fishing lines in the river, came scrambling up the bank.

'Hunters!' he gasped. 'Four hunters! I saw them!'

He raced across and tried to head the ram down towards the far end of the island, but he was too late and the young animal bolted back, disappearing among the trees. A moment later, we heard shots.

The hunters, whoever they were, did not even bother to collect the carcass. I found my young ram lying in the sedge beside the water, where he had dragged himself to die. One of his hind legs had been blasted into a hideous pulp, and there was blood seeping from the shotgun pellet wounds in his flank.

There were three days to go, now, until the Kgotla sat. And we still had to face the Tribal Council.

★   ★   ★

The Tribal Council, which was loosely based on the House of Lords, was composed entirely of influential elders and sub-chiefs, and acted as a steering committee between the Paramount Chief or his representatives on one hand, and the tribesmen – the 'electorate' – on the other. In some circumstances, it actually had the power to overrule the Chief himself. The chairman was Badirwăn Sekao.

On the day before the Kgotla was to gather, the Council met behind locked doors in the empty schoolhouse. The wrangling had lasted four hours.

'You have said that the creation of a game reserve should await the return of our Chief. By that logic, so must all the other cases. So we, who were appointed to act while he was absent, must judge no more cases of stock rustling, theft or even murder until Letsholathebe is with us again. You may all have to wait for justice!' There were times when Badirwăn could have intimidated a rogue elephant. Now, he had had enough of it all. He slammed his hat on his head and stormed out of the meeting. Presently the elders, shamefaced, trickled after him.

'So – what happens tomorrow?' I asked Michael Dithapo as we
followed them out.

'Murder, probably,' he said.

The March Kgotla

The crowd assembled under the Kgotla trees were sitting twenty
deep, and they were very quiet, gleaming with sweat on a burning-
glass morning. I looked around for familiar faces. Tamai, leader of
the Bayei, touched two fingers to his forehead in greeting. 'Good
day, Ma Tau.' The Queen Regent, cool in a floral cotton print, her
hands folded neatly in her lap. The District Commissioner, eyes a
glassy blank, impeccably dressed in a suffocating dark suit. Jack
Ramsden, never less than dapper. Mog, drawing contentedly on
his pipe and trying hard to hide the half-jack bottle of gin that he'd
sensibly tucked into the folds of his jacket. Isaac Tudor, watching
– and watching. 'Rocks' Ledimo the schoolmaster, surreptitiously
rereading the last chapter in his well-thumbed copy of *White Fang*,
and crying quietly when he recalled how the wolves had eaten Bill.
Beloved Badirwãn, craggy face shaded by a wide-brimmed hat.

'I greet the tribe, and I greet the Mother of the People.'
Jack Ramsden opened the proceedings with his customary grave
courtesy, and then went on to review all the arguments in favour
of a game reserve. It was a good start, a sound start – and yet the
moment he resumed his seat there was a murmur of angry opposition from his audience.

*'Did the idea that our wild life might be exterminated come from
yourselves, or perhaps from the white man in white clothes, who is
called Ra Tau? Why do you listen to him, when you know he is a
government man?'*

'He is not a government man!' Jack snapped back, stung by the
grotesque unfairness of the accusation. 'He is just' – he cast about
for the right description – 'he is just a man who lives with a lion
under a tree!'

Some of the tribesmen laughed, but there was an uneasy under-
tone to it.

*'Did you appoint this white man, Ra Tau, to go and find out that our
game was getting finished?'*

'No. He went by himself, and he saw the waste. I have also
seen it.'

'And, before he told you about it, what did you do about this waste?'

Jack winced, but he did not try to evade the question. 'We did nothing,' he admitted, and there was an honest sorrow in his voice. 'No, we did not know that we were squandering our inheritance, until he brought us to the light.'

The DC looked up sharply and then, smiling to himself, scribbled something down in a notebook.

'Oh, Jack!' I thought. 'Please, *please*, stay clear of the Bible. Men have been crucified for "bringing people to the light". That's just the sort of phrase that'll get him thrown out of the Protectorate as a dangerous revolutionary if ever Mafeking gets to hear of it.'

'The ways of white people are always devious. By what token can you be sure that this man, Ra Tau, has not told you lies? In fact, does he not belong to one of those same professional firms we call "the Safari Lion", who are trying to rob us of our game at this very moment? If this thing, this plan, comes to pass, will it interfere with our hunting rights outside the reserve? Can you promise that the reserve will belong to the tribe for ever – or will the government try to steal it from us?'

And so on, and on.

An ancient creaked to his feet. 'I am an old man. I am a very old man indeed. I am so old that everybody else is dead.' His voice quavered out in the still morning, and Michael muttered 'Senile!' between clenched teeth. 'I am so old,' the antique voice continued, 'so old that I do not know what to say about this game reserve, and therefore I say "No!" I hear what is spoken, but I do not understand it, and because that is so I think that we should not be in a hurry over this matter. Why do we not wait for the return of our Chief before we make a decision?' he concluded plaintively.

There was a murmur of approval, and Jack had to struggle to conceal his vast irritation. 'And when our Chief Letsholathebe returns,' he enquired silkily, 'shall he say to us "I left you with much game, but where is it now?" And then will he ask you, "What have you done with all my game, you *very old* man? Is it because of you, because you stood in the path of those of my people who were ready to protect it?" '

Doubt, now. Dissent. Argument. A flood of hostile comment on the hated Safari Lion, punctuated with acrid criticism of the almost equally detested Game Department. There were even poorly camouflaged suggestions of bribery in the government service. I looked at my watch. Noon. High noon.

One of the Bayei rose, and looked majestically about him.

'I am one of those people who has not much to say, and I will speak in short,' he announced confidently. 'What I say . . .'

We never got to hear what he had to say, because Tamai leaned over and, with a terrible smile, whispered something into his ear. The man sat down at once, a sickly expression on his face.

Then came the first flickers of support. An elder named Harry rumbled, 'Even one man can cause great damage to the game, so how can we preserve it when the Safari Lion is loose in our territory?'

'When the High Commissioner, Sir John Maude, came here, he said that you can't shoot an animal more than once, but you can photograph it as often as you want,' said Michael Dithapo. 'So the tourists can come and photograph all our wonderful animals without harming them, and bring us revenue at the same time. If later on we see that the reserve is hurting the tribe in any way we can always cancel the scheme, but in the meantime we must act now, before the outsiders do so much damage that it can never be made good.'

Then everyone had something to say. Make the reserve big enough to provide sanctuary for animals that have fled the guns of the hunters. This plan gives the tribes sole control which they do not need to share with whites. The wise man protects his own cattle, the foolish man leaves them unguarded. Our children will thank us, and the reserve will be entirely in our own hands, so that we can change the laws later on if we want to – although I do not think that we will want to.

'The law that you make for yourself sits less heavily on the shoulders than the law which is forced on you by others.'

In a single word, '*Uhuru*'. This is what Africa means by 'freedom'. Good or bad, the only acceptable laws are those that she makes for herself.

Then, without warning, the debate ended. The Queen Regent had risen from her seat, and in the hushed seconds that followed, the shadow of an eagle raced across the sand. Somewhere, a long way off, an iron cow-bell clanged, and the sound of children laughing drifted up from the river. A boy rode by on a donkey, staring wide-eyed at his elders, and I was startled by the unexpected pricking of tiny claws as Isis crept warily onto my lap. I ran my fingers down her bright fur, waiting, wondering what Elizabeth Moremi was going to say.

'There are always a few who disagree,' she remarked equably. 'When a girl wishes to get married, for instance, all her relatives are called together, and some of them will complain that the bride price is not high enough, but in the end the girl still marries. We should praise the members of the Fauna Conservation Society. I wish that God's light may be with them in the future.'

In a single body, the tribesmen rose respectfully to their feet. I looked blankly at Michael Dithapo, and he smiled seraphically.

'*Yes!* The answer is *yes!* That was her way of saying it. The reserve is approved, and the Kgotla is dismissed. You can go home now.'

But I did not go home, not immediately. Instead, I drove to the camp that we'd set up in the valley of the Kwaai, a place known as The Elephant Crossing. There was a lion I knew who lived there, and I wanted to tell him that he was free.

The Menace of Victory

The Moremi was the first of the game reserves to be wholly African-sponsored, and its creation left the tribesmen in a curiously captious and turbulent frame of mind. They were elated, of course, but all the same there was an element of menace in their jubilation and they remained implacably bitter towards all those who had once seemed to stand in their way.

The safari companies and the government between them reaped the full harvest of that pent-up resentment. The Africans had tasted honey for the first time in decades, and they found it intoxicatingly sweet.

It was at this crucial moment, when minds were already inflamed by suspicion and general animosity, that the Administration committed a truly monumental gaffe.

News leaked out that certain of the British officials had blithely taken it upon themselves to sign agreements with various safari firms, giving them extensive hunting concessions. They had not troubled to inform the tribes of this fact, let alone bothered to consult them in any way. The safari companies had, in turn, swiftly accepted firm bookings from clients for the 1963 season, built a series of base camps, and spent a good deal of the advance payments on equipment, fuel stores, canned luxury foods and various provisions, including the most vital of all: booze. They certainly did not give much weight to the fact that the contracts had not been countersigned by the Batauana.

If N'gamiland had been Kenya, the Congo or somewhere like Algeria – and if the Batauana hadn't been, at heart, a peaceable and law-abiding folk – if the Queen Regent and Badirwän Sekao had not had so sure a grasp – a lot of blood would have flowed. The tribesmen were certain that they had been cynically betrayed, and their rage became almost uncontrollable. The crowds that had once celebrated their triumph were suddenly transformed into bitter and unforgiving mobs.

We were relaxing quietly with the first, blissful drink of the evening when a runner came down to the island with a note for Robert from the District Commissioner. The word 'URGENT' was scrawled in capitals across one corner of the envelope. Robert was wanted at the Residency.

The DC turned out to be in a highly unstable frame of mind. Near to outright hysteria, he informed Robert shrilly that if the Batauana rejected the safari agreements at this stage it would put him personally in what he tremulously described as 'a very difficult position' with the Colonial Office. His masters in Whitehall would blame him for allowing matters to get so far out of hand, and if as a consequence of tribal obduracy the whole hunting scheme were to crash then he would be compelled to hand them his resignation and face a life of disgrace. Moreover, the safari companies could – no, they most certainly *would* – file an enormous claim for damages against the British government. In the circumstances, would Robert help him out of the impasse?

The antipathy between the two men was as volcanic as ever, but Robert had admitted to himself that there was a certain merit in allowing professional safari outfits to operate in the swamps, provided that they were strictly supervised. It would at least reduce, and fairly drastically, all the haphazard shooting and trapping of the past. It would also pour a great deal of money into the tribal coffers.

Robert sought out Jack Ramsden and Michael Dithapo, and the three of them called on Elizabeth Moremi. She seemed, Robert told me later, to have been expecting them.

'Badirwān has been here already,' she said briskly. 'He tells me that the feeling against the government is very high, and I do *not* want a revolution on my hands. Go and talk to him, and see what he suggests.'

Fires danced and flickered throughout the village and dark figures moved against them in silhouette. From where the crowd was thickest they could hear Badirwān's stentorian bellow. Isaac Tudor was standing at the outer edge of the circle, with his hands on his hips. He seemed to be amused.

'Old Blood-and-Thunder is really on the warpath tonight,' he told the trio. 'He has promised to send any man who dares to light even one little match anywhere near the blue touch-paper straight to jail for a long stay. Just listen to him now – he sounds as sweet-tempered as a wounded buffalo. He *knows* just how bad the tribe feels about what's been done to them, but he can't allow the situation to develop into bloody riots by agreeing too openly.'

And he added, angrily, 'I just hope that those damn-fool officials are having a good night's sleep, because if Badirwān fails to impose some kind of order here it could be their last.' He stretched himself, yawned, and smiled. 'If you're still around by breakfast time, come to my house for coffee.' Then he laughed, and slouched off into the darkness.

The tribe was indeed red raw with anger. After they'd spoken to Badirwān the three men went on to plead with the Bayei chief, before visiting every influential elder that they could find. It was dawn by the time they reached home, and they were just able to snatch two hours of sleep before they had to attend a second, emergency session of the Kgotla.

The DC got the reception he had earned. He made a speech that was almost embarrassingly ingratiating, and halfway through his near-apology a group of thirty elders, led by Badirwān, got to their feet and walked over to the fence of the nearby cattle kraal, where they urinated noisily, and in concert. It was the deadliest possible insult.

But somehow Jack Ramsden managed to soothe the irate gathering. A little before noon, the last of the bitterness about the safari concessions began to fade, and in the end the agreements were sanctioned.

'The people who work for the Tsetse Fly Control kill the flies as slowly as possible so that they will last a long time,' one of the elders remarked stonily. 'That is the way they keep their jobs. We hope that the safari companies will also kill game slowly, and keep their concessions.'

The Flaming Torches

It was decided, with universal approval, to name the new reserve in honour of the Royal House of Moremi. An area of 700 square miles had been set aside for the sanctuary, and it was bordered on the north by the Kwaai River and on the south by the N'goha, with the lovely Ruby Island of the Monachira set like a jewel at the western apex.

However, it was one thing to define the reserve, quite another to ensure that everyone respected it. Within two days of the Kgotla, the redoubtable Kweri was called in from Zankuio and offered the post of Chief Game Warden. He accepted, with huge delight, and at once began to plan his tactics for enforcing compliance. He was a born showman, and he used his talent to devise a scheme that would register the fact of the area's new and protected status in the most dramatic fashion.

For over two centuries, the Masarwas had built a grass-thatched hunting encampment in the heart of the Kwaai valley every year. This year, though, Kweri imperiously ordered the evacuation of the entire village. Then, while the hunters and their followers watched in some awe, he put a match to a torch made of dried grass and ran through the deserted encampment setting light to the huts one by one. Finally, he flung the burning brand into the last of the shacks and stood back to watch the flames roar into the sky until the wooden walls crumbled away and the entire settlement was reduced to a pile of smouldering ash. If I close my eyes, now, I can still smell the pungent woodsmoke of that first act of constructive demolition, and see the horde of black drongos that came fluttering through the haze, hawking for the insects that had been driven from their homes in the crevices of the thatch.

The hunting parties, which had been so summarily evicted before their temporary homes were razed, were bundled across to the north bank of the Kwaai, outside the confines of the Moremi, and told to get on with building themselves a new village for what was left of the season. A week later, when the huts had been more or less completed, and the thatching of the roofs could be left to the women, the men were called away to a new project: cutting down termite-resistant mopani poles to serve as stilts for the treetop observation tower which Kweri, in his new and shining status, was going to use as a command post.

Before the work had been quite completed, a pride of lions strolled over to inspect the site and sent Mrewa's terrified wife scuttling up a tree. Mrewa lost his temper and took a shot at one of them, for which he was fined £2 and had his Martini-Henry confiscated for a month.

Green Velvet Safari

Not long after I'd returned from the Kwaai, Isaac strode down to the camp carrying the school exercise book in which he painstakingly noted down the proceedings of the Fauna Conservation Society. He'd stopped on the way to collect my mail from the post office and, while he warmed his hands on a mug of coffee, I sorted through the letters. Bills, bills, yet more bills, an erratic scrawl from Oliver asking when the mainly black Maun football team was going to play against a 'Guphmint' side, and one airmail letter, addressed in a familiar and beautifully elegant hand. Even before I'd slit it open, I knew what was in it: Hector's engagement had made headlines all round the world.

'Something?' asked Isaac when I put the letter down.

'An old friend of mine is getting married in London next month, but I can't possibly go to the wedding,' I sighed.

'But you *must* go!' retorted Isaac triumphantly. 'We have no money!' He opened his exercise book and ran his finger down a column of figures. The total came to £156, two shillings and six pence, which would not pay the game guards for very long. 'We must also get uniforms for Kweri and Mrewa, so that people will know they are proper officials. We need two Land Rovers for patrolling the boundaries. We have to arm the guards with reliable rifles instead of those dangerous old Martini-Henrys. There is plenty of money in England and I think you should go and find some, even if you have to trek there on foot!' It was an enticing argument, especially since there was real merit in it.

'Some bloody fool is certain to ask what we need rifles in a game reserve *for*,' I countered, but half-heartedly.

'Tell them, for shooting poachers!' he snorted. 'Anyway, now I have to go and inform the committee about your decision.'

Before we left Lamorna I had packed the best of my *haute couture* clothes meticulously, layering them between sheets of tissue paper, and the suitcase had lain in the storage hold of the DUKW for four years unopened. Kisi had some trouble with the locks, which had rusted, but in the end he managed to force them, using Robert's favourite screwdriver. Then my head reeled, and I was almost sick with dismay and disappointment. The whole thing seemed filled to the brim with green mould. Creations by Jacques Fath, Dior, Schiaparelli – all irredeemably ruined. So much for the glamour I'd taken so much for granted before I began bleeding myself to financial death in this damnable swamp.

Kisi must have sensed what I was feeling, and he did his best to divert my attention. '*Shoes*,' he whispered encouragingly. 'You must buy some good shoes.'

In point of fact, I can't now recollect the shoes I bought, but I still cherish the memory of the exquisite green velvet suit, the beautiful white leather coat and the wonderful white meringue of a hat made of sparkling feathers. I paid for them with money I'd squirreled away from my magazine article earnings; I'd learned my lesson, once and for all time, when Robert so airily appropriated my £500 lion cub cheque, and I kept all subsequent payments to myself.

256

For two days and two nights I was shaken and buffeted about in the cargo truck on the road to Bulawayo, sharing a broken mattress with a gloomy refrigeration mechanic, a goat, and several regiments of killer fleas, so I needed another forty-eight hours of complete rest when I reached the city. After a series of ruinously expensive telephone calls I also managed to locate Richard, who had left the *Daily Telegraph* and was now heading the news operation for a television station based in Southampton. His secretary answered my call. Sorry, but Sir was out. A message?

'Just say to please meet my flight from Rhodesia at London Airport the day after tomorrow.'

'And who shall I say was calling?' she asked, suspiciously.

A long time ago Richard and I had found private names for each other in a shared, bawdy and joyous Jewish joke.

'Tell mine Abe that it's Rachael asking,' I told her, and rang off.

★ ★ ★

He was leaning on the security rail in the arrivals hall at Heathrow, and the eight years since our parting flew out of the window and it was yesterday again.

Eventually he released me, and held me at arm's length, taking in every detail of my ensemble. Something seemed to amuse him.

'Dear God!' he exclaimed. 'The humiliations I have to endure for your sake. Only you, my pet, would dare to arrive at the world's busiest airport wearing khaki pants and chukka boots. Mind you, I dare say that outfit is going to make the Hardy Amies set at the wedding bile green with envy. None of them will ever have seen anything like it. Tell me, did you bring a lion's tail fly whisk too?'

Hector's wedding at St Margaret's, Westminster, was a gorgeous, glittering affair, but afterwards I had to face the fact that the money was slithering through my fingers and time was running short. Playtime was over.

A publisher friend had put me in touch with the World Wildlife Fund, and they agreed to stage a press conference for me. Sir Peter Scott, distinguished naturalist son of Scott of the Antarctic, took the chair, and Letsholathebe Moremi caught a train down from Southend-on-Sea to lend me support. The hall in the St Ermyn's Hotel was packed, and there were reporters from almost every newspaper of note in Britain. The journalists all seemed enthusiastic, they asked a lot of sensible questions, and we left the meeting in the sure and certain knowledge that it had been a glowing success.

But it wasn't.

That night, the news of one of the greatest British political scandals this century finally broke after months of teasing rumours. Jack

Profumo, Conservative Minister of Defence, was forced to admit that he had been sharing the favours of Christine Keeler with the Soviet naval attaché. His confessions released all the other djinns from the bottle, and every inch of news space and all the television and radio news time was occupied by slavering details of sexual romps in high – and low – places.

The story of how an African hunting tribe had created a unique and important game reserve didn't rate even a passing mention. Nor could the story hold over, to be revived at a less fevered time.

I might, somehow, have weathered even that calamitous setback, but that wasn't the worst of it. I learned, indirectly, that some of the WWF's *éminences beiges* had been decidedly piqued by Peter Scott's impulsive offer to support the Moremi; I have a feeling that even if he *had* consulted them first they would still have found grounds to reject our appeal, for Bechuanaland was not then one of the 'fashionable' locations. 'Peter damn near got the sack because of you,' my informant told me. Letsholathebe had gone back to Southend. Richard had a demanding job and little spare time. I was on my own again.

With nothing more productive in sight, I borrowed a portable typewriter and sent a sheaf of press releases to the provincial newspapers, and a little money came trickling in. But the real problem, I suppose, was that I was too far ahead of my time. Except in a very limited way, when the more picturesque species were involved, conservation was not an Issue then. Greenpeace was a long way off. Nobody was interested, much, in Animal Rights.

In the end, inspiration dried up. I packed my beloved green velvet suit in more tissue paper, and caught a cheap flight back to Africa.

Where there was more trouble waiting for me.

★   ★   ★

The strip of cleared land that served Maun as an airfield was used for football games between the rare appearances of small planes, and Robert was standing in the hot sun when the little four-seater buzzed in. His greeting was almost offensively offhand, but he shrugged off my questions by saying that the Game Department was conducting another witch-hunt, with himself as the sole suspect. The police had mounted a raid on our island camp, arriving unannounced and in an aggressive mood. They had dug up all the ground round Timber's tree in search of contraband ivory. There had been an extended interrogation into Robert's financial background, covering every detail of his affairs, and pointed questions about his political sympathies. Insults had been lavishly exchanged.

258

It was undoubtedly true that Robert had a transcendent talent for encouraging people to dislike him, but even that could not account for this level of persecution. Somebody, somewhere, was looking for a convincing reason to have him deported from the Protectorate. I tried to cheer him up by telling him about my plans for raising more funds, but he was icily dismissive. A few days later, with little subtlety, he contrived an excuse to drive up to Bulawayo on his own.

Even Dingo didn't seem especially pleased to see me back; like all dogs, he had reacted miserably to the sight of packed suitcases, and was still sulking over my prolonged absence. Worse still, while I'd been in England an outbreak of feline influenza had killed almost every cat in Maun. Isis was one of them.

The Elephant Crossing

When Robert came back from Bulawayo he brought companions with him.

'Remember Emm?' he asked enthusiastically as the boat nudged into the bank. 'You met her at the riding school.'

I did remember Emm, but only vaguely. She was small and dark-haired and she seemed to have more than the normal ration of teeth, but apart from that she was unremarkable: Australian-English, an instructress at the riding stables where we usually stayed when we were in Bulawayo. Robert explained eagerly that there was nothing much for her to do at the school at the moment, because Rhodesia was in the grips of yet another recession and riding lessons came fairly low on everyone's list of priorities; so Emm's boss had suggested a trip to the swamps for Emm and her friend Norah, as unpaying guests of the Kays.

I forebore to enquire further, and it was not until we were back in the Kwaai valley that I began to notice a change in Robert's idiom. When he felt a little below par he told everybody that he was 'feeling crook'. This was not at all like him: he had always reacted violently when the children used slang or showed even the smallest trace of the unlovely Rhodesian accent. He also took to saying 'La-di-da!', for no special reason but with infuriating regularity.

He was imitating Emm.

★　★　★

We camped at the Elephant Crossing, where a ribbon of shining water ran between the molapo and a cluster of islands.

The nearest of these islands was a place of unnerving beauty. Green parrots in their hundreds flew there by day, and strange lilies bloomed on the forest floor. There was a stretch of sand between the tree belt and the river, and at night the moon deflected the shadows of the trees back into forest that stretched for a mile or more inland. The sand ran palely to the water, and it bore the massive indentations made by elephant, and the pugmarks of a solitary lion.

We had named this lion Solomon, and he was the only survivor from a pride of seven that had their territory in the light mopani forest surrounding the KuBu (Hippo) lagoon. Originally, the pride had consisted of a black-maned lion, two lionesses – one well past her prime – and four rumbustious cubs whose undisputed leader was Solomon. Robert and I used to set out meat for them whenever their natural prey had been scattered by hunters, and we watched with dismay as, one after another, they fell victim to the guns of white sportsmen and the steel traps of the Masarwas. But Solomon survived. For two years he managed to evade the traps and rifles, and became a wary loner. Then one night he raided the Bushman village, and that sealed his fate: if he wasn't shot or driven away there was an even chance that he'd turn man-eater. The headman sent us an urgent message and we set out to track the culprit. We found him lying up in the mopani, and we chased him in the Land Rover for two miles, until he streaked through the shallow water of the Elephant Crossing and went into permanent exile on the island.

But he wasn't on his island when we arrived there in the winter dusk of that ill-starred safari in 1963. He was out in the molapo and raising hell in the company of eleven other male lions. It didn't take us long to find out why. A pair of lionesses, both on heat, had stormed out of the forest and called up every male within earshot.

Robert didn't wait to see the camp set up. He jolted past me in the Bedford in a spray of sand and dry grass. Emm-and-her-friend-Norah were standing up in the open back of the vehicle. I doubt whether they knew the risk they were running, and I don't think Robert ever gave the matter a thought – or, if he did, he felt secure in his belief that there was no situation, no danger, that he couldn't handle if the need arose. To be fair, the belief was justified. He was always at his best in an emergency, particularly if it was one he'd engineered himself.

I had to find out what was happening, and I drove the Land Rover slowly back through the trees and out into the molapo. Kisi, huddled beside me, was very quiet but his lips were moving. He appeared to be praying.

We watched the lions for a long time and when, eventually, I turned the car round and headed back to the camp I was instantly aware of a marked coolness in Robert's attitude. I couldn't understand why, but he was clearly not in a mood to talk, and when I asked him whether I'd done anything to make him angry he simply told me to get the hell out of his way. He dragged his mattress out of the tent, taking it right down to the edge of the vlei where the mating game was still very much in progress. It was an insanely reckless thing for him to do, and I said so, but his response was an exasperated curse. I left a rifle with him and went back to my own tent, confused and miserable.

Later in the night, towards the hunting hour, the pride began to move steadily away through the underbrush, a diminishing sound-track of lion movement against the sharp yelping of jackals and the eldritch shrieking of hyena. In the morning, the molapo was empty.

★ ★ ★

We spent two days at the Crossing, then returned to our island base on the Thamalakane. Robert's mood was still fairly lethal and it did not improve after Emm and her monosyllabic chum had departed on the cargo lorry for Bulawayo. We talked to each other only when the situation demanded it, and then in the most formal tones. Most of the time he kept out of my company, and I tried not to intrude on his.

Then, about two weeks later, Robert drove into Maun to fetch supplies, and I decided to catch up with my correspondence. There was a sheet of paper in the typewriter, and on it a half-completed letter.

'. . . but thank God it'll soon be over and once I've finally got rid of her, you and I'll be able to run photographic safaris together, darling.' I read no further.

Darling? Who did he ever call Darling? Emm? Not her inarticulate friend, surely? But that single sentence made one thing brutally clear: he no longer saw any rôle, any place, for me in the Okavango. I had long since stopped weeping over the black rages into which he lapsed whenever anyone trod on his ego, and I had acquired a surface toughness hard enough to deflect his sarcasm and his endless, niggling little criticisms. And certainly, I had learned to do without even the semblance of affection. For a long time now I had tried to avoid an open confrontation, but this new threat I could not ignore.

It was I who had opened up the Kwaai valley with him, I who had worked for the creation of the reserve and raised the money to sustain the long campaign – and it was I who was now about to be summarily dismissed. Robert recognized weaknesses when he saw them. Now that the reserve was an established fact, my services were no longer required.

It was very late when he arrived back and I asked him, still hoping against all hope for a reprieve, for an explanation. He was furious, and refused to discuss the matter. In the morning he demanded a divorce.

'This is *my* show,' he hissed at me, white with resentment. 'Up to now, you've had all the publicity; now it's *my* turn for a taste of honey!' *His show*. It had become a matter of personal glory; he wanted sole credit for the creation of the game reserve. He wanted all the world to associate the DUKW, the camp, the Kwaai – the entire bloody delta – with him, and with nobody else. As far as he was concerned, my contribution had been marginal. I was redundant.

There were to be enough strings to be attached to the divorce proceedings to keep a whole flock of kites in the air. I was on no account to tell anybody about it, least of all our children. I was to go on raising funds for the reserve, though, which was – his old cliché – 'bigger than both of us'. He intended to keep all revenues from the apartment block in Bulawayo, and fifty per cent of any money I might make out of a film about the Moremi. I, on the other hand, was to pay half of all the debts incurred in keeping the DUKW in service. There was to be no question of any alimony, which he couldn't possibly afford to pay. Lastly, would I now get myself and my bull terrier bitch Cats to hell and gone out of the camp by nightfall.

And I let him get away with it. Why? Surprise? Post-shock stupidity? Brainwashing? Whichever it was, it took me the best part of eight years to shed the whole addled philosophy of joy through guilt.

I received the *coup de grâce* when Robert suggested, with all his customary insouciance, that I might like to cast in my lot with one of the white hunters in the delta, and conduct safaris in friendly competition with himself and Emm. That Puckish sense of fun. Anyway, I packed my bags, went to Riley's Hotel for the night, and then started out for Cape Town, ready to ride the propaganda trail once more.

There didn't seem much else I could do.

The Chelsea Cubs

Cats and I found a home with friends, as paying guests, and the excellent Professor 'Fuzz' Crompton of the Cape Town Museum lent me an office, and provided me with a platform. Every night I ran 16 mm wildlife films and lectured to large audiences on the dangers that still threatened the game animals of the delta. The fact that two bitterly hostile tribes had buried their ancient grievances to work together for the Moremi had provided a powerful precedent, I explained fervently, and if it succeeded other sanctuaries would follow. It *had* to succeed, too, but the poverty of the tribesmen had to be taken into account . . .

Somehow, I twanged exactly the right nerve, because the response was instant, and overwhelmingly generous. Money poured in. The great Professor Raymond Dart, who first propounded the theory that the *Australopithecus*, 'Southern Ape', whose skull had been uncovered at Taungs in what used to be British Bechuanaland was one of sapient man's earliest ancestors, lent his considerable authority to the campaign. Ian Player, brother of the golfer Gary, and Senior Ranger of Zululand, was in close touch with several important conservationists, and he introduced me to Ken Tinley, then chief ecologist for the Ngorongoza game reserve in Moçambique, who agreed to carry out a full and proper survey of the Moremi. The work was sponsored by an anonymous Cape Town businessman – who also paid the game guards for the next eight months.

Chris Kavanagh of the *Cape Argus*, Anton Stein of the Afrikaans daily *Die Burger*, Terry Spencer of the old *Life* magazine, Michael Moynihan of the London *Sunday Times*, Harry Parker of the *Friend Newspapers* in Bloemfontein and the senior editorial staff of the Johannesburg-based *Rand Daily Mail* did all they could to keep attention focused on the reserve.

In that aspect of my life, at least, I was finally beginning to get somewhere. I went on lecturing at the rate of six evening performances a week and a matinee on Saturdays, which was usually filled by a crowing horde of children. Then, one dreary afternoon, the doorbell rang and I was handed a cable from London. Would I, it said, care to take the chair at an important press conference. 'All expenses paid. Letter follows. Regards Jakes.'

'*All expenses paid.*' The magical incantation. *Open Sesame!*

I had first met Philip Jakes through the World Wildlife Fund in 1963. He had crafted a modest little book about camelias and was so heartened by its success that he conceived a fervent desire to do something bigger; he wanted to produce a film on African wildlife. The Moremi story had still gone largely unheard, but that meant that people hadn't had time to get bored with it. It was a memorable saga, and filled to overflowing with all those heart-tugging, tear-jerking ingredients best calculated to loosen the purse-strings of the great, animal-obsessed British public and extract a reasonable production budget. Jakes hugged the idea to himself for a year, becoming more enamoured of the project by the day, so that by the time he cabled me he had upgraded it from a simple documentary to a full-blown feature film.

In my innocence I never thought to check his credentials, and Fuzz Crompton, who knew as much about film production as I did, thought it might be a good idea. So I left Cats to board with the friends who had lent us their basement room, cancelled the second series of lectures, and flew to England bright with fresh hope.

It might, I suppose, have been all right. The film could just possibly have lumbered off the ground and, all things being equal, given the Moremi the boost it needed, and deserved. Only, Ian Smith chose that precise moment to become Prime Minister of Rhodesia, and the much-heralded opening night of the BBC's second television channel, BBC 2, failed to take place as planned, blacked out by a power failure. The two events between them erased every other story from the front, back and middle pages of every newspaper in Britain. It was the Profumo wipeout all over again. June Kay's luck.

The press conference was thronged by six guests, not one of them a newspaperman, and the total taking amounted to £6 and six shillings. The cheque was pressed into my hand by Muriel, Lady Dowding, wife of the wartime chief of Britain's Fighter Command, and the saintly protectress of the Beauty Without Cruelty League, an organization formed to promote cosmetics which hadn't been tested on animals. It was a kind gesture, but it still left us short of Jakes' target by £34,993 and fourteen shillings.

When the dismal seminar whimpered to a close, Richard did the only practical thing possible. He whisked me off to the nearest pub and filled me with strong drink.

'I do hate to tell you this after all that's happened,' he said, 'but £35,000 wouldn't in any case have hired a documentary crew and their gear for more than about a week, so even if the actors had all agreed to perform for free a feature film was never on the cards. And from what I saw of this afternoon's selection I wouldn't even bid for the ice-cream concession.'

It was true that the artistic component had lacked distinction. In addition to Jakes, there was the Honourable son of a minor peer who yearned for the glamour of Show Business, an unforthcoming cameraman who owned a 16 mm Bell & Howell but couldn't remember any of his film credits offhand, and a leatherette starlet who had once spoken a whole sentence in a long-running TV police series. This dispirited little group finally prised me away from Richard and escorted me back to the tall Georgian house in Chelsea which the Honourable had made available as an operational base.

'What,' asked the Hon, with the distracted air of a puppy which has eaten a shoe and doesn't know whether to throw up on the carpet or out in the garden, 'do we do next?'

As far as I was concerned, there was only one course we could take. If we wanted the publicity, we needed to give the press something they could focus on, not too complicated, a metaphor for the Moremi. The lion was the tribal emblem of the Batauana, so . . .

We found what we needed in the Dublin Zoo. They offered us two fortnight-old infants which were being bottle-reared because their mother couldn't feed them. I flew over to Ireland.

Oh God, but they were beautiful. Small, warm, cuddly, with eyes that were not yet fully open. 'Why couldn't their mother feed them?' I asked a keeper, as the larger of the two cubs made a wobbly attempt to negotiate my lap.

'Ah, well now,' he said, 'd'ye see, this is the third litter she's had in the past two years, poor thing.'

It should have been one litter every two years. But this was Holy Ireland.

At all events, the lion cub ploy worked its little miracle. Duly warned, the photographers turned out in droves at London Airport and there was a pyrotechnic explosion of flashguns as I carried the two wriggling infants off the aircraft, accompanied by a great chorus of 'Oooohs' and 'Aaaahs'. For once, we seemed to have hit the right button.

The press coverage was extensive and, since for a while at least there were no fresh scandals or diversions, sustained. It was enough to attract the attention of a small group of well-heeled patrons who were prepared to contribute a generous slice of the budget – provided that the film company could supply them with hundred-per-cent moth-proof, colour-fast and non-shrink credentials. And they murmured, with the sleek good manners of the moneyed classes, that the presence on the board of a star-struck Honourable and a published authority on camelias did not constitute an entirely satisfactory guarantee.

But none of that was my headache. What mainly kept me in need of aspirin was the task of supervising two boisterous and rapidly growing lion cubs in Chelsea, in between rattling off a stream of articles for various South African publications to help pay our bills.

The cubs' considerable charm was entirely wasted on the neighbourhood. I found that I had to collect the milk and the newspapers in person, because the tradesmen had lost all interest in calling. At night, the cubs and I were shut up together in a converted boxroom, but at least during the day they were allowed the run of the back garden, provided that there was always someone on hand to haul them out of the fishpond, into which they regularly plopped while trying to savage their own reflections.

The Hon's crew and I had already had our first difference of opinion over the matter of names. I admit that 'Cubby' and 'Tiberius Claudius Nero Drusus Germanicus Caesar' might not have been absolutely ideal, but at least they had a ring to them, which is more than could be said for 'Oka' and 'Vango', which was the leatherette starlet's simpering contribution.

While all this was going on, I did my best to push all thoughts of the impending divorce to the back of my mind. Any hint of a rift at this stage might have driven the already uneasy backers into withdrawing altogether, but it was nevertheless becoming increasingly hard to keep the lid on the secret. As time went by, and there was still no sign of a firm commitment, Robert began to fire off furious cables, followed by angry letters and, finally, a series of scalding international telephone calls, all demanding to know exactly what I was doing to protect 'his' interests. The starlet, who doubled as the Hon's *en suite* secretary, tended to open all communications, irrespective, and finally Jakes confronted me with the demand that I explain Robert's latest and most unrestrained cable.

Robert, I insisted fervently, was under great stress, and the stream of abuse was just his way of relieving his inner tensions; it wasn't personal. No, *of course* there was nothing at all wrong between us! Ha-ha-ha! I told everyone else the same story, and the only person I couldn't fool was Richard. The moment he set eyes on me he knew that something had gone irreparably wrong with my marriage.

'You're lying,' he said, when I denied it, and put one finger under my chin. 'Apart from the fact that your eyes are sliding, you *always* touch your hair like that when you're avoiding the truth. Miss Cellophane, 1964! Do you want to tell me about it?' So I did.

He seemed curiously unsurprised.

Marriages Unmade

Like should not always call to like. It is, for instance, seldom a good idea for one ologist (ec, zo, ichthy, ornith or herpet – take your pick) to mate with another of the same genre. This is especially true if both share a conviction that their sole mission in life is to preserve the common blue pigeon, the black rat, the ant, the tick or the common housefly from extinction. In theory, these Planet-Earth marriages should grow greenly to perfection; in fact, most ologists can really only tolerate a life's partner who is content with the background drudgery, and never ever tries to move into the spotlight.

In 1964 there were scalding rumours that the once cosy relationship between Armand and Michaela Denys, celebrated in the endless series of wildlife documentaries they made for television, was largely in the eye of the cameraman; Armand was said to have threatened Michaela with a noisy divorce unless she cancelled all her contracts. Even more famously, Joy and George Adamson, whose *Born Free* had squeezed the tear-ducts of half the world, came to grief when Elsa Worship became a major religion. Hardship and shared dangers, all legends to the contrary, are never going to cement the marital bonds unless one partner defers totally to the other.

Without any doubt, the original idea for a tribal game reserve had come from Robert, and it was he who – crucially – converted the Batauana to his way of thinking. My rôle, as he saw it, was to publicize, first, the Moremi Reserve, and second, Robert Kay. Well, as far as I was concerned I was doing just that.

However . . . it is only fair to admit that I am as great an exhibitionist as anyone else, and although I was ready to work myself to death and penury for a cause I wholeheartedly believed in, I wasn't prepared to back gracefully out of the limelight as well. It was a fact that Robert bitterly resented, and he took the view that I was blocking his light, and somehow obscuring his reputation as a pioneer and an innovator.

By June 1964, it was clear that he had not the slightest intention of halting the divorce proceedings, and in the face of this unwavering determination, my usual defence mechanisms began to fail me. I found that I was always doing or saying the wrong things, offending people I liked, losing friends fast just at a time when I needed them most. Eventually I began to feel a weight

267

that I hadn't noticed before, tugging at my neck. It was a dead albatross.

At Horse Pond Sluice

By the time they were three months old, Cubby and Tiber had totally exhausted the remains of local goodwill, and they'd grown too big for the Chelsea house. But one of the Hon's friends, who had a large house on the Kent coast as well as strong nerves, offered to lend me a wing of it. For their part, the cubs had grown tired of hard pavements and noisy traffic, so they were as relieved as I was to quit London. There was still no bankable money on offer for the film project, and promises were wearing as thin as tempers. The unrelenting barrage of phone calls from Robert, continuing to demand instant action, wasn't smoothing any fur either.

Soon after the publication of *Okavango* he had made another of his regal gestures and, without troubling to consult me on the matter, handed a substantial slice of my first cheque to the tribe. He mentioned this, in passing, during one of his less wrathful calls, and seemed at first mystified and then irritated when my own temper exploded. Moreover, his largesse had unfortunate consequences: the Batauana now appeared to feel that it was my bounden duty to pay them for the privilege of promoting their venture. In addition, they had somehow taken against the whole idea of a film and were giving Robert something of a rough ride, which gave him another psychological stick to wallop me with.

Already distracted with worry, I bitterly resented being asked to solve problems that were none of my making, and from half a world away. I told him so, without mincing my words. Silence. And then a flood of even more vengeful rebukes. In spite of my involuntary donation, the reserve's bank account lurched into the red, and cheques began to bounce. Worst of all, our anonymous benefactor in Cape Town had, without warning, stopped paying the game guards; as I was to learn, the Moremi's new officials had not been troubling to keep him in touch with what was happening. *I must come back at once!*

For once, though, I dug my heels in. It was their mess, and they could simmer in it. I had to have a break from the years of pressure, so I thanked God for the sanctuary of Horse Pond Sluice, and for the fact that Richard was now in charge of TV studios in nearby Dover.

Marguerite, my new hostess, was an enchanting woman, but not long after I'd moved in I was to learn that the house itself had an uncanny atmosphere. It was a big, double-fronted building, and on the ground floor of my wing there was a disused kitchen that I carpeted with sweet straw and turned into a nursery for the cubs. The stairs from the entrance hall led directly up to my bedroom, which had an *en suite* bathroom with a dressing room leading off it. This room was bare now, except for shelves and an old-fashioned wig stand, but there was something hostile about it, and I decided not to store my clothes there.

It didn't take me long to discover that the cubs shared my unease. When I let them out of the kitchen the following morning they hurled themselves joyfully upstairs, bounced across the double bed, raced each other into the bathroom and then skittered across the linoleum floor, to come to a dead halt at the dressing room door. In an instant, their exuberance evaporated. Their hackles rose, Tiber growled uneasily, they backed off and bolted back into the bedroom.

'Oh dear,' said Marguerite when, as obliquely as possible, I raised the matter with her. 'I'm so sorry. I didn't realize that it happened in your part of the house as well.' *What*, for pity's sake? 'Well', she was almost apologetic, 'I hate draughts, and I make a point of shutting all the doors and windows in my bedroom every night. But every single morning, about two o'clock, I'm woken by an icy wind blowing through the room. It lasts for about ten minutes, but the curtains never move.'

Infuriatingly, she knew nothing of the house's history that might have explained the phenomenon, and she'd come to look upon the nightly visitations as the sort of thing you simply had to put up with if you lived in an old house. I asked everyone else in the neighbourhood if they'd ever heard tales of dark deeds and unquiet spirits, but even if they had they weren't saying. But for the rest of the time we spent there, nothing would ever induce the cubs to cross the threshold of that forbidding room.

★ ★ ★

Day by day and little by little I felt the tension that had built up through so many years of unrelenting pressure eased under the benign calm of the soft Kent countryside. But I was, perhaps, becoming a little too complacent, and there had to be a drama. I woke early one morning, to hear Cubby whimpering piteously in the kitchen. I found him wandering restlessly about the room, obviously in great pain. I put him over my shoulder, to 'burp' him in case it was an attack of wind, but that didn't help at all. He turned his head away when I offered him his bottle, and by mid-morning his distress was extreme. Marguerite drove me to a local veterinary surgeon, who took Cubby gently from me so that she could X-ray him. Half an hour later she returned, looking unhappy. 'He has a badly twisted colon, and I'll have to operate at once, but . . . well, he's very bad.'

An age later Cubby was wheeled out on the operating room trolley, still unconscious and with a shaven patch on his stomach. Marguerite and I sat watching him, in deepening misery. His breathing was laboured, and from time to time he gave a tiny moan. But just before midnight the anaesthetic finally wore off and, to our joy and astonishment, he struggled groggily to his feet. I snatched him up just as he was about to pitch headlong off the trolley. We took him home and I spent the rest of the night holding him in my lap, disturbed only by Tiber's attempts to join him.

His recovery was gratifyingly swift, although he did from time to time try to capitalize on his illness by demanding treats he wasn't entitled to, and for some weeks the only symptom remaining was an unpredictably runny tummy. He was still suffering from this undignified condition when Muriel Dowding telephoned. She was, she said, holding a fashion show in London for the Beauty Without Cruelty League and if I cared to bring the cubs she would give me a five-minute slot in the programme. She sent a vast black limousine to fetch us, and after Tiber's playful attempt to eat the chauffeur's cap had been discouraged by a swipe on the nose with an umbrella, the two of them behaved impeccably all the way to London.

It was when the chauffeur opened the door outside the hotel that the accident happened. Cubby, who had been sitting peacefully on my lap, was startled by the sudden roar of the city traffic and instantly lost control again . . . before I could reach the pile of nappies I'd brought along. Somehow, I found myself in the ladies' powder room, half naked, washing Cubby's bottom over one basin while my drip-dry dress soaked in another and the attendant tried to fend off Tiber with a chair. We made it to the catwalk just in time – one wet cub, one dry one and a woman in a clammy frock. But for those five precious minutes, five hundred women clapped in delight as the cubs, fully conscious of their star status, tried to drag me away from the podium, where I was delivering a slightly distracted message about the Moremi. But the message got through, and they contributed a handsome £50 – worth a lot, then.

'Darling,' cooed Muriel as she handed over the notes, 'since the reserve has been *such* a success, I do want you to *promise* me that when you get back to Africa you will please start teaching the lions to live off grass.' *Grass*? 'Yes, it's been foretold in the Bible, so it shouldn't be too difficult.'

I remembered the passage: 'and the lion shall lie down with the lamb.' Well, perhaps, but I rather thought that any lambs trusting enough to lie down with one of the Moremi lions would regret their simplicity pretty instantly.

Cubby reinforced my doubts. We heard him grunting happily and looked down to see him gulping great mouthfuls of chopped meat, still raw and dripping blood, from his lunch-bowl. Muriel winced.

'Well, of course, he's still only a baby,' she said forgivingly, patting his head.

Okavango Bill

'There's a cable for you,' said the Honourable's limber secretary, calling from London. 'Shall I open it?'

I was uncomfortably certain that she already had, so 'Yes,' I said. She read it.

'It says "Emm finally off for good" and it's signed Robert,' she said.

I had to grab the back of a chair to steady myself.

'Are you absolutely sure that's what it says?'

'Yes,' she said, irritably. ' "Emm finally off for good." '

'Thank you,' I said, and burst into tears.

Twelve months of clogging pain began at last to lift. The message was oddly phrased, but it could surely only mean that Robert and Emm were no longer in love. Our marriage could be revived. I wrote back, ecstatically.

Oh, but you see, he hadn't meant that at all. For Emm-off-for-good, read: Emm had ditched him and gone back to Australia, and now he didn't care if he lived or died. And he hated me because it was all my fault. I had written to Tris, trying to comfort him about the impending divorce, and Tris had shown my letter to Emm, who had, for some inexplicable reason, taken umbrage at being described as a scheming little trull and flounced off. Now, as far as Robert was concerned, the divorce still couldn't come soon enough.

I was more stunned by his rejoinder than I have ever been by anything else in my life. I was still in a daze from that when the

271

Honourable phoned. The sponsors, he said without preamble, had withdrawn their backing for the film. In all the circumstances, perhaps I had better return to Africa, he suggested helpfully. I couldn't even cry any more.

★   ★   ★

The next day I took the train back to London, and I did shed tears again, when Cubby and Tiber, uncomprehending and fretful in strange company, were taken off to Molly Badham's zoo in the Midlands. I flew back to Africa on a bleak, grey November's evening, under a sky that sparkled with fireworks because it was Guy Fawkes' Day. As I boarded the aircraft, a new element was suddenly added to deepen my despondency. There is a curious complaint that children sometimes call 'jumping blood', which is usually nothing more than an irritating and uncontrollable tic of the eyelids, and in my case it began the instant I fastened my seat-belt. I tried at first to ignore it, but the involuntary twitching then began to spread rapidly throughout my whole body; deeply alarmed, I asked the air hostess if there was a doctor on the plane.

She looked worried. 'No, not on this trip, I'm afraid. But have a Scotch and some aspirins, and then see your own doctor as soon as possible after we land. But tell me – have you been under some sort of strain? That often brings it on.'

The frightening, purposeless twitching continued unabated for twelve hours, until the aircraft touched down at Kumalo Airport, outside Bulawayo. I had deliberately not told Robert what flight I'd be on, because I needed time to readjust to Africa, and I groaned when I saw him waiting for me in the arrivals hall, ice-cold with anger.

There followed a harrowing scene, in the middle of the crowded reception area, which culminated in Robert bursting into violent and noisy tears, totally uninhibited by the curiosity of all the people who stopped to stare at the spectacle. He shouted that Emm had tried to commit suicide by flinging herself headlong from a galloping horse, was now paralysed, confined to a wheelchair probably for ever.

I called over a grinning porter, told him to collect my luggage and then find a taxi. Robert tried to get into the vehicle with me, then remembered that he'd left his own transport in the car park and allowed me to drive off to a hotel. Once there, now trembling even more uncontrollably, I telephoned Emm's former employer at the riding school.

'Stuff and nonsense,' she snorted briskly. 'She fell off when her dam-fool pony refused a jump and broke a bone or two. Nothing new in that sort of thing for a rider, and she'll heal soon enough. The truth is that she went back to Australia because she was missing her fiancée – and because, in any case, she thought Robert had become a bore.'

I took what I admit was a malicious delight in the news, but even so it did nothing to abate what was becoming a serious nervous disorder. Twitching in every limb, I tottered round to see my doctor in the morning, and he prescribed strong tranquillizers and a long rest. Fat chance. Against all the inner voices of reason, I allowed myself almost immediately to be persuaded to take part in what turned out to be the most devastatingly awful safari in my life.

★　★　★

The divorce hearing was scheduled for mid-December, and in spite of all my pleas the World Wildlife Fund chose this moment to send out their newly appointed 'Okavango Officer', who was to vet the Moremi. My personal problems, they implied, were not of such a nature as to allow a postponement. What I needed was a little personal peace, time to work out what I was going to do with the rest of my life; what I got was a suspicious, profoundly tactless individual, whom the tribesmen loathed on sight and christened, with heavy irony, 'Okavango Bill'. Highly unsociable, he looked on all of us, black and white, with impartial hostility, and he developed a particularly offensive habit of saying 'I find it hard to believe that' whenever anyone tried to explain some of the Moremi's more unusual problems. Most people would have resented these sneering dismissals, and as the tribal elders were men of dignity and status in the community they were doubly offended by this crass and unjustified slur on their honour.

To make a bad situation even worse, early rain had flooded the inland pans and scattered the game to the four corners of the mopani forest. Okavango Bill had been promised herds in teeming clichés. What he actually got to see were distant knots of wildebeest, the odd warthog, impala and a few tsessebe. Next, he discovered that Jack Ramsden was driving the reserve's one and only Land Rover home every night, instead of leaving it to be vandalized outside the deserted government offices; he promptly reported to the WWF that the reserve's property was being misused, for private purposes. He also claimed to have unearthed a rumour that Isaac Tudor, the Moremi's treasurer, had been augmenting his income by poaching rhino on the Mababe Flats. If Isaac had in fact managed to pull off this feat it would have to have been as a time traveller, since the very last rhino on the flats had been shot before the turn of the century. But Okavango Bill never troubled to correct his error.

Meanwhile, Robert continued to pile on the agony for all he was worth and for some unfathomable reason Bill, whose business it was none of, chose to lecture me on Robert's behalf. Wearying of the whole steaming mess, I walked out of the camp one night, intending not to return. Happily, in respect of the longer view, a slavering hyena changed my mind for me.

But all things end, and Bill eventually took himself off back to Britain. Astonishingly, too, Robert muttered a grudging apology. He explained that he had been in despair, and showed me a letter which Emm had written on the ship that was taking her home to Australia for ever.

'. . . absolutely super, *he's only 26, and unmarried!* I haven't been faithful to you, but that's the way the cookie crumbles, isn't it? La-di-da!'

★   ★   ★

In December I returned to Bulawayo, in the run-up to Christmas, when the shops were full of tinsel and good cheer, but Oliver and I were sharing an unfurnished apartment, sleeping on slabs of foam rubber and frying our eggs in a tin pan held over a candle flame. When Divorce Day finally came round I sent the little boy to stay with his brother at the riding school, because whichever way the proceedings went I wasn't going to be fit company for God, man or child that evening.

Happily, the presiding judge turned out to be a man I knew and liked, and he granted me a decree *nisi* as swiftly and painlessly as possible.

Robert was waiting for me outside the courtroom.

'Marvellous!' he beamed. 'Wonderful! I'm free of you at last, and I'm celebrating! Let's go and get ourselves a drink!' I was too stupefied by his effrontery to refuse. And then, may God forgive him, he introduced me to Hugh Islington-Highbury. He had, said Robert with a smirk, 'been saving Hugh up as a post-divorce cheerer-upper.'

'He's just your type!' he cried heartily.

Surprise, surprise. Hugh *was*, in fact, exactly my type at the time, since I hadn't yet learned to steer clear of cads and loafers. And that was the beginning of a five-day rebound that took a full year to heal. With exquisite timing, on Christmas Eve Hugh drove off back to Kenya and his fifth wife, leaving me to wait for his letters, and wait, and wait . . .

★   ★   ★

I was alone again, but at least I had time to examine my situation. I had no settled home, and no income. The royalties from my second book, *Wild Eden*, had long since filtered away into the thirsty sands of the Moremi. The price of calling the media dogs off Hector had amounted to half my reserve capital, and the rest was still locked hopelessly into the block of apartments that I could neither let nor sell.

There is very little, now, to be gained from reflecting that I should have chosen then to break clean away, and start afresh in a new country. Of course, even at the time I did recognize that it would be the most sensible solution, but I was just too emotionally weary to make the effort. Instead, and insanely, I agreed to go on running safaris with Robert 'purely as a business proposition, nothing – er – personal,' he assured me brightly.

The scheme did not get off to a promising start.

Early in the New Year, His Royal Highness Prince Bernhardt of the Netherlands took it into his head to fly out to Bechuanaland to make a close, personal inspection of the Moremi on behalf of the WWF, one of whose elevated patrons he was.

It was a misconceived notion. The Prince had chosen the worst possible time of the year to call. The rains were in full spate, and not only did even four-wheel-drive vehicles bog down in the clinging black cotton soil of the molapos, but the inland pans had flooded and the game animals, now no longer forced to concentrate near the rivers for water, were still scattered throughout the thick forest cover. Accordingly, HRH saw virtually nothing of interest during his mud-bedaubed drive to the centre of the reserve, and that was bad enough; but there was worse to come.

In spite of the rain it was fiercely hot, and the tsetse fly had chosen to swarm out of the trees to gorge on everything that moved. The Prince's convoy was severely delayed, because the Land Rovers kept having to be dug out of the quivering earth of the vleis, so they were two hours late when they finally arrived at the rendezvous where Robert and I, in company with Jack Ramsden and some of the senior tribesmen, were waiting to meet the party. As the leading truck lurched out into the molapo and drove up to us, Robert stepped forward.

'That man Bernhardt and his party with you?' he demanded. Loudly.

The Prince's aides froze. I prayed powerfully, but fruitlessly, that a chasm would open at my feet and swallow me up. I knew then that whatever happened after this, Robert had casually and wilfully signed his own dismissal notice, as far as the professional conservationists were concerned. *Lèse-majesté* of that order would never be forgiven. Nor was it.

When the Prince did finally arrive, he went off with Jack Ramsden as his guide, and we trudged along behind, keeping a nervously respectful distance. Even at that point the sight of a sizeable herd of buffalo or a good pride of lions might just have redeemed the situation. A couple of rooting warthog and a single brace of impala did not.

'*Why on earth did you do it?*' I grated, when the ghastly afternoon was finally at an end. '*What possessed you, to insult him to his staff like that?*'

Robert seemed surprised by my question. He was certainly not in the least abashed. 'Look, he'd kept me waiting, standing out in the sun for two hours, while he was travelling in comfort. And in any case, why the big fuss? It's not as if he was English.'

The inevitable letter from Peter Scott arrived two weeks later. Of course he was truly sorry, but the World Wildlife Fund could not see their way to funding the Moremi: they needed all their money for more important projects. Although their Okavango Officer would, of course, let them know if matters improved in time to come, he felt compelled to say that – and so on, and on.

Neither of us had any money left now, and my third book, *The Thirteenth Moon*, which chronicled the creation of the reserve, was only half-complete. We had to pull our belts in to the very last notch, and the first thing we had to give up was Timber. We could no longer afford to feed him.

The little lion was in an especially playful and affectionate mood that morning, and he bounded happily towards Robert when he saw him approaching. Robert shot him through the head. Then he turned away from the misshapen corpse, stood the rifle carefully in the gun rack, put his head down on the camp table and sobbed and sobbed.

And there was nothing I could do to comfort him.

The Return of Tiberius Claudius Nero Drusus Germanicus Caesar

My next trip to South Africa to solicit funds got nowhere and I raised not a cent. I had spent the last of my emotional capital, and I just couldn't get the message across as effectively as I'd once done. There were daily massacres in the newly independent Belgian Congo, and every new atrocity was being reported in detail, with pictures to emphasize the horrors. The Red Cross were calling for volunteers to aid the survivors, and since I could obviously prove a great deal of practical experience in coping with emergencies in the remote bush, I telephoned their Cape Town headquarters and asked to be enlisted.

They were not encouraging. They wanted recognized medical proficiency rather than resourcefulness, even if demonstrable. The whole matter was resolved, though, by a telegram. It was signed 'Jim-Jim' and it was from a cement-bag manufacturer who had once joined Robert and me on safari. Would I like to join him for a vacation in Switzerland, all expenses paid? Once more, those liberating words: *Hey presto!* all over again. I hoped, though not very confidently, that there would be no strings.

In effect, I was faced with a choice between Suvretta House and the ski-slopes of St Moritz, and the prospect of ending up dead, face down and raped in a Congolese ditch. I didn't honestly think that the Red Cross would miss me.

And there *were* no strings. Jim-Jim wanted understanding female company rather than anything more positive, and for a few days I was happy enough to be with him, savouring a degree of luxury I'd only ever imagined. But the relationship palled when he turned down caviare and *Bœuf Maréschal* and ordered asparagus soup and hamburger-on-a-bun *for both of us!* Looking around, I discovered that there were a great many elegant young women weighed down with diamonds, dining with short and portly middle-aged men who seemed to be able to eat without removing the Davidoff cigars from their mouths. It was not as attractive as I'd hoped it would be. I made my excuses and fled to London.

★ ★ ★

By now Richard had moved to the BBC in Birmingham, where he was the news and current affairs producer. During the staff conference one morning he turned over a newspaper cutting that the group had been discussing; on the back was a photograph of a lion.

'I *know* that lion!' he exclaimed, and the group looked doubtful. 'No, but I do!' he insisted. 'His name is Tiberius Claudius Nero Drusus Germanicus Caesar, and his foster-mother used to read a lot of Robert Graves.' The group looked uneasy. His secretary put down her notebook. 'Yes, of course you do, sir,' she said soothingly. 'Shall I fetch you a nice cup of coffee?'

As it happened, half an hour later I telephoned Richard from London, by which time one of his staff had consulted the zoo and, with a new deference, confirmed that the subject of the picture was indeed Tiberius Claudius Etcetera.

'Marvellous!' he cried. 'Come and stay for a few days, and I'll find a spot on the main regional TV news programme for you if you want to talk about your book, and the Moremi.'

It was freezing when I arrived in Birmingham, and the only warm clothing I had was the ski outfit that I'd wasted so much money on in St Moritz. The BBC studios, when I reached them, reeked of cheap lavender perfume and people were behaving in a very shifty manner. Even Richard stank of the stuff. Without even offering me a cup of coffee he bustled me into the studio and, just before the soundproof door closed, I heard him snap '. . . and for God's sake keep her there!'

The anchorman, a gentle and persuasive studio host called Tom Coyne, began by asking sensible questions about the Moremi, but eventually he pointed to the image on the studio monitor and asked: 'Do you remember this picture?'

Of course I did. It was one of a set that Richard had taken when the cubs were in Chelsea.

'It's Tiberius Claudius Nero Drusus Germanicus Caesar!' I beamed.

'Yes, of course it is,' said Tom, after a pause. 'But, in any event, we've got an old friend here who's dying to see you again.'

The studio door opened. The cub in Richard's photograph had been tiny, still a cuddly three months old. Peering into the studio now was a half-grown lion.

I remember opening my arms and calling his name, at which point Tiberius Claudius Nero Drusus Germanicus Caesar tore loose from his keeper and leapt towards me, crooning delightedly. I think I said something fatuous like 'Darling, you've grown!' I'm sure I cried. I don't honestly remember. But Tom and the studio crew didn't have much experience of lions, and to them the welcoming croon hadn't sounded especially reassuring. Most of them seemed to vanish quite suddenly, but there was one stalwart who kept his nerve and his camera focused on Tiber's glorious head as the lion rubbed his cheek against mine, and clasped his paws around my shoulders. Richard told me later what had happened.

'To start with, we had to lock him up in one of the bigger broom cupboards, but even so I knew you'd sniff him out the moment you walked into the building, so we sprayed the whole place with a lavender-scented aerosol. It just so happens, too, that Tom and most of the others were actually expecting a pretty little cub, so when the people in the studio saw him they mostly took off behind the cyclorama screen. The last shot that we got, before we rolled the closing credits, was of you belting this bloody great lion across the chops while he tried to lick your face, and yelling "Stop it, you fool! You're ruining my make-up!" '

In the hospitality room after the show, when Tiber's leash

had been repaired, I asked eagerly for news of Cubby. 'Oh, he's fine,' said Molly Badham. 'Just fine.' But he wasn't. Cubby was dead.

Runt of the Litter

'A low moon out of Africa said "This way home!" '
— RUDYARD KIPLING, 'JOBSON'S AMEN'

I could have stayed in England, found myself a job, sent for Oliver, and repaired my broken life – but Africa doesn't let go that easily. The smell of the delta was still strong in my nostrils, and I still woke at the hunting hour, listening for the nasal twang of frightened wildebeest, the bronze bells in the throats of stampeding zebra, the challenge of lion, the crazed shrieking of hyena far out in the darkness of the molapos.

Richard put me on the train for London and this time it was harder than ever to say goodbye. And it was the last time I was to see him for six years, because from London I caught the first available flight back to Africa.

The first thing I did in Cape Town was to take a taxi to fetch Cats from the people who'd lent us their basement. The lady of the house was inexplicably evasive, and clearly discomfited by my presence.

'Oh,' she said. 'June. Well, as a matter of fact we actually haven't seen her for a day or two, but I shouldn't worry, because she's taken to wandering off lately. She often goes to play with those children down the road.' And she repeated, 'I shouldn't worry.' That in itself was enough to leave me, illogically, cold with apprehension. I walked down to the house where the children lived, but they hadn't seen her either, not since the day before yesterday.

'A white bull-terrier bitch?' said the woman at the SPCA. 'Yes. We found her running loose, without a collar, and we thought that she'd been hit by a car – that dent in her skull? – so we thought it would be kinder to put her down. Yesterday.'

Yesterday.

I raged through all the kennel ads in the Cape Town newspapers, but nobody was selling bull terriers, so I went to the library and paged through all the recent issues of the *Rand Daily Mail*. There was one litter on offer. I caught the overnight train to Johannesburg, grabbed a taxi at the station and drove directly to the suburban house where

279

the breeder lived. All the way from Cape Town I'd had to fight back the feeling that I was, somehow, betraying the memory of Cats, poor dead Cats who died when I wasn't there to comfort her last moments. I wept for her, and bitterly, but I also knew that I couldn't face telling Oliver about her death until I had another dog to console him.

My meeting with the advertiser was not, however, reassuring. He looked furtive and grubby, and my anxiety made him somehow suspicious.

'Well, there *is* just one other pup,' he admitted reluctantly, after I'd inspected the nine sturdy whelps who were tugging boisterously at the teats of a harassed bitch, who rolled her eyes at me appealingly; her expression said clearly that she wished she'd stayed on the right side of the chastity belt. 'But you wouldn't want her,' he added, anxious to get rid of me. 'She's the runt.'

Cats, too, had been the runt of the litter. 'Where is she?' I asked.

'Nobody's going to buy a dog like *that*,' said the breeder a few moments later, setting a woebegone little object down on the floor. One of her siblings immediately bit her, but, curiously, she didn't yelp. 'I should have drowned her when she was born,' the man continued.

'Too true, George,' agreed his wife. 'Just wasting our good food. The lady doesn't want her, so let's take her to the vet later.'

The runt returned my gaze. Then she waddled over to me and sat down on my foot, with a hideous grin on her face, and waited for me to make out the cheque.

It was a cold day, and the harsh Highveld wind was cutting. I buttoned her down inside my shirt and, after much searching, we found a small hotel of sorts where they didn't mind dogs too much. Then I spent three hours trying to persuade her to eat. She sturdily refused the whole cornucopia of canine delicacies I'd bought her, and then made up for it by bolting down *my* dinner, which happened to be chicken and fried bananas. And chicken and fried bananas were all she would eat for the first three weeks, until we were back in Rhodesia. There, she came across Oliver sitting on the front doorstep, eating his favourite mid-morning snack of puppy biscuits spread with peanut butter, after which she demanded those instead.

Many dogs have owned me, before and since that chill June day, but none as completely as did White Clover of Marlborough, *aka* Piggy-Anne.

The Great Dam

I went back to the delta for a while, but I felt a stranger now, and the joy seemed to have gone out of the place. In August 1965, I drove down the valley of the Kwaai for the last time. There was a particular curve in the river where the current had thrown up a small sandbank and the water had a special, crystal brilliance. I often used to bathe there, lying naked and very still, watching the red lechwe antelope battling furiously for territorial rights, or waiting for the shy, speckled bushbuck to steal out of the forest and come stealthily down to drink. On this journey I deliberately turned my eyes away from the river as I passed it, but Piggy-Anne put her paws up on the window and whimpered.

I found Bulawayo full of ghosts, too. There was no road back to my Rock at Far Lamorna, and the only tenant of my little reed-built hut beside the Thamalakane was the great python that lived in the thatch. Both places had become strangely unreal, as though they'd been emptied of all familiar life, and they had taken on the appearance of fading sepia pictures in somebody else's photograph album. I'd never been there, didn't know them.

So I went to Salisbury, 300 miles away, and took a job as an accountant with a hotel chain that had built an outpost at the vast man-made lake at Kariba in the Zambesi valley.

The creation of the dam was an heroic feat of engineering, with some unheroic human aspects, and the full story was told by the late (and much lamented) Frank Clements in his book *Kariba*. The Kariba gorge enjoys, if that's the right word, what is almost certainly the vilest climate anywhere south of the Equator. For ten months of every year the suffocating heat and humidity combine to give the air a curious, treacle-like quality which makes breathing difficult. As if that was not discouraging enough, it also takes sustained physical effort to get to the wretched place to begin with. The narrow, rutted road from Salisbury swoops through the hills in a white-knuckle series of hairpin bends and blind corners. At that time, air travel was not much of an improvement, because the sole airstrip was usually being picketed by elephants which resented all attempts to shoo them away.

I'd seen my new occupation as a soothingly humdrum, nine-to-five sort of job, and I did in fact spend most of my time in the Salisbury office. But every now and again the hotel would run out of management, and I'd be sent off to the Kariba to deputize until the next hopeful but foredoomed couple arrived. Occasionally, managers came and went so swiftly that I'd be caught between two sets: the departing pair vowing, with tears and curses, never to set foot on the shores of this accursed lake ever again, and the new innocents asking fearfully about the rumour that the entire gorge was haunted by the spirit of the river god Nyaminyami, bringer of terror and creator of disaster. It seldom took them long to discover an equally malign influence closer at hand. The 'luxury chalets' were infested with rats, mice, a regiment of blood-crazed bedbugs and, occasionally, puffadders. At least the public rooms were rather better, especially when the electric lights were functioning.

Two of the main reasons why the lighting failed so often were Andy and Johnnie, a pair of courageous but simple-minded young men who thought they'd discovered an infallible way of making the hotel pay. Andy was blond, a transported Viking, the son of one of our major shareholders; Johnnie was a hard-working professional loafer who'd dropped in casually from somewhere in Switzerland, liked the place, and decided to stay on as unpaid help.

The hotel ledgers were heavily in the red, and the bailiffs were camping uncomfortably in one of the annexe rooms where someone had absent-mindedly locked them. Andy and Johnnie initiated the necessary economy drive by cutting down on electricity. This they did by by-passing the hotel's fuse boxes and connecting the domestic supply directly to the heavy-duty cables that ran from the huge hydroelectric power station above the dam. In a blinding instant every fuse within miles of the place had blown. The hotel was plunged into darkness, the lights within the power station itself went out, and even the glow on the horizon from a distant township was extinguished.

By the time the police arrived, several hours later, having been detained for some time by the herd of elephants which had parked for the night across the main road, the wiring had all been restored to a state of innocence and the guests were quietly enjoying their candle-lit dinners, which included the evening's gourmet special: moth soup.

I had taken Piggy-Anne to the dam with me so that she'd have a little more space to explore for a change. One evening she refused her food, so I took her head between my hands and gently tugged her lower eyelids down to check the colour of the inner surfaces. They were dead-white. Because there was no veterinary service in Kariba I borrowed a car and drove through the night to Salisbury. Piggy-Anne's little body was furnace-hot, and she was breathing with difficulty. We reached the city at four in the morning, and my tolerant local vet, jangled out of his bed by my frantic telephone call, put an overcoat over his pyjamas and drove round. He diagnosed nagana, sleeping sickness, and injected the little bitch with anti-trypanosome drugs.

While she was recuperating, Robert arrived at my apartment with what he thought was a very sensible proposition. He casually suggested that I should remarry him.

★   ★   ★

It was raining when we came out of the Register Office – a full tropical downpour punctuated by flashes of violet lightning and carronades of thunder. I was wet and cold, and my beautiful honey-coloured silk dress was drenched. Robert escorted me across the road to a small bar, bought me a Scotch, then drove me home. He had already parked the DUKW on the grass-patch garden that went with my apartment.

'Right,' he said, in the hallway. 'I'm off.'

'*Off?*'

'Mm, yes. Going out. Friends of mine, the set I go out with these days. They've got a party on. Just got to change quickly.'

I was dizzy with disbelief. I stood in the hall, the water from my soaked clothes making a little puddle on the marble floor, watched him clamber into the DUKW, then made my bewildered way up to the apartment. I sat on my bed, staring at the new wedding ring on my left hand, and wondering what in the name of the Living God it was doing there.

The carnival was over, before it had even begun.

★   ★   ★

Almost immediately after our wedding, I went down with a virulent attack of bilharzia and spent two weeks in hospital. My limbs ached constantly, my joints felt inflamed; even my hair hurt. And then after all that I still wasn't cured. They ran more tests, with negative results, and I had to endure the whole process again.

Nor was I allowed to spend any time convalescing. The latest manager of the hotel at Kariba chose this moment to depart in a cloud of dust, after a hippo bit a biggish chunk out of the tourist launch while the wretched man was still sitting in it. I needed the pay, so I staggered back to the unlovely valley.

Robert telephoned from a remote place he'd wandered off to. Bobbie Wilmot had teased death once too often. 'Of all people, Bobbie should have known better than to take a chance like that!' he said. And he was right. Everybody, *everybody*, idiots and children included, knew that you never ventured onto the islands in the delta without the full FitzSimons Snake-Bite kit, with at least four ampoules of anti-venom.

Bobbie had set out to cross one of the islands on foot, leaving his crocodile crew to camp beside the river. When he was seven miles from his boat he stepped on a cobra, which reared to sink its fangs into his thigh. Somehow he managed to struggle back to the base, but by then the poison had spread throughout his body. He injected himself with one ampoule of serum, but dropped and shattered the second – the last in the first-aid box. His crew drove at full speed, but by the time the boat reached Maun Bobbie had been dead for two hours.

Poor old brave, blunt Bobbie. He had once made me the most resistible offer I'd ever had when we both happened to be checking into Riley's at the same time. I demurred, but he had an ace up his sleeve. 'Ah, come on, June!' he pleaded. 'It'll only take five minutes.'

Sorry, Bobbie. I shouldn't have laughed like that.

I put the phone down, and then I remembered the night on the Mababe Flats when Robert had so wantonly provoked the lioness.

'*I like to flirt with death, too,*' Bobbie had explained then. '*It adds a spice to living.*'

Black Widow

Robert had also begun to take risks again.

He had contracted to conduct a party of Italians on a safari in the Victoria Falls, and instead of sticking to the main tracks – which were bad enough – he chose to take a short cut from Bushman Pits, on the Maun road, through to the border post at Panda-ma-Tenka.

The pits had been dug in antiquity to serve as reservoirs, by the desert-dwelling, lizard-eating, yellow-skinned Bushmen of the Kalahari. The Panda-ma-Tenka road had been surveyed by the Devil and built by his imps to serve as a route to Hell, and there was no more perilous stretch of track to be found anywhere in the whole of the Kalahari. It was true Thirstland, in the most precise and terrifying sense of the word. There were only two boreholes along the 200-mile trail, and the water they yielded was undrinkably brackish and teeming with dysentery bacilli that flourished in the green slime that floated on the cattle troughs. By way of a bonus, the stretch was also infested with vile-tempered elephants, snakes, and swarms of venomous insects.

Robert knew all of this. But, perverse as ever, he nevertheless set out to cross it with only old Rodger as a companion.

The first intimation I had that he'd run into trouble was a spluttering telephone call from the safari operator in Livingstone. Where the hell was my husband . . . two days late . . . clients enraged . . . threatening cancellation, legal action . . . unreliable . . . should have known . . . never again . . . etcetera, et-sodding-cetera, and on and on ad-bloody-infinitum.

But what really worried me was the fact that, while Robert could be infuriatingly unpunctual where his friends were concerned, I had never known him miss the deadline for a safari. The trouble now was that, without a car again, it would have been easier to reach Ultima Thule from Kariba than get to Panda-ma-Tenka. I called the police post there, but they hadn't seen him and they didn't seem especially sorry, either. This meant that he was stuck somewhere on the Bechuanaland side of the border.

In any case, I had problems galore right on my own doorstep. I still had the hotel to run, it was the great Rhodes and Founders holiday weekend and we were overbooked, the temperature was 95°F in the shade, and our big deep freeze had defrosted itself, so that the bulk of our supplies were unusable. Andy went out with a .303 rifle and shot a sizeable antelope to replace the meat in the cold-room, and we hastily altered the menu to feature 'Kariba-style beef goulash'. Then the police came round and asked to see Andy's hunting licence, which he had neglected to obtain. I was frantically trying to make them see the situation from my point of view, when the phone rang.

'Panda on line for you,' said Johnnie, who had been earnestly trying to persuade a middle-aged female tourist to buy a statuette of the river god Tokoloshie, whose heroic genitals had been lovingly reproduced in hippo ivory by the local craftsmen.

'There's an African herdsman just come through,' said a faint voice. 'Says there's a white man dying in the bush on the Bechuanaland side. No, sorry, we can't do anything about it from here . . . it's outside our territory.' He rang off.

And Robert was dying, would have died, if old Rodger hadn't knelt over him for nine hours in the angry heat, holding Robert's arms above his chest so that he could continue breathing, for Robert was black with poison. It transpired that he had pitched his mattress on the ground, neglected to hang a mosquito net, and had been bitten twice on the face and throat by a button spider, the Black Widow, which is almost as deadly as the mamba.

At six in the morning Johnnie woke me. 'Telephone,' he said.

It was Robert, calling from the hospital in Livingstone. His voice was weak, but at least he was alive. Some truck or other, he didn't know whose, had miraculously taken the road and been flagged down by Rodger. The doctors had been pumping him full of serum, and he'd be all right. But – and he paused – he would need a little help with the safari.

I had £17 left from my salary, the most money I'd accumulated in a year, and I spent it on an air ticket to the Victoria Falls. I met Robert in a curio shop being run by one of Kariba's former managers, Robert 'Bob' Hope. My own Robert was grey in the face, looked riven by illness, and was in one of his most winsome moods. Bob helped him to a chair.

'It must have been awful for June,' he said sympathetically. 'She must have been out of her mind with worry.'

'Frankly,' said Robert dismissively, 'I didn't give her a thought. I just felt that the Panda-ma-Tenka road was a damn silly place to die.'

★ ★ ★

In the haphazard way that news sometimes filtered through in the Protectorate, somebody mentioned casually to Robert that Michael Dithapo had been taken ill – so ill that they'd had to send him all the way to Francistown for treatment. Heading for Bulawayo, Robert stopped at the hospital to see if there was anything our cherished young friend might need. He found Michael, sitting on the bare earth outside his ward, his back against the white-washed wall, dying of cancer of the tongue.

Robert knew many of the ministers in Ian Smith's cabinet, and he pleaded with them, if only as a public relations gesture, to have Michael admitted to the modern cancer unit in Salisbury. They shrugged off the idea; apart from anything else, they said, there was no mileage in helping blacks who weren't even Rhodesian citizens. So, in the end, Michael was sent back to the delta, to die in a dark and smoky hut. The stench from his tortured body finally kept even friends like Jack Ramsden away, but the woman Michael loved stayed with him right until the end.

The Poverty Trap

'Lord, I have fed Thy sparrows, do Thou now feed me.'
ANON

Eventually the hotel at Kariba found itself a manager who seemed hardy enough to survive the experience, so I went back to Salisbury for good. The lease on my apartment had expired and I didn't have enough money to renew it, so Oliver and I moved into a disused Nissen hut, which cost us £10 a month to rent. Against that was the fact that it contained no furnishings of any kind. All we had were our two canvas camp beds, so we assembled them, and then set about making the place moderately habitable. First, we begged some packing-cases from a friend in the engineering business, painted them a vivid apple green, and covered the tops with an adhesive oilcloth patterned with pheasants, heads of garlic and bottles of wine. I bought the cheapest pots and a frying pan from the ubiquitous Woolworths, found a paraffin stove at a second-hand store, and retrieved a few plates, mugs and eating utensils from the DUKW when Robert was out of town.

The total effect was impressionistic, but cosy.

Next we constructed a chicken-run, to house the culls that we'd bought at a sale, and we soon found out why the previous owner had let them go. They all turned out to be hermaphrodites, which crowed lustily and didn't lay a single egg between them. The next-door ginger tom relieved us of most of them, and was later sick on our only carpet.

At the time, it wasn't funny. I had to get the two of us out of the poverty trap, and I couldn't look to Robert for help. He was currently preoccupied with someone from the Smart Set, whose hairgrips kept turning up scattered around the upholstery of my car; I didn't use the car much myself, because only Robert could afford petrol.

On a night when the curtains were stirring in the light breeze and there was the scent of quince-blossom in the air, I went out into the garden to think. Orion, hanging bright above the bamboo clump, had no suggestions. My spaniel, Golden Ophelia followed me, and as I stepped down off the verandah she gave the back of my knee a sympathetic nudge.

Puppies! Of course! The perfect solution. What I hadn't considered was the fact that every other dog-owner in Rhodesia was trying to navigate the financial rapids in exactly the same way. Puppies were a drug on the market. A two-year-old could have foretold how it would all end.

Feeding costs hit the roof.

So did my bank manager.

Twenty-two puppies were born within two days of each other.

★　★　★

Piggy-Anne Clover, to give her her more formal title, had been mated to her live-out husband, a rumbustious bull-terrier who regularly won all the red rosettes at the local dog show, and she produced four chubby white piglets. Fine. But the cocker spaniel stud dog had a roan strain in his ancestry and tended to throw every shade from dark red to tricolour, and that wasn't fine because the infant spaniels were so close to each other in age that it was sometimes difficult to tell one litter from another. However, since each bitch had her own private run there seemed to be no problem.

That didn't take P.-A. Clover into account, though.

Kisi adored her, and one evening he waited until I'd let the cockers out for their evening exercise, then slipped in to see her with a pocketful of her Doggy Num-Nums, which she loved. Unfortunately, he then forgot to shut the enclosure door behind him when he left, so that she had the unfettered run of the garage where the four whelping kennels were housed.

When I got back with the other three panting mothers there wasn't a cocker puppy in sight.

I refused to believe my eyes. Not even a full-grown python could have swallowed them all that swiftly. Piggy-Anne Clover was sitting in her own kennel – but facing inwards, with her rump blocking the entrance. She failed to give me her usual effusive greeting when I called her name, but the rump wriggled uneasily. Guilty? Guilty. I hauled her out. In addition to her own demanding young, she had collected eighteen squirming, ecstatic, multi-coloured, and now hopelessly mixed-up spaniel puppies, all of them fighting energetically for their share of her milk.

The kernel of my dilemma, now, was that those puppies had to be sold with impeccable pedigrees if I wanted to remain a member of the Kennel Club. They also had to be sold fast, if I wanted to avoid bankruptcy. At least there was only one tricolour, so he was no problem. Betsy's. I gave him back to her. One down, seventeen to go. I shut my eyes and handed out puppies indiscriminately, relying on the mothers to identify their own. Under the Statute of Limitations, I feel free at last to confess my crime.

★ ★ ★

At last, at nerve-rackingly long last, the twenty-second pup was sold and the breeding kennels were empty and quiet again. As I waved a thankful goodbye to the proud new owner of No. 22, another car scudded down the drive. A sorrowing Leslie got out.

She was broke. She could no longer afford to feed her two bull-terrier bitches and they'd have to go to the SPCA, but please, oh *please*, could I at least take their puppies? She just couldn't bear the thought of having them put down. She buried her face in her hands, and wept.

But no puppy was going to be put down if I could help it. Certainly not while I had a puppy-thief close at hand.

Kisi was hovering.

'Go and tell Clover that I want her,' I said.

Kisi beamed. '*Hau!*' he said delightedly. 'Clover will be *too much* pleased!' He bustled away in search of his treasure. Leslie's children were with her, and Slade tugged at her hand.

'Will the puppies be all right?' he hissed in a stage whisper.

'Of course they will!' Leslie retorted, a trifle snappishly. Her spirits seemed to be recovering remarkably fast. 'June's always a *lot* nicer to dogs than she is to people.'

I peered into the heaving basket. One dog, eight bitches. And they looked suspiciously like an Alsatian/bull terrier cross, a blend which was illegal in Rhodesia. For the second time that season, I swallowed my scruples.

In fact, Clover's milk had dried, so these beauties would have to be raised on patent baby-food. Slade watched me, standing on tip-toe, as I stood in the garage mixing the Pro-Nutro powder with milk.

'I like Pro-Nutro too,' he told me, wistfully.

Kisi fetched a Beatrix Potter bowl that had once been Oliver's. While Clover up-ended each pup in turn and snuffled over them, Slade sat down among them and shared his bowl with the male pup and the prettiest of the bitches.

★ ★ ★

In an attempt to wring at least a little profit out of the kennels I allowed myself to be coaxed into exhibiting three of the

289

adult spaniels at the Agricultural Show in Salisbury. I was leading Ophelia out of the show ring when Oliver ran breathlessly up, wearing the sort of expression he normally reserved for major emergencies.

'Quick!' he panted. 'The police want to see you at once!'

My heart plummeted. 'Oh God, what has your father done this time?' I burst out incautiously, and people began to stare.

'It's not Dad they want,' he said irritably. 'It's you. There's a lioness with a bone stuck to her tooth, and they can't get it off. I said you'd do it for them.'

'Say that again,' I said feebly.

He said it again.

And there was a lioness with a bone stuck to her tooth. She was yelling with rage and clawing ineffectively at her face. Now and again she fell over, because the bone was bigger than she was. She was three months old, and small for her age.

I did the only thing possible. I lay on the floor. The sergeant in charge of the police pavilion looked at me quizzically.

'Do you always lie on the floor when dealing with lions?' he enquired.

'Yes,' I said. 'It gives them confidence.'

The cub was frowning at me, deeply suspicious. I made no attempt to move close to her: instead, I gave the protection call, the odd, placating 'Ah-ow?' that all lions use in moments of stress. The cub blinked, and then trundled awkwardly across the room, still tripping over the bone. Gently, I put my hand on one end of it and anchored it to the floor. She lowered her muzzle to sniff at my fingers and as she did so her small, sharp milk tooth disengaged from the piece of tough gristle that had trapped it.

That was the last time I ever encountered a lion.

★   ★   ★

Once again my luck changed, and this time it was for the better.

The manager of the hotel chain increased my salary, enough for me to give up the lease on the Nissen hut and look for a house. I found a thatched cottage standing on four acres of the wonderful red citrus soil of the Mazoe foothills, about thirty miles north of Salisbury. The mortgage repayments were within my budget, and my bank manager advanced me enough money for the initial deposit.

'Christon Bank' was a hilltop home, overlooking a vista of smoke-blue ridges that stretched away towards the Mazoe valley, where most of Rhodesia's oranges were grown. The stand sloped steeply down to the road, and I found a splendid stonemason named Edison, a small, wiry African who turned out to be a master-craftsman, and who terraced the whole of the hillside and charged me no more than pence for the work. I paid him what he asked, and threw in a generous allowance for his keep.

With Kisi's help I planted an orchard of forty fruit trees, set up chicken-runs and filled the garden with rose bushes, gardenia and trailing clumps of jasmine. I loved my new-found haven, and I had been there for less than a year and a half when, without warning, the capricious gods once more snipped the threads of contentment.

The End of the Road

Even now, after a lapse of seventeen years, I find it hard to write dispassionately about the black and bitter time that followed. I had nothing to look back on, then, and little to look forward to, and I could not even rail against my circumstances because there was no one there to listen to me.

It began when Robert flew to England to collect Toby, his mother, because he insisted that she ought to be living with us again. I took refuge in the thought that time might have softened her; it hadn't, but she was to be the least of my concerns. Robert was away for six months, and the moment he arrived back with Toby in tow I knew that there was something terribly amiss once more. His greeting was perfunctory and Toby was icy, and we lived like three strangers.

After fidgeting about the house for a week, Robert then announced abruptly that he really couldn't go on living in Rhodesia. The country had become quite impossible for a man of his calibre, he assured Toby and me. He borrowed £400 from her and appropriated the Land Rover so that he could go off to investigate the island of St Helena – of all places – as a possible future home. When next I heard from him he reported that he'd burst both front tyres near Maun – which was, by any calculation, one hell of a long way round for anyone who'd been aiming for St Helena. After that, there were no more telephone calls, no letters, and for two months he effectively vanished from the face of the earth.

Oliver and I spent a wretched, anxious Christmas, not materially helped by Toby, who refused to leave her room, or even to accept her modest present from the scrawny tree we'd put up in a corner to add a little cheer to the scene.

And then, in mid-February Robert returned, unannounced and still in a foul frame of mind. No, he wasn't prepared to tell us where he'd been, none of our business. All he would say was that he hadn't actually got to St Helena, because he'd missed the ship; that being the case, he'd decided instead to take a trip up the East African coast.

Two days later he stalked into the kitchen where I was preparing the evening meal and, without preamble, in his customary way, announced bluntly that he'd changed his mind again and intended to apply for a second divorce.

Shot through with misery, I demanded to know what possible cause I had given him for brushing me off so lightly. The question seemed to infuriate him, and he shouted that I had destroyed his will to work, that he was disappointed in Tris, that Toby didn't like Oliver, that this very well-read friend of his hadn't liked my books, that . . . and that . . . and that . . . an unending incantation of wrongs that he'd suffered.

'I want to be free! Just free!' he raged.

It occurred to me then that for over twenty-five years I had unhesitatingly given him everything he had asked for, except the total freedom from restraint or obligation that was what he really yearned for most. Well, if I had, I'd been a loser, too.

In the weirdly unreal discussion that followed I agreed to let him keep the income from the apartments, the Christon Bank cottage, the cars and the dogs. All I wanted was to get away from him, from Toby, from the whole repellent situation. I said I'd move out as soon as I'd found somewhere to live.

'Well, just be bloody quick about it!' he told me. 'And I do *not* want that damn dog of yours. If she's still round by the end of this week I'll shoot her!'

I suppose that was what finally jolted me out of my despair, and made me understand at last that there honestly wasn't anything left for me in Africa. I knew I would never regret the Okavango, never grudge the eight years I'd spent there and the resources I'd contributed, but I also knew that I would have been wiser to have jilted that seductive old enchantress, Africa herself, a quarter of a century earlier.

More immediately, I had nowhere to go, and whatever path I was to take I would have to travel without Piggy-Anne Clover. The kind man who owned her part-time husband said he'd be happy to look after her until I could come back and collect her, but we both knew the break was going to be final. So did Piggy-Anne. She sat still and absolutely silent on the seat beside me when I drove her out to Robbie's home in Mazoe, but as soon as I got out of the car she began to whimper piteously. I handed her over with her basket, her blanket, her feeding bowl and her favourite ball, and both our hearts splintered.

A Foreign Country

'The past is a foreign country; they do things differently there.'
L. P. HARTLEY, *THE GO-BETWEEN*

I left Africa on the Ides of March, 1971 – eight years to the day after the creation of the Moremi Wildlife Reserve. I have never been back, because all I would find there now would be shifting mirages, peopled by far too many wistful ghosts, and I prefer to keep my memories strong and bright.

In the upheaval after Ian Smith's government finally gave way to majority rule, half the Matopos was cordoned off and euphemistically declared a 'curfew area'. No food was allowed in, and Mr Mugabe's Korean-trained troops entered to 'pacify' the 'Ndebele. Both Kisi and Rodger died in the blood–bath that followed.

Mohumagadi Elizabeth Moremi is dead, and so too is her son, Letsholathebe III, who never had a chance to make his mark. His own son, Tawana the Lion Cub, is now Chief Designate of the Batauana, and Elizabeth's second son, Mathiba, is Regent.

Badirwãn Sekao, beloved Badirwãn, died while I was still at Kariba, and Montso Mogalakwe had gone to explain the matter of the murdered herd-boy to his Roman Catholic God. Worst of all, and to my enduring sorrow, Jack Ramsden is dead. Shortly before he died, he wrote me an exultant letter:

'At long last Chief's Island has been included in the Moremi Wildlife Reserve. Wildlife Development Concession has been taken away from the lessee and divided into two. The other half, the area along the Kwaai River to the Batauana Stateland Boundary on the east, is added to the Moremi. Now just imagine how big the Moremi has become – 2,000 square miles, which is only a little less than one third of the Okavango Swamps themselves!'

But it still wasn't all that simple. In a sense, what Robert and I had done was to plug a single hole in a very leaky dyke. The Kalahari Desert was spreading out like an oil slick on water, and erosion was gnawing away at the river banks. Men and elephants were competing to destroy the trees . . . and the deforestation was stripping the cover from the savannahs, so that the light sand soil was whirling away in the hot winds. Setting up a game reserve had at least checked for a while the destruction of the wildlife; what it had not done, though, was to hold back the continuous destruction of the habitat upon which that wildlife depended in order to survive at all.

What was achieved in the end marked a momentous stage in the history of N'gamiland, and the creation of a tribal game sanctuary was a signally important event. Now, with a little more wisdom, I sometimes feel that it might have been better if we had campaigned instead for two trees to be planted for every one that was cut down.

I'm not a great one for wallowing in post-Colonial guilt, but I do sometimes have the uneasy feeling that a great many conservation schemes tend to get carried out at the expense of human beings. The richer nations, who have, by and large, long since wiped out most of their own wildlife, are happy enough to nag away at the present custodians of the world's remaining concentrations of untamed birds and beasts, but their concern for the people affected seems to be minimal. They certainly have a lofty impatience with very poor scratch farmers whose crops are destroyed by, say, zebra, or with Indian herdsmen whose cattle are killed by tigers.

The ultimate creation of the Moremi Wildlife Reserve did, on the other hand, give full recognition to the facts that the tribesmen needed meat to eat and hides to trade; that safari visitors brought with them a great deal of hard currency; that conservation of species could mean more than simply establishing what amounted to a giant zoo. It also set an astonishing pattern for the future: Botswana's Wildlife Department has now created no fewer than eight more national parks. It's a development that would have delighted Robert. In April 1990, when this book was being typeset, I heard that he had died suddenly, in England.

Africa demands a lot from its lovers, and although while I was there I gave it all that I had to offer of heart and endeavour, in a curious, oblique way I still ended up in its debt. But perhaps I have at least paid back a part of the outstanding loan.

One-way Ticket

I would have preferred to quit Africa on a high dramatic note, with a bang rather than a whimper. Instead, my final weeks in Bulawayo were perversely downbeat, bordering at times on low farce. The only farewells to be said were perfunctory ones, for Tris had taken his wife and infant daughter, Sally-Anne, off to South Africa, and Oliver had chosen to follow them. Leslie was building up a satisfying career selling industrial chemicals, and I suspect that we would both have found any attempt at a last-minute reconciliation insupportably hypocritical.

On the day of my departure, Robert at least had the grace to drive me to the airport. He handed the single suitcase containing all my 'European' clothes to a porter and stalked off. I don't know if he looked back, because I didn't watch him go.

Once aboard the aircraft, I squandered a little of my substance on a large gin and tonic and – really for the first time – I began to think hard about my future. The prospects were not reassuring. There was always accountancy as a possible stop-gap, easy but paralysingly boring, and in any case I wanted to turn my life-long love affair with the English language into a career as an author. But England was still virtually an unknown quantity: staying with friends and being squired about the countryside by Richard was one thing; carving out a future there was quite another. And I wasn't at all sure that I was English enough to write about England. I was a deep-dyed Colonial, and if I couldn't have the deep bush I wanted the glamour of the capital cities, and I was damned if I was going to accept anything that savoured of the safe and mediocre.

So. . .? Whichever way you looked at it, I was taking a monumental leap into the Stygian dark, and there was no longer the bolt-hole of Rhodesia if things went wrong.

During the eight-hour flight I put together a preliminary plan. To conserve my capital I would have to impose on my more tolerant relatives until I had found a small flat of my own, to use as a base, somewhere to come back to between writing assignments to the more remote corners of the world. India still beckoned me, but I also wanted to look at Burma, Malaysia and Thailand – the spices and the garlic and the tinkly temple bells of Kipling's 'Road to Mandalay'. Then there were the Americas, Russia maybe, Turkey and – God help me – Lebanon and the Arab peninsula.

This time there was no one to meet me at Heathrow, but I did have a standing invitation to stay with relatives 'until I found my feet', so I took the airport bus through the dispiriting late-winter suburbs to the terminal in the seedy centre of London, and then caught a train to Wimbledon.

★   ★   ★

As things turned out, I wasn't quite as poverty-stricken as I'd anticipated. *The Thirteenth Moon* was doing gratifyingly well, and producing royalties that Robert could no longer touch. I called my cousin Michael Whittaker, a lively and successful fashion promoter with an office just around the corner from Bond Street.

'Darling-lovely-to-hear-from-you!' he carolled. 'I suppose you've come over for the divorce?' I was stunned. I had told no one, not even my sons, about this second, joyless break-up of my marriage. There was a long silence, broken only by the sound of Michael's instinct going into overdrive.

'You hadn't heard,' he said, and it was a statement rather than a question. 'He didn't tell you he was going to get married again? The bride's mama is an old client of mine and I've been invited to the wedding, but I shan't go. The event's scheduled for the eleventh of June in the Scottish parish of – would you believe it? – Pollokshields-with-Titswood. So bollocks-and-tits to him, too!'

So Don Juan Robert had once more excelled himself. Well, I for one did not intend to subsidize his new nuptials. Later that afternoon I cabled my attorney in Rhodesia and told him to withdraw my idiot offer to hand over to Robert half of any royalties that my writing might generate. Even so, I left the rest of the divorce settlement intact, because all I wanted was to be rid of the whole miserable business, once and for all.

I then spent a couple of hours trying to trace Richard, and finally discovered that he'd moved in front of the cameras and was presenting programmes as political editor of one of Britain's more enterprising regional television stations. His production assistant sounded cautious, protective, when I called. He was in the studio, she told me, and after we'd talked for a while she finally said: 'Look, you obviously haven't heard, so I'd better tell you before you speak to him. His wife died, three months ago.'

An hour later, Richard called me back. 'You've been on my mind such a lot lately,' he said, once we'd skated cautiously over the thin ice of mutual grief. 'Listen, I've got some friends coming to dinner on Saturday, so why don't you get the train up to Norwich and spend the weekend?'

He had a beautiful, high-ceilinged apartment with elaborately moulded cornices, Chinese silk carpets, a million books. When the guests had gone, we talked through the night, and at about four in the morning he decided that he was starving. I was, too. But, he explained, he was on a small economy drive, so would I mind something simple? I remembered Richard's idea of simplicity when it came to food: inexpensive herrings, simmered in white wine and served with a cream, mushroom and fresh shrimp sauce. This time, what he prepared was an omelette stuffed with out-of-season asparagus, accompanied by a bottle of Château d'Yquem, which he swore he'd bought at a local wine merchant's closing-down sale.

When this spartan breakfast was over, we went back into the elegant drawing room and sat side by side on the rose velvet Chesterfield, but a silence seemed to have fallen on us. Suddenly he stood up, and pulled me to my feet.

★　★　★

By Sunday evening I'd decided that there was no special reason for basing myself in London, when the ancient city of Norwich, dominated by the great Norman castle keep and the cathedral spire, was so much more beautiful, and so much cheaper. Within a week I'd found my own elegant little flat, but I'd hardly settled in before I was back on yet another waterway – this time in a teak and mahogany pleasure cruiser with Richard at the helm, afloat on the glittering waters of the Norfolk Broads. No dinghy, no crocodile, no fish eagles screaming in the trees and no Kisi-cooked corned-beef meatballs: only stately swans drifting by, and a lunch of tarragon-flavoured chicken in aspic and river-cooled bottles of Bâtard Montrachet.

But we both needed time to let the wounds heal and the scars fade, and the invitation to Richard to edit a glossy magazine in Hong Kong seemed just the sort of assignment we both needed. We were away from England for about two years: a time of travel; of hand-made silk shirts and jade necklaces bought in the New Territories on Kowloon side; the pig-train grunting in from mainland China; chilled glasses of bullshot made by the Chinese barman in the Foreign Correspondents' Club – a man who never forgot a face, no matter how long you'd been away; of the evil Medusa floating round the bows of the boat in the South China Sea; of teak trees and silversmiths in Thailand, and the wonderful tiger-reserve of Ranthambhore in India. Then our money ran out, and we were choking to death in the tropical heat of the pre-monsoon weather, so we headed back to England.

★ ★ ★

For a wedding gift, our adorable Hungarian landlord, Victor, and Priscilla his wife, gave us a Portmeirion china chamber-pot, decorated with roses and filled with early strawberries and a small jar of vanilla-scented sugar. 'What you do,' he explained, 'is, on the aircraft, you buy a bottle of champagne. Then, you dip each strawberry first in the champagne and then in the sugar, and then you eat them.'

They lasted us all the way to Paris.

Glossary and Guide
to Pronunciation

African dialects

Sindebele	– Sin-dá-beelie (S. Rhodesia)
Swahili	– Swa-heelie (East Africa)
Tswana	– (correctly Setswana) Ts-warner (Botswana)

African tribes

Batauana	– baTauana (Children of the Little Lion; 'tau' rhymes with 'cow')
Bayei	– baYei (Children of the Yei)
Herero	– Herr-err-o
Mambukushu	– Mam-bú-kushu
Manica	– Man-eeka
Masarwa	– Má-sarwer (Black River Bushmen)
'Ndebele	– N'-de-beelie (S. Rhodesia)

Names of Africans in text

Chaminooka	– Cham-í-nooker (Manica rain god)
Dithapo	– Dí-t(h)ar-po (Batauana)
Gutwano	– Goot-warno (part-time laundry maid)
Kisi	– Ki-si (cook and ally)
Kweri	– Query (Masarwa Bushman headman of Zankuio village)
Letsholathebe	– Let-sho-la-taybie (Chief Designate, Batauana)
'maGerimani	– 'ma-Jerry-marnie (lit. Many Germans)
Maritsasi	– Marrit-sarsie (Kisi's girlfriend)
Mzenge	– M'zengie (Rodger-alias-Mzenge)
Mohumagadi (Elizabeth)	– Mó-hu-má-hardi Pul-arni Mó-reemey (Batauana Regent)
Pulane Moremi	
Mogalakwe	– Mog-á-lark-wey (Batauana)
N'goma	– N'go-má (Masarwa Bushman)

298

Mrewa	– M'ray-wa (Masarwa Bushman tracker)
K. Oakeng	– Wa-heng (Chief's Representative, Batauana)
Shaka (Zulu)	– Sharker

Names of animals

Duiker	– Dy-ker (small antelope)
Ginyambila	– Gyn-yam-beeler (lit. 'Swallow rock-rabbit'; rock python)
Ingwe	– Ink-wi (leopard – Sindebele)
Piri	– Pir-i (hyena – Tswana)
Tau	– Tow (lion – Tswana; rhymes with 'cow')
Lechwe	– Letch-we (a shaggy red and grey riverine antelope)
Sebogarta	– Sebbo-harter (reed buck – Tswana)
iTendele	– i-Ten-daily (guinea fowl; plural: amaTendele)

Names of trees

Mopani	– Mó-parni (also spelled mopane; hardwood tree, much favoured by browsing animals)
Mochaba	– Mó-charber (the wild fig)
Moselesele	– Mó-seller-seller (Chinese Lantern mimosa, thorny)
Mukwa	– Mook-wá (African hardwood, sometimes used in furniture making)

Place names

Boro (river)	– Borrow
Botletle (river)	– Bot-let-li
Chitabe (river)	– Chi-tarbie
Chobe (river)	– Cho-bie
Gomoti (river)	– Go-mo-ti
Kasaya (Canal)	– Ká-sigh-á
Kunaragha	– Koo-ná-racker
Kwaai (river and valley)	– Kwy (also spelled Kwai; Gwai; Khwaii)
Mababe	– Má-bá-bi
Mahalapwe (small town)	– Má-há-larpie
Matlapanen	– Má-tupper-ning (Bobbie Wilmot's crocodile camp)
Matopi (rapids)	– Má-topey
Matopos (hills)	– Má-tó-pos
Maun (village)	– Mow-n (Mow rhymes with 'cow')
Mohembo (river)	– Mó-him-bó
Mokhokhelo (river)	– Mó-hó-hello
Monachira (river)	– Monna-cheera
N'jelele (mountain)	– N'-je-lay-li
Okavango (Swamps)	– O-ká-vango

Ramowtu (riverine area)	– Rá-mow(as in 'cow')-tu
Savuti	– Sá-voo-ti (also spelled Sivuti)
Thamalakane (river)	– Tá-má-lá-karn
Txatxanyika	– Ká-kun-i-ká
Zankuio (village)	– Zan-key-u
Zibaleanga	– Zibber-lee-anja

Miscellaneous

Dipholoholo	– Dí-pollo-hollo (wildlife, lit. wild cattle – Tswana)
Hau!	– How!
Inkosi	– In-kosi (sir – Sindebele)
Kgotla	– Kot-ler (Tribal Parliament – Botswana)
iKwesi yena shaka lapana nyanga!	– i-Kwesi yenna shaker la-parner-n-yanger! (The starlings are laughing at the moon! – Sindebele)
Mubi	– Moo-bi (bad, very bad, evil – Sindebele)
Kopje	– Copy (a granite hill)
Veld	– Felt (bushveld)
Vlei	– Flay (water meadow)
Molapo	– Mó-la-pó (water meadow, flood plain – Tswana)
Morena	– Mó-reener (sir – Tswana)
Shauri	– Show(as in 'cow')-ri (trouble, the affair of, an elastic Swahili word)

Index